NEGRO EMPLOYMENT IN FINANCE

A Study of Racial Policies in Banking and Insurance

INDUSTRIAL RESEARCH UNIT
WHARTON SCHOOL OF FINANCE AND COMMERCE
UNIVERSITY OF PENNSYLVANIA

Founded in 1921 as a separate Wharton Department, the Industrial Research Unit has a long record of publication and research in the labor market, productivity, union relations, and business report fields. Major Industrial Research Unit studies are published as research projects are completed. Advanced research reports are issued as appropriate in a general or special series.

Major Industrial Research Unit Studies

(Available from the University of Pennsylvania Press or the Industrial Research Unit)

No. 40   Gladys L. Palmer, *et al.*, *The Reluctant Job Changer*. 1962.

No. 41   George M. Parks, *The Economics of Carpeting and Resilient Flooring: An Evaluation and Comparison*. 1966.

No. 42   Michael H. Moskow, *Teachers and Unions: The Applicability of Bargaining to Public Education*. 1966.

No. 43   F. Marion Fletcher, *Market Restraints in the Retail Drug Industry*. 1967.

No. 44   Herbert R. Northrup and Gordon R. Storholm, *Restrictive Labor Practices in the Supermarket Industry*. 1967.

No. 45   William N. Chernish, *Coalition Bargaining: A Study of Union Tactics and Public Policy*. 1969.

No. 46   Herbert R. Northrup, Richard L. Rowan, *et al.*, *Negro Employment in Basic Industry: A Study of Racial Policies in Six Industries*. Studies of Negro Employment, Vol. I. 1970.

No. 47   Armand J. Thieblot, Jr., and Linda P. Fletcher, *Negro Employment in Finance: A Study of Racial Policies in Banking and Insurance*. Studies of Negro Employment, Vol. II. 1970.

No. 48   Bernard E. Anderson, *Negro Employment in Public Utilities: A Study of the Racial Policies of the Electric Power, Gas, and Telephone Industry*. Studies of Negro Employment, Vol. III. 1970.

No. 49   Herbert R. Northrup, *et al.*, *Negro Employment in Southern Industry: A Study of the Racial Policies of the Paper, Lumber, Tobacco, Bituminous Coal, and Textile Industries*. Studies of Negro Employment, Vol. IV. 1970.

Nos. 1-39   Available from Kraus Reprint Co., 16 East 46th St., New York, N.Y. 10017.

NEGRO EMPLOYMENT IN FINANCE

A Study of Racial Policies in Banking and Insurance

(Volume II—Studies of Negro Employment)

by

ARMAND J. THIEBLOT, JR.

Assistant Professor of Management
College of Business and Public Administration
University of Maryland

and

LINDA PICKTHORNE FLETCHER

Associate Professor of Insurance
College of Business Administration
Louisiana State University

With the assistance of

MARJORIE C. DENISON

and

ELSA KLEMP

INDUSTRIAL RESEARCH UNIT
Wharton School of Finance and Commerce
University of Pennsylvania

Foreword

In September 1966, the Ford Foundation began a series of major grants to the Industrial Research Unit of the Wharton School of Finance and Commerce to fund a series of studies of the Racial Policies of American Industry. The purpose has been to determine why some industries are more hospitable to the employment of Negroes than are others and why some companies within the same industry have vastly different racial employment policies.

Studies have proceeded on an industry-by-industry basis, under the direction of the undersigned, with Dr. Richard L. Rowan, Associate Professor of Industry, as Associate Director. As of June 1970, some fifteen industry studies have been published with a dozen more in press or being readied for publication.

This volume is the second in our series of books combining our industry studies and analyzing the reasons for different racial policies and Negro employment representation in different industries. This volume contains our already published banking study (Report No. 9) and insurance study (Report No. 11), plus a final chapter analyzing and contrasting the situation in the two financial industries. Volume I, *Negro Employment in Basic Industry,* published earlier this year, contained besides an analysis of the racial policies of six industries, an introductory part which set forth the purpose and hypotheses of the overall project, and a brief overview of the position of the Negro in industry.

Three additional volumes are now being prepared for publication and four or five others are being planned. Volume III, *Negro Employment in Public Utility Industries* and Volume IV, *Negro Employment in Southern Industry,* are scheduled for publication later this year. In the planning stage are volumes on land and air transportation, retail trade, maritime industries, selected manufacturing industries, and building construction. These nine volumes and the various industry reports should contain the most thorough analysis of Negro employment now extant.

Negro Employment in Finance is primarily the work of Professors Armand J. Thieblot, Jr., of the University of Maryland, who wrote the banking study and the comparative and concluding analysis and of Professor Linda P. Fletcher of Louisiana State University, who wrote the insurance study. Both Drs. Thieblot and Fletcher received their doctoral degrees from the University of Pennsylvania and served on the faculty of the Wharton School before assuming their present posts. Major editorial and research assistance was provided by chief editor, Mrs. Marjorie C. Denison and her statistical assistant, Miss Elsa Klemp, who together also did the proofreading and the index. Administrative problems were, as usual, handled by Mrs. Margaret E. Doyle, our administrative assistant and office manager.

Many others have contributed to this volume. The extraordinary cooperation of numerous industry and government personnel made it possible to obtain material and data not otherwise available. Their request for anonymity precludes our recording individually the great debt which we obviously owe. Dr. John R. Coleman, President of Haverford College, made the initial grants possible as a staff member of the Ford Foundation, and later Mitchell Sviridoff, Vice-President and Basil T. Whiting, Project Officer, assured continued Foundation support and interest. Numerous students added their help, questions, or discussions to improve our own understanding.

In most previous reports, as in this one, the data cited as "in the possession of the author," have been carefully authenticated and are on file in our Industrial Research Unit Library.

HERBERT R. NORTHRUP, *Director*
Industrial Research Unit
Wharton School of Finance and Commerce
University of Pennsylvania

Philadelphia

June 1970

CONTENTS

Part One

THE NEGRO
IN THE BANKING INDUSTRY

by

ARMAND J. THIEBLOT, JR.

TABLE OF CONTENTS

LIST OF TABLES

APPENDIX TABLES

LIST OF FIGURES

CHAPTER I.

Introduction

Although the banking industry is one of the mainstays of the American economy and has always been a necessary partner in new movements in technology and industrialization, it has not been on the forefront of social change. Banking was among the last of the country's major industries to abandon traditional hiring practices and make available responsible job opportunities to Negroes. Not until 1962 or 1963 did the industry begin a noticeable program of hiring Negroes. But once begun, in at least the largest of the nation's banking establishments, the program has been pursued vigorously.

The reasons for banking's long delay are many. On the part of banks themselves, inexperience with untrained job applicants (of whom many are Negroes), fear of a loss of accounts or other reaction from either customers or employees, and a misplaced conception of the prestige image of the industry all had their effect. Many potentially qualified Negro job applicants were undoubtedly deterred by the nature and image of the industry, its level of skills demanded for even entry-level jobs, and its historical hiring patterns. There are many other factors.

The study is concerned with the evolution and present status of Negro employment policies in the banking industry. Basic to an understanding of the acceptance of Negroes by the industry is the nature and structure of the industry itself, which is discussed in the next chapter.

CHAPTER II.

Structure of the American Banking Industry

The history of the American banking industry has been a history of change, for the industry has always been closely associated with the changing requirements and demands of a rapidly evolving economy. The product of the industry is credit, and the demand for credit takes many forms. From the waning years of the eighteenth century through the beginning of the twentieth century America was expanding in all directions. Merchants and traders, the westward moving farmers, the transportation system which had to be built to tie the two together, manufacturers, suppliers, and the general public all wanted credit. And banks arose to fill the need.

By 1820, only forty years after the founding of the country's first bank in Philadelphia, 300 banking institutions were in active operation Twenty years later, there were over 1,000, and by 1860, there were more than 2,000. The numerical peak of 30,900 commercial banks was reached in 1920.

For all its growth and spread in every financal direction, banking remained essentially an infant industry until the mid-1930's. "On the whole, the banking system mirrored the society as a whole—diverse, disorderly, growing rapidly but at an uneven pace of fits, jerks, and starts—enterprising and progressive, but not always overly scrupulous." [1] With relatively easy entry into the industry over most of its history, and with the lure of high profits from the endless credit needs of the burgeoning country—and lacking the machinery to avoid emphasizing swings in the business cycle—the industry contributed heavily to depressions and panics which seemed to come with distressing frequency. Severe banking panics, actually attributable to a wide variety of causes but almost always associated with a general distrust on the part of the American population of its banking system, occurred in 1837, 1857, 1873, 1884, 1893, 1903, 1907, 1919, 1929, and 1933.

[1] Paul B. Trescott, *Financing American Enterprise* (New York: Harper & Row, 1963), p. 38.

2

The failure and forced closings of banks was a serious factor in the industry from its inception until about 1935. It is estimated that one-half of all banks founded between 1810 and 1820 had failed by 1825, and one-half of those founded between 1830 and 1840 had met a similar fate by 1845. In this century between 1920 and 1929, generally considered to be years of previously unparalleled prosperity, 5,411 banks failed, an average of about 600 per year.[2] More than 5,000 failed between 1930 and 1932, and the overall attrition was such during the depression that in 1939, only 14,770 banks remained in operation of the more than double that total which had been in operation twenty years previously.[3]

The industry matured following the stabilizing effect of the Federal Deposit Insurance Corporation, founded in 1934, and since that time the number of bank failures has decreased greatly. There have been fewer than 400 since 1934, and from the end of World War II, failures have averaged only about two a year. The number of banks (including mutual savings banks) in operation as of June 29, 1968, was 14,183, and most of the more recent numerical decreases have arisen from mergers.

Regulation

Regulation of the banking industry has taken many forms through the years, and the demands for tighter or looser control have often caught up the entire country in controversy. The first real trial of the powers of the federal government over the states, which culminated in Chief Justice Marshall's famous decision in the *McCulloch* v. *Maryland* case, involved the constitutionality of a tax imposed by the State of Maryland on the Baltimore branch of the second Bank of the United States.

This was essentially an argument of whether the philosophies of Jefferson or those of Hamilton would have sway in determining the structure of the nation, but as a side effect, it also concerned whether the country would have a central bank or a

---

[2] Charles R. Whittlesey, Arthur M. Freedman, and Edward S. Herman, *Money and Banking: Analysis and Policy* (New York: The Macmillan Company, 1963), p. 532.

[3] The American Bankers Association, *The Story of American Banking*, a pamphlet prepared by the Banking Education Committee of the Association (New York: The American Bankers Association, 1963), p. 66.

diversified system of state banks. The argument was settled in 1803 in favor of national banks and a national currency. This was done without destroying the state banking system but by imposing a tax of 10 percent on all further issues of bank notes other than those authorized by the National Currency Act of 1862, and providing certain other benefits to banks willing to adopt national charters.

The National Banking Act of 1863 attempted to work through incentives rather than prohibitions, and added stability to the banking system without destroying its flexibility. Nevertheless, it had many inadequacies. It did not provide a central banking system, and continued to allow the pyramiding of deposits and other practices which proved to be incendiary in the event of economic downturns, often fanning them into full-scale panics or depressions.

Not until December 1913, when President Wilson signed the Federal Reserve Act into law, was a workable national framework constructed within which a viable commercial banking system could operate. The founding of the Federal Deposit Insurance Corporation in 1934, completed the major legislative activities.

What cannot be detailed here is the complexity and the fantastic profusion of permissions and restrictions, of rules, regulations, and reporting requirements arising from minor federal reforms and from activities of the individual states. The number of these activities make banking the most highly regulated industry in the country. The regulatory diversity results in banks in each of the states of the union holding a slightly different competitive position with respect to banks in other states and with respect to other financial institutions within their own. Thus, the economic concentration in the hands of the few largest banks, the ability to establish branches, the ability to merge with another financial institution, and in general, the entire structure of the industry varies from state to state.

Competition and Services

The banking industry has never had a monopoly on providing financial services. Through the years, other firms, sensing opportunity for competition in some specific financial market served by the "full service banks," have been established. A partial listing of institutions which at one time or another have performed services closely related to aspects of banking includes the following:

Mutual Savings Banks
Stock Savings Banks
Guaranty Savings Banks
Safe Deposit Companies
Postal Savings System
Investment Banks
Trust Companies
Insurance Underwriting Companies
Mortgage Companies
Savings and Loan Associations (State and Federal)
Rural Electrification Administration, Commodity Credit Corporation, Federal Housing Administration, and other loan activities of the Government
Granger Banks
Consumer Finance Companies
Sales Finance Companies
Manufacturers' Finance Corporations
Credit Unions
Morris Plan Banks
Remedial Loan Societies [4]

Not all of these institutions continue to exist, and those which do have neither the power, the prestige, nor the versatility of the commercial banks. But they all perform services which could be or have been performed by the commercial banks exclusively. In addition, more and more corporations are becoming sophisticated in the use of cash, and are finding ways to use it for productive purposes even over short periods such as weekends rather than allowing it to lie fallow. In recent years, many members of the banking industry have been seeking ways to recapture some of the business lost to these competing institutions, and have also sought new markets through service diversification. This has led to considerable augmentation of the traditional deposit, loan, savings, and exchange services offered by commercial banks. Through increased branching, where it is permitted by state laws, banks have protected their image as "retailers of finance," and have followed the customers to their

---

[4] Herbert Spero, *Money and Banking*, 2nd ed. (New York: Barnes & Noble, Inc., 1953), pp. 153-228.

homes in the suburbs. "Drive-in" windows have been provided for the customers' convenience. Credit cards, "special" checking accounts, specialized saving plans, and a variety of new personal trust services have all been instituted.

Many of these new services have been made possible only through increased attention to detail, which has required increased mechanization through computers or specialized book-keeping machinery. The overall result has been vastly increased demand for clerical personnel in the home-office location, a factor which has provided many new job opportunities for Negroes

STRUCTURE OF THE INDUSTRY

The structure of the banking industry is characterized by both decentralization and concentration. It is a highly dispersed industry, but one which is numerically dominated by a few large firms.

Concentration

On June 29, 1968, there were 13,683 commercial banks operating in the United States. Although the number of separate banking organizations makes this country's banking structure unique, a surprisingly large percentage of the banking business is conducted in a relatively small number of institutions. The median bank in the country has something on the order of $5,000,000 in deposits, but there are ten banks each of whose deposits are more than 1,000 times greater than this. Those ten banks are shown in Table 1.

The assets of all commercial banks were $456,827,000,000 at the end of June 1968. Approximately 45 percent of those assets were in the hands of the fifty largest banks, and about 25 percent of the total assets were in the hands of the top ten banks. Among the top fifty banks, assets per employee averaged some three-quarters of a million dollars, and earnings per employee were over $5,000.[5]

The distribution of commercial banks by size of deposit is shown in Figure 1. It can be seen from the figure that the greatest number of banking institutions in the country hold be-

---

[5] Assets per employee were approximately half a million dollars for the industry as a whole in 1968.

TABLE 1. *The Ten Largest Commercial Banks*
1968

Rank by Assets	Bank	Assets	Deposits (Thousands	Earnings of dollars)	Employees	Assets per Employee (Thousands of dollars)	Earnings per Employee (Dollars)
1	Bank of America (San Francisco)	23,961,437	21,502,892	146,162	32,340	741	4,520
2	First National City Bank (New York)	19,355,215	16,643,247	124,789	30,200	641	4,132
3	Chase Manhattan Bank (New York)	19,014,284	16,709,926	119,480	20,688	919	5,775
4	Manufacturers Hanover Trust (New York)	10,439,165	9,202,392	68,531	11,202	932	6,118
5	Morgan Guaranty Trust of New York	10,369,966	8,211,716	78,100	7,004	1,481	11,151
6	Chemical Bank New York Trust	8,967,729	7,640,535	67,258	11,049	812	6,087
7	Bankers Trust (New York)	7,652,980	6,827,713	52,071	9,426	812	5,524
8	Continental Illinois National Bank and Trust (Chicago)	7,373,394	6,301,503	55,918	6,918	1,066	8,083
9	First National Bank of Chicago	6,530,070	5,746,162	50,814	4,718	1,384	10,770
10	Security Pacific National Bank (Los Angeles)	6,288,197	5,711,376	50,549	13,015	483	3,884
	Total or average: ten largest banks	119,952,437	103,897,462	813,672	146,560	818	5,552
	Total or average: fifty largest banks	209,392,282	181,547,992	1,469,439	278,428	752	5,278

Source: *Fortune*, Vol. LXXIX (May 15, 1969), pp. 190-191.

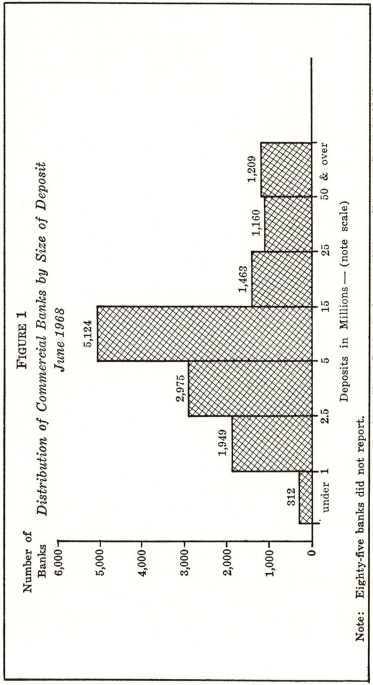

FIGURE 1

Distribution of Commercial Banks by Size of Deposit

June 1968

Note: Eighty-five banks did not report.

Source: *Bankers Directory: The Bankers Year Book,* final 1968 edition (Chicago: Rand McNally and
         Company, 1968), p. 72.

tween $5 and $15 million in deposits, and that less than 10 percent of the total hold $50 million or more. With some arithmetic in Figure 1 comparing the deposits to the total shown in Table 1, it can be demonstrated that *the largest ten banks in the country control deposits equal to the aggregate of about the 10,000 smallest banks,* and the fifty largest banks in the country control deposits equivalent to the aggregate of the smallest 13,000.

The institutions classified as "banks" in the country are either commercial banks or stock savings banks. At the end of 1968, there were also 500 mutual savings banks which controlled more than $64 billion in deposits—making them very substantial institutions, indeed, when compared with the average commercial bank. The mutual savings banks are state-chartered and located almost exclusively in the Northeastern portion of the country. (Because of their concentrated location and because their deposit structures are not reflected by large employment structures, the mutual savings banks have been largely neglected in this study.)

Fewer than half (42.2 percent) of the commercial banks in the country are members of the Federal Reserve System. Generally speaking, however, these are the larger banks, and as a result, they control eight-tenths of the total commercial bank deposits. Almost all banks, whether members of the Federal Reserve or not, are insured through the Federal Deposit Insur-

TABLE 2. *Number of Banks by Type of Operation 1941-1968*

December 31	All	Commercial	Mutual Savings	Member	Non-insured
1941	14,826	14,278	548	6,619	852
1945	14,553	14,011	542	6,884	714
1947	14,714	14,181	533	6,923	783
1966	14,271	13,767	504	6,150	233
1967	14,223	13,722	501	6,071	211
1968	14,183	13,683	500	5,981	211ᵃ
Deposits in Millions of Dollars					
1968	496,070	431,820	64,250	354,928	2,438ᵃ

Source: *Federal Reserve Bulletin,* January 1969, pp. A19, A21.

ᵃ As of June 29, 1968.

ance Corporation. As of the end of June 1968, only 211 banks, or 1.5 percent of the total number were uninsured. Generally speaking, these are smaller banks, and they control only 0.5 percent of the deposits of the industry. These relationships are shown in Table 2.

The commercial banks participating in the survey which are part of this study are listed in Appendix A. They are all large banks, and the combined assets of the forty-seven firms listed ($153,140,000,000) are almost exactly one-third of the total assets of all commercial banks.

Decentralization

Despite the high degree of business concentration seen in the above section, the commercial banking structure in the United States exhibits a higher degree of decentralization than that of any other nation.

> Most economically developed countries have banking systems dominated by a few very large institutions with numerous branch offices. In England and Wales, for example, nearly all the domestic banking business is in the hands of eleven branch banks, and over 85 percent is carried on by the "Big Five"—the Midland, the Westminster, Barclays, Lloyds, and the National Provincial—with much of the remainder done by two smaller branch systems. In Canada there were only nine banks in 1958, operating a total of 4,556 domestic banking offices. In the United States, on the other hand, the "unit" or single office bank is still predominant despite the great increase in branch banking, particularly since World War II.[6]

At the end of 1968, of a reported 13,679 (see Table 3) commercial banks in the United States, 9,733 were unit institutions and 3,946 were branch banks (i.e., banks operating more than one office). These 3,946 branch banks conducted business at a total of 18,777 branches, so that while fewer than one-third of the banks in the country were branch banks, two-thirds of the 28,510 banking offices were operated by these multiple office banks.

-----
[6] Whittlesey, Freedman, and Herman, *op. cit.*, p. 80.

TABLE 3. *The Commercial Banking Industry*
Banks and Branches by State and Branches by Type of Location Within Each State
1968

State	Commercial Banks (Including Mutual Savings Banks)	Branch Banks[a]	Branches	Branches			
				Located in head office city	Located in head office county	Located in counties contiguous to head office county	Located elsewhere in the state[b]
United States[c]	14,179[d]	3,946	19,675	7,295	6,253	2,940	3,187
Alabama	268	76	230	122	87	10	11
Arizona	13	7	273	92	63	72	46
Arkansas	248	72	140	80	54	5	1
California	162	130	2,751	399	380	567	1,405
Colorado	257	2	2	2	—	—	—
Connecticut	135	86	500	142	275	62	21
Delaware	21	11	88	14	43	27	4
District of Columbia	14	13	97	97	—	—	—
Florida	461	6	6	6	—	—	—
Georgia	428	85	235	174	4	8	49
Idaho	26	14	141	12	13	26	90
Illinois	1,074	39	39	39	—	—	—
Indiana	419	188	573	302	271	48	—
Iowa	673	210	281	97	136	—	—
Kansas	601	59	59	58	1	—	—
Kentucky	346	125	285	175	105	5	—
Louisiana	229	114	327	201	117	6	3
Maine	75	44	217	46	84	75	12
Maryland	128	77	501	147	120	145	89
Massachusetts	332	209	881	428	444	8	1

TABLE 3. (*Continued*)

State	Commercial Banks (Including Mutual Savings Banks)	Branch Banks[a]	Branches	Branches			
				Located in head office city	Located in head office county	Located in counties contiguous to head office county	Located elsewhere in the state[b]
Michigan	338	191	1,095	501	389	194	11
Minnesota	724	6	10	10	—	—	—
Mississippi	185	102	293	125	93	44	31
Missouri	667	83	83	83	—	—	—
Montana	135	3	3	2	—	1	—
Nebraska	441	36	36	36	—	—	—
Nevada	9	7	76	20	17	11	28
New Hampshire	109	37	50	23	23	4	—
New Jersey	250	186	822	284	537	1	—
New Mexico	63	43	112	63	40	8	1
New York	444	271	2,492	1,228	716	454	94
North Carolina	121	75	931	149	97	186	499
North Dakota	169	49	67	9	36	21	1
Ohio	526	261	1,128	513	599	16	—
Oklahoma	424	50	51	51	—	—	—
Oregon	51	29	307	60	44	45	158
Pennsylvania	516	245	1,593	456	648	488	1
Rhode Island	20	20	209	56	89	39	25
South Carolina	118	67	344	83	55	49	157
South Dakota	165	39	91	14	31	23	23

TABLE 3. (Continued)

State	Commercial Banks (Including Mutual Savings Banks)	Branch Banks[a]	Branches	Branches			
				Located in head office city	Located in head office county	Located in counties contiguous to head office county	Located elsewhere in the state[b]
Tennessee	303	131	412	259	138	7	8
Texas	1,151	41	42	42	—	—	—
Utah	54	19	112	23	38	9	42
Vermont	51	25	73	11	27	26	9
Virginia	237	149	694	271	115	135	173
Washington	101	54	524	182	130	72	140
West Virginia	195	4	4	4	—	—	—
Wisconsin	606	139	222	45	141	35	1
Wyoming	70	—	—	—	—	—	—

Source: *Federal Reserve Bulletin*, April 1969, pp. A-91-A-92.

[a] A "branch bank" is one which operates two or more offices.

[b] In almost all cases, the branching activities of a bank are confined to the state in which the main office is located. However, one New Jersey, one California, one New York, and two Puerto Rican banks operate a total of fourteen branches in other states. The branches are recorded in the states in which they themselves are located.

[c] Banks and branches in Alaska, Hawaii, and the Virgin Islands are included in the totals but not in the listings.

[d] There is a small discrepancy between the total number of banks shown here and those noted for the same date by other Federal Reserve Board statistics.

Branch banking is a phenomenon of this century. In 1900, there were only 119 branch offices, accounting for less than 1 percent of the total commercial banking offices. At the time, most of the states prohibited the establishment of branch offices. The State of California, in 1909, was the first to relax the legislative and regulatory restraints on branching, but most other states did not follow suit until the 1920's and 1930's. Only thirty-three new branches were opened in the United States in 1938. One hundred and eighty-nine were opened in 1948; 645 were opened in 1958; and it is estimated that over 1,200 were opened in 1968.[7]

A few states, such as Colorado, Florida, Illinois, Texas, West Virginia, and Wyoming still prohibit branch banking, and allow multiple offices only in the event of mergers or in other specified situations. Some states allow branching only in the head office city; some only in the head office county. A few states permit branching in the home office county and in all contiguous counties, and about half of the states permit statewide branching under various restrictions.

A listing of the distribution of banks by state and by the number of branches operating in each state is included as Table 3. (There are some other variations on branching besides those seen in the table. Michigan, for example, allows branching, under some circumstances, into an area formed by a twenty-five mile radius from the home office. Similarly, Virginia allows branching into a five mile radius from the city limits of the city of the home office.)

The banks in Appendix A, which were comprised in our survey, are in locations reflecting seven different degrees of permissiveness toward banking. Eight of the forty-seven are allowed no branches. On the other extreme, one bank alone, the Bank of America, has almost 1,000 branches throughout the State of California. In total, the thirty-nine banks which are allowed branches operate approximately 4,300 of them.

Table 3 also makes clear the great diversity in the number of banking offices located in the various states. Only nine banks, with seventy-six branches, operate in the State of Nevada. At the opposite end of the spectrum is California, with 162 banks operating 2,751 branches. New York is close behind, with a greater number of banks, but fewer branches—319 banks and

---

[7] *Ibid.*, p. 536.

2,205 branches. Texas and Illinois, with 1,151 and 1,074 banks respectively, are the two largest in terms of the number of separate firms. Arizona, Delaware, the District of Columbia, Nevada, and Rhode Island all have fewer than twenty banks. All told, the differences in the number of banking institutions is partially a function of geography, partially of population, and partially of regulation.

Although the total number of banks and branches is large, so is the number of communities which require the services of banks. As a result, many of the smaller unit banks face very little in the way of competition. In the late 1950's, about 60 percent of all unit banks were located in a community with only a single banking office. Eighty-four percent were in communities with only one or two, and only 5 percent operated in areas with competition from more than eight offices.[8]

MANPOWER

In employment, as well as in business and in asset growth, the finance industry has shown more relative growth in the past ten years than any other industrial group except a few service industries and state and local government.

Bank employees work mainly in the densely populated states of New York, California, Pennsylvania, and Illinois, which have the greatest amount of banking services. New York City, the financial capital of the nation, has far more bank employees than any other city. Banking employment is also concentrated, to a considerable extent, in a relatively limited number of large banks and their branches. The top three hundred commercial banks in the country have more than one-half of all commercial bank employees.[9] The 10,000 smallest commercial banks of the country employ an average of about seventy employees each, and the median bank employs about thirteen persons.

Overall employment trends in commercial banking and in the entire financial group, including insurance and real estate, are shown in Table 4. The rapid employment growth can be easily seen in the table. The fact of this growth and the concentration of it in populous areas and large institutions have been factors

---

[8] *Ibid.*, p. 540.

[9] U.S. Bureau of Labor Statistics, *Occupational Outlook Handbook*, 1966-67 ed., p. 612.

TABLE 4. *Total Employment in Banks and in the Financial Industry*
United States, 1963-1968

Employment	Year					
	1963	1964	1965	1966	1967	1968
Banks (SIC-602)	740,600	766,500	792,000	825,200	868,300	911,300
Finance, insurance, and real estate (SIC-60)	2,877,000	2,957,000	3,023,000	3,100,000	3,217,000	3,357,000

Source: U. S. Bureau of Labor Statistics, *Employment and Earnings Statistics for the United States, 1909-68*, Bulletin No. 1312-6 and *Employment and Earnings*, March 1969.

Note: Includes Alaska and Hawaii beginning 1959.

in creating a favorable climate for the introduction of Negro personnel in the industry.

Commercial banks process more than fifteen billion checks every year, and the number of deposit slips, monthly statements, account clearing sheets, and other paperwork related to the primary function is almost inestimable. Therefore, the banking demand for clerical employees is very high. About two-thirds of all banking employees are in this category. In addition to clerks, machine operators, clerk-typists, secretaries, file clerks, and stenographers, banking also includes thousands of jobs which are unique to banks—the teller jobs—which are also listed in the clerical category. The second largest occupational category in banking is that of officials and managers. Some 18 percent—approximately one in six—of the jobs in the industry are on this level. Professional employees—accountants, lawyers, statisticians, and economists—are the third largest occupational grouping.

Blue collar employees, including guards, porters, elevator operators, and various maintenance and service workers, compose a very small part, less than 5 percent, of total employment. We shall see that this skill mix has had significant effect on Negro employment.

The great bulk of jobs in the banking industry are jobs which require numerical manipulations rather than finger dexterity or physical strength, and as a result are jobs which evidence no particular demand for any specific physical characteristics or strengths of either male or female employees. Especially since the Second World War, banks have been turning increasingly to female employees. Women now make up almost five-eighths of all banking employment, and the proportion of females in the work force continues to rise. The occupational and sex distribution of employees for forty-six of the banks listed in Appendix A is shown in Table 5.

Nature of Work

Because of the overwhelming importance of these jobs as the entry level for employment in banking, it will be instructive to examine the nature of the work of the teller and clerical jobs specific to banking. The following listing is taken, in slightly condensed form, from the Bureau of Labor Statistics occupational outlook report series on banking.[10]

---

[10] U.S. Bureau of Labor Statistics, *Occupational Outlook Handbook*, 1966-67 ed., pp. 614-617.

TABLE 5. *The Banking Industry*
Employment by Sex and Occupational Group
46 Commercial Banks Surveyed
United States, 1968

Occupational Group	Total	Percent	Male	Female
Officials and managers	38,195	18.6	32,931	5,264
Professionals	7,073	3.4	5,533	1,540
Technicians	2,790	1.3	2,336	454
Sales workers	767	0.4	631	136
Office and clerical	147,921	72.0	32,835	115,086
Total white collar	196,746	95.7	74,266	122,480
Craftsmen	767	0.4	731	36
Operatives	1,924	0.9	1,510	414
Laborers and service workers	6,104	3.0	4,851	1,253
Total blue collar	8,795	4.3	7,092	1,703
Total	205,541	100.0	81,358	124,183

Source: Data in the author's possession.

Bank clerks handle the paperwork associated with depositors' checking and savings accounts, loans to individual and business firms, and other bank business. Bank clerks known as *sorters* separate checks, deposit slips, and other bank documents, and tabulate them so that they may be charged to the proper accounts; often they use cancelling and adding machines in their work. *Proof machine operators* use special equipment that sorts items and adds and records the amounts of money involved.

Bookkeeping workers, composing one of the largest segments of the clerical grouping, operate posting machinery especially designed for bank use. By and large, their jobs consist of routine typing, calculating, and posting related to banking transactions. Some of the job titles in this group are: *bookkeeping machine operator, account clerk, posting machine operator, recording clerk, Christmas club bookkeeper, discount bookkeeper, interest accrual bookkeeper, trust bookkeeper, commodity loan clerk, bookkeeping and accounting clerk, reconcilement clerk,* and *trust investment clerk.*

Country collection clerks sort the thousands of pieces of mail that come in daily to the city banks and determine which items must be held at the main office and which should be routed to branch banks or to out-of-city banks for collection. *Transit clerks* perform a variation on this job which consists of sorting bank items such as drafts on other banks, and preparing the documents so that they can be mailed for collection.

Exchange clerks service foreign deposit accounts. *Interest clerks* and *mortgage clerks* maintain records relating to interest bearing items.

As of the end of 1964, approximately 700 banks had already installed electronic data processing equipment. Many new jobs, unique to banks, have grown from the use of this equipment, including those of the *electronic reader-sorter operator* who operates electronic check-sorting equipment, the *check inscriber* or *encoder* who operates the machinery that prints information on checks in magnetic ink, and the *control clerk* who keeps track of the large volume of documents flowing in and out of the computer division. This has been an important source of jobs for Negroes.

Commercial tellers, with whom most people deal when they transact business in banks, are mainly occupied with cashing customers' checks and handling deposits and withdrawals from checking and savings accounts during the hours that the bank is open to the public. The duties of the job include verifying the identity of persons to whom payments are to be made, ascertaining that funds are in the accounts against which checks are drawn, checking to see whether deposit slips are correctly itemized, entering passbook or deposit receipt totals, and using a variety of special posting machinery. After public banking hours, the teller is responsible for counting cash on hand, listing currency received, and balancing the daily accounts. Other incidental tasks include sorting checks and deposit slips, filing new account cards, and removing closed account cards from files.

The functions of other teller positions are similar, although they may have special titles such as *savings, foreign exchange, payroll, discount,* or *securities tellers.*

Special Requirements

For the clerical positions, high school graduation is generally considered adequate preparation for beginning jobs. For most of them, courses in bookkeeping, typing, or business arithmetic are desirable. In addition, to these requirements, in the hiring of tellers, employers prefer experience in some related clerical

position. They also pay strict attention to personal characteristics such as neatness, tact, and courtesy. These are particularly important because customers, who deal with tellers far
more frequently than with any other bank employees, often
judge a bank's services principally on their impression of the
teller. We shall see that these factors were long a deterrent to
hiring Negroes for teller positions.

Since tellers handle large amounts of money, they must be
able to meet the standards established by bonding companies.

Banking wages for either clerical positions or teller positions
are not particularly high, and are generally less than or equivalent to clerical positions in manufacturing or government.
Nevertheless, wages have been increasing rapidly from year to
year.

Union Affiliation

Banks have entered into very few collective bargaining agree-
ments with their employees. Despite the recent unionization of
one small, New Jersey bank, and the apparently successful strike
called by a banking union in Seattle, there is no indication that
union activities or unionization in the banking industry is in-
tensifying or becoming anymore common.[11]

EFFECT OF BANKING STRUCTURE ON NEGRO EMPLOYMENT

The aspects of the structure of the American banking industry
which were chosen for discussion in this chapter are all factors
which will be seen in subsequent discussions to have an effect
on the levels of Negro employment found in the industry.

The highly varied industrial location and structure resulting
from regulations affecting the average size of banks, from decentralization, from branching, and from other causes, and the
degree of concentration which locates most of the industry's
employment in a few large banks in a few large cities have an

---

[11] *Wall Street Journal*, January 2, 1968, p. 1. (Four of the banks surveyed
by the author did report some recent union overtures to their employees, but
none developed beyond the "probing" stage.) In a decision announced on
November 7, 1969, the National Labor Relations Board ruled that a single
branch of a bank was an "appropriate unit" for collective bargaining. Since
it is easier to unionize one branch than a large grouping, this decision was
obviously designed to encourage bank unionization. (*Matter of Wells Fargo
Bank*, 179 NLRB No. 79, November 7, 1969.)

obvious effect on the jobs offered by the industry and the population available to accept them. Diversification of services and rapid employment growth have insured that jobs have been available.

The initial instability of the industry, its historical importance as a source of both credit and crisis, its unionization structure, its prestige status, and the general character of its work requirements all affect the image of the industry to Negroes, as a more or a less desirable place to seek employment. The white collar orientation of the industry, the high skill levels required for even entry-level jobs, its increasingly female orientation, and factors growing from services of the industry such as the handling of cash and important documents, all affect Negro employment levels. The evolution of these employment levels will be described and analyzed in the chapters which follow.

CHAPTER III

Negro Employment Levels: National Data, 1940-1968

Until the pattern began to crumble at about the time of the First World War, the banking industry generally eschewed the business as well as the employment of Negroes and most other minority group members. This practice caused the growth through the years of "Granger banks and labor banks, industrial banks and immigrant banks, Hibernian, Germanian, and Scandinavian banks, and a wide variety of styles of private banks. When a group of bank customers felt themselves inadequately served, the way was usually open to start a new bank." [12] (A large number of Negro banks were also founded. See Appendix B.)

As economically-oriented institutions, banks soon enough gave way to the demands for their services by all minority groups; but it is only in the very recent past that minority group members of any sort, and particularly Negroes, were accepted as employees actively participating in the affairs of the organizations.

THE 1940-1960 ERA

During the twenty years from 1940 to 1960, the financial industry was characterized by rapid employment growth—almost three times the rate of all private industry. Of the 475,660 employees in the industry in 1940, only 7,294, or 1.5 percent, were Negro. Twenty years later, in 1960, Negro employment had more than doubled to 19,572. But total employment had more than doubled—to 1,018,046—so that Negroes still composed less than 2 percent of the total work force.

Comparing these Negro employment figures with those for all industry (including agriculture), we find that all industry employed proportionally four times more Negroes than the financial community, and at over 9 percent Negro in their work forces, came much closer to approximating the 10-11 percent

---

[12] Paul B. Trescott, *Financing American Enterprise* (New York: Harper & Row, 1963), p. 268.

Negro population proportion which existed during this period. These statistics are found in Table 6.

Included in the "banking" category as defined by the Bureau of Census were all of the savings and loan associations and various other financial institutions in addition to banks. Also included were the (approximately) seven all-Negro banks and several dozen Negro savings and loan associations. (Fifty Negro savings and loan existed in 1938, of which twenty-two remained in business in 1947.) The number of Negro institutions was not great, and all of them were small. (They are discussed in Appendix B.) Still, discounting their several hundred employees from the already small total number of Negroes in the financial community, and considering that there were well over ten thousand each of commercial banks and savings and loan associations, we see that there remained considerably fewer than one Negro per banking establishment, even in 1960.

During this twenty-year span, the employment composition in banking was shifting rapidly, but it was not particularly a racial shift—rather one of male-female composition. The table shows that females, who were less than one-third of employment prior to World War II, were more than a majority by 1960. Among Negroes, the female employment proportion increased more rapidly than male, and this probably indicates that the traditional jobs held by Negroes in the industry, such as the male-oriented service and maintenance jobs, were giving way in some small degree to female-oriented clerical positions.

EMPLOYMENT CHANGES, 1960-1966

Substantial changes in the racial composition of banking work forces apparently began to take place in the early 1960's. Measurement of the extent of those changes, however, is very difficult prior to 1966. In a few specific areas, where active human relations agencies functioned, data can be found, and we shall present the experiences of banks in several cities in which this was the case in Chapter VI.

In many other areas, however, banks were prohibited by state laws from maintaining records of the racial characteristics of their work forces. For this reason, or from the lack of desire to do so, many banks did not produce statistical reports of the race of their employees until required to do so by federal law in 1966. Thus, extensive data on a national scale are not available for his-

TABLE 6. *The Banking Industry Compared With All Industries*
Employment by Race and Sex, United States, 1940-1960

	Total			Male			Female		
	1940	1950	1960	1940	1950	1960	1940	1950	1960
BANKING[a]									
Employment	475,660	516,240	1,018,046	329,664	261,720	473,771	145,996	254,520	544,275
Negro	7,294	9,300	19,572	6,322	6,780	12,046	972	2,520	7,526
Other racial minorities	351	420	6,236	280	150	2,585	71	270	3,651
Percent									
Negro	1.5	1.8	1.9	1.9	2.6	2.5	0.7	1.0	1.4
All female	30.7	49.3	53.5	—	—	—	—	—	—
Negro female	13.3	27.1	38.5	—	—	—	—	—	—
ALL INDUSTRIES									
Employment	45,166,083	55,813,380	64,639,256	34,027,905	40,060,560	43,466,955	11,138,178	15,752,820	21,172,301
Negro	4,479,068	5,385,900	6,099,089	2,936,795	3,499740	3,643,949	1,542,273	1,886,160	2,455,140
Other racial minorities	191,926	230,460	529,901	159,604	179,040	361,317	32,322	51,420	168,584
Percent									
Negro	9.9	9.6	9.4	8.6	8.7	8.4	13.8	12.0	11.6
All female	24.7	28.2	32.8	—	—	—	—	—	—
Negro female	34.4	35.0	40.3	—	—	—	—	—	—

Source: *U.S. Census of Population:*

1940: Vol. III, *The Labor Force,* Part 1, Table 18.
1950: P-E No. 1D, *Industrial Characteristics,* Table 2.
1960: Vol. I, *Industrial Characteristics,* Part D, Table 213, 214.

[a] Includes savings and loan associations and various other financial institutions.

torical comparison or for illustrating the details of changes in the industry.

Nevertheless, a small field sample of six banks from across the country was taken in 1964. Although not national in scope, it is of sufficient interest to be discussed here. The survey revealed that among 48,250 employees covered, a total of just under 1,400, or 2.9 percent, were Negro. To the extent that these banks were representative of the entire industry, the figures would indicate a modest improvement over the 1960 census results.

Without dwelling on the figures themselves in this small survey, we would like to point out one factor of importance relative to the structure of the banking industry. In these survey banks, 12.1 percent of all blue collar workers were Negro; 2.7 percent of the white collar workers were Negro. Yet the weighted average shows that only 2.9 percent of all workers were Negro. Thus, the relatively high proportion of Negroes among blue collar employees has changed the weighted average by only two-tenths of one percentage point, indicating that blue collar employment is not very important in the industry and that the Negro proportion in blue collar jobs is neither critical nor an adequate indicator of the overall employment pattern.

Another point which bears mentioning takes the form of a caveat against any overly literal interpretation of statistics by occupational grouping in any year.[13] Of the six firms surveyed, two reported no blue collar employees at all. Of the remaining four—all of them large and of about the same size—one showed no professional employees, a different one, no technicians. Only one of the six reported employing craftsmen, and the number of operatives varied from none to 367. Five of these are commercial banks of a similar nature and size, and have similar personnel requirements and job titles; but it would be impossible to say so from their occupational statistics. It is for this reason that little emphasis will be placed on job categories subsequently in this study.

1966 DATA

In the Spring of 1966, all commercial banks with one hundred or more employees were required to file a report on the racial

---

[13] The standard occupational groupings used by banks and other firms in recording their Negro employment patterns follows. In the white collar group are: officials and managers, professionals, technicians, sales workers, and office and clerical workers. In the blue collar group are: craftsmen, operatives, laborers, and service workers.

composition of their work forces with the Equal Employment Opportunity Commission (EEOC), which had been established by Title VII of the Civil Rights Act of 1964. (For the legislative history and the evolution of reporting requirements by banks, see Appendix C.) Because of this reporting requirement, almost all of the larger banks in the country began to keep such records, and as a result, broad-based statistical data are available. The results of a field sample of 738 commercial banks will be presented shortly. First, however, there is a source of difficulty involving the dating of statistical reports which requires clarification if future problems are to be avoided.

Dating of Reports

When the government reporting requirements were established, banks were instructed to submit in March of 1966 data collected at the end of the previous December, January, or February. The Equal Employment Opportunity Commission and other government agencies have always referred to the data thus collected as "1966 data." The author has maintained, and continues to maintain, that these data are much more representative of the policies, procedures, and employment practices of the individual firms during 1965 than 1966, which was a maximum of two months old when the numbers were taken.

The government numbering procedure has the effect of retarding apparent hiring improvement, or any other changes, by one year, and has caused much needless confusion within the banking industry and elsewhere. Nevertheless, because we shall be comparing field sample data with published government reports, we feel we would complicate an already complex situation yet further by failing to be consistent. We shall, therefore, follow the government numbering procedure.

EEOC Data, 1966

Early in 1969, the Equal Employment Opportunity Commission made public the statistical compilations for Negro employment in all industries for 1966. These are extensive data, and will be used heavily for a number of comparisons in later sections of this study.

Summarized totals of employment data for the banking industry, by race and job classification, are shown in Table 7.

TABLE 7.　*The Banking Industry*
Employment by Race and Occupational Group
United States, 1966

Occupational Group	Total	Negro	Percent Negro
Officials and managers	88,107	343	0.4
Professionals	10,787	83	0.8
Technicians	3,811	243	6.4
Sales workers	2,648	13	0.5
Office and clerical	373,251	14,080	3.8
Total white collar	478,604	14,762	3.1
Total blue collar	32,271	7,819	24.2
Total	510,875	22,581	4.4

Source:　U. S. Equal Employment Opportunity Comission, *Job Patterns for Minorities and Women in Private Industry-1966*, Report No. 1, Part II (Washington: The Commission, 1968).

The results from this table can be compared with the 1960 census data seen in Table 6. The rise in the proportion of Negroes employed is most spectacular. In 1966, Negroes were 4.4 percent of total banking employment, up from 1.9 percent in 1960. During this period, the banking industry was continuing to expand in total employment, so that the proportion of Negroes hired was considerably greater than 4.4 percent.[14]

Field Sample Data, 1966

As a complement to the published EEOC data, additional information for 1966 is available from a field sample of some 738 indi-

---

[14] If a firm is expanding and its Negro participation ratio remains the same, then its hiring rate of Negroes is in the same proportion, thus:

A firm of 1,000 employees, 2% black, has 20 Negroes. If it expands by 10%, it will have 1,100 employees. With the same (2%) participation ratio, it will now have 22 Negroes. One hundred new employees were added, 2 of the 100 were Negroes, and hiring proportion remains at 2%.

However:

A firm of 1,000 employees, 2% black, has 20 Negroes. If it expands by 10%, it will have 1,100 employees. With a higher participation ratio (say 5%), it will have now 55 Negroes. One hundred new employees were added, 35 of the 100 were Negroes, and the hiring proportion is 35%.

vidual commercial banks. Although not as complete in coverage
of the industry, these data are in different form than the EEOC
report, and allow certain state and regional breakdowns, evaluation of employment patterns in insitutions of different sizes, and
other statistical accumulations which are not possible from the
published data.

When field sample data are duplicated by figures from the published EEOC report, we shall use the latter. Nevertheless, to illustrate the extensiveness of the field sample and to show the high
degree of similarity of results between the two sets of figures, a
compendium of the sample results has been included as Table 8.

Female employment which appears in Table 8 can be compared
with earlier figures from Table 6. The trend toward increasingly female banking work forces which began in 1940 can be
seen as continuing through 1966, when 57 percent of all employment in the industry was female.

The table also shows that although two of every three Negroes
employed are in white collar jobs, more than nine out of every
ten persons in the industry are in white collar jobs, and the
Negro employment rate for these jobs is therefore considerably
less than that for other races.

RECENT DEVELOPMENT AND TRENDS, *1967 AND 1968*

Data on hand and revised as of March 1969 covering banking
employment for 1967 and 1968 are drawn from a somewhat different population of banks than are earlier statistics. As has
been mentioned, the 1966 statistics were taken from banks subject to the nondiscrimination provisions of the Civil Rights Act
of 1964, which included firms with more than one hundred employees. Subsequent to August 1966, however, all banks holding
deposits of the United States Government (regardless of the size
of deposit) were deemed to be contractors to the government and
therefore subject to the President's executive order 11246 prohibiting discrimination.[15] Under the provisions of this order, all
banks with government deposits and with fifty or more employees
were required to file reports and maintain records on minority
employment. Thus, many additional banks, having between fifty
and one hundred employees, began to keep racial statistics and

---

[15] Letter in the author's possession from Henry H. Fowler, Secretary of
the Treasury, to "The Chief Executive Officer of the Bank Addressed,"
Washington, August 1966.

TABLE 8. *The Banking Industry*
Employment by Race, Sex, and Occupational Classification
738 Banks
United States, 1966

All Employees			376,017
White collar			352,428
Male white collar		144,905	
Female white collar		207,523	
White collar as percent of all employees			93.7
All Negro Employees			16,561
Negro white collar			11,011
Male white collar		3,403	
Female white collar		7,608	
Negro white collar as percent of all Negro employees			66.5
Negroes as percent of all employees			4.4
Negro white collar as percent of total white collar			3.1
Total females as percent of all employees			57.0
Female white collar as percent of total white collar			58.9
Negro female white collar as percent of total Negro white collar			69.1

Source: Data in author's possession.

many of these smaller banks were included in the 1967 and 1968 surveys.[16]

As we shall see in Chapter V, there apparently is a direct correlation between size of firm and proportion of Negroes employed. Thus, by including banks with smaller work forces in our surveys, we eliminate some of the upward bias which systematic sampling error may have introduced into the 1966 figures.

Comparable Statistics, *1967 and 1968*

A most interesting sub-set of the 1967 and 1968 data can be drawn from the more complete statistics available. It consists of the figures from about 1,300 individual banks which had information for both 1967 and 1968. This is a sub-set of *comparable* data, and is invaluable for analyzing growth and hiring patterns between the two years.

The picture of change presented is very encouraging. In 1967, the total employment for these banks was 483,348, and their Negro employment 24,436, making 5.1 percent Negro overall. Between 1967 and 1968, total employment grew by 6.1 percent, raising the work force total to 512,714. Simultaneously, the number of Negroes in banks increased by 24.7 percent, to a total Negro employment of 30,483. In 1968, Negroes made up 5.9 percent of all employment in these banks.

An even more optimistic picture is presented if we look at the growth figures specifically. Between 1967 and 1968, the 1,300 banks created 29,366 new jobs. Six thousand and forty-seven of these were filled by Negroes. If we can assume that the turnover rate for Negroes and non-Negroes already employed was approximately the same, then this means that 20.6 percent of all persons added by the industry (for the "1968" report) were Negro. And if the Negro turnover rate were actually greater than that for non-Negroes, this hiring rate would be even higher.

These data and some similar figures showing the breakdown of the work force by sex are seen in Table 9. Also included in that table are the 1966 data taken from Table 8, which, although not directly comparable to the two subsequent years' figures, are included to illustrate the continuing trends.

---

[16] The average bank in the country in 1968 had 67 employees. See Tables 2 and 4 in Chapter II.

TABLE 9. *The Banking Industry*
Employment by Race and Sex
United States, 1966-1968

	1966	1967	1968
Number of Reporting Units	738	1,300	1,300
Total Employment	376,017	483,348	512,714
Total Male	161,705	188,089	196,844
Total Female	214,312	295,259	315,870
Total Negro Employment	16,561	24,436	30,483
Negro Male	N.A.	10,181	11,816
Negro Female	N.A.	14,255	18,667
Percent Negro Employment	4.4	5.1	5.9
Male	N.A.	5.4	6.0
Female	N.A.	4.8	5.9
Percent Growth, 1967-1968			
All Employees		D.N.A.	6.1
Negro Employees		D.N.A.	24.7
Percent of Total Employment			
Growth Made Up by Negroes		D.N.A.	20.6

Source: Table 8 and data in author's possession.

Overall Statistics, *1967 and 1968*

The more complete data, revised as of March 1969, include an additional 200 banks (approximately) which had figures available for 1967 but not 1968, and approximately 400 which had figures available for 1968 but not 1967. Because they represent the results of larger samples, these data, although unsuitable for analysis of growth, are better indications of the overall employment picture in the industry in each of these years.

For 1967, with 1,500 banks reporting, total employment stood at 535,000, Negro employment at 26,000, and the proportion Negro employed at 4.9 percent. (These numbers are all approximations.) For 1968, with 1,700 banks reporting, total employment was recorded at 667,082, and total Negro employment at 37,396, for 5.6 percent Negro. This information is recorded in Table 10.

Comparing the figures from Table 9 with those on Table 10 reveals that the inclusion of additional banks in the revised data resulted in a decrease in the total percentage Negro recorded.

This decrease could be attributed to a number of causes, of which two stand out. First, the average size of the additional four hundred banks is slightly smaller than that of the first 1,300. Second, many of the reports came from banks located in areas of very small Negro population concentration. Some data on minority employment as well as Negro employment are presented in Table 10.

TABLE 10. *The Banking Industry*
Employment by Race and Sex
United States, 1967-1968

	1967	1968
Number of reporting units (approximate)	1500	1700
All Employees	535,000	667,082
Total male	N.A.	285,200
Total female	N.A.	381,882
All Minority Employees	N.A.	60,824
Minority male	N.A.	25,286
Minority female	N.A.	35,538
All Negro Employees	26,000	37,396
Negro male	N.A.	16,637
Negro female	N.A.	20,759
Percent Minority Employment	N.A.	9.1
Male	N.A.	8.9
Female	N.A.	9.3
Percent Negro Employment	4.9	5.6
Male	N.A.	5.8
Female	N.A.	5.4
Negro as percent of all minority employees		61.5

Source: Data in author's possession; revised as of March 1, 1969.

SURVEY DATA, 1968

In the Summer and Fall of 1968, fifty banks in seventeen cities throughout the country were contacted by the author on the subject of their Negro employment. Forty-nine of these were commercial banks. Forty-seven of the forty-nine consented to participate in the survey, and forty-six of the forty-seven provided detailed statistical data as well as responses to more subjective questions. The institutions which participated in these interviews, and a few words about the survey itself, are to be found in Appendix A.

Although the interviews were national in scope, employing the statistics drawn from them requires some care. These are all large banks by comparison with industry averages. Although they constitute only some 2.7 percent of all banks filing reports in 1968, these banks comprise 30 percent of the total reported employment. Therefore some question exists as to how representative they are of the industry as a whole. (The relationship between size of institutions and Negro employment level will be discussed in Chapter V.)

Even if not particularly representative of the industry as a whole, there is a twofold significance attached to these banks. First, the problems with and concern for Negro employment are predominantly a factor in major cities, and these survey banks are located in a cross-section of the largest cities in the country. Their reactions and their handling of methodologies for increasing Negro employment are the ones which count most heavily. Secondly, these forty-six banks employed 45 percent of all of the Negroes reported in the entire industry in 1968. The various statistical breakdowns for this group of banks are shown in Table 11. In 1968, their Negro employment totaled 8.1 percent of the total work force, and Negro white collar workers were 7.6 percent of the white collar group.

OVERALL TRENDS, 1940-1968

The banking industry in this country has not been a traditional place of employment for Negroes, and even on the verge of 1970 it is anything but overwhelming Negro. The overall trend in the numbers and proportions of Negroes in bank work forces, however, is unmistakeably upward. Figure 2 brings together the available data on the Negro population proportion and the proportion of banking employment. The figure makes it clear that there was a considerable change in attitudes in the industry in the early 1960's, resulting in a dramatic increase in the level of Negro employment.

If the rise is dramatic, one of the factors which makes it so is the lack of change in industry hiring patterns prior to that time. The labor market pertubations which affected employment patterns in most industries after 1940 as a result of the manpower

TABLE 11. *The Banking Industry*
Employment by Race, Sex, and Occupational Classification
46 Commercial Banks Surveyed
United States, 1968

All Employees		205,541
White collar		196,746
Male white collar	74,266	
Female white collar	122,480	
White collar as percent of all employees		95.7
All Negro Employees		16,726
Negro white collar		14,874
Male white collar	3,775	
Female white collar	11,099	
Negro white collar as percent of all Negro employees		88.9
Negroes as percent of all employees		8.1
Negro white collar as percent of total white collar		7.6
Total females as percent of all employees		60.4
Female white collar as percent of total white collar		62.3
Negro female white collar as percent of total Negro white collar		74.6

Source: Data in author's possession.

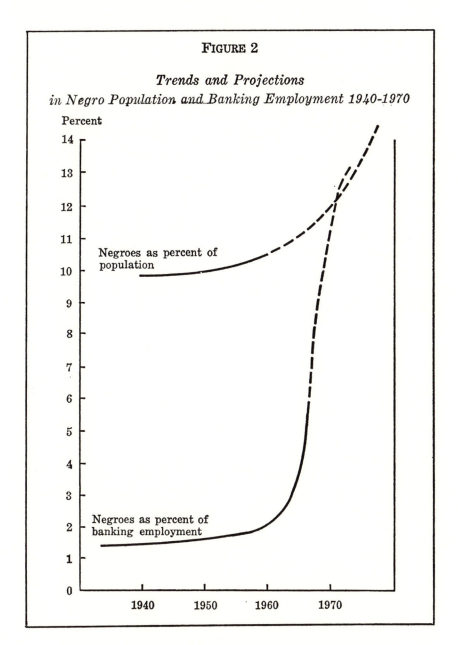

FIGURE 2

Trends and Projections
in Negro Population and Banking Employment 1940-1970

Source: Tables 6, 7, 10, 21, and data in author's possession.

needs growing from the military conscriptions and emphasis on military production were felt by the banking industry, but the shift which came about was in the male-female mix rather than in the racial composition of the work forces. As a result, in racial terms, the industry remained generally more exclusive, less integrated than most by 1960 and had had little previous experience with race issues.

In the 1940 census of the population, reports on the racial composition of eighty-two industrial categories were shown. At that time, compared with the banking group (which included savings and loans, etc.), twelve industries had a smaller proportion of male Negro workers and twenty-two showed relatively fewer female Negroes. In the following twenty years, the racial employment patterns in almost all industries underwent greater change than in banking. In the 1960 census, only three categories, "footwear except rubber," "communications," and "legal, engineering, and miscellaneous professional" still had fewer Negro males; and with a single exception—"mining"—banks employed the lowest proportion of Negro females of any industry.

Thus it was from a very low statistical base that improvement in racial employment began in banking in the early 1960's, and this low base, along with the personnel attitudes which accompanied it, is still very easily recalled by compiance agencies and by qualified Negroes who might otherwise apply to the industry for jobs. Therefore, it is to the detriment of the industry in several ways that it waited so long to embrace equal employment ideas; but in fairness it should be pointed out that there were many factors particular to the banking employment structure which made experimentation with employee patterns seem risky in the eyes of many of the industry's personnel men.

In any event, the level of Negro employment in banking only changed from about 1.5 percent of the work force in 1940 to somewhat less than 2 percent twenty years later, in 1960. After 1960, it increased rapidly, and grew at a rate of just slightly less than a compounded 15 percent per year. The 1968 level was three times that of 1960, and stood at almost 6 percent of the total work force. Projection of the trend illustrated in Figure 2 indicates that banks will be employing Negroes at their population proportion by 1972 or 1973.

Female Advances

Another major trend in banking employment is the status of women in the industry. As mentioned, hiring greater numbers of females was banking's response to wartime labor shortages. During the early 1940's female participation shot up from 30 to 45 percent of the work force. Over the following twenty years, the female employment proportion increased but at a decreasing rate, and probably would have continued a modest increase or stabilized were it not for the sudden increase in clerical work brought about by the introduction of computers, the general spread in the sponsoring of credit cards by banks, and the increased desire for banking services by the general public during the affluent 1960's. These factors made more jobs available for females, and changes in sociological viewpoints during the same time meant that there were more women seeking jobs. The most recent figures show that 57 percent of bank employees are female.

The increase in Negro females as a proportion of total Negro employment started in 1940 at an even lower base, but has changed more rapidly, so that by 1968 their participation ratio was almost identical with the overall female pattern. The Negro female gains are a result of clerical-level hirings, but this is only half the picture. A proper understanding requires realization that the initial low female proportion resulted from the practice of using Negroes, when hired at all, in porter, guard, messenger, maintenance, and miscellaneous service jobs, all of which are male-oriented. Even now, although the female proportion of Negroes is about the same as for non-Negroes, there is a substantive difference in the distribution of the male jobs.

In each job category, the ratio of female to male employees is about the same for Negroes as for non-Negroes. Females of all races are underrepresented in both the high-level—officer and manager, professional, sales, and technical—positions and in blue collar jobs. They are overrepresented in office and clerical jobs. Although the proportion of persons holding office and clerical positions is about the same for Negroes as for non-Negroes, Negroes are overrepresented in the blue collar jobs and underrepresented in the high-level positions compared to non-Negroes. The top jobs are thus predominantly white male, the middle jobs predominantly female, and the blue collar jobs predominantly Negro male.

INDICATIONS FOR 1969

Among personnel men in the forty-seven banks comprised by the survey, none saw any indications that the generally upward trend of Negro representation in banks was coming to an end or even slowing down. And only in a rare case did a bank indicate that its own organization would not change much toward a more heavily Negro racial composition in the near future. One comment representative of this group follows:

> We hired quite a few new people last year when we put in the new credit card. The labor market here is not particularly tight now, so we don't have much trouble getting qualified people this year. There was quite a jump up in Negro hiring last year, but although I don't have the figures, I suspect the rate might be a little lower now.

Comments representative of the more common experience of expanding Negro employment are the following:

> Our hiring went from 25.9 percent last year overall to 41.7 percent in the first quarter of 1968.

> Well, I don't really know [what the hiring rate is] but more than 25 percent of our current applicants are Negro.

> Through May of this year, almost 9 percent of our new hires have been Negroes. This is about three times what it was last year, and doesn't count the NAB program additions.

> We had a 30 percent increase in black hiring last year, and I am sure it will be even more this year.

Finally, and perhaps most typical of all:

> Negro applications and hirings have both doubled in the past five years, and it certainly doesn't look like either is going to be slowing down any.[17]

Interview comments of this sort are not the most positive or persuasive arguments which would be formulated for indicating continued growth in Negro representation in banks; and yet there seems little reason to question them. Those interviewed merely confirm the author's random sampling observations of bank hiring offices: Negroes were present, seeking employment (at least

---

[17] Interviews, various cities, 1968.

during the summer and fall of 1968) in large numbers. By whatever means, the word has apparently spread that employment opportunities are available to Negroes in the major financial institutions.

Perhaps more important, conditions are now much more amenable to the acceptance of Negroes seeking jobs in banking. First, the number of Negroes now generally employed by the average, large, city bank is great enough that the presence of a Negro employee in any department is not a subject of disruptive curiosity. Thus banks are more hospitable to Negroes seeking positions, and the Negroes will be spared the fears of isolation, stares, and other manifestations of close scrutiny attendant to being obviously noticeable in a different (and sometimes hostile) environment.

Second, there is clear evidence that in most such banks, the fears of executives about the internal and external consequences of hiring Negroes, of hiring Negroes for public contact jobs, of promoting Negroes to supervisory positions, of employing Negroes in the personnel function, or using Negroes elsewhere have been largely groundless. These initial deterrents having been overcome, banks are hiring from among the Negro applicants. The indications of this chapter are that the hiring is being done at a rapidly increasing rate.

CONCLUSIONS

The data presented in this chapter have been very carefully selected as the most representative figures available covering the racial employment patterns of the banking industry on a national scale. Systematic statistical errors, where known, have been identified. Nevertheless, the utility of these national data is somewhat limited. It must be remembered that national percentage figures are "average" figures; and in the averaging process, no differentiation can be made between a bank in Lincoln, Nebraska, and one in Jackson, Mississippi. Yet, judging by even superficial analysis, we know from the Negro population proportions of each city that a bank of the same size in each having the national average in Negro employment would be overrepresentative of the Negro population of Lincoln and underrepresentative of it in Jackson. In other words, the national average figures are not a valid standard of comparison for the performance of specific banks.

A second problem concerns the use of averages for performance evaluation at all. Overall trends provide an average against which the performance of an individual bank can be measured, but do not address the question of whether the "normal" pattern is a sufficient one. That question we shall leave to the government agencies charged with evaluating it and to the consensus of individual banking executives. In this study, our focus is to lay before individual bankers as much information as possible about the "normal" pattern for his industry, for his city or area of the country, for institutions the size of his own, etc. By analyzing that pattern, it will be possible to isolate the major factors which seem to have the greatest effect on Negro employment levels. This will be discussed in the ensuing chapters.

CHAPTER IV

Analyzing the Factors Causing Differences Among Industries

The type and quantity of labor demanded or desired by different industries varies with a great number of factors, among them technological and product requirements, job requirements, wage levels, and tradition. The type and quantity of labor supplied or offered to industries is subject to a similar diversity of causes, including wage levels, working conditions, industry image, and perceived welcome. Discrimination and racial bigotry affect demand for minority group members directly and affect supply indirectly through industry image. Let us look more closely at these and related factors as they affect overall employment patterns for Negroes in the banking industry.

JOB REQUIREMENTS, HIGH SKILL

There is no question about the banking industry being very much a white collar industry. In fact, with over 90 percent white collar jobs, it has one of the highest levels in the country of this type of position. Partially, this is required by the particular service offered by the industry, and partially it is a result of a conscious policy to reduce personnel problems in the work force by contracting-out many of the blue collar service requirements such as cafeteria or building maintenance.

The question is does this white collar concentration affect Negro employment, and if so, why? The data on this, while not exhaustive, are consistent enough to give a pretty clear indication that Negro representation decreases with an increasing proportion of white collar positions.

White Collar Comparisons

Table 12 compares banking with all reported employment in the top sixty industries in the country (by employment size) and with the industries which reported the greatest and least proportional Negro representation. The data for this table were drawn from the Equal Employment Opportunity Report (No. 1) which contains the accumulated data from more than 17,500 firms in all industries.[18]

---

[18] U. S. Equal Employment Opportunity Commission, *Job Patterns for Minorities and Women in Private Industry, 1966*, Report No. 1 (Washington: The Commission, 1968), Part I.

Obviously, banking was not one of the leaders in Negro employment in 1966. The industry had about 2 percent of all employment, but only about 1 percent of Negro employment. But banks have a more even distribution of Negroes by job classification than is the case in most industries. The top sixty industries in the country are seen to have had 8.2 percent Negro in their overall work force, but only 2.5 percent in the white collar work force. Banking was 4.4 percent overall, but 3.1 percent in the white collar positions. Agriculture, contract construction, and lumber and wood products, among others, each had more than 12 percent Negro overall but less than 1 percent Negro white collar workers.

Figure 3 is drawn from the same source materials as Table 12, and shows the degree of correlation which exists between white collar employment and Negro employment. Looking at the right-hand side of that figure, we can see that there is a fair correlation between increasing levels of white collar employment and decreasing levels of Negro employment in all major industries. Following the statistical trends in this table would lead us to expect less Negro representation in the banking industry than in electronics assembly or automobile repair, or than in the average of all American industries where white collar employment accounts for about half instead of 90 percent of all jobs.

The next question is why this should be the case. There are two general arguments which can be synopsized briefly. On the one hand is the allegation by the Equal Employment Opportunity Commission (and others) to the effect that racial discrimination is more rampant in industries using higher proportions of white collar employees. This certainly is a possible explanation, but it becomes somewhat less persuasive when it is noted, from the left-hand side of Figure 3, that there is also a direct (though not as strong) correlation between an increasing white collar orientation and the proportion of Negroes in white collar jobs. Thus, if it can be said that industries having a large number of white collar jobs discriminate more against Negroes in general, it must also be said that they discriminate relatively less in the higher-ranking jobs, which would seem odd logic on the part of the discriminators.

The second argument comes from those who allege that white collar jobs are more demanding, higher-skilled jobs for which Negroes are less prepared.

TABLE 12. *Negro Employment in Top Sixty Industries United States, 1966*

Industry	All Employees			White Collar			Blue Collar			Service		
	Total	Negro	Per-cent Negro	Total	Negro	Per-cent Negro	Total	Negro	Per-cent Negro	Total	Negro	Per-cent Negro
Top 60 Industries	25,594	2,090	8.2	11,004	281	2.5	12,628	1,357	10.7	1,962	452	23.0
							Thousands of Employees					
							Actual Number of Employees					
Banking	510,875	22,581	4.4	478,604	14,762	3.1	6,947	1,020	14.7	25,324	6,799	26.8
Industry with greatest overall percent Negro (Personal services)	93,809	34,180	36.4	25,129	1,519	6.0	61,433	30,141	49.1	7,247	2,520	34.8
Industry with greatest percent Negro white collar (Medical services)	1,059,794	174,132	16.4	596,032	42,852	7.2	90,429	17,819	19.7	373,333	118,461	30.4
Industry with lowest percent Negro—Overall and white collar (Pipeline transportation)	15,614	75	0.5	6,536	11	0.2	8,998	41	0.5	80	23	28.8
Among these 60 industries in Negro employment, banking ranked, from the top			46			14			26			25

Source: U.S. Equal Employment Opportunity Commission, *Job Patterns for Minorities and Women in Private Industry, 1966*, Report No. 1 (Washington: The Commission, 1968), Part I, Table A1-4.

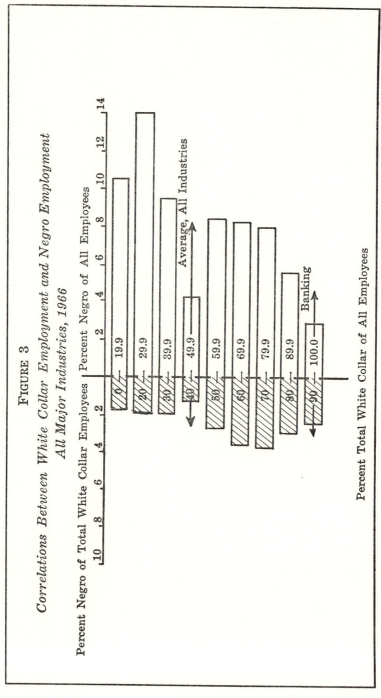

FIGURE 3

Correlations Between White Collar Employment and Negro Employment
All Major Industries, 1966

Source: U.S. Equal Employment Opportunity Commission, Job Patterns for Minorities and Women in
Private Industry, 1966, Report No. 1 (Washington: The Commission, 1968), Part II.

Negro Preparation Levels

There are very few qualified Negro financiers seeking employment in the banking industry. Few members of that race have had any higher-level employment experience with banking and just as few have prepared themselves by garnering the necessary technological skills in college. Given the sociological condition of the country since the turn of the century, the severely restricted job horizons of Negroes until recently, and their general difficulty in acquiring either the experience or the training necessary for higher-level jobs in finance, this should not be unexpected. Even now, there are very few Negroes prepared for the highly specialized top jobs in banking where skill demands require developed sensitivities which are long in forming. But this argument begs the question, for the majority of white collar jobs in banking are not of this sort, being instead entry-level clerical positions, often machine oriented and highly routine. Some entry-level white collar bank jobs, far from requiring carefully developed skills and perceptions, demand little more than manual dexterity. Others, such as the teller positions, require arithmetical facility, an extensive array of good personal habits, and a reasonably sunny disposition as well. But in almost any of the clerical jobs, the minimum experience and skill required is of the high-school-level sort. As with the military so it is very largely true in banks that once the organization scheme has been devised, it can be manned by almost anyone. Therefore, the excuse commonly offered by bankers to the effect that the skills demanded by its white collar jobs are too rigorous for the current state of Negro preparedness is difficult to accept.

Entry-Level Expectations

Banks do prefer, and quite rightly, the best work force input possible for a given cost, and so prefer the experienced or at least the premotivated and adequately trained, not only to keep up standards, but also to protect themselves as much as possible against the dissatisfaction of employees of long standing.[19]

---

[19] *Wall Street Journal*, June 11, 1968: "Nation's Biggest Firms Now Committed to Help Solve the Racial Crisis." Quoting from the article: ". . . Corporate managers have to deal with another delicate problem—white backlash among workers who believe Negroes are getting preferential treatment or not doing their share of the work. 'We have to keep the bank running smoothly,' says Walter A. Hoadley, senior vice president and chief economist at the Bank of America. 'We have to prevent the people who aren't singled out (for special attention) from getting their noses out of joint.'"

A few years ago, when the job market was much looser, banks and other firms with high white collar demands could afford such selection procedures to seek entrants with more than minimal qualifications. In the tight labor markets of the 1960's, this sort of choosiness became a luxury. Almost all of the entry-level applicants seen by banks, white or black, come looking for positions equipped only with high-school-level sorts of minimal skill development. Banks throughout the country are increasingly forced to take up training programs for suitable development of those entry-level skills.

Most banks and other industries whose white collar positions are largely clerical have discovered that once such a training program has been set up, handling the incremental training which may be required by some of the Negroes is not particularly onerous. As a result, the Negro representation among new hires is rapidly increasing, especially in the larger, city banks. Between 1967 and 1968, Negroes were hired at a rate of more than 20 percent nationally, and about 27 percent in sixteen major cities. (See table 9 in chapter 3, and table 22 later in this chapter.) These figures indicate that the gap in Negro proportions between highly white collar industries, such as banking, and others is closing rapidly.

JOB REQUIREMENTS, PUBLIC CONTACT, AND PRODUCT DIFFERENTIATION

After "clerks," "tellers" compose the largest group under a single job title in the banking industry. (See tables 31 and 33 in chapter 6). The job is a demanding one in several respects, and the demands are intensified by the requirements of constant contact with the public. In Chapter II it was noted that certain skills are required, such as arithmetical ability and great care in handling cash. Additionally, there are many specific banking procedures with which a teller must be familiar. The American Bankers Association lists 117 such, which run the gamut from "wrapping coins" to "hold-up procedures," (but which do not, of course, include the instructions specific to individual banks).[20]

---

[20] The American Bankers Association, *How to Train A Bank Teller: A Management Guide*, A Training Pamphlet Prepared by the Committee on Employee Training and Country Bank Operations Committee (New York: The American Bankers Association, 1961), pp. 32-36.

But despite their complexities, learning these procedures and the technical content of the teller's job at least well enough to begin productive service should not take an overly long time for anyone who has demonstrated sufficient proficiency to get through high school. Indeed, the ABA-recommended training course requires but three weeks, and some simple "window" transactions are scheduled for the fourth day.

Customer Relations

The real problem with the teller job is not the job content, but the customer relations. In the words of the American Bankers Association:

> Most people who enter a bank do business principally with the tellers. As a result, tellers have a significant role in customer relations since they come directly in contact with customers more than any other employee in the bank. The success of a bank depends to a great extent on how well the tellers know and perform their jobs . . . An essential part of teller training is the developing of proper attitudes toward the public relations aspects of the job . . . If the customers' impressions, received through their contacts with tellers, are unfavorable, it is likely that they will take their business to another bank.[21]

It is for these reasons that banks are very concerned about the public presentability of those employed in this sensitive job, and the "traits and qualities the officer in charge of hiring should look for and evaluate during interviews," are the following (presented in the order listed by the American Bankers Association): "Appearance, appropriate dress; poise, alertness, self-confidence; voice, mannerisms, ability to communicate; personality, friendliness, cooperative attitude; ambition; dependability; maturity; ability to get along well with people; interest in teller work and banking." [22]

The population which utilizes the services of banks is overwhelmingly white, and it is that population which is the final arbiter of the "appropriateness" of dress or the sufficiency of "friendliness" of a bank teller. For a long time, bankers throughout the country feared that any black would be debili-

---

[21] *Ibid.*, p. 9.

[22] *Ibid.*, p. 15.

tated by his lack of "appropriateness" in one or another of the factors above, and therefore unacceptable to a number of customers who would take their business elsewhere as a consequence of black hiring. Negro tellers were therefore employed by banks which had "Negro branches" and only rarely elsewhere.[23]

Product Differentiation

Another factor which intensifies the sensitivity of this job is the nondifferentiability of the product of the banking industry to the average customer. For handling the checking accounts, holding the time deposits, providing safe deposit facilities, and undertaking the other usual banking needs of customers, there is no essential difference between banks.[24] For most customers, therefore, there is no difficulty—outside of minor inconvenience—connected with changing banks, and the fear of customer reaction for a long time involved a genuine risk to the bank. Under these circumstances, one would expect to find fewer Negroes in public contact jobs generally (and in teller jobs specifically) than in other, less sensitive positions. This was the situation in banks until very recently.

Reaction to Employment of Negroes

In the survey of major banks conducted by the author in the Summer of 1968, one of the questions asked was: "What do you consider to be the greatest lack on the part of the Negro applicants for employment?" Some of the forty-nine bankers who responded gave multiple answers. The responses are ranked by frequency in Table 13.

About half of these responses have direct applicability to the public requirements of the teller job, and it is presumed that five years ago an even greater proportion of the answers would have tended to reflect veiled fears that Negro employees would be unacceptable to customers. Indeed, when asked, the bankers almost invariably admitted that they had harbored great fears

---

[23] For illustration of this point, see Bank F, table 28, in chapter 6.

[24] The author can attest to this personally, having utilized the services of seven different Philadelphia banks in a little over five years of residency. Two of the shifts were caused by dissatisfaction with attitudes of tellers or officers (all white, incidentally) but the balance were purely matters of locational convenience. There are no substantive differences in the type or variety of services offered or their costs.

—which they now agree were overdone—about customer reaction to an inflex of Negro jobholders. The actual reaction reported was very small, as witnessed in Table 14.

TABLE 13. *Bankers' Response to Question: "What Do You Consider the Greatest Lack On the Part of Negro Applicants for Employment?"*
47 Commercial Banks Surveyed
United States, 1968

Reply	Frequency of Reply
1. Basic education	18
2. Poor work history, skill development	12
3. Speech habits, verbal skills	9
4. Lack of empathy with whites, with profit system	7
5. Dress, personal hygiene	6
6. Lack of initiative, motivation	5
7. Lack of acceptable credentials	5
8. Lack of self-confidence	4
9. Super-sensitivity about race	1

Source: Data in the author's possession.

TABLE 14. *Reported Customer Reaction to Visible Negro Employees*
47 Commercial Banks Surveyed
United States, 1968

Type of Reaction	Severity		
	None	Minor	Severe
1. Letters of protest [a]	28	19	0
2. Letters of encouragement	29	17	1
3. Cancellation of deposits	43	4	0

Source: Data in the author's possession.

[a] Includes reaction to summer "hard-core" hiring projects.

Essentially, there were as many customers who either encouraged the banks to hire more Negroes (or congratulated them for having made a start in that direction) as there were customers who complained. Only four banks reported any cancellations of deposits which could be attributed to Negro hiring, and in no case could this manifestation of dissatisfaction be considered severe.

But the fears of reaction which had existed were real. As recently as 1964, in many cities in the South, only a very daring and adventurous personnel officer would have considered undertaking the risk of making his bank the only one in town to have Negro tellers. To break through this sort of situation, concerted action is required—either voluntary or legislated. So long as one personnel man alone had to run the risk of a possible bigoted reaction by customers, there was little reason for him to contemplate hiring Negro tellers, regardless of his personel feelings on the subject. However, if all of the major banks in the city agreed to take on Negro tellers (or were required to) then there could be no major problem, for the only alternative possible to a dissatisfied customer would be to keep his money under his mattress, and this is an alternative which only the hardiest of bigots rich enough to matter would contemplate.

Thus, for banks which had not yet hired Negro tellers, the Civil Rights Act of 1964 and Executive Order 11246 provided not only the necessity but also the excuse to break the racial barriers surrounding public contact jobs. The subsequent hiring of tellers by banks and the lack of difficulties attendant to it invalidated the "fear of reaction" argument and also prevented its use as a "pass the buck" excuse for nonaction—as it may have been used by some bankers.[25]

---

[25] The author made a very informal survey of his current branch bank which does a brisk, if somewhat seasonal, business. On average, three of the tellers in the bank are Negro, three white. The customers are predominantly white, but on the crowded days there are usually some Negro customers as well. Over seven visits, no pattern of any sort was discernible in the racial use of tellers. That is, customers of both races used tellers of both races on a basis which was apparently purely random. The only other pattern which was clear concerned one "favorite" teller, a Negro girl, whose pleasant disposition and efficiency invariably earned her the longest lines of customers.

REQUIREMENT FOR PROFITS

To see how strong a factor the requirement for profits is in affecting Negro employment, we shall compare the experience of commercial banks with those of the Federal Reserve Banks. There are twelve Federal Reserve Banks in the country, one for each of the Federal Reserve Districts. Each of these banks, except for Philadelphia and Boston, has from one to four branches, located for geographical convenience. There are a total of twenty-four such branches. The Federal Reserves are "bankers' banks," and do no business with the general public. Each is a corporation organized and operated for public service, and as such is not a profit-seeking institution. The directors of each of the banks are general businessmen rather than bankers, and not "officers, directors, employees, or stockholders of any bank." [26]

Although major financial policies are closely controlled by the Board of Governors in Washington, this is not so much the case for personnel policies.[27] The banks in no way enjoy a "protected" status and their employees are not on the civil service rolls. The banks are made more conscious of new federal employment policy requirements by their Board of Governors and seem faster to respond to new requirements and directives. But they, too, have had their reviews by human relations commissions, visits from CORE, union organization attempts, and other varieties of external pressures. They are disbursed all over the country; their size in 1966 (including branches), ran from just over fifty employees to almost 3,700; their wages were about the same as those paid by commercial banks: "Our raw wages are some-

---

[26] Board of Governors of the Federal System, *The Federal Reserve System; Purposes and Functions* (Washington, 1961), p. 70.

[27] According to Andrew Brimmer, member of the Federal Reserve Board of Governors, Negro employment in the Federal Reserve Banks is "supported by a strong positive employment policy developed by the Federal Reserve Board;" but Dr. Brimmer goes on to point out: "Despite a strong endorsement by policy officials in the System, the performance is uneven among Reserve Banks." [In: Andrew F. Brimmer, *Employment Patterns and the Quest for Equal Opportunity in Banking*, A Report Before a Conference on Bank Employment Practices Sponsored by U.S. Treasury Department and the Michigan Human Relations Commission, Lansing, Michigan, May 22, 1968 (Washington: Board of Governors of the Federal Reserve System, 1968), pp. 14, 15.] This suggests that, rather than detailed policy directives, the individual Reserve Banks are given suggestions for policy direction and provided somewhat closer review than are commercial banks, but are not subject to employment policy control as such.

what lower, but with fringes may even be a bit on the high side." [28]

In the light of all this, it would be expected that the Federal Reserve Banks might have *slightly* greater Negro employment than commercial banks. In fact, their Negro employment is considerably higher, as seen in Table 15. The table shows that Federal Reserve Banks had more than twice the Negro employment rate of commercial banks. In addition to their having no tellers or other public-contact employees, there are some other job classification differences which become apparent from a study of the table. The Federal Reserve Banks have relatively more blue collar jobs (or at least classified more jobs as such) and these jobs were both more heavily male and more heavily Negro than blue collar positions in commercial banks. On the other hand, white collar jobs in the Federal Reserve Banks were held by a greater predominance of females. Of all the white collar jobs held by Negroes, three out of four were filled by females. The average number of employees in 1966 at the Federal Reserve Banks (545) is fairly close to the average number of employees in a field sample of 738 commercial banks (510). But the Federal Reserves averaged forty-nine Negroes per bank as compared to twenty-two.

The difference cannot be explained by absolute size, relative size, geographical location, government requirements, or wages offered. Job differences and job classification differences, lack of public-contact requirements, closer association with federal policy, and lack of requirements for profits have apparently had effect on managements' policy determinations.

Comparisons with Other Financial Institutions

Other financial institutions which perform services somewhat related to those of commercial banks but do not have the two unique characteristics of the Federal Reserve Banks—closer association with federal policies, and lack of profit requirements—show about the same Negro work force proportions as do commercial banks. Institutions of this sort are: mutual savings banks, trust companies not engaged in deposit banking, currency exchanges and safe deposit companies, and a variety of credit agencies—including savings and loan associations. These institutions have jobs and job classifications similar to those of banks,

---

[28] Interview, June 1968.

TABLE 15.   *Federal Reserve Banks and All Commercial Banks Employment by Race and Sex United States, 1966*

Type of Bank	All Commercial Banks	Federal Reserve Banks
Number of Banks Reporting	738	35
All Employees	376,017	19,080
White collar	352,428	15,786
Male white collar	144,905	5,819
Female white collar	207,523	9,967
White collar as percent of all employees	93.7	82.7
All Negro Employees	16,561	1,727
Negro white collar	11,011	891
Male white collar	3,403	201
Female white collar	7,608	690
Negro white collar as percent of all Negro employees	66.5	51.6
Negroes as percent of all employees	4.4	9.1
Negro white collar as percent of total white collar	3.1	5.6
Total females as percent of all employees	57.0	55.8
Female white collar as percent of total white collar	58.9	63.1
Negro female white collar as percent of total Negro white collar	69.1	77.4

Source: Table 9 and data in author's possession.

although many of them are free from extensive public contact requirements. All of them do require profits. A 1966 field survey of employment patterns in 58 mutual savings banks found that this group had the highest Negro representation in the banking and finance industry, with 5.4 percent Negro overall, and 4.6 percent in white collar jobs.

Companies not engaged in deposit banking, currency exchanges, and safe deposit companies similarly show Negro employment levels slightly higher than those in commercial banks. Credit agencies, security dealers and exchanges, and insurance and other miscellaneous financial services have somewhat smaller Negro employment ratios than do the commercial banks.[29]

THE REQUIREMENTS OF TRUSTWORTHINESS

The close proximity of a great deal of cash, especially when it is changing hands rapidly, provides a very real and understandable temptation for those who would like to find for it a better home than they feel its rightful owner could provide. The degree of temptation varies with the amount of cash and with the looseness of control. In department stores, where tight control is very difficult to maintain, it has been found that many of the losses which had been attributed to shop-lifting customers were actually attributable to employees. Banks have very tight controls, but the amounts handled are much larger than in department stores, and the temptations consequently greater. As a result, banks are very sensitive about the trustworthiness of employees, and seek to do whatever possible to insure themselves against internal thievery and deceit.

Employment Investigations

All of the major banks in the country are members of the Federal Deposit Insurance Corporation, membership in which requires bonding of all guards, tellers, and others who handle money. The FDIC provides relatively stiff penalties for any bank which knowingly employs persons with past criminal convictions of either a major type or involving breach of trust or other crimes against property. For this reason, as well as several others, banks have traditionally been very careful about checking the records of applicants. Checking with the local

---

[29] U.S. Equal Employment Opportunities Commission, *op. cit.*, Part II.

police, running fingerprints through the FBI files, and performing very careful checks of personal and past employment references are quite common. Some banks go further, requiring polygraph tests of applicants for particularly sensitive jobs such as teller or guard. (Only one of forty-seven sample banks in the author's survey follows this practice, and apparently that organization is somewhat sensitive about it, as no information concerning polygraphs was volunteered to the author.)[30]

The primary purpose of these investigations is to identify and restrict from the temptations those who either have demonstrated an untoward desire for large sums of other peoples' money, or whose history is such as to indicate a proclivity in that direction. It is for this reason that banks rely heavily on credit bureau checks to find the stability of the applicants' personal financial situation. Banks also increasingly require physical examinations, where evidences of narcotics addiction can be discovered.

Of the forty-seven banks visited during the author's survey, nine reported that they did no deliberate checking outside of a few spot reference checks, ten checked references extensively, twelve used the services of the FBI, fifteen made at least spot checks with the local police, and twenty-seven made credit checks. (At least six reported requiring physicals, but not all banks were asked about this, and tallies were not kept.)

Effect on Negro Employment

In the large metropolitan areas, where most of the bank hiring that we are dealing with here takes place, the overall crime rate is twice what it is in smaller cities and three times that of rural areas. Dope addiction is almost exclusively a city problem. For whatever sociological reasons, Negroes make up a larger than proportional share of both criminals and addicts, and this affects their employability in some cases. For example, several banks had to seek special dispensation from FDIC in reference to past arrests on the part of "hard-core" youths for summer

---

[30] In states where the practice is legal, many banks do employ polygraph testing as an investigative device in the event of "mysterious disappearance" of funds. The problem here is that the device is nonselective, and the investigators are liable to uncover misdeeds in which they have no particular interest and which, having been discovered, pose serious difficulties to the investigators in determining what should be done with the information. A polygraph investigation into a theft in one bank, for example, turned up the information that two of the tellers (who had had nothing to do with the theft) were homosexual.

employment under the National Alliance of Businessmen program.

But much more important than involvement with crime or past convictions so far as Negro employment is concerned, are difficulties arising from mishandling of personal finances and the risks attendant to this. Undoubtedly this problem will attenuate as the Negro population becomes increasingly middle-class in its outlooks and aspirations, but for the time being the existence of large numbers of jobs in the banking industry for which bad financial or legal history involves considerable risk to the employer makes that industry somewhat less receptive to Negro applicants than would be the case in most industries.

HIGH SCHOOL OUTPUT MATCH

In New York City, where about 40 percent of all high school students who will be gradulated this year are minority group members, the females far outnumber the males. This is also true in other cities throughout the country. Both the female and the Negro proportions of high school graduating classes are increasing, and additionally, more and more of the graduating girls are seeking employment. Those industries which have a high demand for this level of labor input, and such is the case with banks, should show higher levels of Negro female employment than industries which do not have this characteristic. This does not appear to be the case in the banking industry, and we can only assume that the level of Negro female employment would be even lower were so many Negro girls not graduating and entering the labor market.

INDUSTRY IMAGE AND HISTORICAL PATTERNS

If an industry is thought of as a good place to work by any particular segment of the job market, then the members of that segment will be likely to seek employment there, regardless of what the job demands and characteristics actually are. College students, for example, often seek sales jobs during the summer vacation months even though they could generally get more free time, better pay, and far better experience with a blue collar job or other industrial position. An even better example of the pull of "image" is provided by the appeal to young girls of the stewardess job with airlines. Conversely, an industry whose image is such as to be unattractive to some segment of the job market will have much more difficulty appealing to that segment. An image, once established, is very difficult to change.

Banking Image

The stereotype image of the banking industry portrays that industry as conservative, changeless, dull, low-paying, with few opportunities for rapid advancement. The teller line, which sets the image for the clerical-level jobs, currently retains more prestige in the eyes of banks than in the eyes of the potential applicants who often understand the job to be underpaid and requiring extensive technical skills and enforced precision.

There are some other characteristics of the job which serve to frighten applicants. It is apparent from the physical construction of teller windows that little freedom of action for social intercourse is possible on the job between employees, but the constant contact required with bank-using public must be both courteous and extremely careful. It is not a position in which the job holder can enhance his self-image by exerting influence over those with whom he must deal. It is not a job on which a person can ever relax. It has none of the aspects of being a "fun job" and seems more unforgiving than most.

Higher-level jobs in banking often present the same limited appeal to college graduates, MBA's, and others who compare industries in search of a first managerial position. The image of low pay, long training periods, slow advancement, and lack of excitement serves to limit the appeal of the industry.

In sum, banking is not an industry which has been treated well in the public press or by public sentiment. All told, with the possible exception of the popular view of "bankers' hours," there is little inherent in the image of the industry to attract those who are not premotivated to be well disposed toward it; and on managerial as well as clerical entrant levels, there is little reason for Negroes to be premotivated toward the industry.

Negro Experience and Preidentification with Banking

In Appendix B, where the history and status of all-Negro banks are presented, several aspects of banking prior to World War II which served to make Negroes very distrustful of the industry are discussed. The Freedmen's Bank, which was supposed to be a bank run specifically for Negroes and which appeared to many to have the protection of the federal government, failed in the panic of 1873, and in failing destroyed not only the savings but also the faith of many of its depositors in any banking system. Among the all-Negro banks which followed the Freedmen's Bank, a rather high proportion failed in their infancies; this further shook the confidence of Negroes in banking. For many years, the regular commercial banks would not handle the accounts of Negroes, much less accept Negro participation as employees actively associated with the industry.

All of these, and other factors, combine into a general disassociation of Negroes from the industry and, as was also the case with many rural Americans generally, (although from different reasons), Negroes took to storing any excess funds in the cookie jar, or subsequently, in the Postal Savings System. Sociologically, there were many evil connotations connected with the industry, which the upheavals caused by periodic bank panics did little to dispell. Negroes were, and still are, among the hardest hit by depressions, and many were of the opinion that depressions were *caused* by bankers and other financiers.

More so for that race than for other ethnic groups, Negroes have had very little experience with banks as either users or employees. Thus, with some justification, they dislike banks more than most other industries and more than most other ethnic groups do. Therefore there has been little reason for Negroes to aspire to or prepare themselves for employment in that industry as they might for other professions.

Because of these factors, Negroes on all levels lack premotivation towards the industry. Even now, if banks are to be able to recruit many Negro employees having high levels of potential for development, they must be able to make the industry seem attractive to them and present an enticing image. The alternative for banks is to be content with less than the best, watching other industries absorb the most talented Negroes while banks themselves have to undertake extensive training programs.

PRESTIGE AND WAGE LEVELS

As we have mentioned, there usually is considerable difference between the image which an industry has in the eyes of its job seekers and the actuality of the job itself. If the image is positive, industries can often capitalize on it. Going back to a previous example, the airlines are very happy with, and protective of, the excitement and apparent desirability of the stewardess' jobs for the obvious reason that if the image is accepted, then the lines can, to at least some degree, pay their stewardesses with "excitement" rather than with cash. If the job were alternatively conceived of as the hectic, unrewarding, morally and physically dangerous, dead end, flying waitress job it sometimes is, the cash inducements which would have to be offered by the lines to get applicants would have to be considerably higher even than they are now.

Some years ago, despite the sociological and mental demands which we have outlined for the teller's job in banks, the position was considered to have prestige, and as a result banks remunerated tellers (and other employees, by association) partially in this quantity and partially in dollars. But the prestige attached to the job and to working in banking instead of in a manufacturing firm has attenuated. What has happened to banking wages?

Wage Levels

Bankers often seem horrified by the situation, but they are fond of pointing out that clerical wages have been going up rapidly in the last few years, and that managerial entrants are being offered "salaries which would have been unheard of five years ago." [31] It is quite true that bank wages and salaries have been on the upswing; in the last ten years, the average weekly wage of nonsupervisory employees in banking has increased by 50 percent. Highly-placed bank personnel men throughout the country seem overwhelmingly of the opinion that past wage differentials between their industry and others have already been or are rapidly being closed. Of the forty-seven who were asked by the author, two claimed their wages to be higher than manufacturing; four said wages were on par with local nonmanufacturing firms; five felt their wages were at least higher than other banks'; and two professed to have the highest banking wages in the country. Five felt they could not compete with government wage scales (not all were asked); four reported unmeetable competition from some specific local industry; and only four stated their clerical wages were lower than those of-

---

[31] Interview with a southern bank personnel director, August 1968.

fered by other major employers in the area. Twenty-six firms indicated parity in clerical wages with area industry.[32]

Unfortunately, although the consensus here is one of wages trending toward parity, this does not seem to be the case in actuality. Figures released by the U.S. Department of Labor Statistics covering average median wages for 1966-1967 in finance (including savings and loans, insurance, and real estate) and manufacturing show financial wages to suffer by the comparison.[33] These are shown in Table 16.[34] Notice there that although finance employees on average fare better with respect to the male janitors employed (generally taken as the lowest-level job and used as the base standard in the table) than do manufacturing employees in the same jobs with respect to their janitors, this distinction is rather hollow when it is seen that the wages of male janitors in manufacturing are about 20 percent higher than those of their finance counterparts. The final result is that clerical employees in finance in thirty-five of the thirty-six job categories noted make less per hour.

Checking comparative figures in various issues of the *Monthly Labor Review* reveals additionally that the banking industry is the lowest paying segment of the financial group. By those figures, through October 1968, only workers in the garment trades and retail sales, hotel workers, laundry workers, canners, and cigar rollers average to a smaller hourly wage than nonsupervisory bank workers do.

Figure 4 is a composite figure arrived at by using data from several different statistical series. Nevertheless, the indications are pretty clear that banking wages, although they have risen appreciably since 1948, are barely maintaining a proportional lag behind total private industry wages.

---

[32] There are several overlapping categories here, so the frequencies reported in each category do not total to forty-seven. Several bankers said they either would not or could not answer the question.

[33] Donald J. Blackmore, "Occupational Wage Relationships in Metropolitan Areas," *Monthly Labor Review*, Vol. XCI (December 1968).

[34] The table as presented is in a modified format. The Bureau of Labor Statistics showed only wage relatives to average janitorial wages. As these janitorial wages were also presented in the same article, we have simply multiplied them out to arrive at the hourly wage rates.

TABLE 16. *Average Hourly Earnings*
Financial and Manufacturing Establishments in Metropolitan
Areas, 1966-1967

Office - Clerical Occupational Group	Average hourly earnings as percent of average for men janitors		Average hourly earnings	
	Finance	Manufacturing	Finance	Manufacturing
Men				
Clerks, accounting, class A	152	128	3.01	3.03
Clerks, accounting, class B	124	106	2.46	2.51
Clerks, payroll	128	126	2.53	2.99
Office boys	95	82	1.88	1.94
Tabulating-machine operators, class A	148	133	2.93	3.15
Tabulating-machine operators, class B	130	116	2.57	2.75
Tabulating-machine operators, class C	111	100	2.20	2.37
Women				
Bookkeeping-machine operators, class A	121	114	2.40	2.70
Bookkeeping-machine operators, class B	108	103	2.14	2.44
Clerks, accounting, class A	134	122	2.65	2.89
Clerks, accounting, class B	108	98	2.14	2.32
Clerks, file, class A	117	99	2.32	2.35
Clerks, file, class B	95	88	1.88	2.09
Clerks, file, class C	88	84	1.74	1.99
Clerks, payroll	131	110	2.59	2.61
Comptometer operators	101	98	2.00	2.32
Duplicating-machine operators	107	90	2.12	2.13
Keypunch operators, class A	116	104	2.30	2.46
Keypunch operators, class B	104	93	2.06	2.20
Office girls	84	78	1.66	1.85
Secretaries	145	122	2.87	2.89
Stenographers, general	108	98	2.14	2.32
Stenographers, senior	123	108	2.44	2.56
Switchboard operators, class A	121	104	2.40	2.46
Switchboard operators, class B	113	101	2.24	2.39
Switchboard operators-receptionists	116	100	2.30	2.37
Tabulating-machine operators, class A	143	127	2.83	3.01
Tabulating-machine operators, class B	132	114	2.61	2.70
Tabulating-machine operators, class C	105	102	2.08	2.42
Transcribing-machine operators, general	98	97	1.94	2.30
Typists, class A	109	98	2.16	2.32
Typists, class B	95	88	1.88	2.09

Source: Donald J. Blackmore, "Occupational Wage Relationships in Metropolitan Areas," *Monthly Labor Review*, Vol. XCI (December 1968), pp. 30-31.

Note: Average male janitor wages: manufacturing, $2.37; finance, $1.98.

COMBINED EFFECT OF IMAGE AND WAGES

The low pull of the wage levels combined with the lack of other Negro predisposition toward seeking entrance to clerical-level jobs has effects in three areas—the first concerning the quality level of job seekers generally, the second concerning the quality level of Negro applicants, and the third concerning the importance of communications from the banks to potential job seekers.

The attenuation of the prestige image of the most visible banking job (and the lack of a product to identify with) means that more and more applicants come to the bank for employment simply as an alternative to looking for a job at the gas company or at the widget works, and many either will accept the higher wages of those alternatives, or will join the bank as a temporary measure until one of the higher-paying jobs becomes available. Some also join to get the experience necessary to be able to apply for a job with government. The results generally are being felt by the banks in the form of less qualified applicants, higher training costs, and greater turnover.

We have seen that both image and wages have combined to produce even less preidentification by Negroes, so all of these effects are magnified when it comes to them. The results are that banks see fewer employable Negroes than they could, and therefore employ fewer than other industries which do not have these problems. In both cases (and for entrance jobs on managerial levels as well) the burdens on bank communications for recruiting are intensified, and recruiters have to do a better "selling job" on their industry than do recruiters from other firms.

DISCRIMINATION

It is clearly the consensus of Americans, black and white, that the tradition of racial discrimination against Negroes no longer reflects current value orderings of the society and should be scrapped. But tradition is a strong thing, and there is little point to wishing for a different history by recasting the mores of our past society and re-interpreting its actions in terms of our current value structure.

The racial discrimination which was practiced in this country against Negroes a few years ago was in keeping with the then current ideas of acceptable behavior on the part of the majority.

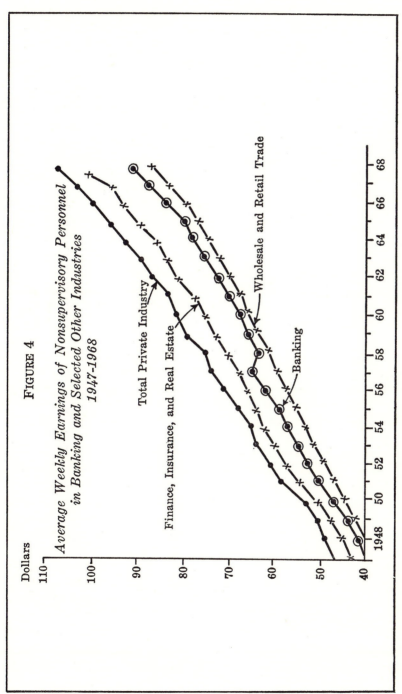

FIGURE 4

Average Weekly Earnings of Nonsupervisory Personnel in Banking and Selected Other Industries 1947-1968

Let us be thankful that ideas of acceptable behavior have changed, and that most persons have agreed that the change constitutes an advancement of the civilization. Let us also admit that some have not made the transition.

There are those who will point out that our current society is so positive about its existing value structure that it has solidified into law proscriptions of discrimination, making illegal the traditions which had supported it. And this is true. However, discrimination, much more so than, say, embezzlement, is a state of mind resulting in an entire behavioral pattern, only parts of which can be given the attention of the law. And anything not specifically covered by the law must be left to tradition.

The sad fact is that even were verifiable discrimination (e.g., refusal to interview Negroes for employment, refusal to serve Negroes in the usual way for the usual fees) completely absent from the society—and it is not—the disguisable sort of bigotry consisting of isolation, nastiness, and various other forms of following the letter but not the spirit of the law will persist and can have the same exclusionary effect. It takes much longer to build the mutual trust and understanding between the races which is required for this form of discrimination to attenuate; and while it is definitely attenuating, it does persist. The question we are facing here is: Is there anything about any particular industry, specifically banking, which would lead one to believe that its officials are *more* bigoted or *more* likely to practice discrimination against Negroes than officials of other industries?

We know that it took longer for bankers to break the all-white tradition of their industry than was required by various others, and we know that the proportion of employment which is Negro is less than the average in most other industries. But if we are to believe that this slowness and relative lack of response is attributable to a higher degree of residue discrimination among bankers, we must be able to demonstrate that something about officials' jobs in banking tends to attract a higher proportion of bigots to that occupation than are attraced to manufacturing. We know, of course, that some bankers discriminate, just as we know some manufacturers discriminate. But we do not know if, or why, more bankers than manufacturers do.

The only sociological factors of which we are aware having general application are two: whites in the lower economic and social classes tend to be more susceptible to practicing discrimination; and among southerners of all classes the tradition that way is stronger. But southerners do not dominate the banking industry and no one would contend that officials of the industry are drawn from the lowest economic orders. There is a somewhat more specialized argument mounted by the EEOC to the effect that although all employers are bigoted, the discrimination becomes more virulent as the jobs involved become more prestigeous; that although some whites are now willing to help Negroes onto the economic ladder, they are willing to help them only onto the bottom rung. The evidence cited for this is in two forms. First, white collar industries employ a smaller proportion of Negroes than blue collar industries; and second, there are extremely few Negroes on top of organizations, and few Negroes in any of the jobs considered especially prestigeous on any level (as secretary to an executive would be on the clerical levels).

We have indicated before, in discussing Figure 3 in this chapter, that we do not find the first of these arguments to be particularly compelling. However, it is undoubtedly true that many corporate leaders, in the interest of prudence, will require a more positive demonstration of potential from Negroes before their promotion to economically sensitive or policy formulating positions than they will from whites with whose aspirations, reactions, and behavior patterns they are more familiar. And since there are relatively more such positions in banking than in manufacturing, the effect of this caution will be more visible. On the other hand, higher-level positions and prestigeous jobs on any level are normally positions of reward for past performance, potential, and a variety of other factors, and are seldom chosen by lot. Experimentation cannot be extreme for jobs which are honestly sensitive. For any of these jobs, it is difficult to say where prudence leaves off and discrimination begins. We therefore can find scant evidence which would support the contention that more bigotry exists in the banking industry than in other corporations, and suggest that insofar as banking employs fewer Negroes the reasons for that must be found in more specific arguments. We do not exclude the possibility that in many of the specific arguments bankers' decision making is influenced by lack of experience with, or lack of understanding of, Negro value structures, motivations, reactions, and general behavior patterns.

CONCLUSIONS

With the exception of the demand by banks for large numbers of high school girls, all of the other factors which we have identified as serving to differentiate the banking industry from manufacturing concerns—including its job requirements, image, and wage levels—also serve to make the climate of the industry less hospitable to Negroes. We have also seen that recent developments in the evolution of the industry are tending to obviate these differences. We expect that banking statistics will much more closely approximate the national averages for Negro employment in the near future. Although the banking industry was one of the last to begin hiring Negroes in any numbers, overt bigotry does not appear to have been the exclusive or even a major cause—except insofar as racial discrimination was a standard behavior pattern of all employers prior to about 1960.

On the basis of the analyses here, and on the basis of the attitudes found among banking personnel managers, some of which were summarized in Chapter III, it is our prediction that the Negro representation in banking will continue to increase at a minimum of 15 and perhaps as high as 22 or 23 percent per annum compounded, continuing the trend which began in about 1960. Unless there is some sharp change in attitude one way or the other toward Negro employment, we shall expect the banking industry Negro employment proportion to approximate the nation's Negro population proportion by about 1972, as shown in Figure 2 in Chapter III.

During this same time period, we shall expect to see somewhat higher Negro representation in the officers and managers job classification, but do not expect that the Negro proportion in those jobs will be as high as for clerical employment.

CHAPTER V

Variation in Negro Employment Within the Banking Industry

Among the forty-six commercial banks which supplied statistical data to the author, Negro employment ranged from a 1968 low of 1.0 percent to 21.2 percent of the work force when the data are arranged by city, the Seattle banks' average of 1.4 percent Negro was low, and the figures ranged up to the sixteen city high of 19.2 percent in the District of Columbia. When the reports from all banks from that year are arranged by states and averaged (excluding the District of Columbia, Hawaii, and Alaska), the employment proportion runs from a low of 0.0 percent in New Hampshire, North Dakota, South Dakota, and Vermont to a high of 10.0 percent in New York. Obviously, the variation around the industry's 5.9 percent average 1968 Negro employment is very great.

The last chapter discussed various aspects of the banking industry which served to differentiate it from other industries and which seemed to affect the relative level of Negro employment. Here we turn our attenion to analysis of factors important to the industry which seem to be responsible for the internal variation in Negro employment within the industry.

To make this analysis, we shall look in turn at historical hiring patterns in various areas of the country and at the availability of Negro applicants; at the affect of organizational flexibility arising from large size and from decentralization; and at the effect of the presence of other minority groups. There are some other differences internal to the industry which will obviously produce variations in Negro employment levels, such as the perceptions of individual personnel officers and the policies of individual banking establishments. These will be taken up in a later chapter.

REGIONAL HIRING PATTERNS

Any discussion of hiring patterns in banking or in any other industry requires attention to the historical patterns of the South. It would be less than realistic to suppose that the traditions of

TABLE 17. *The Banking Industry*
Employment by Race, Region, and State, 1966

Region and State	All Employees	Negro	Percent Negro
South Region			
Alabama	4,943	226	4.6
Arkansas	1,645	87	5.3
Delaware	2,361	74	3.1
D.C.	4,103	493	12.0
Florida	8,211	280	3.4
Georgia	7,659	462	6.0
*Kentucky	1,884	82	4.4
Louisiana	5,595	463	8.3
Maryland	8,482	454	5.4
*Mississippi	—	—	—
North Carolina	10,699	639	6.0
Oklahoma	2,700	73	2.7
South Carolina	3,113	164	5.3
Tennessee	6,926	505	7.3
Texas	17,202	973	5.7
Virginia	9,520	702	7.4
*West Virginia	407	20	4.9
Total	95,450	5,697	6.0
Percent of total banking employment	18.9		
Percent of total Negro employment	25.4		
Northeast Region			
Connecticut	9,163	257	2.8
*Maine	1,936	1	0.1
Massachusetts	18,895	492	2.6
*New Hampshire	115	—	—
New Jersey	16,765	604	3.6
New York	114,338	6,401	5.6
Pennsylvania	33,115	1,065	3.2
*Rhode Island	3,410	53	1.6
*Vermont	743	—	—
Total	198,480	8,873	4.5
Percent of total banking employment	39.3		
Percent of total Negro employment	39.6		

TABLE 17.   (Continued)

Region and State	All Employees	Negro	Percent Negro
North Central Region			
Illinois	24,209	1,252	5.2
Indiana	8,570	299	3.5
*Iowa	1,769	26	1.5
*Kansas	1,103	30	2.7
Michigan	21,095	1,070	5.1
Minnesota	5,581	83	1.5
Missouri	9,514	678	7.1
*Nebraska	1,893	40	2.1
*North Dakota	—	—	—
Ohio	17,752	881	5.0
*South Dakota	141	1	0.7
Wisconsin	4,672	52	1.1
Total	96,299	4,412	4.6
Percent of total banking employment	19.1		
Percent of total Negro employment	19.7		
West Region			
Arizona	5,998	94	1.6
California	80,075	3,081	3.8
Colorado	3,213	83	2.6
*Idaho	2,267	1	**
*Montana	689	2	0.3
Nevada	1,942	23	1.2
*New Mexico	931	—	—
Oregon	7,844	50	0.6
Utah	2,306	—	—
Washington	9,824	71	0.7
*Wyoming	—	—	—
Total	115,089	3,405	3.0
Percent of total banking employment	22.8		
Percent of total Negro employment	15.2		

Source: U. S. Equal Employment Opportunity Commission, *Job Patterns for Minorities and Women in Private Industry, 1966*, Report No. 1 (Washington: The Commission, 1968), Part II, Data for states marked (*) were estimated from a field sample of 738 banks in the author's possession.

Note: Because of the variety of sources used, totals are not identical with those reported in other tables reported in Chapter III.

**   Less than 0.05 percent.

the South concerning Negroes have not had an effect on employment levels there, and normally it would be safe to assume that in banking as in other industries, the progress of the southern Negroes toward employment equality would have been much retarded.[35] Especially because of banking's lack of menial, laborer, and "muscle-power" jobs (and because of most of the other factors mentioned in the last chapter), we would expect the southern employer attiudes to be visible in the statistics.

As a first approximation to understanding the regional differences, the data in Table 17 have been compiled from the overall, 1966 employment statistics. The regional breakdowns used are those of the Bureau of the Census.

Discrimination and the South

Looking at the Negro participation on the table for banks in the individual states provides the first notice that the automatic and offhand dismissal of the South as the ultimate locus of racial discrimination in banking may bear some re-examination. Among the sixteen states which are comprised by the southern region of the country, twelve showed Negro participation at a rate higher than the national average. This compared with only one out of nine for the Northeast, four out of eleven for the North Central region, and none out of ten for the West. (No data were available from three states: Mississippi, North Dakota, and Wyoming.) For the South as a whole, Negro participation was at twice the rate of the West. (The conclusions are not greatly affected by taking the smaller area breakdowns also used by the Bureau of the Census.) The figures in Table 17 also show that for all of the Negroes employed in banking, more than 25 percent were employed in the South, although less than 19 percent of the total banking population was in that region. The situation for the West is almost exactly reversed.

There are some other interesting data which give rise to similar results, and these are the data derived from the tabulation of the number of reporting units in the banking industry which showed no Negro employment at all. The data, taken from a field sample of 738 banks in 1966, are presented as Figure 5, where it is shown that whereas fourteen reporting units from the South, with a total of 1,700 employees, had no Negro employ-

---

[35] Some southerners honestly disagree, arguing that there is no more discrimination in the South than in any other area with equivalent Negro population. We shall develop this point subsequently in the chapter.

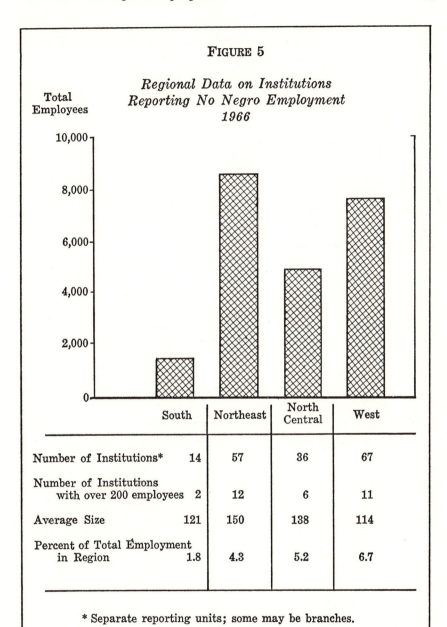

FIGURE 5

Total
Employees

*Regional Data on Institutions
Reporting No Negro Employment
1966*

	South	Northeast	North Central	West
Number of Institutions*	14	57	36	67
Number of Institutions with over 200 employees	2	12	6	11
Average Size	121	150	138	114
Percent of Total Employment in Region	1.8	4.3	5.2	6.7

* Separate reporting units; some may be branches.

Source: Data in author's possession

ment, sixty-seven reporting units from the West had a total of 7,662 employees with no Negroes among them. In total, 1.8 percent of all employees working in the South worked in banks in which they had no Negro co-workers. This compares with 6.7 percent in the West, 5.2 percent in the North Central region, and 4.3 percent in the Northeast.

Growth in Negro Employment

Additional insight into regional patterns can be gained by examining the regional and state totals and breakdowns for 1967 and 1968. These, together with the Negro share in the growth of the industry between the years are shown in Table 18.

The table shows a relative change, both since the 1966 figures of Table 17 and also internally, between 1967 and 1968. Banking in the South region of the country seems to be growing somewhat faster than elsewhere, and in 1968 it represents a greater proportion of the total industry work force; but the Negro representation, while increasing from a high base (relative to the other regions) is not growing at as fast a rate as elsewhere. The "Negro share of growth" column in the table is most indicative of this. Notice that between 1967 and 1968, 12.5 percent of all banking employment growth was Negro in the South, but this is compared with a high of 30.0 percent in the Northeast. (Incidentally, although the South trails the rest of the country in this, 12.5 percent is still slightly higher than the country's Negro population proportion, and it is pleasant to note that were even the lowest rate perpetuated throughout the country gross *statistical* discrimination would eventually become a thing of the past.) Certainly, the case is much stronger in the Northeast which, dominated by New York, shows very great gains for this year. Those gains were sufficient that since 1966, the Northeast region has overtaken the South as the relative leader in Negro employment.

Before moving on, it should be noted that firms representing the industry in four Western states shrank in employment during a period of general banking expansion and it is interesting to see that in all four—Montana, Nevada, New Mexico, and Washington—the Negro proportion of the remaining employment was greater than before. Although these banks had few Negroes to begin with, the Negroes were, by and large, the "last hired"; apparently, they were not the "first fired." We hasten to add that there is no indication that such might be the case in a large-scale

TABLE 18. *The Banking Industry*
Employment by Race, Region, and State
1967-1968

Region and State	1967			1968			Percent Negro Share of Growth[a]
	All Employees	Negro	Percent Negro	All Employees	Negro	Percent Negro	
South Region							
Alabama	4,795	147	3.1	4,962	202	4.1	32.9
Arkansas	1,836	91	5.0	1,919	102	5.3	13.3
Delaware	1,997	73	3.7	2,251	114	5.1	16.1
D.C.[b]	4,282	691	16.1	5,181	958	18.5	29.7
Florida	12,158	401	3.3	12,686	504	4.0	19.5
Georgia	8,431	561	6.7	9,054	663	7.3	16.4
Kentucky	3,653	206	5.6	4,041	261	6.5	14.2
Louisiana	5,838	506	8.7	5,926	406	6.9	*
Maryland	6,806	365	5.4	7,261	419	5.8	11.9
Mississippi	2,615	111	4.2	2,839	134	4.7	10.3
North Carolina	10,565	704	6.7	11,572	751	6.5	4.7
Oklahoma	3,586	93	2.6	3,625	121	3.3	71.8
South Carolina	2,077	112	5.4	2,200	118	5.4	4.9
Tennessee	7,065	538	7.6	7,927	606	7.6	7.9
Texas	18,386	699	3.8	19,632	849	4.3	12.0
Virginia	9,991	699	7.0	10,922	786	7.2	9.3
West Virginia	1,221	83	6.8	1,279	86	6.7	5.2
Total	105,302	6,080	5.8	113,277	7,080	6.3	12.5
Percent of total banking employment		21.8			22.1		
Percent of total Negro employment		24.9			23.2		

TABLE 18. (Continued)

Region and State	1967			1968			Percent Negro Share of Growth[a]
	All Employees	Negro	Percent Negro	All Employees	Negro	Percent Negro	
Northeast Region							
Connecticut	8,392	294	3.5	8,926	345	3.9	9.6
Maine	916	1	0.1	1,119	1	0.1	0.0
Massachusetts	15,590	385	2.5	16,093	490	3.0	20.9
New Hampshire	615	—	—	650	—	—	—
New Jersey	16,575	674	4.1	17,272	855	5.0	26.0
New York	91,530	7,410	8.1	97,262	9,748	10.0	40.8
Pennsylvania	26,763	940	3.5	29,187	1,364	4.7	17.5
Rhode Island	3,390	53	1.6	3,634	70	1.9	7.0
Vermont	457	—	—	484	—	—	—
Total	164,228	9,757	5.9	174,627	12,873	7.4	30.0
Percent of total banking employment			34.0			34.1	
Percent of total Negro employment			39.9			42.2	
North Central Region							
Illinois	28,370	2,113	7.4	30,163	2,395	7.9	15.7
Indiana	9,159	343	3.7	9,637	412	4.3	14.4
Iowa	2,895	42	1.5	3,048	39	1.3	*
Kansas	2,072	88	4.2	2,217	120	5.4	22.0
Michigan	21,665	1,165	5.4	22,690	1,627	7.2	45.1
Minnesota	5,590	96	1.7	5,875	94	1.6	*
Missouri	8,870	530	6.0	9,179	613	6.7	26.9
Nebraska	2,281	46	2.0	2,416	46	1.9	0.0

North Dakota	230	—	—	234	—	—	—
Ohio	22,414	1,095	4.9	23,260	1,312	5.6	25.7
South Dakota	863	—	—	870	—	—	—
Wisconsin	6,428	108	1.7	7,064	143	2.0	5.5
Total	110,837	5,626	5.1	116,653	6,801	5.8	20.2
Percent of total banking employment	22.9				22.8		
Percent of total Negro employment	23.0				22.3		
West Region							
Arizona	6,543	86	1.3	6,903	95	1.4	2.5
California	71,656	2,660	3.7	76,140	3,331	4.4	15.0
Colorado	4,798	93	1.9	4,956	109	2.2	10.1
Idaho	232	1	0.4	245	1	0.4	0.0
Montana	995	—	—	980	1	0.1	*
Nevada	1,694	17	1.0	1,649	28	1.7	*
New Mexico	1,165	5	0.4	1,149	11	1.0	*
Oregon	7,887	58	0.7	7,994	76	1.0	16.8
Utah	2,354	—	—	2,536	3	0.1	1.6
Washington	5,391	48	0.9	5,337	69	1.3	*
Wyoming	266	5	1.9	268	5	1.9	0.0
Total	102,981	2,973	2.9	108,157	3,729	3.4	14.6
Percent of total banking employment	21.3				21.1		
Percent of total Negro employment	12.2				12.2		

Source: Data in the author's possession.

a For Alabama, for example, 167 additional employees were added between the years, of which 55 were Negro. Therefore, 32.9 percent of all new employees added were Negro.

b These figures somewhat off as a result of one bank's figures being counted twice (for both Negro and white).

* Decrease in either total or Negro employment.

banking retraction in heavily Negro areas or cities, but at least the situation is not quite so sensitive as is commonly supposed.

Upward Mobility

The slower Negro employment growth rate in the South region, seen above, brings to mind the related question of whether there is also a slower upward occupational mobility for Negroes in banks in the South. Detailed regional employment breakdowns by job category are not available for all banks, but our 1968 banking survey does indicate that this may be the case. Table 19 contains the aggregate employment data by race, sex, and job classification for forty-six banks located throughout the country. Table 20 presents the same information for the thirteen banks included in the survey which are located in areas defined as "southern" by the Bureau of the Census. These tables show that although the thirteen southern banks have a total Negro proportion which is almost identical to the forty-six bank average, the southern banks' average is made up more predominantly of blue collar Negroes.

Southern banks do not need or have a greater proportion of blue collar workers than banks elsewhere. The tables show that southern banks are 4.5 percent blue collar compared with the national aggregate 4.3 percent. Additionally, responses to a survey question on this point indicated that whereas about 28 percent of the southern banks do at least a significant amount of their own building maintenance, 36 percent of banks outside the South also perform this function. (The other banks contract maintenance to outside organizations.)

POPULATION AND EMPLOYMENT

Measured by its total work force size of just under 800,000 persons in 1965, banking is one of the top twenty-five industries in the country.[36] New York City, with about one-sixth of the total employment, is very much the banking center of the nation, but banks are distributed as cities are throughout the country, wherever industry or commerce abounds. Even so, it is not a uniform distribution. In 1966, banking was among the top fifteen industries in eleven states, according to the total industry

---

[36] U.S. Bureau of the Census, *Current Population Reports,* "Industrial Characteristics of the Population," (Washington: U.S. Government Printing Office, 1965).

TABLE 19. *The Banking Industry*
Employment by Race, Sex, and Occupational Group
46 Commercial Banks Surveyed
United States, 1968

Occupational Group	All Employees			Male			Female		
	Total	Negro	Percent Negro	Total	Negro	Percent Negro	Total	Negro	Percent Negro
Officials and managers	38,195	377	1.0	32,931	263	0.8	5,264	114	2.2
Professionals	7,073	120	1.7	5,533	101	1.8	1,540	19	1.2
Technicians	2,790	202	7.2	2,336	157	6.7	454	45	9.9
Sales workers	767	9	1.2	631	8	1.3	136	1	0.7
Office and clerical	147,921	14,166	9.6	32,835	3,246	9.9	115,086	10,920	9.5
Total white collar	196,746	14,874	7.6	74,266	3,775	5.1	122,480	11,099	9.1
Craftsmen	767	43	5.6	731	42	5.7	36	1	2.8
Operatives	1,924	297	15.4	1,510	180	11.9	414	117	28.3
Laborers and service workers	6,104	1,512	24.8	4,851	1,303	26.9	1,253	209	16.7
Total blue collar	8,795	1,852	21.1	7,092	1,525	21.5	1,703	327	19.2
Total	205,541	16,726	8.1	81,358	5,300	6.5	124,183	11,426	9.2

Source: Data in author's possession.

TABLE 20. The Banking Industry
Employment by Race, Sex, and Occupational Group
13 Commercial Banks Surveyed
South Region, 1968

Occupational Group	All Employees			Male			Female		
	Total	Negro	Percent Negro	Total	Negro	Percent Negro	Total	Negro	Percent Negro
Officials and managers	3,217	18	0.6	2,972	17	0.6	245	1	0.4
Professionals	883	8	0.9	712	4	0.6	171	4	2.3
Technicians	138	9	6.5	109	9	8.3	29	—	—
Sales workers	16	1	6.2	16	1	6.2	—	—	—
Office and clerical	13,283	993	7.5	2,900	297	10.2	10,383	696	6.7
Total white collar	17,537	1,029	5.9	6,709	328	4.9	10,828	701	6.5
Craftsmen	39	2	5.1	38	2	5.3	1	—	—
Operatives	37	19	51.4	35	19	54.3	2	—	—
Laborers and service workers	744	427	57.4	561	302	53.8	183	125	68.3
Total blue collar	820	448	54.6	634	323	50.9	186	125	67.2
Total	18,357	1,477	8.0	7,343	651	8.9	11,014	826	7.5

Source: Data in author's possession.

Note: Three additional Southern banks visited would release no data.

figures reported to the Equal Employment Opportunity Commission.[37]

Generally in these eleven states, the banking industry rated better as an employer of Negroes than as an employer. In other words, although other industries had larger work forces than banking, in most of these states banking had a larger proportion of both Negro white collar and Negro blue collar employees. In itself, this means very little. Consider one of the states, Idaho: there are so few Negroes in banking in Idaho that the percent Negro in the industry rounds off to zero. In fact, there is but a single Negro blue collar employee who was reported from the entire state. But his presence so affects the blue collar employment ratio that banking shows a higher proportion of Negro blue collar workers in the state than any other major industry.

Obviously, there are not many Negroes employed in Idaho; there are not many Negroes in Idaho. In Delaware, on the other hand, 41 percent of all blue collar employees in banking are Negro, but the industry rates only third among major state industries as an employer of blue collar Negroes. The real question is: In which state are banks being more responsive to the call for more Negro jobs?

It is not a bad initial assumption to suppose that Negro employment in banks is related to the Negro population ratio in areas near the bank. Obviously, there are more Negroes in the South than there are in the rest of the country as a proportion of the population, and on this basis, we should expect more Negro employees there. Figure 6 is a chart of Negro banking employment ratios (from 1966) and Negro population proportions (from the 1960 census) for individual states. This figure generally justifies the positive correlation between population and employment, but it must be carefully interpreted. The flaw which obscures the apparently obvious is that the correlations shown between overall Negro population and banking employment do not take into account the uneven distribution of banks.

Surely, there are more Negroes in any town chosen at random in Mississippi than there are in a town of equivalent size chosen at random in Wyoming. However, that fact is not par-

---

[37] These states are Arizona, California, Delaware, Idaho, Maine, Montana, Nevada, New York, Rhode Island, Vermont, and Washington. From Equal Employment Opportunity Commission, *Job Patterns for Minorities and Women in Private Industry, 1966*, Report No. 1 (Washington: The Commission, 1968), Part II, p. 124.

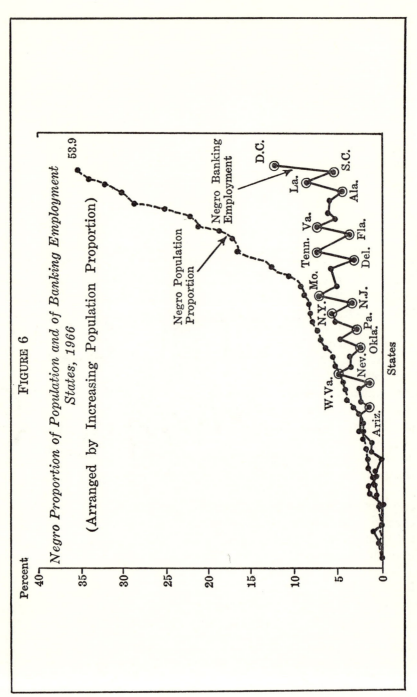

FIGURE 6

Negro Proportion of Population and of Banking Employment
States, 1966

(Arranged by Increasing Population Proportion)

Source: Negro banking employment, Table 17; population, 1960 Census.

ticularly germane. By and large, banking institutions, and especially the larger ones with which we are generally dealing in this study, are located in the urban areas of the country. It is therefore the Negro population proportion of individual urban areas that should be of concern rather than some state or broader region's overall Negro population—a population whose presence does not greatly affect the number of potential Negro job seekers.

City Population Figures

The cities whose banking data we shall investigate in this section are those which were selected by the author for personal visits during the Summer of 1968. There are seventeen cities which represent a reasonably good cross-section of the country, both geographically and sociologically. New York, Philadelphia, and Pittsburgh are all banking centers located in the industrial Northeast, and should provide good representation of that area. Similarly, Chicago, Detroit, and Cleveland were taken from the North Central region. The South and West, as areas of higher problem content, received proportionally higher coverage. In the South, banks were visited in the District of Columbia, Atlanta, Baltimore, Dallas, Richmond, and Winston-Salem.[38] In the western section of the country, banks were visited in Phoenix, Los Angeles, San Francisco, Denver, and Seattle.

For those and other major cities in the country, population data are available on two bases. The first is for the city itself, and the second for the "standard metropolitan statistical area" of which the city is the focus. Even in states which allow extensive branching, the greatest majority of the clerical, check clearing, and bookkeeping functions are located in the downtown offices. And even though some employees commute to the main office or are employed in the suburban branches, we feel the statistical base which should be used for examining the responsiveness of banks to any segment of the local population should be the city itself rather than the standard metropolitan statistical area. However, because of the heavy Negro concentration at the core of most major cities, the use of the central city population will tend to emphasize racial employment statistical discrepancies somewhat, and this point should be borne in mind.

---

[38] Reflecting our policy of not disclosing specific information on specific banking organizations, statistical data collected in Winston-Salem will not be presented in any tabulations where it would show alone, because its dominant banking institution would be too easily recognized.

TABLE 21. Total and Negro Population
United States and Selected Cities
1950-1970

City	1950 (Census)			1960 (Census)			1965 (Estimate)			1970 (Projection)		
	Total	Negro	Percent Negro	Total	Negro	Percent Negro	Total	Negro	Percent Negro	Total	Negro	Percent Negro
				(in thousands)								
United States Total	150,697	15,042	10	178,465	18,860	11	192,852	21,058	11	208,220	23,324	11
Atlanta	331	121	37	487	186	38	515	198	38	540	212	39
Baltimore	950	225	24	939	326	35	930	378	41	920	432	47
Chicago	3,621	492	14	3,550	813	23	3,600	960	27	3,610	1,150	32
Cleveland	915	148	16	876	251	29	811	277	34	805	305	38
Dallas	434	57	13	680	129	19	740	165	22	800	200	25
Denver	416	15	4	494	30	6	502	40	8	510	51	10
Detroit	1,850	301	16	1,670	482	29	1,650	650	39	1,700	800	47
Los Angeles	1,970	171	9	2,479	335	14	2,750	500	18	3,000	700	23
New York City	7,892	748	9	7,782	1,088	14	8,282	1,300	16	8,100	1,500	19
Philadelphia	2,072	376	14	2,003	529	26	2,070	610	29	2,200	700	32
Phoenix	107	5	5	439	21	5	520	40	8	600	60	10
Pittsburgh	677	82	12	604	101	17	607	115	19	610	126	21
Richmond	230	73	32	220	92	42	215	101	47	215	110	51
San Francisco	775	44	6	740	74	10	740	100	14	750	126	17
Seattle	468	16	3	557	27	5	602	40	7	647	56	9
Washington (D.C.)	802	281	38	764	412	54	801	506	63	840	574	68
16 City Total	23,510	3,155	13	24,284	4,896	20	25,335	5,980	24	25,847	7,102	27

Source: The Center for Research in Marketing, Inc., *The Negro Population: 1965 Estimates and 1970 Projections* (Peekskill, New York: The Corporation, 1966).

The population data for the cities which we shall investigate are given in Table 21. Census population is provided for 1950 and 1960, and estimates and projections of the population for 1965 and 1970 are also included.[39]

It is the exceptional city in the table which will not show about double the Negro population of 1950 by 1970. It is obvious from the table that the often-mentioned net in-migration of Negroes to the cities is very much a reality. In 1940 (not shown) the Negro population proportion of these sixteen cities was actually less than that for the country as a whole. It will be two and one-half times as great by 1970, when it is estimated that 12.4 percent of the total population of the country and 30.4 percent of the Negro population will be living in them. Their populations are increasingly composed of youngsters who flock to them to seek education, to find challenging employment, or simply to be "where the action is."

All of these factors are reflected in banking employment. Population, mobility, and youth have contributed greatly to the high turnover rates with which banks must contend. The rapidly increasing numbers of Negroes in the cities means that banks, as major urban employers, must be especially responsive to the needs of this segment of the population. It also means that these banks must be prepared to modify their viewpoints and policies for internal structuring, expansion, customer relations, and loan policies, among other factors, to reflect the new realities, and to appeal to the employability and growing affluence of Negro citizens.

Negro Banking Employment, Sixteen Selected Cities

Table 22 shows the degree to which banks in our sample cities have responded to the call for increased Negro employment. Between the two comparable years, 1967 and 1968, considerable growth is evident. These are entirely "comparable" years, as data are included only from those firms for which information was available in both years. Therefore, the growth results from expansion alone and not from including additional or different firms. On the average, one employee in twelve was Negro, an average which is quite clearly beyond the "hire the handicapped," or "showcase Negro" stage but still very short of matching the

---

[39] The Center for Research in Marketing, Inc., *The Negro Population: 1965 Estimates and 1970 Projections* (Peekskill, New York: The Corporation, 1966).

TABLE 22. The Banking Industry
Employment by Race
Selected Cities, 1966-1968

City	1966			1967			1968			1967-1968 Percent Negro Share of Growth
	All Employees	Negro	Percent Negro	All Employees	Negro	Percent Negro	All Employees	Negro	Percent Negro	
United States Total	376,017	16,561	4.4	483,348	24,436	5.1	512,714	30,483	6.0	20.6
Atlanta	5,174	333	6.4	6,385	436	6.8	6,865	529	7.7	19.4
Baltimore	6,449	423	6.6	4,626	314	6.8	4,915	351	7.1	12.8
Chicago	19,947	989	5.0	17,182	1,547	9.0	18,728	1,774	9.5	14.7
Cleveland	4,092	128	3.1	7,536	462	6.1	7,849	533	6.8	22.7
Dallas	3,408	82	2.4	4,173	172	4.1	4,803	197	4.1	4.0
Denver	2,498	62	2.5	3,198	73	2.3	3,355	91	2.7	11.5
Detroit	11,360	854	7.5	9,447	885	9.4	10,016	1,271	12.7	67.8
Los Angeles	10,396	577	5.6	15,139	795	5.3	16,065	922	5.7	13.7
New York City	68,744	4,380	6.4	67,286	6,953	10.3	72,071	9,057	12.6	44.0
Philadelphia	7,115	300	4.2	13,260	746	5.6	14,545	1,088	7.5	26.6
Phoenix	4,073	65	1.6	5,863	79	1.3	6,120	85	1.4	2.3
Pittsburgh	6,300	147	2.3	2,763	60	2.2	3,072	72	2.3	3.9
Richmond	2,290	188	8.2	4,423	356	8.0	6,095	471	7.7	6.9
San Francisco	13,385	633	4.7	50,348	1,802	3.6	53,224	2,322	4.4	18.1
Seattle	3,146	35	1.1	3,296	35	1.1	3,082	53	1.7	—
Washington, (D.C.)	2,639	322	12.2	4,053	653	16.1	4,310	805	18.7	59.1
16 City Total	171,016	9,518	5.6	218,978	15,368	7.0	235,115	19,621	8.3	26.4

Source: Data in author's possession.

city population ratios. Three out of every ten employees added during 1967 by the 172 banks which make up this sample were Negro. This is a bit higher than the average population ratio of 25 percent for the same cities as interpolated from Table 21, yet the breakdowns for individual cities show some problem areas.

Negro Share in Employment Growth, Sixteen Selected Cities

The Negro share in employment growth, shown in the last column of Table 22 illustrates the best approximation we have for a Negro hiring rate. If we can make the assumption that Negro and non-Negro turnover rates are the same, then this column shows the net gain in Negro employment in 1968 over 1967. This gain compared with the overall bank employment expansion in the city gives what would be, roughly, the Negro hiring ratio. There is a general sort of correlation between the two visible in the figure, but it does not hold when the percentage growth overall is compared with Negro participation in growth. In other words, it is not the fastest growing banks which are hiring the greatest proportion of new Negroes (which would tend to support an argument that in a highly competitive, tight labor market Negroes fare better) but rather the largest banks (or at least banks in cities in which banking is an important industry employing many persons) which are hiring the greatest proportion of Negroes.

Measures of Status and Growth

Our data do not relate employment growth to population change. The 22.7 percent participation of Negroes in employment growth in Cleveland, for example, shows how well Negroes did there compared to whites. But it does not answer the question of how well they *should* have done. Although we do not suggest it as a normative standard for measuring the sufficiency of Negro employment, a benchmark used by many is the population proportion. Under it, the measure of the status of the industry's response would take the form of a comparison between the number of Negroes who would have been hired, had hiring been done along strictly racial lines, and the number who were hired in actuality. There are serious arguments against the use of this measure as a standard, so it should be remembered that we are using this comparison as *one* benchmark rather than *the* standard.

There were 29,366 more people reported working in banking in 1968 than in 1967. At that time, the country had a population ratio slightly above 11 percent Negro, and so if hiring had been done then on racial lines some 3,200 of the new employees would be black. Actually, 6,047 were Negro, and so banks in the aggregate were hiring at a substantially higher than "ratial parity" rate. However, because neither banks nor Negroes are uniformly distributed throughout the country, this overall experience is not reflected equally in the individual cities.

The results of producing similar calculations for regions and individual cities are in Table 23, "measure of status." Only Detroit, of the North Central region, shows a hiring surplus and the net for the three sample cities in the region is negative, indicating a hiring deficit. Yet the overall North Central region shows a surplus. This is in keeping with our findings, and reflects the fact that the region's Negroes are located in a few major cities. A very striking thing in the table is the size of the hiring surplus generated by New York City banks. Alone, this city's banks account for nearly 50 percent of the country's total surplus. Less hopeful are the figures for Richmond and Washington (although see the note on the table for Richmond).

Finally in this series is the "measure of growth" column in Table 23. This column shows that in the country as a whole, every region of the country, and thirteen of sixteen survey cities, Negro participation in employment growth between 1967 and 1968 was higher than the level of Negro employment had been in 1967. The table is self-explanatory.

Again in this instance, the most positive figures are those from New York City. In fact, from all of the tables and figures in this section, New York City can be seen as not only the banking center of the nation, but also as the center for Negro employment.

ORGANIZATIONAL SIZE

In the last section and several times previously in this study there have been strong indications that the most powerful influence on the receptiveness of banking organizations to Negro employees is organizational size. Dr. Andrew Brimmer, a member of the Board of Governors of the Fedeal Reserve System, asked the Equal Employment Opportunity Commission to prepare a

TABLE 23. *The Banking Industry*
Measures of Status and Growth in Negro Employment
United States, Regions, and Selected Cities
1967-1968

Locality	Increase in number of Negro employees 1967-1968	Measure of Status		Measure of Growth	
		Increase expected if hired in ratio to area population (1965 base)	Hiring surplus or (deficit)	Increase expected if hired in ratio to 1967 employment	Hiring surplus or (deficit)
United States Total	6,047	3,230	2,817	1,498	4,549
South Region	1,000	1,595	(595)	463	537
Northeast Region	3,116	832	2,284	614	2,502
North Central Region	1,175	465	710	297	878
West Region	756	207	549	150	606
Atlanta	93	182	(89)	33	60
Baltimore	37	118	(81)	20	17
Chicago	227	417	(190)	139	88
Cleveland	71	106	(35)	19	52
Dallas	25	139	(114)	26	(1)
Denver	18	13	5	4	14
Detroit	386	222	164	53	333
Los Angeles	127	167	(40)	49	78
New York City	2,104	766	1,338	493	1,611
Philadelphia	342	373	(31)	72	270
Phoenix	6	21	(11)	3	3
Pittsburgh	12	59	(47)	7	5
Richmond [a]	115	786	(671)	134	(19)
San Francisco	520	403	117	104	416
Seattle	18	(15)	33	—[b]	—
Washington, D.C.	152	162	(10)	41	111
16 City Total	4,253	3,873	380	1,130	3,123

Source: Tables 18, 21, and 22.

[a] Richmond: Major portion of growth in Richmond came through merger rather than "new hiring."

[b] Banking total employment decreased between 1967 and 1968.

Calculations as follows:

Increase in total employment (1967-1968) times Negro population proportion of city or area (1965) yields "Increase Expected if Hired in Ratio to Area Population." This minus actual 1967-1968 Negro employment increase yields "Hiring Surplus or (Deficit)."

Increase in total employment (1967-1968) times 1967 Negro employment ratio yields "Increase Expected if Hired in Ratio to 1967 Employment." This minus actual 1967-1968 Negro employment increase yields "Hiring Surplus or (Deficit)."

special tabulation by bank size from the 1966 EEOC data.[40] A synopsis of that tabulation is included here as Figure 7.[41]

The distribution seen in the figures shows that the 216 largest banks in the sample, 12.6 percent of the total number of banks had over 60 percent of the employment population, and almost 70 percent of the Negroes. Thus there are not only more Negroes but also a higher proportion of Negroes in the larger institutions.[42]

Confirming these results are our own calculations from the 1966 field survey of 738 banks. Included there were seventy banks reporting a total employment of over 1,000 persons each. The average Negro employment percentage for this group of the largest banks was 4.8 simple (adding the percentages reported by individual banks and dividing by seventy) and 5.5 weighted. Because the weighted average is larger than the simple, the indication is that the very largest of the large banks are also showing the highest Negro proportions.

Because very few large banks exist anywhere except in large cities—and therefore near the greatest Negro concentrations— the locational factor might bear greater weight than the size. To illustrate that this is not the case, we have included Table 24 which shows the banking employment distribution by size of reporting unit in Chicago and New York City. These distributions are based on 1968 employment totals for all of the banks (not "reporting units") in each city which reported figures during both 1967 and 1968. Forty-five banks were included in this category

---

[40] From: Special Tabulation by Equal Employment Opportunity Commission, in: Andrew F. Brimmer, *Employment Patterns and the Quest for Equal Opportunity in Banking*, A Report Before a Conference on Bank Employment Practices, Sponsored by U.S. Treasury Department and the Michigan Human Relations Commission, Lansing, Michigan, May 22, 1968 (Washington: Board of Governors of the Federal Reserve System, 1968), Table 4.

[41] The total employment figure for the industry of 509,214 does not agree with any other 1966 total which we have seen from EEOC. However, the difference is not so great as to cause significant statistical differences.

[42] This result may be over-emphasized by one continuing point of confusion involving the differentiation of "firms" and "reporting units." The data for 1966 is almost invariably based on reporting units rather than firms, and we assume that to have been the case here. The numerical distributions by size of "firm" are therefore skewed to the "under 100," and "100-250" categories, since many of the "firms" recorded there are branches which, presumably, would tend to reflect the employment policies of the home office. On the other hand, insofar as these branches of large (over 500 employees) banks tend to be "white, suburban" branches, the statistical effect is to understate the Negro employment proportion of the smallest banks and overstate it for the largest banks.

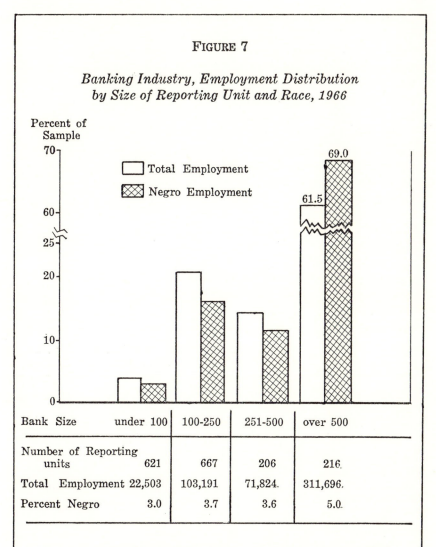

FIGURE 7

*Banking Industry, Employment Distribution
by Size of Reporting Unit and Race, 1966*

Percent of
Sample

Total Employment

Negro Employment

Bank Size	under 100	100-250	251-500	over 500
Number of Reporting units	621	667	206	216.
Total Employment	22,503	103,191	71,824.	311,696.
Percent Negro	3.0	3.7	3.6	5.0.

Notes: (1) The "Under 100" Column was derived as a residual.

(2) Size criterion for classification was "reporting unit" in EEOC tabulation, not total firm size.

Source: Andrew F. Brimmer, *Employment Patterns and the Quest for Equal Opportunity in Banking*, a Report Before a Conference on Bank Employment Practices Sponsored by U.S. Treasury Department and Michigan Human Relations Commission, Lansing, Michigan, May 22, 1968 (Washington: Board of Governors of the Federal Reserve System, 1968), Table 4.

in Chicago, ranging in size from 51 to 6,416 employees. In New York City, where branch banking is allowed, the number of banks included is smaller, but the average size of the banks is larger. All of the banks in each of the cities are facing the same Negro population proportions. The correlation between increasing size and increasing percentage Negro employment is obvious from the table.

The only surprise in the table comes from Chicago where the Negro employment proportion for banks with under one hundred employees is greater than for banks with between 100 and 250 employees. Here it should be remembered that the absolute sizes we are dealing with are very small, and under these circumstances, the presence of a very few Negroes will greatly affect percentage results.

TABLE 24. *The Banking Industry*
Employment by Size of Reporting Unit
Chicago and New York City
1968

| | Bank Size (by total employment) [a] | | | |
	Under 100	100-250	251-500	Over 500
Chicago				
Number of Reporting Units	18	15	6	6
Total Employment	1,403	2,249	1,756	13,320
Negro Employment	80	67	119	1508
Percent Negro	5.7	3.0	6.8	11.3
New York City				
Number of Reporting Units	1	17	6	9
Total Employment	87	2,749	2,000	67,235
Negro Employment	4	226	167	8,660
Percent Negro	4.6	8.2	8.4	12.9

Source: Data in the author's possession.

Note: [a] This distribution is based on 1968 employment totals for all banks in the respective cities for which employment data was available for both 1967 and 1968.

Analysis of the Influence of Size

A number of factors explain why the scale factor is so important to Negro employment in banking. The very smallest banks, ranging in size up to perhaps seventy or seventy-five employees, are essentially in the "family enterprise" stage, in that the president and officers of the firm can know all of the employees by name. Frequently, organizations of this size are highly paternalistic, and the desire may exist to perpetuate a closely-knit employment structure if one exists. This may operate to the exclusion of Negroes except in "traditional" jobs.

In organizations of this size and slightly larger, personnel men may hesitate to add Negroes to the staff for fear of not knowing how to handle racial problems which might arise. A higher proportion of personnel men on this level will be inexperienced with Negro employees, and unfamiliar with the nuances of the equal employment legislation.

The largest banking organizations are able to attract the best managerial talent, and are able to afford sophisticated personnel functions. For example, a number of large banks have established separate "compliance" sections which specialize entirely in activities related to equal employment. Additionally, better communications exist among the largest banks in any given area, and therefore, to a much greater degree than in smaller institutions, personnel men can learn from each others' experiences how to handle problems related to Negro employees.

Another factor in operation in the largest banks tending to increase their Negro proportions is the organizational flexibility associated with large size. Larger institutions can afford not only the facilities, teachers, and materials necessary for extensive training programs, but also can afford the payroll costs of nonproductive trainees for longer periods of time. As a result, the larger institutions can accept persons for employment with lower levels of skill development—and many Negroes are still in this category.

Finally, the very largest banks have both more entry-level jobs —because of their more than proportionately larger paperwork flow—and more Negro applicants.

DECENTRALIZATION

Those states which do not allow branch banking necessarily have a more decentralized banking structure than states which do allow branch offices. We have not produced any direct statistics on the effect of decentralization on Negro employment levels because of the difficulties involved in separating out locational factors and other influences on the statistical results. However, branch office hiring is generally under tight personnel control from the home offices, if hiring is done in the branches at all. Therefore, following the statistical trends above, we would expect to find a higher proportion of Negro employees in a branch office than in an independent bank of the same size.

Our 1968 survey shows that branches do indeed reflect the personnel policies of the home offices. Thirty-nine of the banks visited are located in states which allow branch banking. In twenty-two of those thirty-nine all of the hiring for the entire branch network is done by the main office (or occasionally two main offices). In an additional eleven banks, all of the hiring is done at the main office except for that done for a few far-flung branches. Only four of the thirty-nine banks reported all clerical branch hiring to be done by the individual branches (under home office policy control); in two cases, individual departments in the main offices as well as branches were reported able either to do their own hiring or to utilize the main office as a "hiring service" if desired.

NON-NEGRO RACIAL MINORITIES

One factor affecting the level of employment of Negroes in banking may be the competition afforded them by members of other racial minorities. Our almost exclusive concern in this study has been with Negroes, because they constitute by far the largest of the racial minorities. Members of larger religious and ethnic groups are not as visible and therefore presumably, not as "discriminatable."[43] Members of the smaller racial minori-

----

[43] The American Jewish Committee might, with some cause, dispute this statement. In a survey of the nation's fifty leading commercial banks conducted in about 1965, the Committee found that only 1.3 percent of the banks' senior officers (the top ranking officials listed in the institutions' annual reports) and 0.9 percent of middle management executives (down through the vice-presidential bracket) were Jewish. In New York City Jews make up nearly one-quarter of the population and about half of the college graduates. (From: *Patterns of Exclusion from the Executive Suite: Commercial Banking*, The American Jewish Committee, Institute of Human Relations, New York: By The Institute, 1966, p. 2-3.)

ties tend to be found in numerical concentration in only a few cities or in regional enclaves where there local difficulties are best dealt with locally. Nevertheless, it is instructive to get some feeling for the comparative position of Negroes in banking with respect to the other recognized minorities.

Some data are available from the Equal Employment Opportunity Commission on the relative participation rates in banking of the various recognized minority groups (Negroes, Spanish Surnamed Americans, Orientals, and American Indians).[44] The EEOC presents only employment data. The most recent population data available for minority groups (except Negroes) comes from the 1960 census. At that time, there were about 18.9 million Negroes; 3.7 million Mexican Americans; 890,000 Puerto Ricans; 520,000 American Indians; 464,000 Japanese; 237,000 Chinese; and 176,000 Filipinos.[45] Some appropriate comparisons are found in Table 25.

Employment data for Negroes can often be utilized as indicative of the situation for minority groups generally, but Table 25 shows this not to be entirely the case in banking. Although Negroes make up 76 percent of all of the recognized minorities, they are only 56 percent of the minority employment in banks. Whatever discrimination against minorities by banks these figures reflect, therefore, is either in greater effect against Negroes (and American Indians) or in lesser effect against Spanish Surnamed Americans, and considerably diminished effect against Orientals (who are seen from the table to be positively preferred by bankers).

Another way to look at this is as follows: (We are mixing 1960 population data and 1966 banking data here, so caution is recommended in the use of the absolute numbers.) Of the 179,-323,000 people in the country, 510,875 were in banking, or one person of every 351 of the general population; similarly, one of every 614 minority persons was in banking; one of every 835 Negroes; one of every 364 Spanish Surnamed Americans; one of every 179 Orientals; and one of every 1210 American Indians. Here it is seen that Spanish Americans participate in banking to about the same degree as does the overall population, Orientals to a much higher degree, and the other groups to a much lesser degree.

[44] U.S. Equal Employment Opportunity Commission, Report No. 1, *Job Patterns for Minorities and Women in Private Industry, 1966,* Part I (Washington: The Commission, 1968).

[45] *U.S. Census of Population, 1960,* Vol. 1.

TABLE 25.   The Banking Industry
Negro Employment Compared with Employment of Other Minorities
United States, 1966

	Population (1960)	Banking Population (1966)	Percentage Distribution			
			Population	Banking population	Minority population	Banking minority population
Total population	179,323,000	510,875	100.0	100.0	—	—
Total recognized minorities	24,863,000	40,493	13.9	8.0	100.0	100.0
Negroes	18,872,000	22,581	10.5	4.4	75.9	55.8
Spanish surnamed Americans	4,590,000	12,587	2.6	2.5	18.5	31.1
Mexican Americans	3,700,000					
Puerto Ricans	890,000					
Orientals	877,000	4,892	0.5	1.0	3.5	12.1
Japanese	464,000					
Chinese	237,000					
Filipinos	176,000					
American Indians	524,000	433	0.3	0.1	2.1	1.0

Source: Population Data: *U.S. Census of Population, 1960,* Vol. I.

Banking Data : U.S. Equal Employment Opportunity Commission, *Job Patterns for Minorities and Women in Private Industry-1966,* Report No. 1 (Washington: The Commission, 1968), Part I, p. C44.

Insofar as locational considerations are a factor, the plight of the American Indians, who are heavily concentrated in non-populous and generally bankless regions of the Southwest and Far West, becomes somewhat more understandable, if no less real. But there is no ready explanation, on racial or locational terms, for the industry's affinity for Orientals.

If attenion is directed to internal job classifications, the diversity of experience of the different minority groups becomes even more apparent, as seen in Table 26.

Note that even though the Oriental population is miniscule compared with Negro population in the country, there were almost twice as many Oriental officers and managers in banking in 1966. A similar situation exists (although to a lesser degree) for Spanish Surnamed Americans.

TABLE 26. *The Banking Industry*
Minority Group Employment by Occupational Classification
United States, 1966

| | | Occupational Classification | | | | |
| | | White Collar | | | | |
Minority Group	All Employees	Total	Officers and managers	Clerical workers	Other	Blue Collar
		Number of Employees				
All Employees	510,875	478,604	88,107	373,251	17,246	32,271
Negroes	22,581	14,762	343	14,080	339	7,819
Spanish Surnamed Americans	12,587	11,860	762	10,869	229	727
Orientals	4,892	4,771	655	3,944	172	121
American Indians	433	411	64	334	13	22
		Percentage Distribution				
All Employees	100.0	93.7	17.3	73.1	3.4	6.3
Negroes	100.0	65.4	1.5	62.4	1.5	34.6
Spanish Surnamed Americans	100.0	94.2	6.1	86.3	1.8	5.8
Orientals	100.0	97.5	13.4	80.6	3.5	2.5
American Indians	100.0	94.9	14.8	77.1	3.0	5.1

Source: U. S. Equal Employment Opportunity Commission, *Job Patterns for Minorities and Women in Private Industry, 1966*, Report No. 1 (Washington: The Commission, 1968), Part I, p. C44.

The second part of the table is simply a percentage distribution by job category for each minority group. Once employed in banking, minority group members except Negroes hold jobs distributed about the organization to about the same degree as "anybody else." Although the proportion of officers and managers of all of the minority groups is somewhat lower than the overall proportion, the Negro proportion is very much lower. The distribution of American Indian employment is somewhat surprising on the high side.

As a final index of the relative positions of the various minority groups in banking, Table 27 has been calculated. The banking population of each group in the occupational categories used is taken from Table 26. If minority group members were employed in banking in the same ratio as they were members of the national population, we could find the expected banking population of each by multiplying the "percent of population" (from Table 25) by the total banking employment (510,875 used here). Spanish Surnamed Americans, for example, are 2.6 percent of the population of the country. With perfect distribution of jobs among races, we would expect 2.6 percent of the 510,875 jobs in the banking industry, or 13,283, to be held by members of this group. The actual count shows 12,587, leaving a variance of 696 jobs. This variance is the number of persons who would have to be hired by the industry (or fired, if the variance were negative) in order for the industry to show the same racial distribution as the country does. (The fact that we are using 1960 population data affects the outcome only insofar as the racial *mix* of the population changed in the five intervening years; the change for the country as a whole during that period is not estimated to be significant.)

By similar logic, the occupational classification breakdown of all employees in banking in 1966 was taken as a benchmark, and racial variances were calculated for each job type. These variances are in Table 27.

The table makes it clear that if we are to be concerned about the lack of employment of minority group members in the banking industry the real problem is with respect to Negroes. Orientals are overemployed in every major category except blue collar; the Spanish American experience is mixed. American Indians are underemployed in clerical positions, but not to the same degree or even the same order of magnitude as are Negroes.

TABLE 27. *The Banking Industry*
Numerical Variances by Occupational Classification and
Minority Group
1966

| | | Job Classification | | | | |
| | | White Collar | | | | |
Minority Group	All Employees	Total	Officers and managers	Clerical workers	Other	Blue Collar
All Employees	0	0	0	0	0	0
Negroes	31,061	35,492	8,908	25,112	1,472	—4,431
Spanish Surnamed Americans	696	584	1,529	—1,164	219	112
Orientals	—2,338	—2,378	—214	—2,078	—86	40
American Indians	1,100	1,025	200	786	39	75

Source and explanation: See text.

Some feelings have been reported to exist on the part of non-Negro minority group members that, because of the national attention being devoted to Negroes specifically, the other minority group members were suffering from unfair competition.[46] If we look back at Tables 10 and 25, we can see that between 1966 and 1968 Negro employment proportions not only increased absolutely, but also increased with respect to total minority employment (61.5 percent compared to 55.8 percent for the earlier employment year).[47] But the two tables also show that the total minority proportion increased as well, from 8.0 percent to 9.1 percent. This indicates that although Negroes were being hired at a faster rate, the other minority group members were also being given increased representation in banking.

CONCLUSIONS

In general, this chapter has been devoted to analyzing the effect which the structure of the banking industry has upon the

[46] Interview, July 1968.

[47] Bear in mind that two different statistical series are being used here.

level of its Negro employment. We have sought here to analyze the reasons for the wide variation in employment levels reported by banks in different areas of the country, by banks of various sizes, and under varying degrees of central control.

In pursuing the analysis, we found some interesting results and also some surprising ones. We found, for example, that the cliche: "Nothing is going on in the South" is only partially true. Negroes are actually being employed by banks in the South at a rate which is proportionally greater than that seen in most other areas of the country. On the other hand, we found that, once employed, Negroes in the South apparently face a somewhat more restricted job horizon than they do in other areas. We found that the location of a banking institution by area of the country is not as important as is commonly supposed because, by and large, Negroes who are potentially job applicants to the banking industry live in the urban areas from which the majority of banking employment is drawn. The Negro population of these areas has little relationship to that of the state or region in which they are located.

Examining the data from individual cities, we did not find as close a correlation as we had expected between Negro population proportions and employment levels. We did find, however, that the banking industry in New York City comes closer than that in any other which we investigated to hiring Negroes and non-Negroes in the ratio which the relative population figures would indicate. This is important for several reasons. In the first place, the banking industry in New York City alone employs approximately 10 percent of the total work force of the industry. Secondly, the banking industry in New York City is actually adding Negroes to its work force at a rate which is greater than the population figures would lead us to expect. Thirdly, the banks in New York City, as the collective financial center of the country, are in a better position to communicate their Negro employment policies and experiences to banks located in other areas. The major institutions in the city are among the largest in the country, and therefore are able to afford, economically and organizationally, the experimentation necessary in the personnel function to develop the most effective procedures for molding large numbers of Negroes into their work forces.

The effect of organizational size on Negro employment levels was found to be greater than it is generally considered to be. We feel that there is a combination of factors bringing about this result: More Negroes apply to the larger banks; the banks themselves have had more experience with Negroes on the work force, are more sophisticated in their understanding of the entry-level Negroes' motivations, aspirations, and behavior patterns, and they are better able to afford special training and other personnel activities which might be required.

Finally, in this chapter, we investigated the experiences of Negroes in banking compared with those of other racial minority group members, and found that Negroes are underrepresented in the banking industry even compared with other minority group members. Although both groups are being hired at an increasing rate, Negroes are making up a larger and larger share of the total minority employment in the industry.

CHAPTER VI.

External Influences

Of the external influences at work affecting Negro employment levels in banks, the major one is undoubtedly that which has emanated from the regulatory efforts of various government agencies. However, these regulatory efforts could not have been effective were it not for the prosperity and general upward trend in the state of the American economy over the past several years, which has allowed the creation of new jobs and permitted some personnel experimentation; additionally, these regulatory efforts might have been very different had it not been for the social pressures of NAACP, CORE, and others in the years preceding national legislation.

SOCIAL PRESSURES

The banking industry was relatively free from the forms of demonstrations practiced by the Negro social pressure organizations during the early 1960's. Such sit-ins and picketing as did occur before banks became subject to Executive Order 11246 in late 1966 were generally in support of demands for increased Negro employment. A sampling of the news media reveals that such picketing was carried on by the National Association for the Advancement of Colored People in East St. Louis in August of 1963,[48] and in Detroit during the same year.[49] During May of 1964, the Congress of Racial Equality conducted massive sit-ins and business disruptions in San Francisco to support increased Negro hiring. Included as a target of CORE's "harrassing techniques" were the San Francisco branches of the Bank of America, the country's largest bank, which had recently been commended by the California Fair Employment Practice Com-

---

[48] "Lay-Downs' at Bank," *New York Times*, August 13, 1963; "Bank Protest Barred," *New York Times*, August 17, 1963.

[49] "NAACP picketing of Detroit S & L halted as board pledges to weigh demand," *Business Week*, October 14, 1963, p. 38.

mission for its hiring of minorities.[50] In 1965, the NAACP in one instance added a call for a general boycott by Negroes and white sympathizers of a small savings and loan association which it was picketing.[51]

With the inclusion of banks under federal regulations prohibiting discrimination in employment,[52] organized social pressures began to take on a slightly different form. Not only did the form of the pressures change, but the organizations promoting them were generally different. In December 1966, an organization known as the Committee of Conscience Against Apartheid alleged that its members had withdrawn at least $23,112,190 from two major New York City banks as the opening stage of a boycott protesting the banks' involvement in the economy of South Africa.[53] Early in 1967, the City of New York announced its intention to use the city treasury as a social instrument in helping depressed neighborhoods by choosing as depositaries to hold city money "ghetto" neighborhood banks that agreed to help finance small business enterprises in their areas.[54]

In June of 1967, through the State Treasurer, Adlai Stevenson, III, the State of Illinois issued an order prohibiting the depositing of state funds in banks which discriminated in providing mortgage funds or other banking services. The primary thrust of this action was said to be "setting a needed precedent in breaking the 'gentlemen's agreement' among bankers and the real open-occupancy financing." [55]

---

[50] "Race Issues Rife in San Francisco," *New York Times*, May 22, 1964; "Who's to Decide if a Banker is 'Biased'?" *Business Week*, June 13, 1964, p. 29.

[51] "NAACP Continues Picketing at Suburb & Co.," *Philadelphia Tribune*, August 14, 1965; "NAACP Halts Picketing at Collingdale," *Evening Bulletin* (Philadelphia), Sept. 8, 1965.

[52] "President Issues Rules to Bar Bias in Banks," *Sunday Bulletin* (Philadelphia), August 28, 1966.

[53] "Boycott Is Pushed Against 2 Banks," *Evening Bulletin* (Philadelphia), December 7, 1966; "Editors Battling Apartheid," New Pittsburgh Courier, December 10, 1966.

[54] "City to Favor Banks Aiding Ghetto Firms," *New York Times*, January 12, 1967.

[55] "Stevenson Raps Banks Over Bias," *New Pittsburg Courier*, June 24, 1967.

Churchmen,[56] government officials,[57] banking associations,[58] and bankers themselves [59] have all joined in urging other bankers not only to improve the employment opportunities for Negroes, but also to become involved in helping to meet urban crises by providing low-cost funds for Negro housing projects or business undertakings. The calls for improved employment opportunity for Negroes since 1966 have generally taken the form of exhortations by individuals connected with Negro social pressure groups rather than by mass actions by the groups themselves.[60]

The progression of social pressures as seen above, although not an exhaustive account of the activities which have taken place, is representative of their general direction. Prior to 1966, they generally took the form of direct pressures such as sit-ins or other harassing techniques and were conducted by the Negro advancement organizations. The goal was to promote the hiring of Negroes into responsible jobs in the banking industry. Since 1966, when the banking industry became subject to more powerful federal regulation on discrimination in hiring, the primary goal of social action groups seems to have shifted away from employment and toward urban involvement. Sit-ins and harassments have generally given way to speeches and exhortations by both individuals and a wide range of organizations.

If the trends in social pressures on the banking industry continue in the indicated directions, and there is no reason to suppose that they will not, then the banking industry will have to be very careful over the next few years in defining the limits of its involvement in social responsibility for it is clear that those limits will be tested. We shall see in Chapter VIII that banks themselves (at least the large, urban ones) have already undertaken numerous social activities beyond providing employment.

---

[56] "Episcopalians Put $720,000 in Negro Banks," *New Pittsburgh Courier,* October 26, 1968.

[57] "Ghetto Lending Urged on Bankers," *New York Times,* November 11, 1967.

[58] "Ghettos Need Bank Loans, Lending Officials Are Told," *Evening Bulletin* (Philadelphia), March 4, 1969.

[59] "Banks Urged To Help Meet Urban Crises," *Evening Bulletin* (Philadelphia), October 21, 1968.

[60] "Bankers Urged To Help Ease Racial Tension," *Evening Bulletin* (Philadelphia), October 17, 1967; "Negro Leader Assails Bankers on Ghettos at Conference Here," *Philadelphia Inquirer,* October 30, 1968.

Union Pressures

Another form of external social pressure which might be thought to influence Negro employment levels is that provided by unions. Unions are usually considered to have a modifying effect on managerial prerogatives in hiring Negro employees. This aspect of union pressure, of course, can have at most a miniscule effect on an industry as little unionized as is the banking industry. There is, however, another point with respect to unions which is of concern to banking personnel managers—the converse of the effect of unions on Negro employment—and that is the effect of Negroes on the unionization of banks.

Twenty-two of forty-seven banks included in the author's survey were questioned as to the feelings of the bank personnel manager on whether Negro employees would have more of a tendency to support a union's organization attempt in the bank than would their white counterparts. The responses provide little in the way of direction. Five banks felt their Negro employees would be more inclined to support a unionization attempt, five felt they would be less inclined, nine felt there would be no difference between white and Negro employees, and three preferred not to express an opinion.

However, only two banks could speak authoritatively on the subject, having undergone a unionization attempt subsequent to the time when they had hired a significant number of Negroes. In those instances, the banks reported that Negro employees were, in the words of one, "against the union all the way." [61] The evidence of these two banks may countermand the fears felt by other banking managements which have not experienced an actual organizational attempt. It suggests that unionization and Negro employment are at least independent situations in the banking industry.

BROAD ECONOMIC TRENDS

As of the Spring of 1969, the American economy continues to be in the throes of an unparalleled expansion and a continuing period of prosperity. This particular period of prosperity began before Negroes were hired by the banking industry in any numbers. Although some economists fear that the rate of growth of the economy is decreasing and a mild recession may be in

---

[61] Interview, August 1968.

store sometime during the next two or three years, it is obvious that the banking industry has not had the opportunity to test its personnel policies with respect to Negroes in a recessionary period.

In most industries, Negroes are considered to be the "last hired, first fired." Many researchers therefore fear the sociological consequences of a recession on the Negro community. Evidence relating to this point in the banking industry is scant. But we did have some indication in the last chapter that when four Western states suffered a contraction in banking employment during 1968, the Negro proportion of the remaining work force was greater than it had been before. How much this point can be generalized to a highly competitive job market situation such as would result from an economic recession is very difficult to say. However, it should be noted that banks in general have an extremely high turnover rate in the normal course of affairs (largely attributable to the high proportion of young females on the work forces) and have very horizontal employment structures with short lines of upward movement in any given job position. It is therefore reasonable to assume that in the event of a recession of moderate strength, the banking reaction would probably be more one of not hiring to augment the work force than one of laying off existing employees. The effect on Negroes would therefore more likely be one of a contraction of the employment opportunities of Negroes not yet hired. There is no question that in a highly competitive labor market, Negro applicants, who at the moment tend to be more often marginal applicants, could easily be passed over. There is also no question that a continuation of the tight labor market which now exists in many city markets will work to the benefit of Negro job applicants

GOVERNMENT PRESSURES

Government pressures take two general forms. The first is through legislating whatever regulations and sanctions are deemed necessary, to restrain discrimination or promote job opportunities, and the second is through the promulgation of attitudes which serve to set the level of expectations of industry members as to the "seriousness" with which government views the legislation it has enacted.

Acting either alone or in consort with various other forms of social and broad economic pressures evidenced above, government activities have almost always been a spur to increased Negro employment. The next sections evaluate the effects of both legislation and governmental attitudes on a local level in three specific job markets before returning to the national situation.

New York City Experience, 1945-1966

The legislation on minority employment rights traces its history to the "New York State Law Against Discrimination," which established what is now known as the New York State Division of Human Rights in 1945.[62] This law established the pattern for similar legislation in the majority of other states and undoubtedly influenced the form of the Civil Rights Act of 1964.

We have already seen from the national statistics that the progress of racial and ethnic minorities in banking was very slow from the end of World War II until the late 1950's. During this period, the New York Commission Against Discrimination (predecessor of the New York State Division of Human Rights) made a number of informal investigations into complaints concerning banks. At the end of August 1958, the Commission tabulated its activities in this area.[63] A study of that tabulation gives some insights into the speed of progress.

The complaints themselves are of relatively minor significance. There were fifty-two filed against banks or trust companies during the thirteen year period by forty-seven different persons, almost 90 percent of whom were clerical workers. Forty-nine of the fifty-two complaints were in New York City. Over 60 percent of them alleged discrimination because of color and the majority of complaints arose from dismissal from employment actions. Five of the cases remained open as of the end of August 1958, but of the twenty-nine complaints of color discrimination which were closed, "probable cause" was found in only three. These were "adjusted by conference and conciliation," in the words of the Commission. However, in a pattern often followed by compliance agencies, the Commission did not restrict

---

[62] *New York State, Law Against Discrimination* (1945), Art. 15, Executive Law, Ch. 118, Sec. 296.

[63] *The Banking Industry: Verified Complaints and Informal Investigations Handled by the New York State Commission Against Discrimination, July 1, 1945 - August 31, 1958*, (in the files of the Commission). (Mimeographed.)

itself to investigation of specific allegations, and in 55 percent of the cases some discriminatory practices or policies were disclosed and adjusted, whether or not they pertained to the specific complaints made.

As a result of the informal investigations, the Commission was often able to collect data on Negro employment and employment trends. The statistics, presented as Table 28, are spotty at best, and not meant to be precise. Total employment figures were reported as of some specific day during the year reported, and it was not the same day in each case. Often it was an approximate number. The number of Negroes reported was sometimes based on managerial estimate and sometimes on head count; confusion was occasionally evidenced between Negro and Puerto Rican job holders.

It is interesting to note the progression of Negro employment during this period when employment levels were not subject to federal pressures but were taking courses largely determined by the philosophies and policy determinations of individual bank officers under the spur of the state law. As might be expected under these circumstances, there is considerable variation in the results.

Overall in the eight examples cited, there were about five times as many Negroes employed in 1956-1957 as there were in 1949-1950, which indicates some progress even though employment in the base years was very low and the banks were growing rapidly. It is well to remember that the early 1950's were not characterized by social activism on the part of corporations, and as a result the progress made by Negro employees advancing in the firms was much more likely progress based purely on merit. If there was such a thing as a "traditional Negro job" evident at the beginning of this period, it was for male Negroes in the guard, messenger, and porter categories. There were still many Negroes in these jobs six years later; but additionally, there was the beginning of representation in a wide variety of clerical positions, an increasing number of public contact teller jobs, and even a (very) few managerial and official positions.

One of the banks was running what was obviously a "Jim Crow" operation, using its Negro employees almost exclusively in its black branches in Harlem and Washington Park. For the period, this probably did more good than harm, as the only black branch manager noted among the eight cases appeared in

TABLE 28. *Negro Employment, Various Banks* *
New York City, 1945-1958

Year	Employees Total	Employees Negro	Notes
			Bank A
1949	2,800	0	None had ever been employed.
1950		5	All girls hired for clerical positions.
			Reportedly, one Negro applicant had received serious consideration for a position as a cost accountant, but failed the physical examination.
1951	3,000	16	Clerks, typists, machine operators, trainee, messenger, and cleaning women.
1952		22	
1954	4,000	36	15 clerks, 8 machine operators, 5 typists, 3 messengers, 2 junior bookkeepers, 1 bookkeeper trainee, 1 stenographer, 1 matron.
1956	6,200	117	Including now two junior tellers and a junior teller-trainee.
			Bank B
1950	3,000	0	None had ever been employed.
1952		5	Two supply clerks, three female clerical workers.
1954		9	Seven clerical.
1955		12	Eight clerical
			Bank C
1950	2,500	75	All working in branch offices. All except one teller were armed messengers or porters; all males.
1951		76	One stenographer added. Five other Negroes had been hired in clerical positions, but had left.
1954		115	25 clerical workers, 90 messengers, etc.

TABLE 28 (Continued)

Year	Employees Total	Employees Negro	Notes
			Bank D
1948	8,000 (including foreign)	3	All clerical positions.
1949		30	Includes teller trainee, registered teller, dividend clerk, clerk-typist, draftsman, librarian, plus twenty employed as cleaning women, porters, matrons, and elevator operators.
1950		37	Seven additional Negroes hired including 4 pages and 3 clerical workers.
1952	7,100	50	Approximate number.
1953		75	Estimated.
			Bank C and D
1955		200-250	Various clerical positions. No Negroes on staff strictly as janitor or porter.
1957	13,000	300	Includes an assistant head of files and a chief checker in documentary division.
			Bank E
1952	1,000	24	Fifteen as guards or in maintenance jobs.
1953	2,500	( )	Entire maintenance staff Negro. Additionally, there were 40 clerical workers.
			Bank F
1947	1,900	( )	Twenty-four clerical workers, 20 were at Harlem branch. Negro messengers used throughout system.
1948		( )	Thirty clerical workers. One head bookkeeper. Four other clerical promotions during the year.
1953		90	Some Negroes in each of 77 branches. Branches in Negro areas (Harlem and Washington Heights) very largely Negro, but managers and assistant managers white.

TABLE 28. (Continued)

Year	Employees Total	Negro	Notes
			F Branches of E and F Bank
1954		90	Includes one assistant manager.
1955			Promoted to manager. Also one head teller.
1956	1,450	100-120	Seventy-five guards and messengers.
			Bank G
1947		5	Two file clerks, 1 messenger, 1 junior clerk, 1 typist.
1949		20	
1950		30	
1951		41	
1953	8,000	105	Two tellers of 700 employed.
1954	9,500	122	
1955		171	Positions include assistant section head, teller, head bookkeeper and bookkeeper, senior and junior clerk, stenographer, typist, clerical machine operator, messenger, and guard.
1956	10,600	256	Includes also section head, elevator operator, telephone operator, and investigator.
			Bank H
1950	341	1	One real estate inspector. One Negro real estate appraiser had been employed but resigned to take position as executive vice president of a Negro savings and loan.
1951		4	One real estate inspector still employed, 3 typists.

Source: Condensed from: *The Banking Industry: Verified Complaints and Informal Investigations Handled by the New York State Commission Against Discrimination*, July 1, 1945.

*The Commission study gives names of the individual banks involved but there is no advantage to reporting them here. All save the last were among New York's ten largest.

Note: All figures are approximate.

this bank. Another bank was, with equal obviousness, trying to avoid establishing "traditional positions" for its black employees by assigning them to various jobs in the organization but employing none in janitorial or porter positions.

However, few sociologists or other investigators felt that the apparent advances made by Negro workers in gaining entry to the industry were sufficient. One unpublished 1957 study of attitudes and practices toward minority hiring and upgrading in suburban areas adjacent to New York City felt:

> The postwar attitude of management toward Negro workers in our limited sample does not appear to have undergone any drastic change. Business officials in the interviews we conducted speak more often than not in the same terms as those quoted [in 1946].
>
> *   *   *   *
>
> Circumstances have changed since World War II. Negroes have benefited, like nearly everyone else in the country, from the present economic boom . . . [but] . . . private industry still has far to go. Negroes are still frequently the last to be hired and the first to be fired. Furthermore, they are not being provided with the [right] kind of motivation.[64]

The authors of the above study reflect a position which seems pervasive to the point of universality among researchers into minority hiring by major firms in New York City or elsewhere: that "something is being done, finally, but it is not enough." This attitude is especially prevalent among compliance agencies.

A report prepared eleven years later by the Equal Employment Opportunity Commission for the Commission's hearings on discrimination in white collar employment in New York City, January 15-18, 1968 echoes the same sentiments:

> On the basis of the 1966 data, banks and insurance companies as a whole rate high in overall white collar employment of both [Negro and Puerto Rican] minorities, compared to major corporate employers in manufacturing and those in publishing, advertising and broadcasting. . . .

---

[64] Bernard Rosenberg and Penny Chapin, *Management and Minority Groups: A Study of Attitudes and Practices in Hiring and Upgrading* (unpublished: in the files of the Industrial Research Unit of the University of Pennsylvania, 1957), pp. 147-148.

Actually, only two or three [among the ten or fifteen largest firms] in each of the two industries had made significant progress in equal employment by 1966 and were continuing to make progress in 1967. Many of the larger firms were still doing poorly. Some of them still exclude Negroes and Puerto Ricans completely from managerial and professional jobs.[65]

This last paragraph might seem somewhat harsh in light of the fact that by 1966 the banking industry in New York, both in absolute numbers and relative to the size of its work force, employed more Negroes in white collar jobs than any other major industry in the city except hospitals. The Commission is absolutely correct in pointing out that many banks, and some very large ones among them, were not contributing to the Negro employment gains. Table 29, taken from the EEOC report verifies the wide disparity in Negro participation in nine dominant banking firms. Notice that the firms labeled "F," "H," and "I" had no Negro employees in technician, professional, or official and manager categories. (Firm "D," more than likely defines "technicians" somewhat differently than do the other firms, a problem which we have encountered before.)

The nine firms in Table 29 are very definitely dominant firms in the industry. Their total white collar employment of 52,173 is five times the aggregate of the forty-six smaller banks also included in the survey. Their average work force size is 5,797, compared to 235 for the smaller banks. Comparing the 7.1 percent Negro white collar participation in the large banks with the 4.4 percent rate of the smaller firms reflects the fact that large banks in general provide more than average proportional job opportunities to Negroes.

Between 1966 and 1967, the EEOC noted considerable change in the level of Negro utilization by the large banks.

The nine large commercial banks as a group made substantial gains in Negro employment in one year, their participation rate for Negro white collar workers rising from a collective 7.1 percent to 10.2. One bank moved from 9 percent

---

[65] Equal Employment Opportunity Commission, *White Collar Employment in the New York City Financial Community* (Summary of Report). (New York: The Commission, 1968), pp. 2-3.

TABLE 29. *The Banking Industry*
Percent Negro Employment In White Collar Occupational Groups
New York City
1966

Occupational Group	Total Number of Negroes	Total NYC Banking	46 smaller banks Total	Percent Negro Nine dominant banks									
				Total	A	B	C	D	E	F	G	H	I
Officials and managers	77	0.7	N.A.	0.7	0.6	1.0	0.7	2.1	0.7	—	—	—	—
Professionals	35	1.1	N.A.	1.3	1.0	3.8	2.7	1.2	2.8	—	0.9	—	—
Technicians	57	5.2	N.A.	6.2	1.8	1.3	3.3	18.6	—	—	—	—	—
Office and clerical	4,638	8.2	N.A.	8.8	11.6	9.8	10.3	9.7	8.9	5.2	4.7	3.1	2.8
Total white collar	4,811*	6.7	4.4	7.1	9.0	8.3	8.0	7.9	7.1	4.5	3.8	2.7	2.2

Source: Equal Employment Opportunity Commission, *White Collar Employment in the New York City Financial Community* (Summary of Report). (New York: The Commission, 1968), Tables 4, 5, and Appendix E.

* There is a discrepancy of four persons in this column total which is not accounted for by EEOC.

to 13.4 percent and another from 7.9 to 12.8 percent. Even the bank with the lowest percentage increase rose by 1.1 points, from 4.5 to 5.6 percent.

Total white collar employment in this group jumped by 7,179, with an increase of 2,377 in the number of Negro white collar employees. . . . this suggests that one of every three hires was a Negro, a rate proportionately five times higher than that in the past.[66]

These are obviously tremendous gains in one year and the hiring rate reported for Negroes is extremely high. The Commission's report added an emphatic caveat:

However, these gains must not be misinterpreted. The vast majority of the new Negro employees (2,229 of the 2,377) were placed in office and clerical work.[67]

Actually, this is itself an optimistic note, for it indicates that in ten years the "traditional" jobs in banking in New York City had moved up from the porter-messenger-guard type positions to general clerical. And the 148 Negroes hired directly into the higher-level white collar positions represent about one-fifth of the total number of Negroes employed on all levels, both white collar and blue, which could be accounted for in seven major banks and one small one ten years previously.

Obviously, the EEOC is right to suggest that more could be done in providing job opportunities to Negroes in New York City. On the other hand, it is difficult to conceive of situations in which "more" could not be done. If banks throughout the country had equaled the experience of New York City during this period there would be little cause for concern.

The Baltimore Experience, 1959-1967

It took the Baltimore Community Relations Commission ten years to get the commercial banks of Baltimore to agree to provide quarterly statistical reports showing their involvement with Negro employment and their rates of Negro hiring. The Commission's Tenth Annual Report, for 1966, measures the progress which had occurred in banking in the preceding nine months:

---

[66] *Ibid.*, p. 14.

[67] *Ibid.*

Total employment of Negroes rose from 6.5% to 8.3% of the work force in the banks while "white collar" employment showed a similar rise from 5.5% to 7.0%. About one in five new employees during the first six months of 1966 was a Negro.[68]

In the first six months of 1966, 176 Negroes had found new white collar employment and 199 in all job classifications in Baltimore's seven commercial banks. The Commission recognized the gains: "These figures represent encouraging progress in the involvement of Negroes in the commercial banks of Baltimore." [69] The inevitable disclaimer follows: "The breakdown of the figures, showing in more detail where the increase and new hiring took place, is disappointing, however." [70]

The report then continues, to show that Baltimore's banks had no Negro officers, and that during the six months of new hiring, only two Negro administrative assistants and four Negro administrative trainees had been hired. Finally, it asks for higher banking wages (to cut down turnover during the early months of employment), and for more sophisticated recruiting methods and improvement in interpersonal relationships (to hold and attract qualified Negro employees).

A somewhat later report by the same Commission gives detailed information on Negro employment and hirings by Baltimore's commercial banks for 1966 and the first quarter of 1967.[71] These data are in Table 30, where it is seen that Negro white collar employment rose from 6.6 percent to 7.7 percent over the twelve months, and Negro overall employment from 7.9 to 9.0 percent. These numbers (which do not reconcile exactly with the Commission's previous, 1966 report) show a 24.7 and 19.7 percent growth in Negro white collar and general employment respectively (which the Commission would call a 1.1 percent rise in each case, were it to follow similar examples in its 1967 report). This is substantial growth, and reflects an aggregate hiring rate for the seven banks of 17 percent Negro

---

[68] Baltimore Community Relations Commission, *Tenth Annual Report, 1966* (Baltimore: The Commission, 1966), p. 20.

[69] *Ibid.*

[70] *Ibid.*

[71] Baltimore Community Relations Commission, *A Summary of the Employment of Negroes in Commercial Banks in the Baltimore Metropolitan Area* (Baltimore: The Commission, 1967).

TABLE 30. *The Banking Industry*
Employment by Race
Baltimore Metropolitan Area
1966-1967

For Quarter Ending	All Employees			White Collar		
	Total	Negro	Percent Negro	Total	Negro	Percent Negro
3/31/66	4,627	366	7.9	4,302	283	6.6
6/30/66	4,858	411	8.5	4,535	326	7.2
9/30/66	4,716	395	8.4	4,418	321	7.3
12/31/66	4,803	416	8.7	4,502	335	7.4
3/31/67	4,869	438	9.0	4,561	353	7.7

Source: Baltimore Community Relations Commission, *A Summary of the Employment of Negroes in Commercial Banks in the Baltimore Metropolitan Area* (Baltimore: The Commission, 1967), Table III.

over the period, at least a fair proportion of which must be attributed to the activities of the Commission. Nevertheless, the Commission is again quite right to point out the lack of Negro officers in Baltimore's banks and the relatively heavier representation by Negroes in the entry-level and low-paying jobs of lower-skill demands. Table 31 shows a representative quarter's job classification breakdown for Negro and non-Negro employees.

More than 25 percent of non-Negro employees in the Baltimore banks are seen to hold jobs in the two highest classifications, compared with slightly over 1 percent of Negroes. Machine operator, junior clerk, and various blue collar jobs account for seven out of ten Negro employees, compared with three out of ten non-Negro employees in these generally unglamorous jobs. (It is interesting to note that about as many of Negroes as whites are in teller jobs, despite the general sensitivity of that position.)

In addition to being low-paying, the jobs held most frequently by Negroes are also generally entry-level positions. One explanation for this occasionally offered by bankers but disclaimed by Negro interest groups is that Negro turnover is higher than for whites, which would tend to increase the proportion of Negroes in the entry-level jobs. The Commission's 1967 report contains

TABLE 31. *The Banking Industry*
Employment by Race and Occupational Classification
Baltimore Metropolitan Area
March 31, 1967

| Occupational Classification | Employees | | | | Percentage Distribution | |
	Total	Non-Negro	Negro	Percent Negro	Non-Negro	Negro
Officers	585	585	—	—	13.2	—
Administrative assistants	558	553	5	0.9	12.5	1.1
Administrative trainees	69	67	2	2.9	1.5	0.5
Senior clerks	512	492	20	3.9	11.1	4.6
Machine operators	627	507	120	19.1	11.4	27.3
Tellers	924	840	84	9.1	19.0	19.2
Stenographers	268	267	1	0.4	6.0	0.2
Junior clerks	782	681	101	12.9	15.4	23.1
Clerk typists	224	206	18	8.0	4.7	4.1
Other trainees	12	10	2	16.7	0.2	0.5
Total white collar	4,561	4,208	353	7.7	95.0	80.6
Service employees	308	223	85	27.6	5.0	19.4
Total	4,869	4,431	438	9.0	100.0	100.0

Source: Baltimore Community Relations Commission, *A Summary of the Employment of Negroes in Commercial Banks in the Baltimore Metropolitan Area* (Baltimore: The Commission, 1967), Table I.

data not only on employment levels but also on hirings. There do seem to be some statistical aberations in the Commission's tables, and so our Table 32, which follows, should be used only as possible indication of turnover differences rather than a precise measure, but it does seem to show that Negro turnover in Baltimore in late 1966 and early 1967 was considerably higher.

What does all of this indicate about the status of Negroes in banking in Baltimore? It is most instructive to look back a few years in order to obtain some base data for comparison. In the Third Annual Report of the Baltimore Community Relations Commission (under its previous title of "City of Baltimore

TABLE 32. *The Banking Industry*
Turnover Rates by Race
Baltimore Metropolitan Area
Fourth Quarter, 1966 and First Quarter, 1967

	Negro Employment		Non-Negro Employment	
	4th Quarter 1966	1st Quarter 1967	4th Quarter 1966	1st Quarter 1967
Employment at beginning of quarter	395	416	4,321	4,386
Employment at end of quarter	416	438	4,386	4,431
Net gain during quarter	21	22	65	45
Hired during quarter	65	88	325	448
Left during quarter	44	66	260	403
Quarterly turnover rate [a]	10.9	15.5	6.0	9.1
Indicated annual turnover rate	52.9		30.3	

Source: Baltimore Community Relations Commission, *A Summary of the Employment of Negroes in Commercial Banks in the Baltimore Metropolitan Area* (Baltimore: The Commission, 1967), Table I.

[a] Defined as number of employees who left during quarter divided by average employment during quarter.

Equal Employment Opportunity Commission"), we find that in 1959, seven years before the data shown above were collected, not only were there no Negro officers in the commercial banks of Baltimore, there were no Negro employees at all.[72] In October of that year, the Commission had been forced to postpone a conference of the City's commercial banks called to illustrate to them the positive experiences of a large New York City bank with Negro hiring because six of the larger banks invited refused to attend. It required threats of investigations and hearings by the Commission to obtain the attendance of all but two of the banks at a rescheduled conference but even then in the

[72] City of Baltimore Equal Employment Opportunity Commission, *Third Annual Report* (Baltimore: The Commission, 1959), p. 8.

Commission's words: "Those representatives who did attend were reluctant to discuss the issue." [73]

Between October 1959 and October 1966, not only had the open feelings of hostility toward integration on any level in banking been overcome, but one out of every twelve jobs in the industry had become Negro held, and about one person in eight or nine being hired was Negro.

Washington, D.C., December 1965

In December of 1965, the Commissioner's Council on Human Relations of the Government of the District of Columbia prepared a survey of employment in banks, savings and loan associations, and insurance companies.[74] Thirteen of the District's fifteen banks were included. (One "Negro bank" was not included, and one other bank refused to provide detailed data.) The Council found that among the 3,632 persons employed, 474, or 13 percent, were Negro, but that over half of the Negro employees were in the two lowest job categories, as "unskilled" or "maintenance" workers.

The Council's statistics provide both positive and negative inputs. On the positive side, proportionally more Negroes (13.0 percent of the work force) work in the District's banks than do in the banks of almost any other city, or than do in the savings and loan associations (7.2 percent Negro) or insurance companies (10.2 percent Negro) in the District. On the other hand, only two of the 474 Negroes held jobs as officers in these thirteen banks, and the Nation's Capital is the most heavily Negro populated major city in the country.

The Commissioner's Council noted:

> With the exception noted [a bank founded by an "interracial group"], all District banks employed Negroes in 10 percent or less of skilled positions. These proportions were constant, whether the banks were large or small, new or old, whether or not the bank had adopted a formal "equal employment" policy. . . . There is no correlation between formal, or informal, equal employment policies and the level

---

[73] *Ibid.*

[74] Government of the District of Columbia, Commissioner's Council on Human Relations, *Summary of Survey of Patterns of Discrimination in Banking, Savings and Loan Associations and Insurance Industries—Washington, D. C.* (Washington, The Council, 1966).

of equal employment achievement. . . . There are few indications that the banks are promoting these equal employment policies with any vigor.[75]

Whether the Council's overt pessimism is warranted, the survey does show very few Negroes in the highest job positions, and the report provides one of the best breakdowns available of job categories. With some rearrangement and the addition of the "percent of column totals" figures, the survey's results are reproduced as Table 33, where the wide disparity in job distributions among whites and nonwhites should be noted.

TABLE 33. *The Banking Industry*
Employment by Race and Occupational Classification
District of Columbia
December 1965

Occupational Classification	Employees				Percent Distribution	
	Total	White	Non-white	Percent non-white	White employees	Nonwhite employees
Executives						
President	12	12	—			
Exec. Vice Pres.	12	12	—			
Senior Vice Pres.	38	38	—			
Vice President	77	77	—			
Unspecified[a]	13	13	—			
Total	152	152	—	—	4.8	—
Junior Officers						
Asst. Vice Pres.	79	79	—			
Treasurer	3	3	—			
Asst. Treasurer	30	30	—			
Cashier	17	16	1			
Assistant Cashier	72	71	1			
Unspecified	80	80	—			
Total	281	279	2	0.7	8.8	0.4
Chief Clerks						
Chief Clerks	8	8	—			
Asst. Chief Clerks	33	31	2			
Total	43[b]	41[b]	2	5.0	1.3	0.4

[75] *Ibid.*, p. 2.

TABLE 33. (Continued)

Occupational Classification	Employees				Percent Distribution	
	Total	White	Non-white	Percent non-white	White employees	Nonwhite employees
Tellers						
Head Tellers	53	53	—			
Senior Tellers	108	106	2			
Tellers	431	387	44			
Unspecified	1	1	—			
Total	593	547	46	8.0 [b]	17.3	9.7
Clerical						
Secretaries	126	124	2			
Clerk-typists	153	143	10			
Clerks	807	753	54			
Machine operators	324	275	49			
Unspecified	839	774 [b]	63			
Total	2,249	2,071 [b]	178	8.0 [b]	65.6	37.5
Unskilled [c]	98	50	48	49.0	1.6	10.1
Maintenance	216	17	199	92.1	0.6	41.9
Total	3,632 [b]	3,157	474 [b]	13.0 [b]	100.0	100.0

Source: Government of the District of Columbia, Commissioner's Council on Human Relations, *Summary of Survey of Patterns of Discrimination in Banking, Savings and Loan Associations and Insurance Industries—Washington, D.C.* (Washington, by the Council, 1966), p. 12.

[a] Some institutions provided no breakdowns within the larger categories. Such figures were reported as "unspecified."

[b] *Sic*, minor arithmetical problems are indicated which we have not attempted to correct.

[c] Includes runners, guards, chauffeurs, messengers, and kitchen staff.

National Legislation and Compliance Attitudes

The examples taken from the individual cities, above, have two things in common. First is that under the spur of legislation and the active interests on the part of human relations commissions and other compliance groups, Negro employment levels showed a marked improvement. Second is that compliance organizations are almost invariably pessimistic about the results which have obtained, regardless of what those results reflect. The same is also true in dealing with national legislation and national compliance agencies.

Appendix C scans the legislative and regulatory history of activities by the federal government relating to equal employment opportunity (without detailing the content of the legislation). There it can be seen that in recent years, the number of agencies involved and the complexity of the legal requirements have grown immensely. So has the amount of time which bank managements in general devote to personnel activities, and personnel managers specifically devote to civil rights activities.[76]

Much of the thrust of the national compliance agencies' activities has been devoted to sensitizing top managements in banks to the problems of Negro employees. The more sophisticated compliance groups recognize that this is a much more important factor than any imposing of sanctions.[77] It is probable that this is the reason that most compliance agencies on all levels are extremely hesitant to issue a statement of unqualified optimism on any aspect of the banking employment situation; for the momentum of the advance of Negro employment will be lost if bank managers are allowed to become complacent about their activities to date.

Simultaneously, the sanctions available to the compliance groups have occasionally been applied. As of the end of 1968, four small southern banks had lost their federal deposits because of refusals to take action to meet the equal employment opportunity requirements. This action "has served notice to the entire banking industry that the Treasury Department will use sanctions for noncompliance when it is necessary." [78]

There can be no doubt that this strategy on the part of compliance groups—consisting of working from the top of firms down, of being perpetually dissatisfied with results so far re-

---

[76] The President and the Chairman of the Board of one of the country's largest banks report that they now spend two-thirds of their time on personnel problems. From: "Why Citibank is More than a Bank," *Business Week*, November 16, 1968, p. 83.

[77] Interview with an officer of a Federal compliance agency, September 1968.

[78] Robert A. Wallace, before the U.S. Commission on Civil Rights, San Antonio, Texas, December 13, 1968, quoted in "Federal Banks Increase Minority Employment Nearly One-Third in One Year," *Fair Employment Report*, December 23, 1968, p. 131.

corded, and of showing judicious amounts of regulatory muscle —has had considerable effect on the level of Negro employment in the banking industry. Very few bankers pretend that the same results would have been obtained had the activities of the federal, state, and local governments not been so visible. There are, however, no firm indications whether increased legislation will result in the Negro employment augmentations seen in the largest of the city banks to spread to the numerous, smaller establishments located throughout the country.

Effects of the Regulation on Smaller Banks

The effects of the regulations in influencing equal employment policy formation have been seen primarily in the larger, city banks. These banks seem to operate not in fear of the sanctions which could be imposed against them (although these could be severe) but rather in fear of the adverse publicity which would accompany their imposition. The smaller banks are not so conscious of publicity. Additionally, they are shielded by their numbers from the federal compliance agencies. With over 13,000 commercial banks in the country, any individual, smaller bank is invisible to compliance agencies unless in flagrant violation of the regulations, or unless specific complaints call the bank to the attention of these groups.

Although many smaller banks, particularly those in outlying areas outside of the South, are unfamiliar with the details of the federal regulations, most know that some form of sanctions are possible in the event of noncompliance with equal opportunity provisions. Many of these smaller banks are believed to feel that a dissatisfied Negro employee will be likely to file a formal complaint with a government agency rather than use internal methods for due process and grievance redress, thereby bringing the firm to the government's attention.

Under these conditions there would be logic to a bank's being particularly careful in screening Negro applicants in order to avoid government notice, and the result would be fewer Negro job opportunities in these banks. We have no evidence that this pattern is pervasive among smaller firms in the banking industry, but do not doubt that were it so, increased legislation would provide little remedy.

Overall, legislation and regulations have been effective in sponsoring the beginnings of Negro employment, and the activities of the compliance agencies have been effective in promoting sensitivities to this cause and in furthering employment gains. Considering, however, the already complex regulatory base (as seen in Appendix C) and considering that many firms have not yet understood or assimilated the existing regulations, there seems little need for additional regulation in this area unless they can be more effectively communicated to the smaller firms.

CHAPTER VII.

Some Problems of Negro Employment

As is the case in most other industries, the employment of Negroes in banking has created some problems for managements with which they did not have to deal a few years ago. In this chapter, we shall examine the problem areas which are usually cited and which potentially have application to an industry as skill-structured as is the banking industry. The analysis will be concentrated in three general areas. First, we shall evaluate the impact of Negro hiring on white employees; second, we shall examine the severity of the problems with the behavior patterns which many Negroes bring to the workplace; and third, we shall investigate the possibility that there may be some incremental costs to employers who currently have larger numbers of Negroes in their work forces.

IMPACT ON WHITE EMPLOYEES

There are three areas of potential difficulty associated with the impact of increasing number of Negro employees on the whites who were there before them. First, there are the upsets which are sometimes associated with the initial employment of Negroes; secondly, there is the possibility that when any given department or section of an organization reaches a certain percentage Negro, whites will tend to no longer apply for jobs there; thirdly, there are situations which can arise from the integration of facilities such as water fountains or washrooms.

Reaction of White Employees

Before banks generally became integrated in their employment structures, the greatest fear on the part of managements was the reaction which might be felt from white customers of banks, but there was also some question, especially in the South, as to how employees would accept Negroes as co-workers. In an earlier chapter we found that the fear of bank managements as to the reaction of their customers was largely unfounded, and that

124

even when Negroes began to be placed in sensitive, public contact jobs, customer reaction was minimal. In Table 14 (in Chapter IV) the reactions evidenced by customers were classified, and those reactions were found to be about evenly split between positive and negative.

The concern by most banks for the sensitivities of their employees was understandably less than that felt for their customers. A very few of the banks interviewed by the author indicated that concern in this area had been a major factor accounting for their lateness in beginning Negro hiring. The reaction of the employees reported by the forty-seven banks which were included in the survey bears out the fact that this was not a significant factor. These are categorized in Table 34.

TABLE 34. *The Banking Industry*
White Employee Reaction Reported to Influx of Negroes
47 Commercial Banks Surveyed
United States, 1968

Type of Reaction	Severity		
	None	Minor	Severe
Voluntary white terminations	40	7	0
Isolation of Negroes	43	4	0
Other expressed resentment	32	15	0
Favorable employee reaction	42	5	0

Source: Data in the author's possession.

In the cases involving voluntary terminations or early retirements noted among white employees, in Table 34, no more than two persons were known to be involved from any one bank. (Some banks, particularly in the Northeast felt that a few more employees may have terminated for this reason without indicating to management why it was that they were leaving.) In any event, we can see that there were very few examples of expressed dissatisfaction on the part of white employees and very little obsruction from them to their banks' providing employment opportunities to Negroes.

The probable cause for this overall lack of disruption, aside from the relatively high class of person which chooses a bank as a place to work, is the very deliberate way in which most banking establishments added Negroes to their work forces. The rate of growth of Negro employment in most banking firms has been slow enough to forestall any feeling of being threatened with job displacement on the part of whites already employed. (Also involved is the high turnover rate which banks have experienced over the past several years.)

All Negro Departments

Considering the short time that Negroes have been hired by the banking industry in any significant numbers, it is reasonable to anticipate higher concentrations of Negroes in entry-level jobs than elsewhere, and this of course exists. During interviews, however, it was found that very few banks reported any significant concentrations of Negroes in such areas as custodial and cafeteria services. Only one bank showed a custodial force that was entirely Negro. In other jobs, however, there were some significant concentrations. Twenty of the forty-five banks which responded to a question asking if Negroes were found in higher concentrations in some jobs than in others indicated higher than proportional numbers of Negroes in the proof and transit sections, with figures ranging as high as 30 percent of employment in those sections. Twelve of the banks, all of them located in eastern urban centers, reported high concentrations of Negroes on the night shift. One of those banks indicated that 60 percent of its night employees are Negro, and this bank and several others felt that the Negro proportion on the night shift was changing more rapidly than they thought desirable.

For banks which have night shift requirements in urban population centers, it is apparently becoming increasingly difficult to lure white employees, and specifically white female employees, to the center city areas for work at night—despite shift differentials and other benefits. Although it is obvious that none of the night shifts reported have become exclusively Negro, several large banks are anticipating the time when this will happen. A few others are also looking forward to the time when similar results may obtain in the proof and transit section, in data processing sections, and in other machine-oriented departments. Those banks which feel that this sort of *de facto* internal segregation might harbor potentially serious problems for the future, might be well advised to devote attention to seeing whether these jobs can be made more attractive to everyone or can be distributed throughout the organization rather than having them clustered in a single location.

Facility Integration

The integration of facilities, such as locker rooms, washrooms, and water fountains has occasioned serious difficulty in some industries.[79] There were, however, so few Negroes in the banking industry during the period when segregation was a general practice in this country that separate facilities were seldom constructed. Therefore, banks have inadvertently been spared any problems connected with their integration.

NEGRO BEHAVIOR PATTERN PROBLEMS

Although it is generally true that the behavior patterns which Negroes newly entering the job market bring with them to their place of work are also shared by the majority of whites of the same social class and background, it is also true that banks have been unfamiliar with both until recently. Generally speaking, the most qualified Negro applicants for jobs in banking as elsewhere were absorbed by those progressive employers who began hiring Negroes before they were really compelled to do so. When the combined compulsions of government activities and social pressures forced the balance of firms to begin hiring Negroes, those firms found that the number of Negroes required who could meet the entry-level skill demands could not be found. Therefore, many firms were forced to re-evaluate their entry standards, such as the requirement for a high school education, and other evidences of past achievement, in order to obtain a sufficient number of Negroes. These same standards then had to be applied to whites seeking entry-level employment. In a large number of cases, the result has been that bank managers must now contend with new employee behavior patterns, from both whites and blacks, from which their higher entry-level requirements had protected them in the past.[80] These new patterns show up in work efficiency, in attitudes, and in a few other areas.

---

[79] Herbert R. Northrup, *The Negro in the Rubber Tire Industry*. The Racial Policies of American Industry, Report No. 6 (Philadelphia: Industrial Research Unit, Wharton School of Finance and Commerce, University of Pennsylvania, 1969), pp. 117-119.

[80] Interview with Herbert R. Northrup, "On Hiring Hard-Core Jobless," *U.S. News and World Report*, October 14, 1968, p. 85.

Work Efficiency

It is very difficult to measure the actual output efficiency of employees without engaging in an extensive study program on this point alone. There are, however, certain manifestations of work behavior which are related to efficiency and about which many have felt concerned for some time with respect to Negroes. Absenteeism, tardiness, and mysterious disappearances from the place of work are among the areas most often mentioned as sources of difficulty. The response of forty-seven bankers interviewed on their experiences with Negro as compared with other employees in these three areas are classified below in Table 35. The table shows that a great majority of the banks interviewed found no differences between the races. It also shows, however, that no bank considers its Negro employees to be superior in regard to these work habits.

TABLE 35. *The Banking Industry*
Reported Work Habits of Negroes Compared with Non-Negroes
47 Commercial Banks Surveyed
United States, 1968

Response	Frequency
Reporting for Work on Time	
No difference seen between races	31[a]
Others better	10
Negroes better	0
No comment	6
Regularity of Attendance	
No difference seen between races	30[a]
Others better	11
Negroes better	0
No comment	6
Terminating Employment Without Giving Notice	
No difference seen between races	29
Others better (less frequently)	10
Negroes better (less frequently)	0
No comment	8

Source: Data in the author's possession.

[a] Includes four exclusions of "Hard-Core" employees in each case.

Also closely related to work habits is the question of turnover. Turnover among Negro employees in some industrial occupations has been characterized as "amazingly high." [81] This factor perhaps deserves special consideration in the banking industry, where our data indicate the average turnover rate of all employees for 1967-1968 in our survey banks was already something over 32 percent per year.

The forty-seven banks interviewed were asked whether their turnover rates had been analyzed and if they had any feelings about the primary composition of that turnover. Remarkably few of the banks had made any calculations or analyses of Negro turnover differentials. Only eleven commented on Negroes at all. Of those, three banks felt their Negro employees had turnover rates which were the same as for others in the work force; three other banks felt that the Negro turnover rate was somewhat more; and one felt it to be twice as high. Additionally, there were some more complex feelings. One bank stated that Negro female turnover was less than other female turnover, but that Negro male turnover was higher than other male. Finally, one bank said that although Negro turnover averaged out to about the same as for others, there was less "averageness" to the ratio; that bank felt the probability that a Negro employee would leave in the first week or two was very high, but that if this period was passed, the probability was also high that a Negro would stay permanently.

Only two banks had actually performed analyses of turnover by races. One of these found Negro turnover to be almost twice as high as for whites, and the other found it to be five percentage points higher. (They are both eastern, urban banks.) There are two structural factors which might be thought to influence the results seen: time on the job, and sex. Females, and especially young females, have higher turnover rates than do males. But since the male-female ratio among Negroes is about the same as it is among non-Negroes, this factor should not affect the turnover ratio. On the other hand, time on the job very definitely is a factor. Banks which had analyzed their turnover on a time basis found that 60-78 percent of their yearly turnover was made up by persons who were in their first year of employment. Because a much higher proportion of all Negroes working in banking establishments has been recently hired, we should

[81] *Ibid.*, p. 83.

expect the overall Negro turnover rate to be somewhat higher as a result.

Communications Difficulties

We have already noted some of the difficulties which bankers have experienced with their Negro applicants concerning poor basic education, poor work history and skill development, and bad speech habits and verbal skills. Except for some communications difficulties, these factors are not specific to Negroes, but grow from a sociological experience of urban poverty—which has been the lot of a proportionally larger number of Negroes than whites. Thus, the consequences of this experience are more often seen in banking employment among Negroes than among whites. For bank managements, this has often meant that additional training has had to be undertaken at the workplace, and training of a more basic sort than banks had previously had to perform.

A problem more specific to Negroes is that of verbal usage and general communications. One of the manifestations of this may have been seen above in the somewhat larger proportion of Negroes reported to terminate their employment without giving notice or telling the employer of their plans. To at least some degree, the communication breakdown seen between the employee and the management is a result of the employer not recognizing the sociological gap between himself and a Negro employee, and therefore presuming a communication pattern when none exists.

These difficulties are intensified when it comes to "hard-core" or other culturally deprived employees. Two fairly typical stories illustrate this communication problem. In Chicago, a young, "hard-core" Negro employee repeatedly reported to work unshaved. After several warnings by a supervisor, the case was referred to the bank's personnel department, where careful questioning was required to find out that the youth had never used a safety razor and was afraid of cutting himself with the straight razor which he owned.[82]

A similar story comes from a West Coast bank which reported that one Negro employee had come fairly close to being fired when he offered as an excuse for not reporting for work the fact that "his hog was stole." Only after the bank was able to ascer-

---

[82] "Chicago Banks Hiring 'Unemployables' as Part of Federal 'Jobs Now' Project," *American Banker*, August 8, 1967.

tain that a "hog" in slum parlance is a Cadillac did the excuse make any sense.[83]

Attitudinal Problems

The attitudes which employees bring with them to the workplace are partially conditioned reflexes. The child of a father who felt well-disposed towards his workplace and respected his employer will be more likely to have similar feelings himself than the child of a father who did not. Upbringing, environment, and personal ambition all have a part to play in setting the attitudes of a new employee, and again it seems that in much of American industry, the problems connected with poor attitudes are most visible among the Negro employees.

In response to a statement by "an official at one big company" that a "fairly high percentage of Negroes as compared to whites are totally irresponsible in their attitudes toward the company, the public, and their jobs," and engaged in "an unhappy and disconcerting degree of theft" and similar activities, the director of a Negro activist organization replied that these attitudes and activities were "common everyday occurrences" in Negro society—because Negroes have been excluded from the mainstream of society.[84]

Fortunately, as was the case with other problems with Negroes in the banking industry, the attitudes of Negroes in the industry toward their jobs and/or their employer do not show the grave cause for concern occasionally reported in other industries. Thirty-nine of forty-seven banks of our survey answered a question asking for a comparison between the attitudes of Negroes and other employees. Nineteen of those responding felt Negroes held the same variety of attitudes as non-Negroes; thirteen felt that others were better, and seven felt that Negroes were better. Four comments were also received concerning polarization of attitudes among Negroes—that is, that the good attitudes were very good, and the bad were very bad.

A question related to the preceding one was asked about the self-confidence exhibited by employees on their jobs. Here, twenty-eight bankers responded, with half indicating they could

---

[83] Interview, July 1968.

[84] "Nation's Biggest Firms Now Committed to Help Solve the Racial Crisis," *Wall Street Journal*, June 11, 1968.

see no difference between the races, and only ten finding that perhaps their Negro employees did not yet feel fully at home.

These results can be interpreted to mean that the banking industry has attracted neither a large number of "Uncle Toms" nor a large number of "black power" types or other activists. We found similar results previously when we examined the propensity of Negro employees to join unions in banks. It is possible that Negro job seekers do some self attitudinal-prescreening before looking for work in an institution closely associated with the "establishment" such as a bank. The true activists, in other words, do not bother to apply. The same, undoubtedly, is true on the part of a number of the truly unprepared.

THE COSTS OF NEGRO EMPLOYMENT

The problems that we have covered so far, including lack of qualifications and preparations on the part of Negroes, attitudinal incompatibility, job demands, white employee or customer reaction, and discrimination on the part of bank managements are among the arguments most frequently raised to explain why more Negroes are not currently employed in the banking field. There are two other important factors which need to be investigated: One of these is the number of Negroes who apply for jobs in banks—a point which we shall discuss in the next chapter; the other, less frequently mentioned argument is that employing a Negro or other minority group member is more costly than employing a white.

We have seen that, by and large, the skill level, the credentials, and the work history which the banks see offered to them by entry-level Negro applicants is lower on the average than it is for whites. Additionally, many firms are exhorted to seek deliberately "underqualified," the "culturally disadvantaged," and the "hard-core" to provide them with not only the opportunity to work, but also the rehabilitational training and special handling necessary to bring them to a performance level acceptable to the firm and its customers. Most of these "culturally disadvantaged" are Negroes. It is reasonable to assume, therefore, that banks which have a large number of Negroes are undertaking more special training and a wider variety of training than are banks employing very few Negroes. It is also possible that the level of competence demonstrated on the job by these employees is somewhat more costly to banks which have a large number of Negroes.

On the other hand, if the additional training procedures which may be required for new Negro employees can be effected by existing staff through increased sensitivity, reorientation of techniques, or other devices requiring only the redirection of discretionary managerial time, if the training period is not so lengthy as to be overly costly to the firm, and if the results of the training are reflected in skill levels and behavior patterns accepable to the firm—then there is no reason why a pattern of employment which includes greater numbers of Negroes should be more costly. It is even possible that, because of training procedures, increased sensitivity, and special attention, post-training efficiency and behavior patterns might be better (less costly overall) than would have been the case had standard employment procedures been followed.

Statistical analysis on this point, comparing operating efficiencies among some twenty large banks having widely different proportions of Negro employees has led us to the conclusion that there is no cost-related variable associated with employing Negroes which is strong enough to affect earnings per employee. The coefficient of correlation between change in earnings per employee and change in Negro employment was calculated as —.000256.

SOME PERSPECTIVES OF PROBLEMS WITH NEGRO EMPLOYMENT [85]

It would be surprising indeed if the employment of Negroes in banking had not brought with it some problems which bank managers had not had to face before. Yet it seems clear that the banking industry has suffered less and has seen fewer difficulties and disruptions in integrating its work forces than have many industries. This is partially a result of the Negro applicants to the banking industry being better prepared and better attitudinally adjusted to the rigors of work force participation than many of their counterparts who apply to more industrial firms. With a few exceptions in the custodial sections of banks, the lowest of banking jobs is half-way up the industrial scale found in many other firms. As a result of this, Negro (like

---

[85] During the investigations and interviews to collect the data which has been presented in this study, some perspectives were gained into bankers' reactions to the problems stemming from Negro employment. These were felt to be of sufficient interest to be included here. They are opinions of the author and should be interpreted as such.

white) applicants to the industry apparently go through something of a process of self-screening; the worst do not apply.

Undoubtedly, all banks would prefer better qualifications, better past histories, more premotivation, and more evidenced ambition from Negroes. Some banks, and particularly the smaller ones which are relatively less experienced, continue to indicate they feel that having finally made the effort of offering opportunity to the disadvantaged, that they should be rewarded by gratitude and superior performance. They are looking for "dream Negroes" and they have seldom found them. Nevertheless, banking managements' experiences with Negroes have seldom been especially trying. Banks have been almost uniquely free of the incidents between employees which have marred the integration of some industrialized firms. They have been protected by the high level of sophistication of their existing work forces, by the characteristics of the bank work environment, and by the deliberate, careful way which most carried out the integration of their establishments. Banks broke no new ground in providing employment to Negroes; but although this retarded the entry of Negroes to the industry, it made the subsequent transition less painful.

Not only was the transition sociologically tranquil, it has also been economically unobtrusive. Undoubtedly, there are costs associated with the employment of Negroes which would not have been experienced had they not been hired. We can find no relationship, however, between a gross measure of the performance of banking firms and the relative level of Negro employment. Nevertheless, organizational changes have been required in both the structure and the behavior patterns within management.

Organizational Changes

The organizational structure of most banking firms has had to be modified within the past few years to reconcile them to the fact that among Negro applicants (and increasingly for all applicants) the level of skill development and motivations which individuals bring to the job are in need of remedial attention. Especially among the urban banks, where this is a particular problem, firms in the industry have had to take up remedial education to supplement the appalling level of learning which is the unhappy output of today's city school system. To banks, this means training in reading, writing, and arithmetic as well as in specific requirements related to banking's needs. This has already required considerable redirection of managerial activities in banks, and more will be needed in the future. (Banks have every right to expect better levels of performance from the output of the city school systems, and might be well advised to consider pressures in this direction as an excellent avenue for social involvement.)

Another area in which banks face new problems is with attitudes seen among Negro employees—toward work itself as well as the work place. Many bankers new to dealing with Negro employees undoubtedly have difficulty in sorting out how they, themselves, should react. Extremely few bankers are openly racist; on the other hand, extremely few bankers are experienced enough with Negroes to be "openly open." Most are bombarded by conflicting statements and personal experiences and often do not know how to react. As an example, consider the story of the stolen "hog" earlier in this chapter. Any bank personnel manager is sufficiently at home with the expected behavior and speech patterns of a white employee that, being informed of the stolen "hog" he would automatically question the employee further to find out what really did happen. But in reacting to a Negro making the same statement, many bank managers would hesitate.

Closely alligned with this problem is one of communications verbiage. Some bankers have attempted to ape the patois of the slum, but the sounds made are not only silly, they are also transparently insincere. For example, one eastern bank (not included in the survey) has issued a recruiting piece titled "Break Into the Bank, Baby," which appears in comic book form. This may be a sensitive recognition of the different social values of the slum, but one suspects that those to whom it has appeal might find more compatible employment in another field. Even in the interests of promoting the sociological benefits of increased Negro employment, there is little reason for bankers to compete with parking lot operators for sources of employees.

In training, discipline, and other necessary on-the-job communications, many bankers have shown a propensity to cover their confusion as to what constitutes a proper reaction toward Negroes by formalizing the personnel structure. Many bankers apparently feel more comfortable in dealing with Negro employees if they have some rule or standardized procedure, such as an internal regulation to fall back on. For example, rather than face the individual sensitivities of new Negro employees on some matter such as proper dress on the job, a bank might instead institute a formalized procedure, such as an internal "charm school" in which proper dress, speech, and poise are taught. Such devices, of course, must extend to all equally, regardless of race.

As a result, many personnel activities in banks are becoming more structured and more bureaucratic. To the degree that this has brought about a more orderly personnel activity in banking by replacing unnecessary traditions and limiting the whimsicalities of autocratic control, it has benefitted the industry. Insofar as it has substituted unnecessary bureaucratic procedures, it is dysfunctional.

Nevertheless, it is probably true that having to contend with the sensitivities of Negroes in their work forces has generally had the beneficial effect of requiring personnel departments to be more careful, more diverse, more imaginative, more attuned to the needs of the work force, and generally more sophisticated. This is an unexpected and seldom mentioned positive outgrowth of Negro employment.

How far personnel departments have come in this is the subject of the next chapter.

CHAPTER VIII.

Banking Activities in Support of Increased Negro Participation

Despite the problems, and sometimes to overcome them, bank managers have undertaken a large number of activities in support of increased Negro participation. These activities have spanned the entire range of the personnel function. Additionally, many banks have also become involved in other projects closely related to the urban Negro crisis which, although not concerning employment directly, are part of the new social involvement pattern of banks.

AFFIRMATIVE ACTION

"Affirmative action" is: "positive or firm or aggressive action as opposed to negative or infirm or passive action." [86] It has been interpreted by an undersecretary of the Treasury as follows:

> "Affirmative action" means applying management techniques and controls over personnel actions that are normally applied to any program that you want to succeed. It means analyzing the methods, procedures and results of personnel actions to determine whether they have resulted in the exclusion of qualified or trainable workers because of race. It also means taking direct and appropriate corrective action if discrepancies are found between policy and practice.[87]

There is no consensus among bankers as to what the requirement for affirmative action actually calls for. As part of the interview in the banks sampled, two questions were asked concerning affirmative action: (1) How does the bank interpret "affirmative action?" (2) Do you feel that this carries the connotation of "discimination in reverse?"

---

[86] Section 301 (1), Exec. Order 10295, 26 Fed. Reg. 1977 (1961).

[87] Robert A. Wallace, before an Equal Employment Opportunity Workshop (New York: September 26, 1967), in "Equal Employment Opportunities," *Proceedings of the Workshop on Equal Employment Opportunities sponsored by the American Bankers Association* (New York: American Bankers Association and American Jewish Committee, 1967), p. 6.

All forty-seven banks were asked the first question, and there were, essentially, forty-seven different answers. Most of the responses reflected specific (although often vague) activity goals, such as "encouraging Negro applicants," or "insuring the company from top to bottom is attuned to equal employment opportunities," or "taking any action beyond what you would normally take to gain Negro employment," or "establishing liaison with minority group members who are willing to do some preselection for us," or even "doing what is right." Several bankers felt affirmative action meant "doing exactly what we are doing now." Only three banks, two southern and one midwestern, felt it meant "equal treatment regardless of race." (It is interesting to note that the personnel policies and practices manual of that midwestern bank contains no reference to equal employment opportunity.)

The question on whether affirmative action carried with it connotations of "reverse discrimination" was not asked in all cases. But among twenty-two responses collected, fourteen bankers felt it did, only seven felt it did not, and one bank felt that "preferential recruitment but not preferential hiring" was implied.

Whatever "affirmative action" does actually mean, it is fortunate that many bankers are better at practicing it than vocalizing it. Most of the larger banks throughout the country, although they may interpret "affirmative action" in different ways, have instituted programs aimed at increased minority utilization. A typical program was outlined in a letter from a major, southern bank to the Chairman of the Equal Employment Opportunity Commission in response to a question from the Commission in early 1968. It contained seven major points, summarized below.

(1) Our company has established an equal employment opportunity policy which has been communicated throughout the bank among both officials and employees, and to the community through employment advertising.

(2) We recruit administrative and management trainee candidates at most of the major Negro colleges and universities in the state. We also visit all of the predominantly Negro high schools in the area in recruiting clerical employees.

(3) We have established contacts and sound working relationships with several influential members of the minority communities and have outlined our equal employment op-

portunity policy and enlisted their support in referring applicants.

(4) We have worked very closely with almost all of the governmentally supported programs aimed at preparing minority groups for more meaningful employment. We have also worked closely with the Urban League and State Department of Labor to obtain qualified applicants.

(5) We have carefully reviewed our battery of tests in order to determine absolute minimums for the particular tests that are relevant to given jobs. We have also experimented with pictorial and non-verbal tests in an attempt to minimize the effect of heredity and environment.

(6) Our interviewers have been encouraged to utilize their interviewing skills in determining applicants who seem to possess maturity, initiative, and sound judgment but who might not measure up to our minimum requirements on all of our clerical tests. A number of these applicants have been hired for entry level positions which would utilize their strongest qualifications.

(7) We have encouraged supervisors to promote their minority employees from entry level jobs to more responsible positions in order to provide positions for which marginally qualified applicants might be considered.[88]

We shall look more specifically at several of the areas which are raised here, such as recruiting, testing, and training later in this chapter. Many banks do have affirmative action programs covering areas similar to those noted above and reflecting change from older personnel practices in varying degrees.[89] (Some of these are included in the next chapter.) Before we examine the more specific aspects of these programs, however, we shall have to acknowledge that in practice many equal employment opportunity programs are constructed more for the purpose of public relations than for the purpose of setting personnel procedures. The Plans for Progress program, consisting primarily of a public

---

[88] Letter in the author's possession.

[89] A nice summary of a bank's affirmative action program in the public domain is that by Mr. David Rockefeller, President, The Chase Manhattan Bank, before the Federal Equal Employment Opportunity Commission, New York, January 16, 1968. We would do it injustice by summarizing it here, but the full text is available from the Public Relations Department of The Chase Manhattan Bank.

posture of affirmative action in minority employment on the part of many of the nation's largest firms, has come under fire for this very point. In analyzing the statistics for firms which were and were not members of the program in New York City in 1966, the Equal Employment Opportunity Commission found that minority utilization in the "Plans for Progress" firms was "substantially lower" than for companies not party to a comparable public pledge. [90] This has led to some question as to the continuing utility of that program, especially now that minority representation reports (another aspect of the Plans for Progress program) are required of all banks with over twenty-five employees.

In a similar vein, one large California bank supplied the author with a copy of a special edition of the company's newsletter magazine as evidence of the distribution to employees of information concerning the bank's stance on equal employment. In the magazine's lead article, entitled "Equal Employment Opportunity in Practice," pictures are included of fourteen orientals, nine Negroes, two persons who are possibly Spanish-Surnamed Americans, and twenty-three others. In the balance of the magazine, other stories of general interest to the bank's personnel are included. In these stories, photographs containing recognizable pictures of 292 persons are included. Among the 292, exactly three are Negro: one of these appears as the subject of a picture in a photo contest, and the other two are seen serving punch at a branch opening. We have no doubt that this is unintentional, but it does provide what may be a sad insight into the sincerity of the lead article.

Another example comes from an interview in a southern bank in which a personnel manager spoke at great length and in glowing terms of the effectiveness of a Negro preinduction training center in providing well-qualified Negro entry-level employees for his organization. Unfortunately, a check in the records revealed that over a two year period, only one employee in the bank had come from that organization.

Many bank organizations devote more effort than perhaps they should to telling the government and interviewers what they feel the interviewers want to hear. There is no question that bank participation in many of these areas is overstated. But there is

---

[90] "EEOC Looks Into New York City Employment Patterns, Finds Minorities Substantially Under-Represented in White Collar Jobs," *White Collar Report* (No. 567), January 18, 1968, p. B-3.

no evidence that a "conspiracy of hyperbole" exists among bank managers, and it is only reasonable to allow for some aggrandizement through self-recognition and self-praise; often this is the only specific recognition that bank personnel managers have received for their efforts in this field during the last two or three years. And even discounting this factor, the evidence is very clear that at least among many of the nation's larger banks, changes in personnel activities reflecting a new awareness of minority groups have come at an increasing rate and with increasing sensitivity.

In a remarkable number of cases in banking, this new sensitivity seems to flow from the top of the organization. In only two cases among the banks interviewed did the author find indications that the personnel manager had actually a higher degree of commitment to Negro employment than the bank's president to the point where the personnel manager felt he was undertaking new programs at his own risk. In part, this is a result of very good communication of equal employment needs and requirements to at least the larger banks which are in a position to hire a large number of Negroes. Both the Department of the Treasury and the American Bankers Association have figured strongly in this by arranging workshops and devoting conferences to these activities. A new, high-level committee within the American Bankers Association, the Bankers Committee on Urban Affairs, has recently been formed to evaluate existing programs and formulate new ones for involving the banking industry in not only providing jobs and job training, but also in other areas of social responsibility such as housing and business assistance.[91]

Part of any affirmative action program requires spreading the sensitivities developed among the officers of a corporation to the level of first line supervision. This is often portrayed as an extremely difficult procedure, but although it is clear that a positive stance must be taken with many first line supervisors, the approach need not be harsh. An excellent example of the handling of this situation is provided in the next chapter. Here let us examine some of the specific programs in recruiting, selecting, and training employees which have been undertaken by banks.

---

[91] American Bankers Association, *A Program for Urban Progress* (Washington: American Bankers Association, Bankers Committee on Urban Affairs, 1968), p. 2.

RECUITING

Using turnover data and other sources, it is estimated that the forty-seven survey banks interviewed 458,800 persons in order to hire 70,417 during 1967. This indicates that in the average bank, 6.5 persons were interviewed in order to fill one job. The weighted average selection ratio is somewhat smaller than the simple average, indicating that smaller banks have been somewhat more selective than larger ones.

The nearly half-a-million applicants recruited by the industry were contacted through all of the usual recruiting techniques. Depending upon the traditions in individual cities and on the condition of the specific labor market, walk-ins, referrals, employment agencies, classified ads, and direct high school and college recruiting are all used. None of these sources is predominant in the industry for applicants. Walk-ins are the most common source in many cities, but where tight labor markets prevail, employment agencies are often mentioned. Referrals are often a major source of applicants as well.

Banks have undertaken special activities in connection with all of the employee sources in order to promote a larger flow of Negro applicants. The number of Negro drop-ins can be stimulated only by banks' indicating a general attitude of acceptance through other recruiting sources, and through the general expression of an equal employment policy in practice. The Department of the Treasury's Compliance Section has frequently exhibited a fear that Negroes were not applying to banks for employment. But although this may have been true as recently as two or three years ago, the author's spot check of banking hiring offices revealed that there is no longer great need for concern on this point. Thirty to fifty percent of persons seen there were Negro.

Special efforts involving classified advertising are somewhat difficult to evaluate. All banks which use classified ads indicated that they have requested the EEO tag lines as required by law, but since these tag lines appear in all classified advertising, they can provide no informational input to Negroes seeking employment, and therefore can have little effect. About one-half of the firms interviewed indicated that they had at some time or another placed ads in predominantly Negro papers, either of an institutional nature or actually seeking applicants. One bank mentioned that it knew of one employee acquired because of this form of advertising, but most bankers felt that such advertising was of token significance either for finding new employees or for aiding the image of the bank.

A few years ago, there were a number of private employment agencies specializing in minority group members, but these firms generally catered to blue collar and service occupations and few banks used their services. Some of these firms continue to exist, but on higher levels their functions have been generally taken over by the profusion of quasi-public Negro self-help organizations and firms engaged in "vestibule" training.

In the deep South, bank association with these groups, while growing, is still relatively limited. The surplus supply of qualified Negroes in the South is only now being absorbed to the point where banks have to seek "substandard" Negroes and install special training programs. In other areas of the country, banking involvement with these groups is heavy. One New York City bank alone reports that it cooperates with more than fifty antipoverty agencies, public and private, as well as five agencies serving the handicapped. Most of these are providing special sources of minority group recruitment. There are forty-two such programs in the city of Cleveland, alone, although the Cleveland banks do not deal with all of them.

Banks are involved with organizations or programs bearing such acronyms as PACT, TAP, CAMP, STEP, JOIN, WEB, AIM, MIND, CEC, WCEPT, CEP, BEEP, and others. Opportunities Industrialization Centers (OIC) have proved to be rather popular among bankers in cities where they exist, especially in Philadelphia. Dissatisfaction with this program was noted in only two cases. About half of the bankers interviewed mentioned the Urban League and the National Association for the Advancement of Colored People specifically, but six bankers felt dissatisfaction with the ability of local chapters of the Urban League to send referrals to the banks. The general feeling seems to be that although the Urban League's referrals are of a high quality and have definite skills and educational backgrounds to offer, there are not many referrals offered.

By far, the most popular of all of the special programs is that of the National Alliance of Businessmen, a program for providing employment for the hard-core jobless and summer jobs for disadvantaged youths. The NAB program was only about six months old when most of the banks interviewed were seen, and there was still some confusion as to the details of the program. But by that time, approximately 1,862 jobs for either the hard-core or for summertime employment had been pledged, and a fair number of them filled. Bankers' reaction to the employees hired under this program seemed optimistic, and although two banks reported bad initial experiences, most felt the program was working well, with about the normal drop-out rate. Few of the jobs filled had to be especially created.

Although few banks have had any luck with using local Negro businessmen or ministers as a referral source, four banks had obtained a few applicants in this way. One final example will perhaps make obvious that at least not all banking involvement with these special programs exists simply for its public relations aspects. One of the major New York City banks, for its own use, tallied the number of employees hired as a result of special-program minority group recruiting. It found that over approximately one year's time, more than 950 persons had been hired from these programs (including 400 young people hired for summer work). Although not all of this employment was drawn from predominantly Negro groups, the involvement is nonetheless extensive.

The type and degree of college recruiting performed by banks varies with the size of the organization. Many banks recruit throughout their states, and a few of the biggest cover major universities throughout the country. In the South, banks generally recruit at the Negro colleges to some degree, but they report the competition for the highly skilled to be intensive—not only from other industries, but also from the larger California, Chicago, and New York banks. Generally, banks have reported little success with acquiring Negro managerial candidates from the colleges. Many, however, have found that local junior colleges are often an excellent source of clerical employees. Especially in the South, many of the more ambitious Negro girls will apparently enter junior college with the expectation of staying only for a year or so, reasoning that this puts them at a competitive advantage for good clerical jobs. Both they and their schools are anxious that they be employed as rapidly as possible since job seeking rather than graduation is the primary goal. This has been found to be a source of prized employees at many banks.

Recruiting at high schools is almost always missionary recruiting, consisting of talks at career days, tours, occasionally sponsoring summer programs, and often trying to attract the attention of high school counsellors to steer qualified applicants to the bank establishments. Very little direct recruiting is or can be done. New programs in this area which look promising concern potential high school drop-outs who are being given the opportunity to work part time and go to school part time until they complete their studies. Banks involved with these programs almost always report them to be among their best and most rewarding. We shall discuss some of them subsequently.

The final, major recruiting source for bank employees is other employees. Referral systems, whether or not they include a "bounty" are often the most important source of applicants. We have already noted that there has been some dissatisfaction with referral systems from EEOC because it was felt they tended to perpetuate the existing, low-minority racial mix in banks. Some banks, too, have indicated that they have avoided referral systems for fear of increasing the general dissatisfaction of the work force because of the number of friends of employees who might have to be turned down.[92] Four of our surveyed banks said that they were trying to overcome the first of these difficulties by making a special communications effort to Negro employees to refer in friends. Concerning the second point, although some referred applicants are inevitably turned down, banks which employ this recruiting system extensively report few difficulties with it. The selection ratio among employee referrals—that is the number of applicants who have to be seen in order to fill one job—is about three or four to one compared with seven or eight to one among walk-ins.

In the interview survey, bankers were asked for estimates of the racial ratio of their job applicants. Except in Phoenix, where Negroes are not the largest minority group, the minimum estimate was that 20 percent of those seeking work were Negroes. In New York and Philadelphia, the average was over 50 percent, and ranged as high as 85 percent for walk-ins. In the light of these figures, it is fairly obvious that Negroes do apply for jobs in banking, especially where they know that other Negroes are employed.

SELECTION

Standard procedure employed by banks in selecting new clerical-level employees consists of a screening interview, followed by a battery of tests, followed by interviews in greater depth. The

---

[92] This reaction has received judicial sanction in at least one case involving a textile mill. *Shirley Lea et al.* v. *Cone Mills Corporation,* U.S.D.C., Mid. Dist., N.C., July 29, 1969.

final selection of persons for employment is usually made by the personnel office, but occasionally by individual departments. Traditionally, banks have required a high school diploma for all full-time jobs. This requirement is now becoming a rarity in the industy. Almost all banks require employment and personal references, make credit checks, police checks, and occasionally other investigations as well.

It is currently in vogue to speak of the selection process as one of "screening-in rather than screening-out" applicants, but it is the inevitable nature of any selection process to screen out when the number of applicants exceeds the number of positions open. Most banks have interpreted "screening-in" to mean that they should examine their entry-level requirements very carefully to make sure that they are at the lowest possible level compatible with the position being filed. And in point of fact, since the entire training of personnel managers is to avoid filling jobs on a "first come first served" basis but rather to secure the best qualified employees at the least cost, most bank personnel managers continue to choose the best qualified, regardless of where the minimum standard level may be. Most will now, however, under a *ceteris paribus* condition give preference to a Negro applicant. For managerial positions, many report that a Negro applicant will be accepted over a white if the Negro's qualifications are 80 percent as good.

Overall, very little in the way of visible creativity can occur in the selection process itself. Most banks have relaxed their standards to some degree since 1965. Only three of our sample banks revealed that they continued, in 1968, to require a high school diploma for all jobs within their organizations; twelve others continued to require the diploma for all except special-program entrants (such as NAB or OIC) ; and five banks give preference to applicants holding a diploma. The remainder have dropped the requirement, generally without noticeable ill effects. The type of work offered by the banking establishments, and their general reputation, have insured that 90 and 95 percent of those currently applying to the industry come equipped with the high school diploma.

Testing

The tests normally used by banks for clerical-level applicants consist of mental ability tests (such as the Wonderlic Personnel

Test, the Otis Self-Administering Test of Mental Ability, or the Science Research Associates' SRA Verbal Form), tests of clerical abilities (such as the Minnesota Clerical Test, the Hay Number Perception Test, the Psychological Corporation's General Clerical Test, or the Short Employment Tests—developed by the Psychological Corporation specifically for the banking industry), and various proficiency tests for special skills (typing tests, stenography tests, language usage tests, office machine tests, and proof machine work samples). A number of other, less widely known tests are also used by individual banks.

All employers have been affected by recent regulations concerning the use of tests from the Equal Employment Opportunity Commission, various state human relations commissions, and the Secretary of Labor.[93] All of these agencies are fearful that employment tests, and especially mental ability tests, either contain inherent cultural biases, or may be being used by employers to unfairly exclude Negro applicants. The Secretary of Labor's order, which initially covered federal contractors employing 2,500 or more persons, contractors employing 1,000 or more beginning in September 1969, and all other contractors beginning in February 1970, is especially far-reaching. Essentially, it requires that all employers covered by the order who use tests to judge qualifications for hire, transfer, or promotion maintain statistical evidence that the tests are valid for the purpose used, and contain no inherent racial bias.

Although purporting to cover the validation of employment tests, this order actually contains verbiage suggesting a new definition of "unfair discrimination" and seems to cover all selection techniques. A portion of the order is reproduced below:

> Selection techniques other than tests may also be improperly used so as to have the effect of discriminating against minority groups. Such techniques include, but are not restricted to, unscored interviews, unscored application forms, and records of educational and work history. *Where there are data suggesting that such unfair discrimination exists*

---

[93] " 'Guidelines on Employment Testing Procedures' Adopted by Equal Employment Opportunity Commission," *White Collar Report* (No. 496), September 8, 1966, pp. C-1 to C-3.

Pennsylvania Human Relations Commission, *Affirmative Action Guidelines for Employment Testing* (Harrisburg, Pennsylvania: The Commission, 1967).

Willard Wirtz, *Validation of Employment Tests by Contractors and Subcontractors Subject to the Provisions of Executing Order 11246*, a memorandum to the Heads of All Federal Contracting Agencies, September 9, 1968.

(e.g., differential rates of rejecting applicants from different ethnic groups or disproportionate representation of some ethnic groups in employment in certain classes of jobs), then the contractor may be called upon to present evidence concerning the validity of his unscored procedures as well as of any tests which may be used. . . . If the contractor is unable or unwilling to perform such validation studies, he has the option of adjusting employment procedures so as to eliminate the conditions suggestive of unfair discrimination.[94] (Emphasis added.)

It is difficult to draw from the definition of "unfair discrimination" implied above any connotation other than that any selection procedure which does not provide hiring ratios in proportion of population percentages is unfairly discriminatory. A literal interpretation of this passage would require the implementation of quota systems which both Title VII of the Civil Rights Act of 1964 and Executive Order 11246 are very careful to avoid.

This most recent order of the Secretary of Labor was not yet in effect when our interview survey of the industry was conducted, and so no reaction to it could be collected. Subsequent conversations between the author and several bank personnel managers did reveal that some banks may be considering abandoning tests entirely as a selection device, but using them subsequent to hiring as a gauge of additional training which may be necessary, and to locate persons better in their initial job assignments. Several bankers expressed the hope that the American Bankers Association might coordinate validification studies for a number of banking jobs, which studies would apparently be acceptable under the Secretary of Labor's order.[95] This would not be an easy task for the American Bankers Association, or anyone else, for there are also some problems with how to validate a test for minorities. George K. Bennett, President of the Psychological Corporation, in commenting on the 1966 EEOC requirements for validating tests for minorities asked: "What is meant by this? Empirical validation? Content validation? How much generalization? Is it intended that if a test is equally valid

---

[94] Willard Wirtz, *op. cit.,* pp. 8-9.

[95] The American Bankers Association compiled information and made recommendations on test usage in 1952 in: American Bankers Association, *Clerical Testing in Banks* (New York: American Bankers Association, Customer and Personnel Relations Department, 1952).

for both groups but that the disadvantaged score lower a correction factor should be used? Such factor would be an indication of reverse discrimination and, moreover, would have to be used on a judgmental basis since cultural deprivation is not all-or-none but a matter of degree."[96]

Many feel that "critics of testing are not advocating test reform, but rather test abolition." [97] Banks will not be able to tell whether this is the case until they see the method and degree of enforcement of the existing regulations.

TRAINING

The special requirements of bank jobs, and the high degree of efficiency and precision needed throughout the clerical levels but especially in the teller functions, have meant that banks have always been involved with special training programs. Stenography, typing, filing, and similar skills of a more general application have long been offered by secretarial schools, and are options in most of the public school systems in the country. High schools and secretarial schools, however, do not offer teller training.

In recent years, the larger banks have found it necessary to supplement the special training programs required for their special job positions by more extensive teaching of basic skill development and refresher courses on the clerical levels, and many have instituted courses on the managerial level and executive level to sensitize top management personnel not only to technological and business advances but also to human relations problems and techniques. The training offered by one of the larger, midwestern banks now consists of eight different courses in general orientation to the bank, its operations, and its customer relations policies; six courses in communications, dealing with telephone training, effective speaking, letter-writing, etc., and six courses for secretarial training including typing and stenographic skills. Additionally, clerical training is effectuated with the help of nine courses ranging from the fundamentals of typing to advanced keypunch training; supervisory and management

---

[96] George K. Bennett, "Ability Testing and the Culturally Disadvantaged," a document from The Psychological Corporation marked "Draft—10/6/66."

[97] Thomas E. O'Reilly, "Equal Employment Opportunity: A Mandate for Today" (unpublished thesis, the Stonier Graduate School of Banking Conducted by the American Bankers Association at Rutgers—The State University, 1967), p. 64.

courses span the range from first line supervisor to officer level and consist of twenty-three courses ranging from basics through creative thinking, problem-solving, conference leadership, and productive selling, to clever management techniques and officer development seminars stressing behavioral sciences. Finally, four courses are offered for in-house off-duty formal education.

This range of programs typifies the approach of the larger banks, but does not reflect the changes occasioned in training structures by the industry's involvement with the special needs of minority group members. A more imaginative approach is being formulated by one of the major competitors of the bank whose program is outlined above. That program is being set up with a "quasi-university" approach—that is, an offering of courses is provided (twenty-five courses initially, but expanding) for which employees may sign up as desired. The courses are run on a semester basis, taking up to two hours per day—all on company time, with full wages. The courses fall into four basic areas: (1) A "socialization" course for disadvantaged entrants consists of remedial training, instructions in personal finance, hygiene, work force participation requirements, and other "vestibule training." (This course is on a more concentrated time scale, and takes place outside of the bank, but with full salary during the training period.) (2) Education courses are offered in vocabulary, arithmetic, and other areas. (3) Skill development courses are offered, not only for such things as teller position requirements, but also—for the girls—in charm, poise, etc. (4) Management development courses dealing in finance, behavioral sciences, etc. are also given. This training is supplemented by a career counseling program designed to aid clerical-level personnel in preparing themselves for promotion.

It should be no surprise that smaller banks do not have training programs as extensive as these. Most banks of all sizes have some relationships with the American Bankers Associations' American Institute of Banking, which provides courses and instructions in many cities.

In addition to the in-house training and skill development programs, banks engage in two other types of training programs: special training for the "hard-core," and special programs with high schools.

"Hard-Core" Programs

Through local chapters of the American Institute of Banking, special training programs for the "hard-core" unemployed are currently being conducted in New York City, Boston, and Wichita among others. The New York program involves thirty-four local banking institutions which have entered into a consortium arrangement to hire and train more than 700 "disadvantaged ghetto residents" for banking careers over a twelve-month period. The six week program involves thirty-two hours of classroom work each week, with teaching and counseling provided by the New York City Board of Fundamental Education, and on Friday afternoon of each week, the trainees—all of whom are hired prior to beginning training—return to their employing institutions where they report to a "buddy" who helps them make the transition into the work place. This six-week program is followed by an additional forty-six week period during which participants spend twenty-six hours of the work week on the job and the remaining nine hours in further classroom training. (This program has extensive federal funding.)

A similar program in Boston involves a group of seven banks, cooperating with the Opportunities Industrialization Center there, to train about sixty-five disadvantaged persons for achievement of proficiency in office skills. (This program also has funding through the United States Department of Labor.)

In Wichita, fourteen banks, in cooperation with the Urban League, structured and privately funded a seven-week skill training program conducted at a local vocational school. The program was designed to provide the trainees with a banking orientation. Remedial training was not involved, and trainees were not paid for classroom work.[98]

Two other very extensive programs in New York City have been established by banks which are not part of the AIB consortium there. Perhaps the most ambitious project is one sponsored by the First National City Bank under contract with the Department of Labor. This is an eighteen-month project which began in the Fall of 1968 and has as its goal the training of 700 persons for proficiency in clerical skills, language, and mathematics. All of the trainees are full-time employees of the bank, and during their sixteen to twenty-six weeks of off-the-job training, earn $65.00 per week. On graduation, they are automatically continued in employment by the bank, and all receive a ten-dollar raise. The bank expects its own financial involvement to be more than $150,000 for administrative and other services not covered

---

[98] A summary of the New York City program can be found in: "34 New York Financial Units, AIB, Join to Train, Employ Ghetto Youth," *American Banker*, July 8, 1968.

by the contract with the government. About 200 persons were covered by the program as of September 1968.[99]

The Chase Manhattan Bank also undertook an extensive special training program involving full-time off-the-job training in December of 1967. That program, called "Job Opportunities in Business" was undertaken without federal funding. It is one of the few such training programs in the banking industry which is oriented toward male trainees. Trainees are accepted in groups of about twenty, and the program consists of three phases. The first phase lasts six weeks, and includes forty hours of classroom training each week in oral and written communications, literature, basic economics, arithmetic, and orientation to the business world. Trainees receive $1.60 per hour pay during this time. During the second phase, trainees begin working, receive regular full-time salaries, and continue their remedial education on bank time. This phase may last for up to one year, and includes up to two hours per day of remedial education. The third phase is a follow-up phase of no specific time duration, and provides on-the-job coaching, individual development, and up-dating of educational achievements for any trainees who appear to need additional remedial education for specific positions. Other staff members may participate in this phase of the program on a voluntary basis.[100] This program has not been inexpensive, for the bank estimates that it has made an investment of more than $1,000 per student involved.[101] However, it has provided three significant benefits: it has achieved some sociological good by providing broader job horizons to trainees than they otherwise would have had; it has provided the bank with some well-trained new employees; and it has given the bank wide publicity at what would be modest cost for an advertising campaign of equivalent

---

[99] "Wirtz Visits Bank's School for Unemployed," *New York Times*, September 12, 1968, p. 71.

[100] The Chase Manhattan Bank, N.A. *Job Opportunities in Business Program* (New York: By the Bank, 1968). See also *Wall Street Journal*, December 23, 1969.

[101] "Training The 'Hard-Core'—A Top Banker Tells His Story," *U.S. News and World Report*, August 12, 1968, p. 51; the cost per employee estimate may somewhat understate actual costs. An officer of the New England Merchants Bank reported to the author in conversation that the "hard core" training program in which his organizaion participates (the AIB program mentioned earlier in the chapter) has a cost of $202,000 over a two year period. During the first year, twenty-six trainees were put through the program of whom twenty finished. This works out to a cost per trainee of approximately $5,000.

coverage. The program has been covered in *Newsweek*, and *U.S. News & World Report*, by the *American Banker*, *The New York Times*, *The Christian Science Monitor*, the Chicago, Illinois *News*, *The New York Post*, the Miami, Florida *Herald*, and even such papers as the Wooster, Ohio *Record*. Television and radio time in New York City has also been devoted to the project.

There has been more activity of this sort in New York City than anywhere else in the country. (There is also, of course, more banking and more Negro banking employment in New York City than anywhere else in the country.) Programs are also under way in Philadelphia, through the Opportunities Industrialization Center, in Los Angeles, through the Los Angeles City Board of Education, and in other cities. One of the most interesting of the new training programs is not supplied to the disadvantaged, but rather consists of making available the special training facilities of the larger, commercial banks to the membership of the (Negro) National Bankers Association. Through the American Bankers Association, and with financial aid from a government grant, twenty-two Negro trainees were placed, one each with an ABA member bank, for an intensive, year-long course of experience at the department head level. After the year of exposure to decision making in a large commercial bank, the trainee is expected to return to a black-owned NBA bank in a managerial position. (Management inexperience has long plagued the twenty-two Negro-controlled banking institutions now in existence. See Appendix "B.") The commercial banks sponsoring trainees pay them $7,000 to $9,000 during their year with them, and are responsible for seeing that the training offered can be applied to the black community.[102] This project is still in its formative stages.

Relationships to Schools

Many banks throughout the country, and with greater ranges of size than those which engage in the special programs noted above, have established special relationships with their local school systems whereby students in danger of dropping out are given the opportunity to work part time for pay in the bank. Very few adverse comments have been heard from bankers using this sort of a program, in that the programs not only pro-

---

[102] "White & Negro Bank Associations Launch Joint Project for Training Black Bankers," *Fair Employment Report*, April 28, 1969, p. 53.

vide sociological good, but also are an excellent source of pre-motivated, full-time employees. Very little specific classroom training is required, and the students actually perform productive work during their training. Thus, costs are relatively light, and the program can be engaged in by banks of almost any size.

The best documented, and perhaps largest, program of this type is sponsored by the First Pennsylvania Bank in Philadelphia. Several other banks in Philadelphia, as well as five area high schools, participate in the program.[103]   Other company-sponsored training programs which involve on-the-job training for high school students are taking place in banks throughout the country. Often, these programs, too, provide not only sociological benefits for the bank, but also good public relations within the community.

OTHER BANKING ACTIVITIES

We have mentioned several times previously our conviction that the banking industry will be asked to expand its social responsibilities, especially in the area of urban affairs. In the past few years, individual banks, or local groups of banks, have provided financial support, either directly or through intermediary social organizations, to urban low-cost housing development, and to the development of black entrepreneurship and black businesses. The extent of this support has been significant. A quick scan of a few newspaper clippings, all from 1968, revealed the following: Philadelphia banks agreed to make up to $5 million in credit available to the city's low-income housing and rehabilitation program; [104] a group of Philadelphia banks announced a $2 million loan fund primarily to help Negroes establish new businesses in their neighborhoods; [105] a fifteen member bank group in Chicago had agreed to provide $100 million for interim financing of low-cost housing; [106] a San Francisco bank announced plans to advance

---

[103] For information on this well-documented program, contact the Personnel Department, The First Pennsylvania Banking and Trust Company, Philadelphia, Pennsylvania.

[104] "Banks Pledge $5 Million in Housing Aid," *Evening Bulletin* (Philadelphia), February 26, 1968.

[105] "Philadelphia Banks Join Agency, Form Loan Fund for Negro Ghetto Firms," *Wall Street Journal*, April 2, 1968.

[106] "Bank Group to Finance Low-Income Housing Plan," *Wall Street Journal*, April 5, 1968.

up to $100 million in real estate loans in minority areas throughout California; [107] eighty financial institutions advanced $100 million for homes in the Bedford-Stuyvesant section of Brooklyn; [108] a group of Philadelphia mutual savings banks provided a pool of $20 million for real estate mortgage loans.[109]

Evidence of an additional $68 million pledged by banks in New York City, Philadelphia, Houston, and Boston is found in Appendix "B." All told, these individual and group efforts—and probably there are many others not included here—have made available very close to $400 million in special loans or loan funds for low-cost housing and Negro business financing. Although this is a considerable sum of money, the fact that it is provided by individual banks or groups of local banks has deprived the industry of the additional publicity benefits which would have been derived through a more concerted effort. Everyone is familiar with the insurance industry's famous billion-dollar pledge, but relatively few realize the existence and significance of the banking industry's activities in these fields. (Undoubtedly, one of the functions of the American Bankers Association's Bankers Committee on Urban Affairs will be to insure that future activities of the banking industry in this area are well-directed, and do not go unnoticed.)

SUMMARY

Overall, it appears that, although the banking industry's involvement with locating, employing, and training Negroes for the industry commenced slowly, it is now moving very rapidly, especially among the larger banks. Even though they seem to have difficulty defining precisely what it means, bankers do seem to be undertaking affirmative action in opening up job opportunities, and in recruiting and training Negroes and other disadvantaged persons. At the same time, bankers have been expanding their social responsibilities to include increased attention to urban problems. There are some exceptions among the smaller banks, but these activities have been almost exclusively within the purview of the handful of largest banks in the country, and even among them there are banks not participating in the changes taking place within the industry.

---

[107] "California Banks Join Drive to Aid Easier Ghetto Loans," *New Pittsburgh Courier*, July 20, 1968.

[108] *Ibid.*

[109] "Mutual Banks Aid Philly Homebuyers," *New Pittsburgh Courier*, October 12, 1968.

CHAPTER IX.

Policy Statements

In order to find out the extent to which equal employment opportunity has been formalized into policy statements, the personnel policy manuals were collected from four of the survey banks, one from each of the census regions. They reveal some interesting differences which reflect the divergence of reactions we have seen previously in the banking industry.

EQUAL EMPLOYMENT POLICY STATEMENTS

The manual obtained from the southern bank contains the strongest policy statement. It was given prominent display on the first page of the "employment practices" section of the personnel manual in late 1968, and reads as follows:

> It is the policy of this Bank to adhere to the requirements of Title VII of the Civil Rights Act of 1964, the Age Discrimination Law of 1968, and to all other legislation having to do with equal employment opportunities. We do not practice any form of discrimination, both in compliance with the law and as a matter of principle. We have long since informed our sources of manpower supply, and our management personnel, of our position of nondiscrimination in recruitment, training, and promotion.

> As part of the Bank's continuing affirmative action in being an equal opportunity employer, [name supplied] has been designated as the Bank's Equal Employment Officer. He will assure compliance throughout the Bank and with all equal employment laws and regulations; he will see that Bank personnel are assigned and utilized both for the Bank's best interests and so as to achieve maximum individual development and opportunity, regardless of race, color, religion, national origin, sex, or age; he will represent the Bank at conferences and other meetings related to equal

employment; and he will be available to discuss with any employee the Bank's equal opportunity practices.

Although this is a rather positive statement of an equal employment policy, it appears from its verbiage to have been influenced as much by a desire to satisfy the requests of the compliance agencies as to inform employees or request their participation in affirmative action. Other policy statements and personnel procedures in the same section of the manual do not dwell on past activities of the department.

Partially, this omnibus statement may have been included in reaction to the short-sighted views which characterized many compliance reviews conducted by federal agencies before they became more experienced. At that time, there appared to be something of an inclination on the part of those conducting reviews to be overly interested in not only written policy statements on equality of opportunity, but also in documentation that the bank had or would inform manpower suppliers, advertising agencies, and others of the policies of the bank, and would appoint in writing a high-ranking officer of the corporation as the equal employment opportunities officer.

The personnel policies manual of one of the largest of the eastern banks does not contain as directed a statement. The first section of the manual deals with "employee advancement and compensation," and contains the following statement:

> In considering candidates for advancement, the supervisor is required to make an objective selection based on merit. Included in this judgment are the individual's past performance, education, and work experience, as well as his aptitudes, interests, and attitudes. The choice of one member of the staff over another should be based on length of service only if both candidates are equally qualified in these fundamental respects. Race, color, creed, national origin, age, or sex are never to be impediments to advancement.

Another reference to the equal employment activities of the bank can be found in the manual, under "changes in employee status: placement." This is an extremely strong statement:

> The bank will not tolerate discrimination based upon race, color, creed, national origin, age or sex; disregard of this Bank policy will lead to disciplinary action. New employees

are selected upon their qualifications . . . and the requirements of the job for which they are being considered.

The policy manual of a smaller, western bank also contains
more than one reference to equal employment considerations.
Under "personnel aims," one of the ten aims mentioned is: "To
respect individual rights and to insure fair, courteous and con-
siderate treatment without regard to race, creed, color, national
origin, sex or age."

Making up the first page of the "policy statements," which
follow, another equal employment statement appears:

> It is our policy to select the best person available for each
> job opening. Hiring is based on ability to perform a specific
> job and on potential for growth and advancement. Race,
> color, religion, sex, age, or national origin will not be con-
> siderations.

Finally examined was the personnel policies manual of one of
the major north central banks. It contains no mention in its
102 pages of equal employment or race. (Worse, it contains one
passage on working conditions—smoking during working hours
—which seems to discriminate against females.)

This last experience—of not containing a policy statement in
the personnel department policy manual—seems to be a common
situation in the banking industry, even among the large banks
interviewed. Only eleven of the forty-seven banks surveyed said
that a statement appeared in their policy manual, although all
except four indicated that some method of distributing a policy
of equal employment opportunity had been undertaken at one
time or another. Fifteen banks had statements in employee
handbooks (or a separate statement given to all new employees);
seventeen had given space to these policies in the bank's house
organ (although there were indications in the last chapter that,
unless carefully handled, such statements can do more harm
than good); and in eighteen cases a letter from the president,
chairman, or some other official had been sent to all employees
at one time or another.

But it remains difficult to understand why so many banks,
even those which are apparently practicing affirmative action in
employment are so hesitant to include a statement to that effect
in the policy manual, or to make a continuing effort to insure
that all employees are kept aware of the policy. A suggested
draft of a policy statement prepared by the Department of the

Treasury for distribution at workshop meetings and, on request, to other banks, does not suggest that extensive verbiage is necessary for policy statements. The Treasury suggested draft is reproduced below:

> It is the policy of this (Bank) to implement affirmatively equal opportunity to all qualified employees and applicants for employment without regard to race, creed, color, sex, or national origin and positive action shall be taken to ensure the fulfillment of this policy. This obligation includes:
>
>> Hiring, placement, upgrading, transfer or demotion
>> Recruitment, advertising, or solicitation for employment
>> Treatment during employment
>> Rates of pay or other forms of compensation
>> Selection for training
>> Layoff or termination
>
> This policy of the (Name of bank) is consistent with the requirements and objectives set forth by the Presidential Executive Order 11246.
>
> The objective of the (Bank) is to obtain individuals qualified and/or trainable for the position by virtue of job related standards of education, training, experience and personal qualifications.
>
> Responsibility for ensuring compliance and continued implementation of (Bank)'s policy on equal employment opportunity is assigned to the (Officer and title).
>
> The responsible on site official and the (Bank) will review this policy every twelve months and measure progress against these stated objectives.

Despite the obvious grammatical and syntactical difficulties with this suggested draft, the elision from "policy" to "obligation," the lack of mention of age discrimination, and the reference to the Executive Order rather than the Civil Rights Act, there appears to be no reason why a statement of this sort should not be included in the personnel manuals of all banks.

AFFIRMATIVE ACTION STATEMENTS

One of the difficulties in disseminating an affirmative action pattern throughout an organization which is often voiced by bank personnel managers is the inability to communicate such policies with first-line supervisors. An excellent example of the spreading of such policies is included in the text of a speech presented by the personnel director of a major, southern bank to his personnel supervisors in June 1968. It covers the special problems of the disadvantaged, and then goes on to specify policy adjustments which the bank will require of first-line supervisors.

In presenting the policy changes to his supervisors, the personnel manager emphasized that reasonable policy adjustments in the method of selecting people would be made until such time as the minority group member should be able to compete more successfully on a merit basis. He also emphasized a willingness to provide extra time and training to allow Negroes to meet the high standards of his organization. The procedural policy changes themselves seem to make up an extremely well-balanced and sensitive program, and are presented in their entirety, below:

1. *Aggressively recruit* a certain percentage of "higher risk" people who with make-up orientation and skill training will have success on the job. The personnel department interviewer is the most skilled person to seek out and recommend the deserving applicants to you. Set priority jobs for Negroes. Some may be absorbed into existing easy-to-learn jobs. Where possible, jobs may have to be restructured to allow the person to grow into the position. Opportunities may be available to employ a person on a trial basis such as summer employment or maternity leave replacement. Entry level jobs may have to be redefined to the extent that they cannot be used for staffing higher level positions.

2. *Accentuate the positive* and use human potential with some innovation. In interviewing an applicant, instead of looking for what is wrong with the applicant, we need to look for what is right. Test results are not the sole determining factor. A person may score low because he is a slow reader but possesses other qualities which will permit success on the job. Carefully review the aptitudes and potentialities present in all forms of the personal interview.

3. *Broaden orientation program* jointly with the personnel department to include pre-work counseling—without which regular skill training often fails. Subjects should range from grooming, money management, transportation, baby-sitting, job expectations, work rules, cooperation, application

to duty, adaptability, communications, merit salary, benefits, company objectives, job titles, grievance procedure, to the more complex attitudes towards job, themselves, and community. Create a learning situation in which the trainee feels identified with the bank and its growth.

4. *Coach during training*, giving extra support to the learning process. Motivating the person to learn the total job and to expand beyond is almost as important as the actual training. Assign a work "sponsor" (the buddy system) for close personal training. Support techniques do cause a higher initial training cost but result in a more dependable worker over the long run. Make-up training as distinguished from normal training is necessary to bring a person up to standard in time available. Simple brochures available from manufacturers on "do's" and "don'ts" of the job are helpful.

5. *Frequent follow-up* is particularly important to monitor the progress or lack of progress of the individual. Because of deficiencies in background, careful supervision and more frequent appraisal is a must. Need for bank services and other needs should be recognized early and appropriate referral made with close contact continued until satisfactory solution.

It is difficult to imagine a finer statement of an affirmative section procedure; moreover, this statement was produced for internal use by the bank, and not for publicity.

CHAPTER X.

Determinants of Industrial Policy

Throughout this study, we have devoted our attention to cataloging the responses of managements in the banking industry, under varying conditions, to the economic, regulatory, and social pressures which have been associated with Negro employment advances over the past decade. In this concluding chapter, we shall assimilate that information in order to gain insight into the policy formulation patterns specific to the banking industry which those responses have produced.

In following the statistical presentations of the chapters, one factor which is readily apparent is that the banking industry delayed longer than most the inclusion of Negroes in its work force and the provision of meaningful job opportunities to members of that race. A second factor, equally apparent, is that once the banking industry did begin to act, it did so with reasonable vigor—at least on the clerical levels. From the 1940-1960 average of approximately 1.75 percent, Negro employment levels began to increase at a compound rate of about 15 percent per year. By 1968, the level had reached about 5.95 percent, and our current statistics on the rate at which Negroes are being added to the industry show that about one person in five now being hired is Negro.

A third factor which is also characteristic of the new employment patterns in banking is that the gains in Negro employment have been overwhelmingly on the clerical levels. Even our most recent statistics show that there are very few technical, sales, professional, managerial, and official positions held by Negroes. Finally, we have seen that there is considerable internal divergence within the industry in the Negro employment levels found.

We shall examine each of these factors in turn, and also discuss briefly the degree of social involvement now becoming apparent among banking managements.

162

INITIAL RESPONSE

Although the banking industry was among the last in the country to adopt an equal employment policy and provide meaningful job opportunities for Negroes, it is not apparent from our studies that overt discrimination was a major cause of this. Almost every aspect of the specific job requirements of the banking industry is unfavorable to the employment of Negroes, and additionally, there are several unique characteristics of the industry —especially those concerning its image—which have been important in holding back the initial entry of Negroes into meaningful jobs.

Job Characteristics

The lack of any significant number of blue collar job openings in banking has meant that the normal entry level requires a fairly high degree of skill development. Additionally, the skills demanded by the overwhelming majority of those entry jobs are such as can be performed equally well by either males or females. As a result, during the labor-short World War II years, the industry turned as a source of a new labor supply to females rather than to Negroes. Unlike many other major industries, banking arrived on the verge of the 1960's without any previous substantial experience with Negro employees.

One of the factors to which bank managers themselves call attention as having been important in delaying the acceptance of Negroes into the main body of the banking work force was a fear on their part of the potential reaction from employees and—more importantly—from customers. There is no way of knowing the degree to which this claim reflects an honest fear rather than an over-reaction on the part of banking managers or a methodology by which they transfer blame for inaction to other personnel within their organizations. But it is true that because of the structure of the banking industry and the sameness of the services rendered by individual banks a more violent customer reaction could have been a real possibility.

Image

Probably the most important reason for the continued inaction of banks in regards to Negro employment was the fact that the industry was under very low compulsion to become involved. The economic and work force considerations important to the industry were generally such that despite a rapid expansion in employment between 1945 and 1960 there were few pressures on the banks to seek sources of supply of entry labor alternative to the "safe" white, female, high school output. Sociological considerations were such during this period that very few Negroes bothered to apply to the banking industry. Also during this time, Negro advancement organizations were concentrating on industries which seemed to offer much greater potential gains. As a result, the banking industry was left very largely to its own devices and the image-conscious traditions of the industry seemed to have held sway, retarding the Negro employment progress.

Depositors in banks have always been interested in the security of their funds, and therefore in the security of their banks. Much of the decision making of the banking industry has therefore been traditionally aimed at presenting to depositors and to the general public an image of safety and conservatism—not only in the handling of monies, but also in the conduct of all banking operations. As a result, banks have usually been very slow to espouse new causes—whether in industrial, technological, financial, sociological, or organizational areas. Banks have seldom been the agents of change, and have usually shown an inclination to let others lead and bear the high initial risks of innovation. It is not unlikely that this same "wait and see" logic was applied by the banking industry to Negro employment. Without any compelling reason to hire Negroes, the banking industry felt no necessity to be on the forefront of sociological change.

ACCELERATING ACCEPTANCE ON CLERICAL LEVELS

Prior to 1960, a few banks, predominantly in New York City, experimented cautiously with customer and employee reactions to Negroes on the work force in other than custodial, guard, or service positions, and an occasional bank probed business relations by placing a few Negroes in jobs where they would be dealing primarily with other Negroes. But these experiments probably were not as important to the acceptance of Negroes throughout the banking industry as was the increasing acceptance of Negroes in industries elsewhere.

Lack of Artificial Barriers

It must have become apparent to the banking industry in about 1960 or 1961 that, although there was no overwhelming necessity to hire Negroes, there was also no longer any compelling reason *not* to hire them. Only then did the banking industry hiring patterns begin to change; but once changes began they spread through the industry with relative rapidity.

Part of the reason for this pattern, too, lies in the nature of the standard entry-level job in banking. In many other industries, artificial barriers had been erected through the years to protect the economic position of unskilled whites against erosion from inroads made by the expanding job horizons of Negroes no longer content with menial or agricultural work. There is convincing evidence that many of the segregation laws of the deep South were economic rather than sociological in their origins, and had the aim of making it more expensive to hire Negroes. However, once these laws were in effect, the barriers which they formed were interpreted as sociological and could only be battered down by concerted effort.

Within the banking industry, on the other hand, the barriers to Negro employment were very largely ones arising from the nature of the work itself. There was little need to erect elaborate devices to keep Negroes out of the industry, because under the prevailing educational and sociological patterns, very few Negroes could or would consider the industry in any event. This, coupled with the fact that the industry's attitude toward Negroes had been generally one of inaction rather than antagonism, meant that once affirmative action was undertaken it could proceed smoothly. As hiring did begin, bankers soon found that the fears which they had felt about possible disruptions attributable to white employee and white customer reaction were largely groundless allowing methodologies for including Negroes in the industry to be worked out easily.

The Negro population did not change so significantly from the 1950's to the 1960's that Negroes became significantly more attractive to banking managers. But several other factors were in effect in the 1960's encouraging bank managements to become more involved. In addition to the fact that it soon became a characteristic of the decade to expect special efforts from all employers to hire Negroes, one of the most important spurs to changing the attitudes of management was the increasing and continued pressure from government regulations and the threat of the possible loss of government deposits.

Additionally, the job market and economic conditions of the 1960's were considerably different than they had been during the 1950's. Profits were good, and most firms, including banks, were expanding rapidly. Personal mobility was increasing, so that banks were under pressure to seek out new personnel—not only to meet expansion needs but also to replace turnover losses. Simultaneously, the job market became exceptionally "tight," especially in keypunch and other jobs related to the new automation technologies. Banks, and especially the trend-setting urban banks, had to seek new sources of employees; and Negroes seeking industrial entry or job advancement were readily available. Together these factors encouraged new attitudes on the part of banking managers which, when tested by experience, produced the new hiring patterns which we have seen.

Drawbacks

With the current rates of hiring Negroes at approximately 20 percent on average for all banks, almost 30 percent for the major banks included in our survey of the industry, and well over 40 percent in certain of the major firms in New York City and Chicago, the banking industry is now adding Negroes to its work force faster than is the case in most other industries. There have been, however, two continuing drawbacks in the banking industry.

Being late entrants to the job markets for Negro clerical-level personnel, banks everywhere outside of the South found that the fairly small pool of well qualified Negroes had largely evaporated before they began to probe it. As a result, the experience of some banks in hiring Negro employees may have been that they found confirmation of the stereotype of ill-preparation, lack of motivation, and incompetence that many had anticipated. Fortunately, because these stereotypes had been feared, in many cases bank managements were prepared to combat them with affirmative action, and therefore were not unwilling to experiment internally with special training programs, buddy systems, and other special personnel procedures. These activities eased the transition to more heavily Negro work forces, and also seem to have had the beneficial side effect of producing a more organized, more sophisticated personnel function in these firms.

A second continuing drawback, often voiced by bank managements, has been the lack of an acceptable methodology for communicating the affirmative action stance of the firm to first-line supervision. Fortunately, here too there is evidence that practices are being worked out to communicate these ideas to supervisors and to insist on performance without being either fatuous or brutal.

CONTINUED LACK OF ACTION ON MANAGERIAL LEVELS

Despite escalating activities in increasing the numbers of Negroes on the clerical levels of banking organizations, there are still very few Negroes in higher positions in commercial banks. Partially this is because the supply of qualified applicants is limited. In discussing the effects of the job image perceptions of the banking industry on potential Negro applicants to it, we noted that there is very little reason for Negro college graduates to be premotivated toward, or attracted to, the banking industry. Additionally, banks which do extensive college recruiting have all noted the fierce competition among industries for the top quality Negro college graduates. Finally, the supply of "instant Negroes" who can walk directly into middle management banking jobs is limited and subject to the same competition.

Caution

It appears most probable that the lack of advancement of Negroes to managerial ranks in banking is at least partially attributable—in addition to the above factors—to the same "wait and see" attitude exhibited by bankers in beginning Negro employment at all. Advances in banks are always cautious, and there remains a flavor of experimentation with hiring Negroes for the higher-level jobs. Many bankers are not yet fully convinced that Negroes on managerial levels will be first, employees of the bank—and incidently, Negroes—or whether they will be first Negroes—and incidently, employees of the bank. As a result many of the officer-level jobs which are going to Negroes in the banking industry currently are in personnel or in public relations functions where the primary duties often consist of dealing with racial questions.

It is clear from the thrust of the recent governmental concerns that banks will be under increasing pressure to include greater numbers of Negroes at higher levels in their organizations. It was also apparent to the author that banks have not worked out the methodology for employing Negroes at high levels effectively. Three of the five Negro bank executives who were interviewed by the author volunteered (they were not asked) information indicating dissatisfaction with their current jobs, salaries, acceptance by their organizations, or advancement potentials.

INTERNAL DIVERGENCE

The more than 13,000 commercial banks of the country are joined together by an extensive network of correspondent relationships, by clearing house associations, by the Federal Reserve System, and by bankers associations on several levels. However, these are most often business relationships not involved with the internal organization of banks. Mechanisms for communications among banks concerning development of personnel procedures and policies are somewhat limited.

Communications

The American Bankers Association, through its Personnel and Management Development Committee, does provide guidance and opportunity for exchange of ideas at annual meetings. Additionally, the personnel officers in the larger banks in many cities do have more or less formalized groups which meet, usually over lunch, to discuss matters of mutual concern. However, in these and other areas, the communications pattern for reaching the smaller city and country banks is somewhat limited. Large meetings in the banking industry among personnel men usually have as either a direct or ancillary purpose the aid or indoctrination of small banks—and the sharing with them of the experiences of the large organizations. However, the effectiveness of this is limited. In the first place, such meetings are usually ill-attended by the smaller banks which, like smaller organizations everywhere, often cannot afford to send men to participate. In the second place, experience is always one of the most difficult things to communicate, especially when environmental differences exist which require that the communication be understood at some level of abstraction.

Managerial Reactions

Because of the variation in the structure which exists in the banking industry, because of its extent, and because of the lack of a mechanism to provide a concerted response pattern on the part of bankers to questions concerning Negro employment, considerable divergence does exist within the industry. The degree of sophistication exhibited by personnel men varies tremendously, and as a result it is often difficult to separate the normal response pattern of the industry from any number of differently motivated responses. Bankers from different areas of the country or representing banks of different sizes will view and interpret differently not only their environmental conditions, but also the strengths of the stimuli which are impinging upon them concerning Negro employment. We know, for example, that some bankers are overreacting to the thrust of government pressures. Fearing further constraints on their managerial prerogatives, they have grown defensive and will not change employment policy until specifically required to do so. Similarly, we know that some bankers have overreacted to the black militancy visible in the news media, and that others have improperly estimated the organizational and economic costs of hiring Negroes.

This lack of communications patterns and possible overreactions on the part of bank managements have greater effect on the smaller banks than on the more sophisticated, city institutions. This is undoubtedly one of the factors which explains why the greatest divergence in apparent policy responses is based on size of institution rather than on location or on the Negro population of the area in which the bank operates.

CONCLUDING OBSERVATIONS

Aside from the slow start of the banking industry in providing meaningful job opportunities to Negroes, the policy patterns exhibited by the industry reflect consideration and concern for furthering the state of Negro economic advance. If the present hiring rates continue, and if the affirmative patterns exhibited by the industry leaders continue, then there will be few areas for continued concern. Over the next several years, in addition to continuing the progress begun, there seem to be three areas which will be of critical importance.

First, the industry must work toward developing a more effective methodology for bringing the smaller banks into the mainstream of thinking on banking personnel activities in racial relations. Second, the industry must work toward devising methodologies for recruiting or training greater numbers of Negro executive personnel. Third (a point covered in a previous chapter), the industry must determine the extent to which it will be willing to participate in social responsibility outside of the employment sphere. The continuing urban orientation of the industry will require that it give attention specifically to urban problems. There will be a variety of pressures on the industry attempting to influence it to devote its considerable talents to one

Appendix A

SURVEY PARTICIPANTS

During the Summer and Fall of 1968, the author visited fifty banks of various sizes, but all of them large, located in seventeen cities throughout the country. Not all of the banks visited provided usable statistical information. One of the fifty was the Federal Reserve Bank in Philadelphia. As Federal Reserve banks are not subject to Executive Order 11246 or other employment regulation by the Treasury Department, data collected on employment there is not included (although it was much appreciated by the author).

In a different vein, two southern commercial banks, one in Atlanta and the second in Dallas, were unwilling, despite careful introductions and the availability of local and national references of some worth, to provide information—statistical, opinion, or otherwise—in person, by phone, or by mail. A fourth bank, located in another southern city, provided opinions but no statistical data. It is for this reason that the number of "surveyed banks" seen from time to time in the study varies. Usually it is forty-six for statistics, and forty-seven for opinions.

In all of the interviews, the degree of friendliness or cooperation extended the author, while always high, was generally speaking, directly proportional to the level of Negro employment in any given bank. The case could therefore be structured that the employment picture presented by the sample banks is overstated to the degree that these three survey members would provide no data. However, external statistical sources indicate that racial employment at all of these particular three was about on a par for their areas, so the effect here is not large, and should not affect the statistics. Left, then, are statistics from forty-six major bank interviews (and opinions from forty-eight).

The banks which did participate in the survey responded to a structured interview comprising a minimum of sixty questions and requiring from one to three hours to complete. Tabulations of the responses to those questions are included in various places in the study, and specific insights provided by the interviewees are quoted from time to time. Special pains have been taken to insure that no bank is identified with any of the positions taken by this study, or is identifiable from them.

The banks which are listed on the following pages are those which were kind enough to participate in the survey. The author is particularly grateful to them for their time, cooperation, and insights. They are listed by assets and rank, as of June 1968.

SURVEY PARTICIPANTS

Banks	1968 Assets ($ Million)	National Rank
1. Bank of America (San Francisco)	22,357	1
2. First National City Bank (New York)	18,153	2
3. Chase Manhattan Bank (New York)	18,087	3
4. Manufacturers Hanover Trust (New York)	9,588	4
5. Chemical Bank (New York)	8,588	6
6. Continental Illinois National Bank and Trust Company of Chicago	6,595	8
7. First National Bank of Chicago	5,751	9
8. Security First National Bank (now Security Pacific: Los Angeles)	5,487	10
9. Wells Fargo Bank (San Francisco)	4,788	11
10. Crocker Citizens National Bank (San Francisco)	4,248	12
11. United California Bank (Los Angeles)	4,225	14
12. Mellon National Bank (Pittsburgh)	3,860	15
13. National Bank of Detroit	3,537	17
14. The Cleveland Trust Company	2,282	19
15. The First Pennsylvania Banking and Trust Company (Philadelphia)	2,213	21
16. Philadelphia National Bank	1,962	22
17. Detroit Bank and Trust Company	1,882	23

SURVEY PARTICIPANTS
(Continued)

Banks	1968 Assets ($ Million)	National Rank
18. Harris Trust and Savings Bank (Chicago)	1,807	24
19. Manufacturers National Bank of Detroit	1,799	25
20. Seattle-First National Bank	1,748	26
21. Republic National Bank of Dallas	1,636	28
22. Pittsburgh National Bank	1,566	31
23. First National Bank in Dallas	1,487	34
24. Union Bank (Los Angeles)	1,464	35
25. Girard Trust Bank (Philadelphia)	1,451	36
26. The Citizens and Southern National Bank (Atlanta)	1,390	38
27. Wachovia Bank and Trust Company (Winston-Salem)	1,388	39
28. National City Bank of Cleveland	1,319	40
29. Valley National Bank (Phoenix)	1,318	41
30. The Fidelity Bank (Philadelphia)	1,238	43
31. Central National Bank of Cleveland	1,108	47
32. Maryland National Bank (Baltimore)	943	57
33. The Riggs National Bank (Washington, D.C.)	877	64
34. The First National Bank of Atlanta	812	72
35. First National Bank of Arizona (Phoenix)	742	76
36. American Security and Trust Company (Washington, D.C.)	701	84
37. First and Merchants National Bank (Richmond)	698	86
38. First National Bank of Maryland (Baltimore)	638	89

SURVEY PARTICIPANTS
(Continued)

Banks	1968 Assets ($ Million)	National Rank
39. National Bank of Washington (D.C.)	540	106
40. First National Bank of Denver	530	109
41. Denver United States National Bank	471	123
42. State-Planters Bank of Commerce and Trusts (Richmond)	425	140
43. People's National Bank of Washington (Seattle)	400	148
44. The Arizona Bank (Phoenix)	324	180
45. The Colorado National Bank of Denver	287	193
46. Mercantile Safe Deposit and Trust Company (Baltimore)	229	233
47. The Central National Bank of Richmond	205	260

Source of assets and rankings: *Bankers Directory: The Bankers Blue Book.* Final 1968 ed. (Chicago: Rand McNally and Company, 1968), pp. 68-69.

Appendix B

NEGRO BANKING

INTRODUCTION

In a slave society, almost as a matter of definition, the subjugated faction has considerable difficulty in acquiring wealth or engaging in entrepreneurial activities in competition with the slave-owning class. But when slavery gives way to segregation, or when under slavery the prohibitions against economic activities are not severe, the suppressed are often allowed or even encouraged to take over the jobs generally considered to be unglamorous. At one time, unglamorous jobs included any sort of production or trading activity, but in recent history they have been more specialized to manual labor, personal service, and supply activities to their fellows of the same caste. Negroes in this country subsequent to emancipation were very definitely at a severe competitive disadvantage to whites in all job categories, but the pressures were somewhat less severe for these unglamorous categories.

Lack of freedom in job opportunity is not without its mitigating aspects if it is based on a mutually exclusive principle. If barbering, tailoring, cooking, or catering, for example, are considered to be the personal service jobs which should be left to Negroes, and they are in fact left to Negroes, then the opportunity for excellence and for a reputation of some sort is possible to a Negro going into one of those trades. The reputation of Jewish domination of money-lending (as differentiated from banking) owes its origins to such practices in medieval Europe, where the handling of money was considered beneath the dignity of the aristocracy.

Unfortunately (or perhaps fortunately in the long run) for American Negroes, the great in-migration of central and western Europeans towards the close of the last century brought men of low aristocratic pretention who, willing to compete for the jobs previously considered inferior, prevented the formation of Negro "monopolies" in any particular trades. In some occupations concerned with supplying goods and services to the Negro communities, however, Negroes still held a competitive advantage. Bank-

175

ing was one such service. Certainly a Negro banker, especially in his role as a provider of funds, is a source of greater potential understanding as well as a symbol of race pride to the Negro community.

The market for Negro banking until after the turn of the century was one subject to parallel development, a modification and outgrowth of the earlier mutually exclusionary principle. The white bankers were afraid of Negro borrowers and uninterested in Negro depositors. The institutional handling of Negro funds was to be left in the hands of Negroes, and Negro banking was to be encouraged. Many now are surprised by the number, but there have been, to date, at least 135 banks owned and operated by Negroes for Negroes in this country since 1888.[110]

Many factors appeared amenable to Negro banking in addition to its being a profession made possible by white disinterest. Banking provided an outlet in the Booker T. Washington sense for the Negro elite, as the prestige of the banker's job was open to any Negro able to organize and capitalize it. The initial capital required for any small bank was not excessive, and we shall see shortly that there were some Negroes who had managed to accumulate reasonably large fortunes. Because banking has no requirements for raw materials, selling on the open market, or using commercial channels of distribution, founding a bank was not subject to the same sorts of restrictions that manufacturing or trading operations were under segregation.

Unfortunately, the experiment in independent Negro banking was not entirely successful. Negro banks suffered severely from infant mortality, and for the seventy-five Negro banks which failed prior to 1936 whose life spans we know, the average life was only 8.9 years. In bankruptcy, many were unable to recover sufficient assets to provide any dividend for depositors at all. Few were able to provide for over 50 percent dividend.

---

[110] According to one source (Robert Kinzer and Edward Sagarin, *The Negro in American Business* (New York: Greenburg Publisher, 1950), p. 102), the *Negro Year Book of 1912* compiled some 103 institutions operating under the title of "banks." We are able to confirm directly only about a quarter of this number. Our data show forty-nine Negro banks had been founded by this date, of which twenty-seven remained in operation. We suspect that the *Negro Year Book of 1912* included all banks which had been founded and, additionally, all savings and loan associations. The numerical progression of Negro savings and loan associations has been largely lost to history, but the first was founded in Portsmouth, Virginia in 1883, and eighty of them were reported by Kinzer and Sagarin as operating in 1929.

In this Appendix we shall examine the history of Negro banking, and analyze the reasons for its lack of success. Some twenty Negro banks do exist today, but half of those have been founded since 1963. Only six can trace their origins to before the Second World War. This indicates something of a resurgence in this area of Negro endeavor, and we shall also evaluate the modern Negro banks.

To understand the circumstances connected with the rise of Negro banking and to evaluate some of the investment decisions made, we shall have to examine some aspects of Negro life going back to before the Civil War.[111]

The Development of Negro Wealth

Before the Civil War, real estate constituted the chief type of wealth in the southern part of the country, and some of this was in the hands of Negroes. Negro property-owning traces its origin back at least as far as one John, of Lancaster, a free Negro who was assessed for eight acres of land and a horse by the Pennsylvania tax levy of 1779.

By 1960, when the ratio of Negroes to the total population of the country was actually higher than it is today, a fair number, though not a large proportion, of Negroes were freedmen or progeny of freedmen,[112] and the extent of their wealth was respectable. Harris points this out in an example from Louisiana:

> At New Orleans in 1836 there were 855 free Negroes who owned 620 slaves and other property assessed at $2,462,470. By 1963 their holdings had increased about fourfold. In appealing to the State in that year for permission to exercise

[111] Here and subsequently in this section, I am deeply indebted to Dr. Abram L. Harris, late Professor of Economics at Howard University and the University of Chicago, whose book, *The Negro as Capitalist*, written in 1936, I have drawn from heavily. Dr. Harris's work is beautifully constructed, scholarly, objectively neutral in tone, and well worth the reading if copies can yet be found. (It is apparently being reprinted and should soon be available again.) In the balance of this section, I have footnoted Dr. Harris only for direct quotes, but almost all of my historical material is taken from him, as his is the only detailed source extant on the subject. (Philadelphia: The American Academy of Political and Social Science, 1936.)

[112] The first census of the United States, in 1790, showed 757,208 Negroes who constituted 19.3 percent of the total population. Seven point nine percent of the Negroes were Free Negroes. By 1860, the census of that year showed the percentage of Negroes to the total population had fallen to 14.1 percent and their numbers were 4,441,830. Eleven percent, or 488,070, were Free. These data are found in Kinzer and Sagarin, *op. cit.*, p. 27.

the right of suffrage these "gens de couleur" claimed that they paid taxes on more than nine million dollars' worth of property. This was hardly an overstatement of their wealth because in 1860 the value of the slaves and real estate held by the wealthy free Negroes of Louisiana was variously estimated at from ten to fifteen million dollars.[113]

Apparently, the Negroes in Louisiana were particularly prosperous, but not uniquely so. The estimated five hundred thousand free Negroes in the country at the eve of the Civil War had real and personal wealth at their command conservatively said to amount to $50,000,000, of which half was in the southern states. In addition, Harris estimates that one in five of the free Negroes had obtained manumission through self or family purchase, adding at least $10,000,000 to the total wealth owned which was none the less real for its odd form.[114]

Outside of agrarian operations, the free Negro entrepreneurs were engaged in generally small operations of the personal service sort, such as barbering, running livery stables, tailoring, cooking, saloon keeping, catering, and the like. Merchandising and manufacturing, commercial undertakings requiring skillful bargaining, accounting, and capital, were uncommon, although individual accounts can be found of Negroes operating such diversified trades as coal dealing, sail-making, and agricultural machinery manufacturing.

The financial position of the free blacks before and after the War was ever precarious, although there were some notable exceptions, such as Cyprian Ricaud, a plantation owner in Iberville Parish, Louisiana, whose wealth included ninety-one slaves in 1851, or Thomy Lafon whose estate at his death in the late nineteenth century was assessed at a half-million dollars. The more common state of affairs was widespread poverty, which led to the organizing of a number of mutual assistance societies, often but not always of a fundamentally religious or social nature. The earliest of these, the Free African Society, dates to 1778, and by 1850 it had become the first of over 100 societies with a membership approximating 8,000. The rapid growth of these societies indicates that they were obviously being responsive to a felt need. Operating as mutual funds, they generally provided sick benefits and death payments on the basis of monthly dues of about

---

[113] Harris, *op. cit.*, p. 8.

[114] *Ibid.*, p. 9.

twenty-five cents per member. Some were large enough to maintain deposits in commercial banks, but they generally did not lend or invest funds, leaving this function within the community to a few individual Negro money lenders and note discounters.

Until the Civil War, these last named individuals were about the only source of credit to Negroes. White banks, savings banks, and home building associations frequently denied them the privilege of even becoming depositors. Sometimes this denial was effected by the charter of the institution and sometimes by enactment of the state legislatures. In Harris's words:

> Undoubtedly race prejudice was at the root of these discriminations. Yet when it is remembered that the majority of free Negroes controlled only small sums of money and that the cost of carrying their deposits was relatively great, banks may have had an economic reason for excluding them in many cases.[115]

We shall see subsequently that Harris's observations on the size of deposits and their cost may not have been unfounded.

As borrowers, too, Negro merchants undoubtedly had great difficulty securing credit, although in view of the variety of businesses conducted, at least some source of institutional money had to be available to them. Then as now, the lack of credit facilities for capitalization of specifically Negro enterprises was held to be a cause for serious anxiety, and as early as 1851 a convention of colored people met in New York to discuss forming a bank to provide credit for Negro homesteaders and entrepreneurs. By the outbreak of the Civil War, several other plans to the same end were afoot in New York, Philadelphia, and elsewhere, but none of them came to fruition.

With emancipation, the specific obstacle of slavery gave way to the common obstacles to economic advancement of the poor, which were shared by the majority of Negroes: (1) low wages and high competition for jobs; (2) civic and educational handicaps; and (3) the difficulty of obtaining capital and credit. Many felt that the greatest of these was the last.

A few years after emancipation the stage was set for the birth of Negro banking. Slowly, but surely, some Negroes were managing to accumulate funds, either individually or jointly, for which they desired a depository. An economically-based class

---

[115] *Ibid.*, p. 22.

structure was developing rapidly with a Negro elite arising from the operation of service enterprises, or, less frequently, from real estate ownership and operation. But so far, there had been little Negro experience with banks as such. This was to come with one of the grand experiments of the reconstruction period, the Freedmen's Saving and Trust Company.

THE FREEDMEN'S BANK

The organization of the Freedmen's Bank is very closely tied with the usage during the War of military banks as depositories for the savings of Negro soldiers. Whether because of the required allotment system sometimes used, or from thrift, many of the colored soldiers desired a place to store all or a portion of their wages until the end of the war. To satisfy this need, several generals organized military banks, which also came to be used by Negroes outside the army. At War's end these banks had accumulated upwards of $200,000 of unclaimed deposits of Negro soldiers who had died or disappeared, and feelings arose that a permanent savings bank should be formed to protect these deposits and to serve the general financial interests of the Negro populace. Congress acted, and on March 3, 1865, President Lincoln signed the bill creating the Freedmen's Savings and Trust Company, subsequently renamed the Freedmen's Bank.

The Freedmen's Bank began auspiciously. By March 1866, it had accumulated over $185,000 from the military banks and sufficient general business from its fourteen branches to have a balance due depositors of some $200,000. By 1872, there were at least 70,000 depositors scattered over the Southeast, and the bank held deposits of over $3.6 million. By 1873, deposits had grown to $4.2 million, a level which would not again be reached in Negro banking until the First World War. In 1874, the bank failed. It failed owing $2,939,925.22 to some 61,131 depositors who between 1875 and 1883, were able to recoup only 62 percent of their funds as dividends in bankruptcy.

The Freedmen's Bank was not a typical banking institution. It held a special congressional charter and was outside the National Banking Act of 1864. It was managed by trustees, with no stockholder capital. It was allowed to open and operate branches but was not meant to engage in general banking. Its investment potential was initially circumscribed, and two-thirds of its deposits were to be in government bonds, with the remain-

ing to be left as an "available fund." It was not supervised and
no security was required of its officers nor penalty provided for
their misconduct. Because of the nature of its founding, it was
able to attract many depositors by cloaking itself with an "official" character hinting strongly at government sponsorship.

Neither was the Freedmen's Bank a typical Negro bank. It
was run, presumably, *for* Negroes (although it never restricted
its business specifically to that race), but in the beginning it
was not run *by* Negroes, and until 1870, few Negroes were employed in any capacity. It was meant to be a philanthropic venture into mutual trust savings under the control of public-spirited
white citizens who, as officers and trustees, were to look upon
their services as contributions to a charitable cause and were
therefore to receive no loans, wages, or any other remuneration
save necessary expenses.

Both the character and the charter of the bank were changed
during the nine years of its existence: the charter not until 1874,
but the character beginning in 1866. The panic of 1873 should
not have affected the bank as much as many smaller banks, but
the "reckless speculation, overcapitalization, stock manipulation,
intrigue and bribery, and downright plundering" rampant in the
country between 1866 and 1873 were reflected in the activities
of the bank's management.[116]

After 1870, the bank was headed by H. D. Cooke, who was also
president of the First National Bank of the District, and a cousin
of Jay Cooke, the nation's leading private banker. When Jay
Cooke's Northern Pacific bond venture fell through in 1873 and
his own bank failed, it took with it his cousin's First National
Bank of the District and set off the violent phase of the panic of
1873. The tie-in was direct, as the Freedmen's Bank was being
used by the First National as a source of funds for both the firm
and its officers and a repository of worthless paper. The Freedmen's Bank did not survive H. D. Cooke. When the First National failed, the failure precipitated runs on the Freedmen's
Bank, which had come to be looked on as sort of branch of Jay
Cooke. In eighteen months, the Bank lost $2 million in deposits,
and although it remained open under the new management of
the famous Negro leader, Frederick Douglass, the doors were
closed by him on June 28, 1874.

---

[116] *Ibid.*, p. 33.

The Freedmen's Bank failed not only because of the speculation and dishonesty of its previous management, but also because of its high operating expenses and heavy investment in fixed, illiquid assets, notably real estate. Considerable assets had been tied up in office buildings and furniture.

The important aspects of the failure of the Freedmen's Bank have been summed up as follows:

> The country began to be filled with rumors, usually based on fact, concerning the state of affairs of the Freedmen's Bank, and there were consequently runs on the bank. The business depression, lower realty value, corruption, stealing, disregard for the interests of the depositors, and manipulation of funds—these were the combining factors in bringing about the end. The controlling banks themselves failed, and the trustees, who had deposits in the bank and knew of its coming failure, were quick to withdraw their money, while they continued to solicit the funds of the Negroes. And *because the bank was identified with the endeavors of the newly-freed Negro, anyone who dared to raise a cry against the mismanagement was charged with being anti-Negro;* inasmuch as the enemies of the Negro were not interested in the bank, and the friends were effectively silenced with the anti-Negro charge, there was no exposure of the condition of the bank.[117] (Emphasis added.)

Despite its failure and its failings, the operation of the bank subsequent to 1870 had some value as a training ground for a few Negro bookkeepers, clerks, and tellers; and it provided a means of acquainting Negro shopkeepers and other businessmen with "high finance." It also encouraged thrift and the acquisition of property among Negroes, not only in the home offices in New York and Washington but throughout the South, wherever its thirty-three branches were located.

With the failure of the Freedmen's Bank, Negroes were again left without an institutional financial structure. The wealthy Negroes and those with adequate collateral were generally able to participate in the white organizations as depositors or borrowers. But the white banks' continued unwillingness to serve the needs of the small Negro saver left this class again demanding institutions geared to them. Harris presents these views perhaps more cogently:

---

[117] Kinzer and Sagarin, *op. cit.*, pp. 63-64.

White banks, it was more and more alleged, would not supply the Negro businessman with necessary capital and credit. In consequence, Negro leaders maintained that the organization by Negroes of their own banking facilities would meet this need. The degree to which white banks have been motivated in this attitude by racial instead of economic considerations is hard to determine, but from our investigation we do know that the policy of many white banks is to discourage the deposit business of Negroes as a general rule. The adoption of this policy has been attributed by several white officials to two main causes. The first is the probability of losing the large business of white clients who refuse to patronize public establishments frequented by Negroes in large numbers. The second and more important cause is the high cost involved in handling the deposit accounts of Negroes whose monthly balances are as a rule below the average and whose withdrawals are unusually heavy and frequent.[118]

This was answered by the rise of the Negro banks.

NEGRO BANKS

The great surge in banks operated for Negroes by Negroes began in 1888 and ended with the great depression, roughly forty years later. During those forty years, records show at least 135 Negro banks were founded. All save nineteen of these had failed by 1933, and only six of that group remained in 1958.

The progression in the number of Negro banks is shown in Figure B-1, and the progression of aggregate total resources, as far as they are known, in Figure B-2. These figures make apparent that the relative prosperity of Negro banking institutions, at least as measured by total resources and the number of foundings and failures, was not highly dependent on general economic conditions. Except for the period 1910-1915, in fact, the growth or retraction of Negro banks seem countercyclical. Six institutions were founded during the year of the great panic of 1907, for example, and twenty-two Negro banks failed during the five years of prosperity preceding the Great Depression of 1929. Some other factors were obviously involved in the failure of these banks, and actually there is enough commonality among the 129 failures to admit of some tentative generalizations.

---

[118] Harris, *op. cit.*, p. 54.

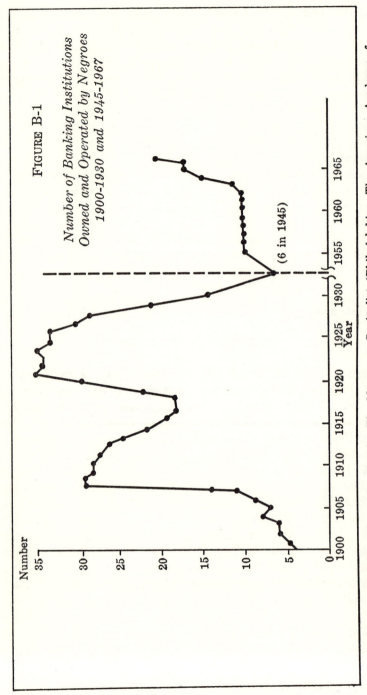

FIGURE B-1

*Number of Banking Institutions
Owned and Operated by Negroes
1900-1930 and 1945-1967*

(6 in 1945)

Source: 1900-1930: Abram L. Harris, *The Negro as Capitalist* (Philadelphia: The American Academy of
         Political and Social Science, 1936), Appendix IV.

         1945-1967: National Bankers Association

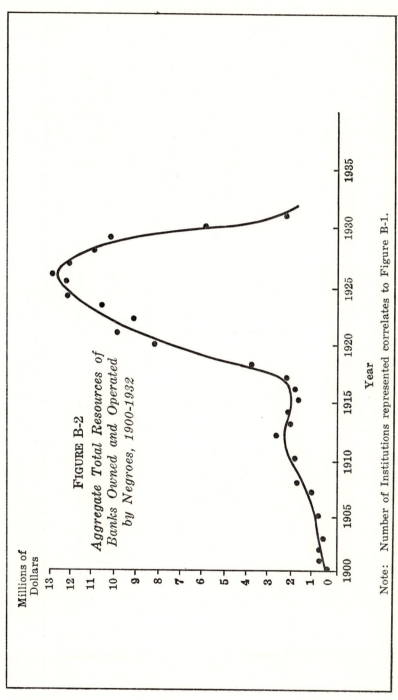

Millions of
Dollars

FIGURE B-2

*Aggregate Total Resources of
Banks Owned and Operated
by Negroes, 1900-1932*

Year

Note: Number of Institutions represented correlates to Figure B-1.

Source: Abram L. Harris, *The Negro as Capitalist* (Philadelphia: The American Academy of Political and Social Science, 1936), Appendix IV.

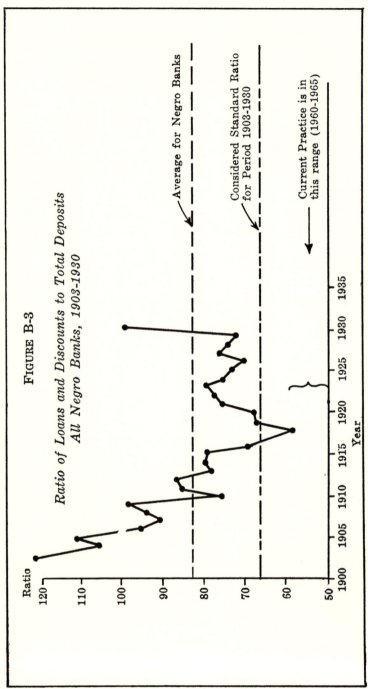

FIGURE B-3

*Ratio of Loans and Discounts to Total Deposits
All Negro Banks, 1903-1930*

Source: Abram L. Harris, *The Negro as Capitalist* (Philadelphia: The American Academy of
Political and Social Science, 1936), Table VI.

Negro Bank Failures

Among the factors which most often contributed to the failure of the Negro banks were overexpansion of loans, accepting often worthless securities and real estate as collateral which resulted in an overcommitment to illiquid investments; misconception of the nature of banking, ignorance of banking methods, and pilfering and fraud on the part of bank officers; and an inability to develop a sufficient mercantile and industrial deposit business. We shall look at each of these in turn.

Loans and investments.—Figure B-3 shows the ratio of loans and discounts to total deposits for the Negro banks between 1900 and 1930. Current banking practice (1968-1969) shows this ratio to be on the order of 50 to 60 percent, but in 1928, 66 percent was considered to be a sufficiently conservative norm.[119] The average for the Negro banks was almost invariably above the "normal" figure, and the average for all of them over the twenty-eight years was 82.6 percent loans to deposits. In other words, in comparison to the standard practice of the times, the Negro banks evidenced a tendency to expand loans and discounts disproportionately to total deposits. Partially this was the result of an inability to secure sufficient deposits, a point we shall return to, and partially from a desire to maximize returns.

In conjunction with a tendency to accept real estate and worthless or illiquid bonds from bank-related or subsidiary real estate-based concerns as collateral, this loan policy had the effect of debasing and solidifying the bank's asset structure, and reducing or eliminating its flexibility in fielding the vagaries of the economy.

As we have seen earlier in this section, much of the wealth accumulated by Negroes prior to 1900 was in the form of real estate. There were few Negroes in manufacturing or merchandising above the retail store level, and as a result marketable securities of corporations were not commonly held, even among the affluent. Among the poor, the only "investment" was in mutual death benefit associations or other fraternal or social organizations. Some of these associations formed their own Negro banks to act as depositories of their funds, and at least four of these banks failed when their officers proved unable to disassociate themselves from the associations or treat them in a businesslike way.

---

[119] *How to Analyze a Bank's Statement* (Bankers Publishing Company, 1928).

Real estate speculations had their effect as well. **Three Negro** banks were helped to failure through investment in bonds of theater-owning real estate corporations which proved unable to operate their properties at a profit. But the real culprit was often simply the inability of Negro borrowers to provide property other than real estate as collateral. Much of the property tendered was overvalued and many cases have been uncovered of property subject to prior lien being accepted as collateral by inattentive loan officers.

More generally, the problem was simply one of too many fixed and unproductive assets. A difficulty ancillary to this was the understandable desire on the part of most Negro bank managements to add to their aura of prestige and respectability by buying luxurious bank buildings and furnishings, which were often out of scale with the volume of business conducted. At times this sort of real estate absorbed 40 percent of the bank's total assets.

Except for the largest of the Negro banks, such as the Douglass National Bank in Chicago, almost none of them held any substantial amount of government bonds or readily marketable securities as investments. An example is provided by the Binga bank, also a large Chicago bank. When this bank failed, it held a total of only about $45,000 worth of negotiable securities as investments plus fifty-nine loans secured by some $85,000 of industrial stocks and bonds. The total of 861 loans outstanding amounted to a little over a million dollars which included $283,-000 in unsecured notes and $671,000 of loans secured by real estate. Additionally, $800,000 of the bank's resources were tied up in mortgages on Negro property. None of this real estate was particularly salable in 1930, and it is no wonder that the bank could not meet its obligations. It would probably have been in serious trouble even without the help of the $379,000 of unsecured loans made through dummy accounts to ventures in which the president was personally interested.

Deposit structure.—We shall take up the questions of dishonesty and incompetence in the next section, but before we do there is one more operational factor of the Negro banks' business which deserves mention, and that is the general structure of deposits in these institutions.

The Negro banks were never large. The average of total deposits per bank did not rise above $100,000 until after the First World War, and the maximum, in 1929, was scarcely above $350,000 per bank. This included demand deposits, savings deposits, and time and demand certificates of deposit. Besides being small in absolute size, the deposits were ill-structured. A few examples should suffice.

The Savings Bank of the Grand Fountain United Order of True Reformers was one of the first Negro banks. It existed from 1888 until 1910. At the time of its failure, there were 5,500 depositors. The average deposit was only $31.80. There were a large number of deposits of $2.00 or less, and only one private account of more than a thousand dollars.

The Mechanics Savings Bank was one of the largest of the Negro banks, and was organized in Richmond in 1902. When it failed in 1922, its deposits aggregated almost half a million dollars. The average savings deposit was $180 and the average commercial deposit was $127. But 62 percent of the savings deposits were under $50, and among its commercial accounts were 110 customers (almost 10 percent of the total number) who were allowed to maintain balances which *aggregated* only $49.63.

The Metropolitan Bank and Trust Company was organized in Norfolk, Virginia, in 1919 on the heels of the postwar boom. When it was suspended in 1931, almost 85 percent of its 3,797 depositors were maintaining balances of under $50.00. There were 462 depositors with claims to less than $1.00.

It is easy to demonstrate that the time, and therefore personnel, required in a bank is proportional to the number of transactions rather than the size of transaction. There is very little difference in bank costs between handling a check or deposit for $150.00 or one for fifteen cents. But it is obvious that the profit potentials of the former are much greater.

Unfortunately, no information is available on the relative staffing levels of these Negro banks and white banks of the same size at that time. Nor do we have information on the deposit structures of the small white banks. But certainly the deposit structures portrayed above (which, incidentally, are typical rather than extreme examples) are not conducive to profitable banking.

Dishonesty and incompetence.—It is never pleasant to write of dishonesty and incompetence, to assess guilt, and to assign blame. It is especially unpleasant to speak of it in small banks wherein the traditional widows and orphans, among others, have reposed their trust. But in fact, dishonesty and incompetence have contributed to the failure of, literally, hundreds of banking institutions in this country, and the Negro banks have had their share of both.

Among Negro bank failures, incompetence seems to have played the larger role, although the dividing line between gross neglect and willful misconduct is more difficult to draw than might be imagined.

Many of the Negro banks should not have been chartered in the first place. But state bank departments appear to have been willing to wink at personal speculations by Negro bank officers and at interlocking subsidiaries in the interests of building as "strong" a Negro banking structure as possible to promote "parallel race development."

This racial policy, which was felt to benefit everyone, was especially emphasized in Virginia, North Carolina, and to a lesser degree in the other southern states. It could not be projected if state banking departments gave the impression of not encouraging the Negroes to develop their own institutions.

Although this practice served to reflect and to reinforce the social convictions of the period, it was hardly designed to insure efficient and trustworthy bank managements. As is so often the case when economic institutions overindulge social whims, the long-term exigencies of economics could not be avoided; instead of promoting a sound parallel Negro banking structure, these policies helped to destroy it by destroying its fiduciary credibility.

There were some dishonest men in Negro banking, and indeed, charges were pressed on three or four. But even in these cases there is insufficient evidence to substantiate even an impression that banks were founded for dishonest purposes. The more common pattern consists of large withdrawals from dummy accounts, large unsecured loans to officers, false entries and erasures, or other loose practices in the confusion surrounding the last few weeks of the failing firms. Generally speaking the real damage had already been done through previous mismanagement or poor supervision of employees.

A good deal of the blame for this must be laid simply to lack of training and experience on the part of the managers. And the blame for that must devolve to the white banks, banking institutions, and regulatory authorities. For where were aspiring Negro bankers to acquire the experience with "good banking practices"? Where could they find skilled tellers, bookkeepers, clerks, or other employees? To whom were they supposed to apprentice themselves? Whose experience could they follow in making sound investments?

Even today there are very few Negroes in managerial positions
in the white banks; in 1900 there were none. Only in late 1968
was any mechanism established to provide outside training for
Negroes working in Negro banks, and that project is still in the
experimental stage; in 1900, there was none. The Freedmen's
Bank did provide a training ground for a few managers and
employees between 1870 and 1873, but the first Negro bank was
not established for fifteen years thereafter. There was also very
little in the way of self-help. The National Bankers Association,
the Negro equivalent of the American Bankers Association, was
not founded until 1927. So if confusion of goals resulted, if
there were evidences of loose control and bad banking practices,
it should not be much of a surprise.

Summary of historical development.—We have seen above that
the experiment in Negro banking was not highly successful. For
every eight Negro banks formed between 1888 and 1928, one remained in 1936. The failures arose from a variety of causes,
but predominant among them were overexpansion of loans; commitment to unproductive and illiquid investments, especially real
estate; an absence of commercial and industrial business or other
large accounts; and incompetence, dishonesty, and lack of training among bank managers.

Negro banking suffered severe attrition during the late 1920's
and was further hurt by the Great Depression; but it did not dis-
appear. By the beginning of the Second World War there remained seven all-Negro banks. Three more were founded in the
postwar boom years, 1946 and 1947; one in 1963; four in 1964;
two in 1965; and three more in 1967. These banks obviously
exist for a different purpose and under different conditions than
did their predecessors.

THE MODERN NEGRO BANKS AND THE
RATIONALE OF THEIR EXISTENCE

There has been a resurgence in the number of Negro banks
in recent years, and that resurgence will undoubtedly continue
apace as long as national emphasis and interest centers on and
encourages "black capitalism," "black control of black business,"
and similar philosophies. But separatism is one of only two
understandable reasons for Negro banking to exist in the late
1960's.

Separatism

Separatism versus integration has been an issue since emancipation. Frederick Douglass, during the reconstruction phase following the Civil War, attempted to lead his fellows into the mainstream of America. With the help of a still-"abolitionist" congress he sought political and economic equality for Negroes. The road was not easy. Following severe southern reactions around the close of the last century, it became evident that the strengths of a number of economic and sociological factors had been overly discounted. Southern whites were demanding and enforcing segregation. From among the Negroes, two leaders arose who reflected the new realities, albeit in different ways.

Booker T. Washington favored accommodation with the whites together with internal economic development. "His aim was to curry favor, to advance slowly through education and race improvement, to assure the whites that he neither sought nor desired integration for the Negroes.[120] In Washington's words:

> In all things that are purely social we can be as separate as the fingers, yet one as the hand in all things essential to human progress.[121]

Simultaneously with Washington's plea for accommodation, and partially in reaction to it, was W. E. B. DuBois's call for militancy:

> In the decade previous to the First World War, DuBois denounced the spirit of compromise, and demanded that Negroes stand up and fight for their full rights as human beings and as Americans. He called for the advance of Negroes in business, declared that the separate economy was being forced upon the race, but [sic] laid the foundations for a long range program of integration through militant struggle against all compromise.[122]

The arguments for and against separatism continued apace, but by the early 1960's, it seemed the battle had finally been won. The movement towards enforced integration which had

---

[120] Kinzer and Sagarin, *op cit.*, p. 41.

[121] Washington, speech at Atlanta, Ga., quoted by Kinzer and Sagarin from E. Franklin Frazier, *The Negro in the United States* (New York: The Macmillan Company, 1949), p. 41.

[122] Kinzer and Saragin, *op. cit.*, p. 45.

begun on the state level a few years previously was given the sanction of the federal government under which conditions it was more or less grudingly accepted by the majority of the white population. The country at least should have been free of one of the points of the dilemma of separatism versus integration.

Almost immediately, when the dust of change had settled, and to the surprise of many "establishment whites," new, again militant Negroes emerged as leaders under the banner of black power and black separatism. Roy Innis, director of the Congress of Racial Equality at the time of this writing, believes that "integration is as dead as a doornail." [123] Seeking ideological support by drawing analogies between his philosophical stance and that of the revolutionaries of 1776, he is demanding, under threat of revolt and chaos, federal funds for a separate economy.

> . . . We want the transfer of institutions within the black community to the management and control of the people themselves. Nixon should support the concept of community control of schools, welfare, sanitation, fire, police, hospitals, and all other institutions operating in the so-called "ghettos." [124]

Unfortuately, it is the militance which is most visible to the white community in the requests of the Innises and others on the more extreme "Black Fringe." But by association, the white reaction spreads to reject even the arguments of the simple economic separatists. Over recent years most of us have lost sight of the economic arguments, many of them cogent, for separatism—for the society within a society. Unfortunately, Mr. Innis has lost sight of them as well. For now, just as during the Reconstruction period, although to a lesser degree, there is insufficient Negro professional and managerial talent and insufficient Negro capital to make the scheme work even if the overwhelming practical difficulties such as geographic feasibility could be worked out and a consensus could be gained on the merits of the idea. At some stage in the past such a scheme might have worked, but at the moment the offering of it serves no useful purpose and only promotes further interrace bitterness.

The point of all this is that the argument for economic independence which seems to be accepted by many as both new and

---

[123] Interview, "When Negro Leaders Look Ahead . . ." *U.S. News & World Report,* November 25, 1968, p. 60.

[124] *Ibid.*

exciting is, in fact, neither. It is old and pragmatically in-
feasible, and although the desire for it as evidenced, for example, in the call for "black banks for black people," is in some
ways understandable, it is best left unheeded. If there are to
be specifically black banks, they need other justification.

Economics and Sociology

To a very large degree it is difficult to find justification for
modern black banks. The usual arguments are economic and
sociological, and they deserve some attention.

Any functions which Negro banks can perform can be done at
least as well by white (integrated) banking firms. There is no
longer a need, as existed in 1895 or 1925, for a specifically Negro
place of deposit of Negro funds. The white commercial banks,
even in the South, have long ago realized that they would not
lose white customers by accepting Negro depositors, and by the
use of sliding charges on deposit accounts have protected themselves, as have the modern Negro banks, from the onus of too
many unprofitable small accounts.

As a source of funds either for personal finances or business
capitalization, Negro banks can claim no particular advantages
save those arising from a better rapport with and understanding
of potential borrowers. And this has its disadvantages as well
as benefits, for the possible Negro borrower whose request for
a loan is denied for sound banking reasons will be even more
disenchanted with a Negro bank which refuses his request for
funds than with a white bank where, at least, he can feel his
request was denied through the bigotry he has been taught to
expect.

Again, concerning funds for slum development or other worthwhile black community projects, which are almost by definition
economically high-risk, the Negro banks are still generally too
small to participate on any level above tokenism. To illustrate,
financing for "Progress Plaza" and "Progress Aerospace Enterprises," two black-owned, black-operated Philadelphia undertakings of Rev. Leon Sullivan sprang from $100,000 seed capital
raised by Sullivan himself through his church members to which
was added some $2.5 million of construction loans and long-term
financing arranged though a major Philadelphia bank.[125] Again,

---

[125] *Evening Bulletin* (Philadelphia), November 21, 1968, and "In the
Black," *Philadelphia Magazine*, June 1968, p. 83.

in October, 1958, ". . . five of Manhattan's largest banks agreed to provide up to $50 million to help minority businessmen. A consortium of 23 Houston banks has pledged $7,000,000 for the same purpose, a nine-bank group in Philadelphia, $6,000,000, a group in Boston $3,000,000." [126] Except for the seed capital, which was private rather than institutional Negro money, the other funds mentioned here, over $68 million, are all from white commercial banks.

This is not to demean or to belittle the Negro banks. Their total aggregate resources in 1967 were less than three times the amount pledged above, and it is no more reasonable for them to be involved than it would be for the (hypothetical) Cattle Exchange Bank of Greencastle, Pennsylvania.

The Negro banks are not economic giants, and they have little in the way of discretionary capital available for high-risk ventures. This is seen in Table B-1, which shows the status of this segment of the industry compared with the industry as a whole. In this decade, Negro banks have grown rapidly in numbers and in assets, but taken together they command less than four one-hundred-thousandths of the resources of the industry. Together, in 1967 they were less than one-tenth the size of the Pittsburgh National Bank, which was ranked twenty-eighth in assets by *Fortune's* survey.[127]

There is an argument occasionally raised which takes the position that the shadow of the black banks is larger than they, that their presence causes the regular commercial banks to act differently than they would alone. A passage from an Atlanta study illustrates this point:

> As in the case of insurance, Negro banking has aimed at satisfying a definite need—to provide a range of credit assistance to Negroes. *An important side effect has been to force a reconsideration of loan policies in white banks* which welcome Negro depositors but are generally not interested in extending loan services.[128] (Emphasis supplied)

---

[126] "The Birth Pangs of Black Capitalism," *Time*, October 18, 1968, p. 99.

[127] "The 50 Largest Commercial Banks," *Fortune*, June 15, 1968, p. 208.

[128] Harding B. Young and James M. Hund, "Negro Entrepreneurship in Southern Economic Development," *Essays in Southern Economic Development*, ed. Melvin L. Greenhut and W. Tate Whitman (Chapel Hill, North Carolina: The University of North Carolina Press, 1964), p. 135.

TABLE B-1.   *Resources, Growth Rates, and Size of Banks Owned and Operated by Negroes Relative to All Commercial Banks 1940-1967*

Year	Number of Negro Banks	Total Assets Negro Banks ($ Million)	Asset Growth Negro Banks (Percent)	Total Assets All Banks ($ Billion)	Asset Growth All Banks (Percent)	Negro Bank Assets as Percent of Total
1940	8	Approx. 5.0	—	Approx. 68.0	—	.0074
1960	10	58.0	—	246.8	—	.0235
1961	10	62.7	8.1	254.2	3.0	.0247
1962	10	71.3	13.7	274.2	7.9	.0260
1963	11	76.9	7.9	298.9	9.0	.0257
1964	15	84.0	9.2	325.5	8.9	.0258
1965	17	93.4	11.2	357.2	9.7	.0261
1966	17	106.9	14.5	387.1	8.4	.0276
1967	17	162.2	51.7	421.1	8.8	.0385

Sources: (1) Federal Deposit Insurance Corporation (as reported by National Bankers Association).

(2) National Bankers Association, *NBA Salary Study.* A report prepared for distribution to NBA member banks (Washington: Xeroxed, 1968).

Were this argument valid, of course, those cities in which the commercial banks were faced with the competition of Negro establishments should be as Meccas for black businessmen. However, the authors of the above quote went on in the same paragraph:

> There has been no real competition from white banks for Negro business loans; a survey of major Atlanta banks revealed but few Negro business loans on their books.[129]

One of the largest of the Negro banks is located in Atlanta and has been there since 1921.

Employment

From a sociological viewpoint, one of the most powerful arguments for the black banks is that they provide service to the community as a training ground and place of employment for Negro tellers, bookkeepers, clerical workers, and managers. For all save the last category, this is both insignificant in any sort of absolute terms and unnecessary, at least since 1964. Negro bank employees do apparently receive somewhat higher wages than employees in white banks of similar size, although about the same as the average for all nonsupervisory employees in commercial banking. Negro bank officers salaries are somewhat less than those of officers in similar-sized white banks.[130] These relationships are shown in Table B-2.

To at least some degree these data reflect the fact that, although small when compared with commercial banks, these banks are large and prestigious institutions in the Negro community. There is also the possibility that the figures reflect marketplace considerations. One woman personnel officer from an all-Negro bank reported: "We have a lot of trouble hiring qualified people. They would rather go and work for the big, downtown banks." [131]

This view finds corroboration in the Atlanta Study mentioned previously:

> The barrier to organization of the [new Negro banking] enterprise has been locating persons with training and experience in banking. Negro banks in other cities can ill

---

[129] *Ibid.*

[130] National Bankers Association, *NBA Salary Study*. A report prepared for distribution to NBA member banks (Washington: Xeroxed, 1968).

[131] Interview by the author, Chicago, October 29, 1968.

TABLE B-2. *Average Annual Wage Comparisons*
Negro and Non-Negro Banks

	1966	1967
Officers		
NBA banks (13 all-Negro banks)	$8,539	$9,899
All FDIC banks of under $25 million deposits	9,330	10,072
All commercial banks	N.A.	N.A.
Employees		
NBA banks (13 all-Negro banks)	$3,713	$4,113
All FDIC banks of under $25 million deposits	3,127	3,752
All commercial banks	4,294	4,495

Sources: (1) National Bankers Association, *NBA Salary Study.* A report
prepared for distribution to NBA member banks (Washing-
ton: Xeroxed, 1968).

(2) *Monthly Labor Review,* various issues, 1966 and 1967, Table
C-1.

afford to release some of their trained employees in whom
they have made a heavy investment. The problem is made
all the more acute by the fact that Negroes have not been
in responsible managerial positions in banks other than
those operated by Negroes.[132]

The portion of the difficulty laid to regular commercial banks
is treated at length elsewhere. But there is one final reason for
the continued existence of a parallel all-Negro banking structure.
As promised, it is an argument which is understandable, has
considerable validity, and provides a rationale for these banks:
Negro banks provide a comfortable place of employment for
Negro managers, and they provide an outlet for Negro enter-
preneurial activity.

In one view:

The Negro banking industry has long been a source . . . of
race pride. . . . The banker symbolizes, perhaps more than
anyone else, the successful businessman of the community,
and the race, anxious to demonstrate the extent of its suc-

[132] Young and Hund, *op. cit.,* p. 136.

cess in the business world, has looked hopefully upon its banking efforts.[133]

In this regard, the Negro banks are not significantly different from a variety of immigrant or other nationalistically-oriented banks. The opportunity to do what one wishes—even to the founding of a bank—should be available to anyone willing to bear the risk. Naturally, if it is a Negro who feels such an urge, the resultant bank will be a "Negro bank." If the institution is successful in competition with the regular commercial banks of the area, certainly no harm has been done and considerable personal and perhaps some sociological good has resulted.

---

[133] Kinzer and Sagarin, *op. cit.*, p. 102.

Appendix C

LEGISLATIVE AND REGULATORY HISTORY
AFFECTING BANKS

Legislation and regulations of American industry relating to equal employment opportunity for all races take three separate forms. Congressional legislation concerning merit employment can trace its history to the Civil Service Act of 1883.[134] For a long period, the application of this act was essentially reserved to outlawing religious discrimination. Congressional action dealing indirectly with racially equal job opportunity was slow during the depression period. Antidiscriminatory references can be found in the Unemployment Relief Act of 1933, the National Industrial Recovery Act of 1933, and others; but it was not until 1940 when the Ramspeck Act sanctified a 1940 Civil Service rule prohibiting racial discrimination that Congress adopted a philosophy of "equal rights for all." [135]

In order to forestall a threatened Negro marching on Washington in 1941, President Roosevelt opened the second phase of the legislative progression on equal employment by issuing Executive Order 8802 on June 25, 1941.[136] This was the first of the important executive orders and created government-wide machinery which was meant to implement a national policy of nondiscriminatory employment and training through the Fair Employment Practices Committee (FEPC) as an independent agency responsible solely to the President. The executive order also began an era in which continued efforts to secure equality of employment opportunity fell almost exclusively within the province of the Chief Executive.

The FEPC was authorized to receive and investigate complaints, but had no direct enforcement powers. It had to rely on moral suasion and negotiation to effectuate any recommendation it made. The FEPC passed out of existence when its funding was not renewed in 1946. And from 1946 until 1961, most of fair employment activities took place in the individual states.

---

[134] The Pendleton Act (Civil Service Act), 22 Stat. 403 (1883).

[135] Ramspeck Act, 54 Stat. 1211 (1940); Exec. Order 8587, 5 Fed. Reg. 445 (1940).

[136] Executive Order 8802, 6 Fed. Reg. 3109 (1941).

During this period, however, two more commissions were created. One was the Committee on Government Contract Compliance, established by Executive Order 10308 on December 3, 1951,[137] and the second was the President's Committee on Government Employment Policy, established by Executive Order 10590 on January 18, 1955.[138] Both of these commissions were replaced on March 5, 1961, by the President's Committee on Equal Employment Opportunity (PCEEO), which was formed by President Kennedy's Executive Order 10925.[139] The Executive Order 10925 (as amended by a subsequent order, 11114)[140] was important not only because it consolidated the government's activities in this area into the hands of a single agency, but also because it required for the first time "affirmative action." (Banks were not subject to this order.)

All told, up until this time, there had been at least nine executive orders (not all of them are cited here) which had some effect on equal employment opportunity. However, there had been no Congressional action since 1940, with the exception of the Civil Rights Act of 1957 which, dealing almost exclusively with voting rights and education, had little effect on employment. Congress finally moved, in 1964, to pass the Civil Rights Act of that year, Title VII of which prohibits discrimination in employment on the basis of race, creed, sex, and national origin. The Act also established the Community Relations Service (now attached to the Department of Justice) and the Equal Employment Opportunity Commission (EEOC).

With Title VII of the Civil Rights Act of 1964 (which became effective in July 1965), came the beginning of increasing complexity involving enforcement of equal opportunity in employment. The EEOC can act only in the event of complaint, must defer to state human relations or fair employment practice commissions, and can only conciliate the parties unless the matter is of sufficient public importance that, through the Attorney General, the courts find it necessary to issue an injunction where discrimination may be found to be intentional. Four groups are thus involved in the enforcement procedure; the individual complaining about discrimination can bring a civil action; the De-

---

[137] Executive Order 10308, 16 Fed. Reg. 12303 (1951).

[138] Executive Order 10590, 20 Fed. Reg. 409 (1955).

[139] Executive Order 10925, 26 Fed. Reg. 1977 (1961).

[140] Executive Order 11114, 28 Fed. Reg. 6485 (1963).

partment of Justice can intervene in that action (or where the Attorney General feels a pattern of discrimination requires a remedy he may bring a civil proceeding of his own); the state fair employment practices commissions are expected to enforce their respective laws; and the federal Equal Employment Opportunity Commission has the function of conciliation and persuasion.[141] Notice that this situation is complicated by the fact that the Commission, under the law, is obliged to defer to state action and local laws where such actions and laws are consistent with the objectives of Title VII. Thirty-six states plus the District of Columbia are considered as having enforceable statutes.[142]

Although many considered that the Congressional action in passing the Civil Rights Act of 1964 should have filled whatever legislative vacuum existed, making further executive orders unnecessary, President Johnson responded to pressures placed on him by various civil rights groups and issued Executive Order 11246 less than a year later, on September 24, 1965.[143] This executive order differs from all but a handful of executive orders on all subjects in the past in that it is not a modification or an explanation of existing legislation, but rather has the weight of new law.[144] It is currently the most important tool in the federal arsenal. It abolished the President's Committee on Equal Employment Opportunity, and transferred those functions to the Secretary of Labor. Simultaneously, the Secretary established within the Labor Department the Office of Federal Contract Compliance (OFCC) but continued in effect as a temporary measure the previous rules, regulations, orders, instructions, and directives issued by the President's Committee.

Contractors covered by the order must permit access to their books, records, and accounts "pertinent to compliance with the order, and all rules and regulations promulgated pursuant thereto," during normal business hours.[145] In other ways, too, the

---

[141] Arthur B. Edgewarth, Jr., "Civil Rights Plus Three Years: Banks and the Anti-Discrimination Law," *The Banker's Magazine*, Vol. CL, No. 3 (Summer 1967), p. 26.

[142] *Ibid.*, p. 27.

[143] Executive Order 11246, 30 Fed. Reg. 12319 (1965).

[144] Opinion of a knowledgeable lawyer interviewed by the author in Washington, September 1968.

[145] National Association of Manufacturers, *Summary Analysis of Revised Regulations of the Office of Federal Contract Compliance*. Report prepared

executive order goes far beyond the Civil Rights Act of 1964. It eliminates some of the specific limitations on the authority of the federal government to regulate employment practices in the area of nondiscrimination. The Civil Rights Act does not require "affirmative action" of the kind required by the executive order, and the authority of state agencies administering state equal employment laws is specifically protected by the earlier congressionally established legislation.[146]

One obvious difference between the Civil Rights Act and the Executive Order is that the latter applies only to contractors with the federal government. There had been some question as to whether the relationship between a bank and its depositor is a contractual one. Consequently, Treasury Department regulations were amended, on August 25, 1966, to provide that all banks designated as depositaries of public monies subsequent to November 30, 1966, in accepting them would thereby agree to an amendment of their contract of deposit with the Treasury Department to incorporate an equal employment opportunity clause.[147] This applied to all banks, regardless of the size of deposits, which had more than fifty employees.

The Office of Federal Contract Compliance delegated the burden for insuring the enforcement of Executive Order 11246 to the federal contracting agency having "predominant interest" in the affairs of a particular industry. In the case of the banking industry, this agency is the Department of the Treasury. This brings in the third stage of regulatory pressure on the banking industry; for the Department of Labor (through the OFCC) and the Department of the Treasury (through its contract compliance section) are perfectly within their rights to issue rules, orders, and regulations amplifying or explaining the executive order 11246. In the banking industry, these have primarily taken the form of regulations concerning testing and testing procedures, although in other industries the contracting agencies' requirements have gone considerably beyond those of the

---

by the law department of the National Association of Manufacturers for distribution to its members (Washington: The Association, 1968), p. 15.

[146] *Ibid.*

[147] "Equal Employment Guidelines for Depositary Banks," *Banking* (Journal of the American Bankers Association), (February 1967), p. 47; the amended Treasury Department regulations are found in 31 Fed. Reg. 11388 (1966); their effect on banks can be found in "Guidelines for Compliance by Depositary Banks," 31 Fed. Reg. 15024 (1966).

executive order.[148] To date, the Department of the Treasury has been content with preparing and distributing suggested drafts of policy statements and affirmative action programs to be applied by banks if they so desired.[149] Treasury has also sponsored a number of conferences and workshops with groups of banks throughout the country.

The confusion attendant to the administration of Executive Order 11246 within the contracting agencies is apparent from the following passage:

> The Secretary has designated an Assistant Secretary as the Treasury Department Compliance Officer, who is responsible to the Secretary for carrying out the duties and responsibilities of the Department under Chapter 60 of this Title [41] and the provisions of this subpart. In his office the Contract Compliance Officer has established an Office of Employment Policy, the Associate Director of which is designated as the Principle Deputy Contract Compliance Officer. He is assisted by Contract Compliance Specialists. Additionally, the bureaus and offices of the Department have designated Deputy Contract Compliance Officers to assist the Department Contract Compliance Officer in the administration of the Executive Order, as amended, with respect to contractors for whom the respective bureaus and officer have been designated as compliance agency units.[150]

Given the duplication of agencies and the complex administrative set-up within each one, it is difficult even to ascertain the circumstances under which a compliance review might be performed on an individual bank. Apparently, such a review can

---

[148] (Department of Defense) "Defense Contracts Compliance Program: Factors which Indicate Compliance (No date on publication data) from the files of the National Association of Manufacturers. This report lists fifty-five factors which must be specifically met by contractors to indicate compliance. The Atomic Energy Commission has similar requirements: (Atomic Energy Commission) "Equal Employment Opportunity (Non-Discrimination in Government Contractor Employment)" TN 4200-26, Chapter 4208, July 21, 1967 (in the files of the commission).

[149] These undated, suggested drafts were issued October 30, 1968, and are available from the Equal Employment Opportunity Office, United States Treasury Department, Washington, D. C., 20220.

[150] Text of Treasury Department Regulations, (41 CFR Ch. 60, Sec. 10-12.802 Administrative Responsibility) found in "Equal Opportunity in Financial Institutions," *Labor Relations Reporter*, Vol. LXX (Jan. 13, 1969), p. 24.

be initiated by either Treasury or by OFCC. According to an officer with OFCC, in the majority of cases, Treasury will do the initiating, but OFCC can request Treasury to perform a compliance review on a certain bank or group of banks within a certain time period. In either event, the review is actually conducted by Treasury. Subsequent to Treasury's investigation, a report is sent of the results and findings to OFCC for what a Treasury official calls "filing" and what an OFCC official calls "review." [151] In any event, it is possible that OFCC, on reviewing (or filing) the report from Treasury, might be dissatisfied with the conclusions reached. If this is the case, OFCC indicates no unwillingness to reopen an investigation. It is thus possible for an individual institution to be reviewed by both agencies seriatim.

Overall, it is conceivable that an individual bank's activities might be reviewed in succession by a city commission of human relations, a state fair employment practices commission, the Equal Employment Opportunity Commission, the Department of Justice, the Department of the Treasury, and the Department of Labor. Civil suit can also be brought by an individual who feels he might have been wronged. Obviously, the legal and regulatory hierarchy has become extremely complex.

---

[151] Interviews by the author at the Office of Federal Contract Compliance at the U.S. Department of the Treasury, September 20, 1968.

Index

Part Two

THE NEGRO
IN THE INSURANCE INDUSTRY

by

LINDA PICKTHORNE FLETCHER

TABLE OF CONTENTS

v

LIST OF TABLES

APPENDIX TABLES

CHAPTER I.

Introduction

The American insurance industry is older than the United States and, in broad terms, has experienced a continuous and immense growth similar to that of the country. The efforts of the first insurance entrepreneurs were the foundation of an industry that now includes many insurers that are giant financial corporations and, in the aggregate, employs more than one million persons, two-thirds of whom are in salaried occupations. It is not surprising, therefore, that the insuring enterprise is one of the most influential elements in many aspects of the national economy.

One significant economic activity in which insurance companies are constantly engaged is that of employee recruitment. It is this area—the development, status, and problems involved in racial employment policies and practices of the insurance industry—that is analyzed in this study.

SAMPLE SELECTION

The initial, and perhaps most difficult, step in conducting the research for this study was selecting the insurers that were to be asked to participate in the project. Three criteria were required if the chosen sample was to be representative: (1) both large and small companies had to be surveyed; (2) a balanced geographic distribution of corporations was essential; and (3) all types of organizations (in terms of legal form, kinds of insurance written, and other factors) should be included.

On the basis of these criteria, 183 insurers, which as an aggregate are domiciled in twenty-five states, were asked to cooperate in the study. The approach letter addressed to each corporation contained an explanation of the objectives of the project and a request for a personal interview with the appropriate executive of the organization.

Of the total number of insurers contacted, five (2.7 percent) issued a negative response and twenty-eight (15.3 percent) did not reply to the inquiry. The remaining 150 companies (82.0 percent) agreed to participate in the project.

THE INTERVIEWING PROCESS

The personal interview method of gathering data was selected because it was felt to be the most accurate technique for obtaining pertinent information, despite the procedure's inherent subjective influence and other imperfections. Extracted and isolated employment statistics, percentages, and other numerical data do not reveal insurer attitudes toward Negro employment, participation in community Negro advancement programs, and similar facts. Hence, the interviewing process is superior to other possible devices, especially since statistical data on employment can be secured during the discussion.

A series of questions were prepared prior to arranging the meetings with the participating insurers and provided the format of all the interviews, although other matters arose during the course of individual discussions. The following basic questions were asked of the representatives of all the insurers that were surveyed:

(1) How are job openings made known? What is the relative importance of each of these avenues in terms of cost and results (applicants and new employees)?

(2) What are the components of the screening process?

    (a) Résumé and personal appearance;

    (b) Verification of résumé (police record, former employers, credit rating);

    (c) Tests (mental, aptitude, manual) and minimum scores.

(3) What is the relative weight of any remaining criteria?

(4) Are qualified applicants offered specific jobs in specific locations or are they allowed to select from among several job openings for which they are qualified?

(5) Does the company have training classes to prepare persons for employment?

(6) Are employees given formal training to upgrade their skills so as to enable them to transfer to more desirable jobs?

(7) Is there provision for tuition rebate plans and/or company sponsored after-work classes to encourage the acquiring of higher academic diplomas?

(8) Does top management take a strong stand in any phase of the application-screening-training areas?

(9) What are the primary criteria for promotion in typical jobs? Is there any formal policy or periodic merit rating or do superiors reach promotion decisions by subjective and informal appraisals of overall effectiveness?

(10) Who makes employment and promotion decisions?

    (a) Centralized-decentralized;

    (b) Personnel department;

    (c) First and/or second level supervisory personnel.

(11) Has the organization made any special efforts to hire Negroes?

(12) Has the federal government or other agencies voiced any complaints regarding Negro employment in the company?

(13) What, if any, impression does the company have of what other employers are doing about Negro employment?

(14) How does Negro employment in the firm compare to that of others in the industry?

(15) Does the company feel that business enterprises have an obligation to ease job qualifications in order to employ Negroes?

(16) How are lower managers informed of the prohibition against employment discrimination?

The insurers also were asked to provide basic employment and organizational data, as well as other relevant information.

During the later stages of the study, twenty-nine of the original 150 participating insurers were asked to complete written questionnaires as a substitute for the personal interview previously requested. Data pertaining to the remaining 121 insurance companies which were included in the initial sample universe were obtained by interviewing only fifty-four of those corporations. This approach was possible because of the parent-subsidiary relationship frequently encountered among the participating insurers. That is, as an aggregate, the fifty-four insurance organizations actually interviewed established corporate policy (including employment practices) and compiled statistical data for an additional sixty-seven insurers.[1] Hence, the fifty-four interviews produced information for 121 separate entities.

---

[1] The fifty-four companies interviewed either wholly owned or controlled a total of 250 insurers. The parent corporations, however, formulated administrative policies for only the sixty-seven companies indicated above.

CHAPTER II

The Structure of the Insurance Industry

Insurance as a technique is defined by academicians and practitioners in numerous ways. A definition of insurance is relevant to this study for two reasons. First, it is necessary to delineate between insurance provided by private as opposed to governmental mechanisms. Second, it is essential to eliminate from the scope of this study insurance-like devices such as service or parts replacement contracts sold by retailers along with a given product. For the purpose of this study, therefore, insurance shall be defined as the transfer of pure risk through a two-party contract. Accordingly, the following data are relevant only for those entities that meet this definition.

CATEGORIES OF INSURERS

Currently accepted usage categorizes an insurance company according to the type of product (referred to as "coverage") it sells. The four broad types of coverages and, therefore, categories of insurers are (1) life, (2) health, (3) property, and (4) liability (historically termed "casualty"). Each of these classifications usually is referred to as a "line" of insurance. For all practical purposes, however, there are only two rather than four lines of insurance: life and property-liability. This narrowing of categoies is permissible because most insurers of tangible property write both property and liability insurance; similarly, there are few insurance companies that are organized to write only health insurance since both life and liability insurers may be licensed to market the health product.

Most state insurance laws prohibit a single corporate entity from writing both life and property-liability coverages. An insurer may be chartered, therefore, as a life *or* a property-liability insurer, but not as both a life *and* property-liability company. As a result, an organization—for example, a life company—that wishes to extend its marketing efforts to all four lines must form a subsidiary or related affiliation to conduct the property-liability business.[2]

Life Insurance

The term "life insurance" includes three basic types of products: ordinary, group, and industrial. A life insurer may be authorized to write business in any one or all of these three areas.

Most consumers are familiar with ordinary and group life insurance policies. The nature of the industrial contract, however, is not as commonly understood. Two primary factors differentiate industrial contracts from their ordinary and group counterparts. First, industrial life insurance is issued for small amounts, usually less than $1,000; and, second, the premiums on these policies generally are collected weekly or monthly at an insured's home by a service agent.

Property-Liability Insurance

Corporations that write both property and liability coverages are known as "multiple line" insurers. Since, as previously stated, most nonlife carriers underwrite both property and liability policies, these two lines customarily are combined and viewed as one type of product for analytical purposes.

Property insurance provides financial protection against loss or damage to an insured's property caused by fire, windstorm, hail, explosion, riot, aircraft, motor vehicles, vandalism and malicious mischief, riot and civil commotion, smoke and marine perils. Liability insurance indemnifies an insured for expenses he incurs in connection with injuries to persons or the property of others for which the insured is responsible under the law of negligence. The property-liability category also includes such diverse products as glass insurance, burglary and theft insurance, aviation insurance, and fidelity and surety bonds.

Health Insurance

As was indicated earlier, health insurance may be written by either life or property-liability companies. This coverage may be extended to provide benefits for medical expenses incurred and/or lost income arising from an illness or injury. Other terms used

---

[2] It is pertinent to note at this point that many of the largest property-liability insurers have organized life companies.

to describe health insurance policies include "Accident and Sickness Insurance," "Accident and Health Insurance," and "Disability Insurance."

DOMINANT LEGAL FORMS

Most state laws do not list the various legal forms that may be adopted in organizing an insurance company. Nevertheless, there are some types of legal entities that are sanctioned statutorily for some lines of business but not permissible for other categories of coverage. Despite the wide variety of acceptable organizational structures, the stock and nonassessable mutual types are the legal forms most frequently adopted by insurers in all four categories.

Stock Insurance Companies

A stock insurer is a corporation owned and controlled by stockholders who seek a profit on their investment. About 27 percent of all property-liability insurance companies are stock corporations.[3] Despite their numerical minority, however, stock companies produce slightly over 70 percent of the aggregate property-liability net premium volume and hold approximately 75 percent of the assets of all nonlife insurers.

In the life insurance field, slightly more than 90 percent of all life companies are owned by stockholders. Contrary to their numerical predominance, however, stock life insurers have issued only about 46 percent of all life insurance in force and control just 30 percent of the aggregate assets of the entire life industry.[4]

Of those private organizations operating in the health insurance field, about 56 percent are life or property-liability companies. In addition, there also are forty-two monoline insurers writing only health insurance. The combined property-liability and monoline health insurers represent 58.5 percent of all health benefit organizations and have received 61 percent of the premium income attributable to all health coverages.[5] The remaining 39 percent of income from the health benefit market was dominated by such noninsurance devices as Blue Cross-Blue Shield plans and group practice prepayment arrangements.

---

[3] *Insurance Facts 1967* (New York: Insurance Information Institute, 1967), p. 15.

[4] *Life Insurance Fact Book 1968* (New York: Institute of Life Insurance, 1968), pp. 96-97.

[5] *1968 Source Book of Health Insurance Data* (New York: Health Insurance Institute, 1968), pp. 44, 49, 50.

Nonassessable Mutual Insurance Companies

A mutual [6] insurance company is one owned and controlled (at least theoretically) by its policyholders. The corparation's management is administered by a board of directors that is elected by policyholder vote.

There are over 2,000 mutual companies in the property-liability field.[7] Despite the fact that they represent nearly 70 percent of all organizations operating in this line, mutual insurers produce only about 27 percent of all property-liability net premiums and account for only approximately 24 percent of the assets of the property-liability companies. Five of the largest twenty property-liability groups (companies under common management), however, are mutuals. This fact is of significance to a legal form analysis since these twenty groups, as an aggregate, are the recepients of over half of the total net premium production of all property-liability companies.[8]

Mutual life insurance companies comprise approximately 9 percent of all life insurers. This percentage is deceptive, however, since these mutual life corporations control approximately 70 percent of the assets of the entire life insurance industry and have issued 54 percent of all life insurance in force.[9]

Life companies dominate in the area of health coverages written by insurers and are credited with writing over 90 percent of all health insurance policies. As a result, life corporations also held the vast majority of assets attributable to the operations of all insurers in the health benefit area.

Summary

Athough the insurance industry consists of a relatively large number of companies, the vast majority of its business transactions are conducted by a small number of very large insurers. Hence, the dominant type of legal entity in the insurance industry must be considered from two aspects: numerical superiority and market share.

---

[6] For all except definitional and the most technical purposes, nonassessable mutual insurers are referred to simply as mutual companies. Accordingly, this terminology will be adopted throughout the remainder of the study.

[7] *Best's Insurance Reports—Fire and Casualty: 1967-1968* (Morristown, New Jersey: Alfred M. Best Co., Inc.), p. xii.

[8] *Ibid.*, p. 152.

[9] *Life Insurance Fact Book 1967*, (New York: Institute of Life Insurance, 1968), p. 98.

In the life and health field, the majority of companies are stock corporations. Mutual insurers, however, command the largest share of the life and health market.

In the property-liability area, the most common type of organization is the mutual form. From the standpoint of business written (i.e., market share), stock companies are predominant.

MEASURES OF CONCENTRATION

Market share concentration is gauged in the insurance industry primarily in terms of four measures. Since each criterion involves some concepts completely unrelated to those underlying the other measures, it is possible to derive four separate, and valid, conclusions concerning market share concentration, each of which may be quite different from, and not reinforce, the other three measures.

The four criteria of market share concentration are (1) assets, (2) insurance in force, (3) annual premium volume, and (4) geographic variations. The measures generally are used to determine (1) an individual company's position in its segment of the industry (life, property-liability, or health insurance) and (2) the relative importance of the various legal forms of companies (mutual, stock, and so on) in its segment of the industry and each company's rank within this categorization by legal form.

Assets

If the size of a given product segment of the insurance industry is expressed in terms of total assets, the amount of assets held by an individual insurer is one indication of that company's share of that portion of the market. The greater the amount of an insurer's assets in relation to the corresponding total assets held by the industry, the larger the market share commanded by the company. This is attributable to statutory regulations that require a company to maintain a given asset level in support of its insurance in force. Similarly, the greater the total assets held by the insurers of a particular legal form in relation to the total assets of all insurers within the same segment of the industry, the larger the market share controlled by those types of insurers.

Stock life insurers account for about 30.1 percent of all assets held by life companies. The remaining 69.9 percent is controlled by mutual life organizations. Since, as previously indicated, only 9 percent of the life companies are mutual in form, it is clear that they dominate the life insurance business. Moreover, of the total 154 mutual insurers, nine (6 percent) hold approximately 80 percent of the asset accumulations of all mutual life entities.[10]

In terms of assets, therefore, nine mutual companies—which represent only half of 1 percent of the total number of life insurers—control about 70 percent of the life insurance market.

Stock insurers, which represent approximately 26 percent of all property-liability companies, hold 74 percent of this portion of the property-liability industry's assets. Moreover, fourteen of the twenty largest property-liability insurance groups are organized as stock companies. On the other hand, mutual property-liability companies of all types, which number about 2,000, account for slightly under 24 percent of the assets attributable to the insurers operating in this area.[11] The property-liability industry's pattern of asset concentration thus is similar to that observed in the life field: a relatively small percentage of companies (about 26 percent) control the vast majority of assets held by all such insurers. Stock insurers, however, do not have as significant a percentage of the aggregate assets attributed to property-liability operations as do mutual companies in the life area.

Health insurance statistics are incomplete with respect to assets, insurance in force, annual premium volume, and geographic variations. The deficiency is the result of several factors: (1) the smallness of the health insurance portion of the industry, (2) the infancy of the health insurance concept, and (3) the difficulty in isolating data caused by the overlapping activities in the health area of life and property-liability companies. The result of the lack of statistics is, for all practical purposes, the inability to measure market share concentration applicable to the health portion of the insurance industry.

Insurance in Force

For a given segment of the insurance industry, the total dollar amount of coverage owned by all policyholders is referred to as the aggregate "insurance in force." This measure is an important indication of market share concentration since, by definition, it encompasses all insureds in a given classification, the total amount of insurance possessed by those policyholders and, hence, the

---

[10] *Life Insurance Fact Book 1967*, *op. cit.*, pp. 97-98.

[11] *Best's Fire and Casualty Aggregates and Averages 1967* (Morristown, N. J.: Alfred M. Best Co., Inc.), p. 1.

amount of the total product distributed by insurers. "Insurance in force" thus is comparable to another industry's total sales. Logically, the larger the portion of total sales (insurance in force) attributable to an individual company and/or companies of a particular legal form, the greater the total market share commanded by that company and/or companies.

Mutual corporations have issued about 55 percent of the total life insurance in force and stock life insurers account for the other 45 percent. Less than 10 percent of the companies in the life insurance industry, therefore, control approximately 55 percent of the market in terms of insurance in force. Moreover, of the aggregate number of mutual companies, 6 percent (about nine) dominate 83 percent of the mutual insurers' market. The fifty largest life companies, as determined by the amount of insurance in force, are listed in Table 1.

Insurance in force is not a measure of concentration applicable to property-liability and health insurance companies. Statistical data are available in the property-liability and health areas only in terms of amount of assets, annual premium volume, and geographic variations.

Annual Premium Volume

Annual premium income is one of the most accurate and widely accepted indicators of market share concentration among insurers and measures the revenue derived from the sale of the companies' product: insurance.

Exact figures are not available for the mutual-stock insurers' share of total life insurance premium income. On the basis of the amount of life insurance in force, however, it may be estimated that mutual insurers (i.e., 10 percent of the companies) receive about 55 percent of the annual premiums collected by the life insurance industry. The remainder is controlled by stock insurers.

Annual premium volume of property-liability companies is measured in terms of net premiums written. "Net" premiums written are defined as the direct and/or reinsurance premium income retained by insurers, less payments made for reinsured policies. The annual premium income of the combined property-liability lines generally is distributed as follows: 69 percent is paid to stock companies and 27 percent is received by mutuals. Stock

TABLE 1.   *The Fifty Leading*
Life Insurance Companies Ranked
by Insurance in Force, 1967

Company	Amount of Insurance in Force (Million $)
Metropolitan Life Insurance Company	129,993
The Prudential Insurance Company of America	121,677
The Equitable Life Assurance Society of the United States	56,373
John Hancock Mutual Life Insurance Company	43,440
The Travelers Life Insurance Company	40,512
Aetna Life Insurance Company	39,587
New York Life Insurance Company	36,720
Connecticut General Life Insurance Company	21,608
Occidental Life Insurance Company of California	17,713
The Lincoln National Life Insurance Company	16,036
The Northeastern Mutual Life Insurance Company	14,524
Massachusetts Mutual Life Insurance Company	13,710
The Mutual Life Insurance Company of New York	11,889
Continental Assurance Company	11,455
New England Mutual Life Insurance Company	10,933
Mutual Benefit Life Insurance Company	9,405
American National Insurance Company	9,003
The National Life and Accident Insurance Company	8,661
Connecticut Mutual Life Insurance Company	7,641
The Western and Southern Life Insurance Company	7,618
The Penn Mutual Life Insurance Company	7,291
Provident Life and Accident Insurance Company	6,705
Franklin Life Insurance Company	6,510
Bankers Life Company	6,491
The Minnesota Mutual Life Insurance Company	6,135
United Benefit Life Insurance Company	5,190
General American Life Insurance Company	5,001
State Mutual Life Assurance Company of America	4,945
State Farm Life Insurance Company	4,841
Phoenix Mutual Life Insurance Company	4,645
The Life Insurance Company of Virginia	4,432
National Life Insurance Company	4,221
Southwestern Life Insurance Company	4,057
Northwestern National Life Insurance Company	4,006
Provident Mutual Life Insurance Company of Philadelphia	3,997

TABLE 1. *The Fifty Leading*
Life Insurance Companies Ranked
by Insurance in Force, 1967
(Continued)

Company	Amount of Insurance in Force (Million $)
Home Life Insurance Company	3,968
Pacific Mutual Life Insurance Company	3,946
Liberty National Life Insurance Company	3,744
The Guardian Life Insurance Company of America	3,721
The Union Central Life Insurance Company	3,654
Washington National Insurance Company	3,237
Jefferson Standard Life Insurance Company	3,141
Life and Casualty Insurance Company of Tennessee	2,882
Southland Life Insurance Company	2,863
Acacia Mutual Life Insurance Company	2,597
Equitable Life Insurance Company of Iowa	2,261
Kansas City Life Insurance Company	2,000
The Fidelity Mutual Life Insurance Company	1,983
The Paul Revere Life Insurance Company	1,789
Teachers Insurance and Annuity Association of America	1,440

Source: "The 50 Leading U. S. Life Companies," *Best's Insurance News-Life Edition,* May 1967, p. 11.

insurers obviously have a major share of the market in terms of annual premium income.

Within the stock category, the fifty largest companies—which as an aggregate represent 6 percent of all stock property-liability insurers—have a combined annual net premium income equal to 47 percent of the amount paid into the entire property-liability industry.   The fifty largest property-liability companies, as determined by annual premium volume, are listed in Table 2.

TABLE 2.   *The Fifty Leading*
Property-Liability Companies and
Groups Ranked by Net Premiums Written, 1967

Company	Net Premiums Written (Thousand $)
State Farm Group	1,082,087
Travelers Group	1,000,635
Allstate Group	905,253
Continental Insurance Companies	816,120
Aetna Life and Casualty Group	793,694
Hartford Fire	773,523
Insurance Company of North America Group	670,313
Continental National American Group	624,137
Fireman's Fund American Insurance Companies	590,659
Liberty Mutual	586,027
Home Insurance	487,561
U. S. F. and G. Group	448,428
Nationwide Group	392,679
Royal-Globe Companies	373,266
James S. Kemper	347,380
Farmers Insurance Exchange	312,485
Employers' Casualty Group	283,742
Connecticut General-Aetna Group	280,358
Employers Mutual Casualty Group	263,979
St. Paul Fire and Marine	256,622
Crum and Forster	243,325
Great American Group	239,873
Maryland American General	227,478
Reliance Insurance Group	223,437
SAFECO Group	188,380
General Accident Group	184,080
Sentry Insurance	180,706
Chubb and Son	177,276
American Mutual Liability Group	176,800
Government Employees Group	173,536

TABLE 2.   *The Fifty Leading*
Property-Liability Companies and
Groups Ranked by Net Premiums Written, 1967
(Continued)

Company	Net Premiums Written (Thousand $)
General Motors Acceptance Corporation	172,986
Commercial Union Group	146,821
Transamerica Group	144,018
General Reinsurance	141,330
Glens Falls Group	136,563
American Re-Insurance Company	126,455
Ohio Casualty Group	116,694
United Services Auto Association	106,851
Hanover Group	106,829
Zurich-American Group	106,653
Swiss Reinsurance	105,472
Security Insurance Company of Connecticut	101,736
Detroit Automobile Inter-Insurance Exchange Group	95,789
Inter-Insurance Exchange, Auto Club of Southern California	90,769
New Hampshire Group	90,344
Western Casualty and Surety Group	88,911
Northwestern National Group	79,901
Northwestern Mutual Group	79,029
Atlantic Mutual Liability Group	78,155
Lincoln National-American States	72,126

Source: *Best's Fire and Casualty Aggregates and Averages* (Morristown,
N. J.: Alfred M. Best Co., Inc., 1967), p. 29.

The above analysis of the annual premium income of life and
property-liability companies includes the health insurance premiums written by each of these categories of insurers. Of the total
health insurance premium income, approximately 90 percent is
attributable to life insurer operations with less than 10 percent

being received by property-liability companies. Presumably, mutual life insurers and stock property-liability corporations predominate in this field.

Monoline health companies, which receive only a small portion of total health premiums, have the following type distribution pattern: over 55 percent of the total monoline premium income is earned by mutual monoline health insurers and the remainder (45 percent) is written by stock monoline health companies.

In the entire health area, then, the largest share of the insurance market as measured in terms of annual premium income is commanded by mutual corporations.

Geographic Variations

The insurance industry and its product not only are measured quantitatively by assets, insurance in force, and annual premium volume, but by geographic concentrations. The latter measurement may be made on a regional basis by analyzing the (1) number of policies in force, (2) amount of insurance in force (for life companies) or annual premiums written (for property-liability and health insurers), and/or (3) the number of insurance companies domiciled in a state. Or, the market may be gauged on the same three bases for each state.

In terms of regional concentration, statistical data are available on the amount of insurance in force in each of four regions in the United States. Table 3 reveals that the greatest total amount of life insurance coverage is in the North Central region of the country, followed by the Northeast.

As Table 3 demonstrates, however, the smallest proportion of life insurance in effect is in the South region where a majority of Negroes still dwell. Moreover, although the South has the greatest number of domestic insurers, insurance companies in this area nevertheless tend to be small. In terms of employment potential, then, the smallness of the insurers causes only a few job openings to arise because the companies' operations do not require large staffs, white or black. On the other hand, in the North Central and Northeast regions, a substantial and increasing share of the Negro population now lives primarily in large cities where many major life insurance companies have their home offices. These also are the areas where the greatest total of life insurance is in force, thus affording new and expanding work opportunities for Negro employment.

TABLE 3. *Life Insurance in Force*
in the United States and Negro Population Percentages
by Region

Region[a]	Total Life Insurance in Force (1967) (Million $)	Percent of Negro Population (1966)
South	182,555	55
North Central	289,565	20
Northeast	269,285	17
West	243,284	8
Total	984,689	100

Source: *Life Insurance Fact Book 1967* (New York: Institute of Life Insurance, 1967), p. 20, and U. S. Bureau of Labor Statistics, *Social and Economical Status of Negroes in the United States, 1969,* U. S. Bureau of Labor Statistics, Report No. 375 and Current Population Report, Series P-23, No. 29, 1969.

[a] Geographic definitions are as follows:

South: Alabama, Delaware, District of Columbia, Florida, Georgia, Kentucky, Maryland, Mississippi, North Carolina, South Carolina, Tennessee, Virginia, and West Virginia.

North Central: Illinois, Indiana, Iowa, Kansas, Michigan, Minnesota, Missouri, Nebraska, North Dakota, Ohio, South Dakota, and Wisconsin.

Northeast: Connecticut, Maine, Massachusetts, New Hampshire, New Jersey, New York, Pennsylvania, Rhode Island, and Vermont.

West: Alaska, Arizona, Arkansas, California, Colorado, Hawaii, Idaho, Louisiana, Montana, Nevada, New Mexico, Oklahoma, Oregon, Texas, Utah, Washington, and Wyoming.

Table 4 shows that the regional distribution of property-liability written premiums follows the same concentration as does life insurance. The potential impact on Negro employment, therefore, is likely to be the same as that noted for the life industry.

TABLE 4. *Property-Liability*
Direct Premiums Written and
Negro Population Percentages by Region

Region[a]	Total Direct Premiums Written (1967) (Thousand $)	Percent of Negro Population (1966)
South	3,235,903	55
North Central	5,245,620	20
Northeast	5,614,958	17
West	5,402,901	8
Total	19,499,382	100

Source: *Insurance Facts 1967* (New York: Insurance Information Institute, 1967), pp. 35-36, and *Social and Economic Status of Negroes*, see Table 3.

[a] For geographic definitions see Table 3.

Information is not available concerning the number of companies writing health insurance on a regional basis. The only fact definitely known is that there are insurers licensed in each state to sell this type of coverage. Data also are incomplete concerning the number of policies issued in the various regions. Information is available, however, concerning the regional distribution of written premiums in the health field and is presented in Table 5.[12] This tabulation reveals that the largest amount of health premiums was written in the North Central region, followed closely by the West and Northeast. The smallest premium income was produced in the South. The health insurance industry thus is subject to conclusions made above concerning life and property-liability insurers.

---

[12] It should be noted that there is no available analysis of the per region (or state) written premiums to delineate those attributable to life, property-liability, and monoline health insurers.

TABLE 5.　*Health Insurance Premiums Written*
and Negro Population Percentages
by Region

Region[a]	Total Premiums Written (1966) (Thousand $)	Percent of Negro Population (1966)
South	1,475,246	55
North Central	2,567,951	20
Northeast	1,789,035	17
West	1,963,768	8
Total	7,796,000	100

Source:　*1967 Source Book of Health Insurance Data* (New York: Health Insurance Institute, 1968), pp. 34-35, and *Social and Economic Status of Negroes*, see Table 3.

[a] For geographic definitions see Table 3.

MANPOWER

The data in Table 6 reveal that nearly 1.3 million persons were employed in the insurance industry at the beginning of 1967. Approximately one-third of this aggregate works as sales personnel and two-thirds are in nonsales activities. One-half of the industry's total employees are classified as clerical or "other" personnel. The "others" category includes the industry's few janitors, building maintenance, and other peripheral personnel. Managerial, professional, and technical employees comprise the balance of the nonsales labor force.

Table 6 thus reflects the fact that the industry is characterized by the employment of a great mass of clerical workers. Since this large clerical force includes many relatively unskilled jobs, the companies would seem to offer excellent employment potential for Negro (especially female) workers. This advantage is further enhanced by the location of many insurance offices in center cities that are convenient to Negro residential concentrations.

On the other hand, and as is true of many industries, few Negroes are employed in sales activities. The absence of Negroes in the sales area is due, among other things, to a reluctance to

TABLE 6. *Insurance Industry
Employment by Occupational Group
United States, 1967*

Occupational Group	Number	Percent of Total
Sales	415,000	32.9
Nonsales		
Managerial	160,000	12.7
Professional and technical	55,000	4.4
Clerical and other	630,000	50.0
Total nonsales	845,000	67.1
Total insurance personnel	1,260,000	100.0

Source: U. S. Bureau of the Census, and Institute of Life Insurance. Based on tabulations sponsored by the Institute of Life Insurance in conjunction with the March 1966 Current Population Survey.

alter the industry's traditional employment practices, an element discussed in a later chapter.

As indicated by the data in Table 7, the insurance industry's aggregate work force is almost evenly divided between males and females. By product line, slightly less than 60 percent of the total work force is associated with life insurance. The aggregate sales staff is distributed in about identical proportion between life and nonlife employment.

Nonsales personnel in the industry are about equally divided between home office and agency (field, brokerage, or other) offices. As will be explained later, since home office operations are directly under the control of policy making officers, that locale seems to afford greater Negro employment potential than decentralized field, agency, or brokerage offices that are independently managed.

Earnings

The insurance industry is not noted for its high salary scales. An indication of the wages within the industry is given by a Bureau of Labor Statistics industry wage survey of nonsupervisory employees in selected occupations and regions in life insurance companies during October-November 1966. Among the

TABLE 7. *Insurance Industry*
Employment by Sex, Line of Insurance, and Type of Work
United States, 1967

Employment Characteristics		Number	Percent of Total
SEX			
Male		660,000	52.4
Female		600,000	47.6
Total		1,260,000	100.0
WORK RELATED TO			
Life or Life and Nonlife Insurance		720,000	57.1
Nonlife Insurance Only		540,000	42.9
Total		1,260,000	100.0
TYPE OF WORK			
Sales: More than 50% of Income from Life Insurance	205,000		16.3
Less than 50% of Income from Life Insurance	210,000		16.7
Total Sales		415,000	33.0
Nonsales: In Home Office of Insurance Company	435,000		34.5
In Agency, Field, Brokerage, or Other Office	410,000		32.5
Other Nonsales		845,000	67.0
Total		1,260,000	100.0

Source: U. S. Bureau of the Census and Institute of Life Insurance. Based on tabulations sponsored by the Institute of Life Insurance in conjunction with the March 1966 Current Population Survey.

fourteen (of a total of thirty-four) occupational categories predominantly staffed by men, nationwide average weekly salaries ranged from $332 for class A actuaries to $76 for class C tabulating-machine operators. Averages of about $125 a week were recorded for most of the jobs in which men were in the majority.[13]

Women were dominant in the clerical occupations studied. The average weekly salaries for some numerically important clerical jobs staffed by women were: $63 for class C file clerks, $66.50 for class B typists, $70.50 for class B keypunch operators and $74.50 for general stenographers. Among all the occupational categories predominantly staffed by women, nationwide average weekly salaries ranged from $106.50 for class A correspondence clerks to $63 for class C file clerks.[14]

On a regional basis, average weekly earnings usually were found to be the highest in the Middle Atlantic region, the largest region in terms of employment, while those in the Middle West were usually the lowest.

As is discussed more fully in Chapter V, the wage levels enumerated above generally are below those available in comparable positions in other industries. As a result, the wage schedules in the industry tend to complicate the recruitment of both Negro and white employees, particularly at the clerical level.

Unionization

The insurance industry traditionally has been an overwhelmingly nonunion one. The only current union of importance—the Insurance Workers International Union, AFL-CIO—has a membership (approximately 35,000 in 1966) comprised almost exclusively of industrial life insurance agents. The significance of this organization is declining, however, since the demand for industrial insurance is constantly decreasing and the union admits to almost no success in organizing "ordinary" agents and office workers. Neither the "ordinary" agents nor office employees considers a labor union necessary.[15]

---

[13] U. S. Bureau of Labor Statistics, *Industry Wage Survey: Life Insurance-October-November 1966*, Bulletin 1569 (October 1967), p. 2.

[14] *Ibid.*, pp. 2-6.

[15] Harvey J. Clermont, *Organizing the Insurance Worker: A History of Labor Unions of Insurance Employees* (Washington, D. C.: The Catholic University of America Press, 1966), pp. 217-218.

Because of this long prevailing general negative attitude toward unionization, the analysis in Chapter V of the factors encouraging or discouraging Negro employment in the insurance industry will indicate little or no union impact on the insurer's racial employment practices.

MAJOR MARKETING METHODS

Insurance is marketed through (1) agents, (2) brokers, and (3) direct writing systems. The type of system used varies by line of insurance. In addition, there are numerous variations within each of the three broad marketing categories for the different lines written.[16]

All three distribution systems enumerated above are found in both the life and property-liability insurance industry. The most commonly used channel of distribution in the life area is some version of the agency system while, on the other hand, many of the property-liability insurers simultaneously use more than one of the three distribution approaches.

Agency System

Under the agency method, a life insurance agent represents only one insurance company and frequently is referred to as an "exclusive agent." In the property-liability field, however, most agents have contracts with more than one company.

Life Insurance. The organization of the agency operation in life insurance has primarily two forms: (1) the general agency system and (2) the branch office system. In some cases, both forms are used by a company.

A life insurer utilizing the general agency system divides its marketing area into geographic territories. Each territory then is assigned to a general agent who, as an independent contractor, is responsible for, and has control over, that territory. The general agent is entitled to a commission on all business that is written within his territory. The commissions received from the insurer are used by the general agent to (1) compensate any agents he hires to develop business in the territory and (2) absorb the administrative expenses of his organization.

---

[16] Since most health insurnace is written by either life or property-liability companies, the following discussion is limited to the latter two classifications of insurers.

Under the branch office system, a life insurer establishes "districts" (which are comparable to the territories of general agents) throughout its areas of operations. A salaried employee of the insurer (referred to as a branch office manager) is placed in charge of each district. The branch manager's main functions are to recruit agents in his area and to direct their work. The remuneration of a branch office manager consists of a salary and periodic bonuses of a given amount for increases in volume of business attributable to the production of the agents under his supervision.

Whatever the legal and/or technical differences between the branch office system and the general agency system in the life industry, one specific difference is pertinent to this study: control by the home office over agency operations, including hiring practices. Under the general agency system, in its purest form, complete control of all aspects of the agency's operation is in the hands of the general agent; he is an independent contractor and the insurer that the general agent represents has no authority to direct the agency's activities. The corporation, therefore, is unable to control the number of Negro agents or clerical employees hired by the general agent. On the other hand, a branch manager is an employee of a life insurance company. Accordingly, the insurer is able to direct the branch office's personnel activities. The insurer can require that both Negro agents and clerical employees be hired in all branch offices. The effectiveness of, or interest in, the control of field hiring policies will vary, of course, among the different companies.

Property-Liability Insurance. The agency system of the property-liability industry encompasses two types of agents: (1) independent agents (the sum total of which are sometimes referred to as the "Independent Agency System" or the "American Agency System") and (2) exclusive agents.

In property-liability insurance, the independent agent is an independent contractor but has much broader authority over the distribution of the insurance contract than does the general agent in the life insurance area. Traditionally, the independent agent issues all policies he sells, collects the premiums, and, as far as his companies are concerned, retains the exclusive right to solicit renewals from his policyholders. None of the insurers that the independent agent represents has any control over the way in which the agent's administrative operations are conducted. Hence, the number of Negro agents and clerical employees hired by an independent agent cannot even be influenced by an insurer. Moreover, any suggestive "interference" by the latter in an agent's employment practices, if persistent, probably would result in the agent terminating his relationship with the insurer. This could be extremely detrimental to the company if the agent is one that produces a profitable and sizeable amount of business.

As previously indicated, the exclusive agent marketing method is not used as extensively by property-liability insurers as by life companies. Exclusive agents agree to represent only one insurer (or a group of insurers under common management) and the company (or group) retains the right to solicit renewals from policyholders. This type of agent is neither an employee of the company nor an independent contractor. Because of this quasi-employee/independent contractor status, an insurer—if it so chooses—is able to exercise some degree of control over the activities of exclusive agents, including the employment of Negroes.

The branch office system used in the property-liability lines is very similar to the life insurance branch office technique. In the nonlife lines, the branch office serves only one company (or a group of companies) and the branch manager, as an employee, is under the supervision of his company and the branch office employees are the employees of the company. Accordingly, the insurer has extensive control over its field force and is able to issue directives concerning the number of Negro employees hired by the branch managers.

Brokerage System

The life and/or property-liability insurance salesman who acts as an agent of a potential insured, rather than as the representative of an insurance company, is known as a broker. A broker may be a general insurance practitioner who sells all kinds of insurance or he may function only in one line of the insurance business. Moreover, a broker has contracts with a number of different companies. Like the general agent, therefore, his employment practices, including the number of Negroes hired, are not subject to control by any of the insurance companies with which he is under contract.

Direct Writing System

An insurance company that does not use agents in marketing its product is known as a "direct writer." The contract is marketed directly by the insurer to the insured, usually through the mail or by salaried employees. Direct writers, therefore, are able to maintain complete control over the employees that are engaged in sales activities. These insurers, then, can employ as many or as few Negro sales employees as are desired. Direct writers are much more common to property-liability lines than to the life insurance field. Where direct writers do exist in the life industry, they usually are subsidiaries of property-liability companies.

CHANGING OPERATIONAL PROCEDURES

Total employment in the insurance industry increased by 19 percent from 1960 to 1967. On the basis of this record, it is reasonable to presume that the industry's level of employment in the years following 1967 will not be static. For example, such occurrences as an expansion of the market for insurance and a resulting manpower need and/or attrition among existing employees will cause the employment figures to fluctuate. In addition to these somewhat common events, however, operational innovations will affect the employment pattern and total manpower needs within the insurance industry.

Dispersion of Home Office Activities

A relatively recent trend in the insurance industry is decentralization of home office functions by the larger life and property-liability insurers. The main objective of decentralization is to improve efficiency and speed in providing administrative services to policyholders. The net effect of this dispersion probably will be an increase in clerical employment within the industry. This conclusion follows from the realization that home office decentralization entails the establishment of offices in several geographic regions in each of which are performed the functions previously ascribed only to the home office. In short, a regional duplication of jobs results in an increase in the total number of clerical employees needed by an insurance company. Home office decentralization and its corresponding increase in numbers and geographic areas of jobs could be an important element in expanding Negro employment, both in terms of absolute amounts and regions. The outcome will depend on the attitudes of insurers toward Negro employment and the level of competence or skills needed to perform the newly created jobs.

Holding Companies

One of the most recent and widespread of the organizational changes within the industry has been the formation of holding companies. The general motivation behind the trend is a financial one although the specific reason varies between life and property-liability corporations.

Basis of Holding Company Trend. Life companies traditionally have played a dominant role in marshaling savings and making them available to borrowers as long-term investment funds. This role, however, has been steadily changing. For example, the ratio of total premium collections to total disposable personal income has diminished from 6.28 percent in 1935 to 3.87 percent by 1967. This indicates that individuals have been finding life insurance a less attractive medium for accumulating savings than the offerings of competitive financial establishments.

Moreover, the life industry's portion of total institutional savings has decreased from over 50 percent (in 1947) to about 25 percent (in 1967). The organizations that have gained from this decrease are savings and loan institutions, noninsured pension funds, state and local retirement funds, investment companies, and credit unions.

In an attempt to improve the performance of their organizations, various life companies have turned to the holding company device as a means of broadening the base of their services and products and gaining wider discretion in their portfolio investment selections. It is too soon to determine whether the effort will succeed. Evidently many insurers believe the results will be positive since the number of holding companies being organized is increasing in geometric ratio.

Current market prices of the stock of many property-liability companies reflect their depressed level of profits. The unfavorable earnings of this segment of the insurance industry, which is attributable primarily to adverse underwriting results, has caused a severe decline in the flow of capital funds to these insurers. As a result, many property-liability companies have sought to diversify their activities by forming holding companies that will control not only the existing insurance operations but also other types of profitable business activities. The objective is to attract capital that may be used in any or all of the holding companies' enterprises, but primarily in its insurance operations.

Effect of Holding Companies on Employment. Although many of the largest life and property-liability companies have organized holding companies for the purposes cited above, state regulatory laws present serious restrictions that may affect the extensiveness of this movement. There does seem to be some indication, however, that the various state insurance laws will be modified to some degree to accommodate the insurers' formation of holding companies.

Barring regulatory difficulties, the effect of the holding company trend on employment within the insurance industry undoubtedly will be to increase the total number of employees. As insurers expand their operations to other activities, there will be a corresponding absolute increase in number of employees. This is true whether the employees are new or workers already employed by an existing organization acquired by the holding company. All these employees, even though perhaps performing functions in noninsurance fields, will be under the ultimate control of the insurer behind the holding company. The sphere of insurer influence on total employment in the nation, therefore, will increase as the holding company trend grows to maturity. Hence, a successful holding company trend that culminates in broader and expanded corporate activities and new employment positions could result in advantageous employment opportunities for Negroes in the insurance industry. The fulfillment of this potential depends, of course, on each corporation's commitment toward increasing the number of its Negro employees.

Expansion of Computer Applications

The vast majority of an insurer's home office operational procedures are clerical in nature. It is not surprising, therefore, that insurance companies were among the first business firms to use electronic computers. A few life companies installed such equipment in the first half of the 1950's, and by 1963 the overwhelming majority of life insurers had adopted the use of electronic data processing equipment (EDP).

The property-liability portion of the industry, however, appears to be behind the life segment in the application of electronic data processing techniquues to clerical operations. Actually, the property-liability insurance operation is ideally suited for adaptability to electronic data processing. For example, the automation of insurance bookkeeping improves accuracy and eliminates the extremely high cost of manual paperwork. It has been estimated that the average cost of processing a new policy on computerized automobile coverages is approximately 40 percent less than the expense associated with manual accounting methods. Further, previously issued policies that are renewed may be processed on computers with savings in the vicinity of 80 percent. In addition to policy issuance and administrative procedures, every step in nonlife rate calculations and claims processing may be stated numerically. Another justification for the use of EDP by property-liability insurers is the rising need for rapid communication with field offices, rating bureaus, and agencies.

The Stanford Research Institute contends, in a study of the property-liability industry, that:

> The Institute believes that within the next ten years:
>
> (1) All major companies in the P & C property-liability industry will use EDP for internal accounting and management information and controls.
>
> (2) All major companies will have data transmission facilities direct to their branches and agents throughout the country; to employee group administrations; and to other organizations such as state motor vehicle departments, state insurance departments, rating and statistical bureaus, and claim adjusters.
>
> (3) The individual agent will be directly connected into the computer facilities of each of his major companies.
>
> The speed with which these changes will occur will depend on the willingness of all parties to cooperate in joint development of compatible equipment and systems.[17]

It is probable, therefore, that the expansion of electronic systems into the insurance business will proceed at an increased pace. The effect of this expansion on the insurance industry's total employment pattern, however, is uncertain.

On the one hand, automation will result in the elimination of many low-skilled clerical jobs. Moreover, it is these jobs, as is explained in detail in Chapter V that seem to offer the numerically largest employment opportunities for Negroes. On the other hand, there will be a demand for trained computer personnel. This demand, according to one estimate, could result in the hiring of 10,000 trained computer personnel. To the extent that existing or new Negro employees are trained to perform in this capacity,

---

[17] Stanford Research Institute, *Planning For the Future of the National Association of Insurance Agents*, I (Menlo Park, Calif.: Stanford Research Institute, 1967), p. 23.

higher-level jobs may be made available to them.   Nevertheless, the net effect of automation on the insurance industry probably will be to decrease total nonsales employment, an occurrence that could affect Negro employment adversely.

Mutual Funds

Acquiring or forming a mutual fund is one of the newest, and most rapidly growing, trends among life insurers.   More than sixty affiliations between insurers and mutual funds have been consummated and several well-known insurers are planning to establish their own funds.   This innovation underlines the change in the attitude of life insurance companies that, through the years, have found it increasingly difficult to market fixed-dollar policies because their value is eroded by inflation.   As previously mentioned, the result has been a decrease in the percentage of total savings received by life companies.   To combat this situation, insurers have turned in increasing numbers to the combined mutual fund and insurance product concept.

It is still somewhat uncertain as to how the new life insurance-mutual fund "package" will be marketed.   Some mutual funds will continue to operate independently of their parent insurers.   In this case, then, the addition of the mutual fund product to the life companies' operations probably will not affect insurer employment patterns, either in the sales or clerical area.

Gradually, however, it is expected that insurance salesmen will be trained to offer to customers a package product combining mutual funds and life insurance in a ratio determined by the customer. If this package makes life insurance more attractive to investors, and therefore aids in increasing sales, there may be a net increase in the number of salesmen in the life industry.   On the other hand, failure by insurers to orient their sales personnel in the marketing technique applicable to the combined product probably will culminate in a loss of the agents' market to more efficient competition, such as mutual funds not affiliated with insurers. This possible outcome could only discourage individuals from entering the sales end of the life insurance industry. Moreover, the licensing examinations applicable to mutual fund salesmen may further discourage entrance into the agency area and eventually result in a decline in the existing total number of salesmen if the package gains consumer preference over life policies alone.

The newness of the life insurance-mutual fund product innovation and the possible detrimental as well as beneficial effects on the sales force of the life insurance industry prohibit a definitive conclusion to be made concerning future sales employment. Nevertheless, there seems to be a tendency within the industry to regard mutual funds as a positive stimulus, and one that will create a need for more salesmen, whether black or white.

As far as clerical employees are concerned, an existing mutual fund that affiliates with an insurance company, but retains its individual entity and activities, should cause neither an increase nor a decrease in the insurer's clerical staff. The clerical staff of an insurer that absorbs or creates a mutual fund probably will be increased to the extent that specialized clerical employees are needed. Barring a requirement for distinctive talent, however, most insurers should be able to fulfill their needs through the use of existing employees made available because of attrition due to automation or through some other type of adjustment of the current clerical staff. New Negro (or those of any other racial group) clerical employees therefore will not be necessary.

Variable Annuities

Similar to mutual funds in purpose are the variable annuities offered by an ever growing number of life insurance companies. Stated in the simplest terms, a variable annuity provides income benefits (such as retirement income) that tend to vary inversely with changes in the purchasing power of the dollar. If the purchasing power of the dollar declines, variable annuity benefits increase so that an annuitant's real income is not affected by inflation or deflation.

Also like mutual funds is the uncertainty of the effect of variable annuities on the employment structure of the life insurance industry. This is primarily the result of the fact that life insurers are just now beginning to adopt the concept. The main thrust, if any, on employment will be in the sales area and here, as in the mutual funds, any change in the total as well as Negro employment picture will be dependent on the sales stimulus provided by the introduction of variable annuities and similar equity contracts.

Mass Marketing of Property-Liability Insurance

The concept of mass marketing has existed in life insurance for over fifty years under the nomenclature of group insurance.

Group life insurance accounts for a substantial portion (35 percent) of the life insurance industry's total life sales and group health insurance transactions constitute a major portion of such premiums written (65 percent) by all types of insurers.

The mass marketing concept has not been developed in the property-liability lines in a manner parallel to the growth in the life area. This ostensibly is because group property-liability insurance is considered to be an "illegal" product in most states. According to a survey of state insurance commissioners, the illegality of group property-liability insurance is based on the fact that it is considered to be (1) fictitious grouping and (2) unfairly discriminatory.[18]

The reasons for the prohibition of the use of group marketing techniques in the property-liability lines are highly suspect. In fact, the same two arguments enumerated above were advanced in opposition to the introduction of group life insurance but were quickly silenced by a highly vocal consumer demand for the group life and, eventually, the group health product. The main reason for restricting the mass marketing of property-liability insurance seems to be the continuous opposition of agents to the concept, as expressed most forcibly and effectively by the *National Association of Insurance Agents (NAIA)*.[19]

The basis of the organization's opposition is the preservation of the status quo of property-liability agents. The fear is prevalent among the agents represented by the NAIA that the mass marketing concept will result in the ultimate destruction of the agents' market and hence the current *Independent Agency System.*

Despite the agents' active opposition, however, it appears that the mass marketing concept will become increasingly important in the property-liability industry because of (1) the continuously mounting high costs and corresponding losses of insurers in providing various types of coverage and (2) consumer (mainly union and employer) demand for group property-liability insurance. For example, substantial savings in administrative (including commission) costs can be realized through group purchases and sales, thus acting as a positive influence on property-liability costs. In addition, union interest in the cost and benefit advantages of group automobile coverage seems to indicate that the latter is viewed potentially as a new fringe benefit. There is little doubt

---

[18] *Irving M. Field, Employee Group Property and Liability Insurance* (Eugene, Oregon: University of Oregon, 1967), p. 27.

[19] *Ibid.,* p. 94.

that the political power of unions eventually will offset the attempts of the National Association of Insurance Agents to restrict extension of the mass marketing concept to property-liability insurance.

The net effect of the mass marketing technique on the aggregate employment of nonlife agents probably will be negative. Moreover, most insurers anticipate that the decline will occur first among the relatively large number of marginal and part-time producers. To the extent, then, that the few existing Negro insurance salesmen are marginal and/or part-time producers, their ranks probably will be diminished. The decline in the total property-liability sales force may be even greater if insurers elect to sell and service the group product through salaried group representatives rather than through agents. This marketing technique may become more important because employers and other group consumers often prefer to deal with salaried group representatives rather than with agents. In this area, then, employment potential exists for Negroes only among those insurers willing to hire Negroes as salaried group representatives.

On the positive side, the distribution of property-liability lines on a group basis probably will result in an increase in the number of clerical employees that comprise the industry's work force. As previously indicated, proportionately fewer agents will be needed whether the group product is sold by agents or salaried group representatives. On the other hand, and again regardless of the type salesman utilized, additional claims and group service personnel will be necessary to handle part of the administrative functions previously performed by the agency force. The extent of the increase, however, must be based on conjecture. To a great degree, the group administrative functions can be automated. Further, as the use of EDP equipment increases within the property-liability industry, employees whose functions are replaced by automation may be transferred to the company's group department. It thus is unrealistic to try to estimate exact clerical employment increases; rather, the only conclusion that accurately may be drawn is that the clerical employment of property-liability insurers probably will increase due to adoption of the mass marketing technique. Moreover, the increment could result in additional Negro employment if the industry so desires.

The Rise of Direct Writers

The direct writing system is not in reality a new marketing innovation. The total property-liability market controlled by direct writers, however, has increased so substantially during the last ten years that their impact logically may be considered to be the same as if these insurers represented a new facet of the industry. In fact, it seems that the increased share of total property-liability premium volume commanded by direct writers is a factor that, along with the mass marketing concept, probably will be responsible for the anticipated employment changes that the Independent Agency System is expected to experience in the future.

Direct writers in the property-liability field operate primarily in the automobile insurance market. Since automobile coverages account for more than 40 percent of all property-liability premiums written, direct writers are significant in projecting possible employment changes among independent agents.

The success of the direct writers is attributable to their (1) lower prices, (2) aggressive promotional activities, and (3) selective underwriting standards. The lower rates are primarily the result of lower acquisition costs. That is, the salary paid by direct writers to their salesmen is much smaller than the commission paid to independent agents who produce the same type business for their companies. The selective underwriting practices also result in lower costs since such procedures are designed to restrict coverage to insureds with lower-than-average losses. The effect, of course, is lower-than-average premium rates.

To combat the financial advantages and market share control of direct writers, agency property-liability insurers have introduced (1) administrative procedures for reducing costs of conducting their business, (2) new policies that are competitive in price, and (3) new marketing concepts. It is the third innovation, combined with the extent of the market controlled by direct writers, that poses the threat to the independent agents. Automobile insurance is considered to be the independent agents' most important sales area; thus, if it is diminished by mass marketing techniques and/or the continued market growth of direct writers, the inevitable result will be the eventual elimination of a portion of the existing property-liability agents, whether black or white.

White collar workers also should be affected by the success of the direct writers, but not as dramatically as the members of the independent agency system. Direct writing companies utilize clerical employees to perform many of the operations assumed by agents. If the nonagency insurers continue to command an increasing share of the property-liability market, one result will be the need for additional clerical employees. As indicated in preceding sections, however, such an anticipated increment must be balanced against the negative employment effects of EDP. Moreover, the direct writers have long been noted for maintaining low administrative expense ratios. This factor could be instrumental in sustaining the number of their clerical employees at the existing level. In short, it is highly unlikely that the continued growth of direct writing companies will result in a substantial increase in the number of their clerical workers. As a result, clerical employment opportunities for Negroes probably will not be created in the insurance industry as the market of the direct writers expands.

CHAPTER III

Negro Employment Prior to 1967

Negroes initially entered the insurance industry either as unskilled workers (laborers or porters) in white companies or as owners, agents, managers, or other employees of insurers owned by and operated for Negroes. The absolute number as well as the percentage of Negroes employed by insurance companies, however, have remained small since the industry was first penetrated by Negroes. Even though the period since World War II has been characterized by the efforts of a number of major companies to improve their Negro representation and many organizations in the industry currently are actively seeking Negro workers, the status of Negro employment by insurers generally has not been changed. The reasons why this situation still prevails are placed in better perspective by a broad analysis of the history and present status of Negro employment in the insurance industry. The purpose of this chapter is to analyze the extent of Negro employment in the industry prior to 1967.

EARLY NEGRO EMPLOYMENT

Table 8 shows Negro employment during 1940, 1950, and 1960 as reported by the Census Population.[20] In 1940, most of the industry's Negro employment—especially in the white collar categories—probably was provided by Negro owned and/or operated insurers.[21] According to the companies interviewed in connection with this study, Negro employment by white insurance organizations did not begin its ascent until the World War II era. The proportion of Negro workers increased slightly between 1940 —a year when all nonwhite employees were reported as a composite figure—and 1950. This increment was due to various factors, the most significant of which was the extreme war time labor shortage being experienced by all employers. These unusual

---

[20] Prior to the 1940 Census of Population, such statistics were gathered for the insurance and real estate industries as a single category.

[21] See Appendix A for a history of Negro insurance companies.

36

TABLE 8. *Insurance Industry*
Total Employed Persons by Race and Sex,
United States, 1940-1960

Year	All Employees			Male			Female		
	Total	Negro	Percent Negro	Total	Negro	Percent Negro	Total	Negro	Percent Negro
1940	531,900	10,140*	1.9	342,820	7,380*	2.2	189,080	2,760*	1.5
1950	750,720	15,600	2.1	419,460	9,030	2.2	331,260	6,570	2.0
1960	1,072,849	22,474	2.1	585,399	11,170	1.9	487,450	11,304	2.3

Source: *U.S. Census of Population:*

  1940: *The Labor Force,* Industrial Characteristics, Table 1.
  1950: P-E No. 1D, *Industrial Characteristics,* Table 2.
  1960: PC (2) 7F, *Industrial Characteristics,* Table 3.

* Nonwhite employees.

influences were not present beginning in 1950 and consequently, there was no similar appreciable change in Negro employment from 1950 to 1960.

Hence, although the two decades following 1940 resulted in a doubling of the insurance industry's total work force, and Negroes experienced, in absolute terms, increased job opportunities, their share of total employment remained at 2.1 percent between 1950 and 1960. As Table 8 further shows, the only noteworthy percentage gain occurring during 1950 and 1960 was made by Negro females.

The World War II impetus that resulted in the opening to Negroes, for the first time in many cases, of clerical jobs in insurance companies was continued in some states by the enforcement of antidiscrimination legislation. The first such law was enacted by New York. The statute became effective on July 1, 1945 and provided for the creation of the New York State Commission Against Discrimination.[22]

One of the most important products of the Commission's activities is its report on complaints and informal investigations pertaining to the insurance industry's minority employment from July 1, 1945 to September 15, 1958.[23] This study is of significance for three reasons. First, insurers domiciled and/or operating in New York state at that time (and currently also, for that matter) provided a substantial portion of all jobs in the industry, in terms of both home offices and field locations. Second, the report covers years for which little Negro employment data are available from other sources. Finally, the positive influence attributable to the Commission's activities is demonstrated by the improved Negro employment situation at the time the report was rendered.

The Commission processed a total of eighty-one verified complaints and conducted six informal investigations relating to employment discrimination by fifty-five companies or insurance agencies. Forty of the fifty-five accused had only one complaint filed against them and the remaining fifteen had two, three, or four complaints filed against them. By September 15, 1958, seventy-three of the eighty-one verified complaints and all six of the informal investigations had been closed.

---

[22] This Commission is now called the New York State Commission for Human Rights.

[23] New York State Commission Against Discrimination, *The Insurance Industry: Verified Complaints and Informal Investigations Handled by the New York State Commission Against Discrimination, July 1, 1945—September 15, 1958* (New York: The Commission, n.d.).

Of the eighty-one complaints, forty-five (56 percent) involved discrimination because of color.[24] Among the seventy-three complaints that were resolved were forty-two of the forty-five filed on the basis of color. The forty-two were resolved as follows. Probable cause was found in eleven cases (26 percent). No probable cause was found in twelve cases (29 percent). Fifteen (36 percent) of the complaints were discharged with a ruling of an existing discriminatory policy—other than that alleged—having been adjusted. Three complaints (7 percent) were withdrawn and one (2 percent) was deemed to have involved no unlawful practice.

In addition to the numerical analysis of charges of discrimination the Commission's report includes a section on employment trends for twelve insurers and eight agencies. Nine of the twelve corporations were found to have had an increase in Negro employment between July 1, 1945 and September 15, 1958 and the remaining three showed no increase. For seven of the companies that increased Negro employment, the actual change was minimal, averaging little more than six additional black employees per company. Total employment in each of these seven organizations generally exceeded 2,000.

Two of the nine New York companies, however, recorded a substantial improvement in Negro employment during the thirteen year period studied. One, with a total employment of approximately 4,500 added 200 Negroes to its personnel rolls. The second, with a labor force of 2,500 increased its Negro employment by a total of fifty workers.

Progress in other locales was slower than that observed in New York City. A 1952 study of Negro employment in Akron, Ohio, for example, noted that only seventeen of the 1,250 workers employed in banking, finance, insurance, and real estate firms in that city were Negroes and all were engaged as janitors and porters.[25] Similarly, a study of Negro employment in Chattanooga, Tennessee during 1951-1952 revealed that

> three insurance companies have their home offices in Chattanooga and provide a large proportion of the total employment opportunities in finance, real estate and insurance. There are many other insurance and real estate agencies and four banks. Negroes are generally employed in these businesses

---

[24] Other noncolor complaints were based on national origin, creed, and unlawful inquiry.

[25] Akron Committee for A Community Audit, *The Akron Community Audit* (Akron: The Committee, 1952), p. 35.

only for custodial duties, but a significant exception occurs in the Chattanooga branch offices of four Negro life insurance companies. They employ staffs which total about 75 persons, engaged in administrative, clerical, sales and collection work.[26]

Table 9 further reinforces the conclusion that Negro employment in the insurance industry was low and that there was not available a variety of job opportunities. Few Negroes were employed as agents even by 1960. Hence, despite some progress in Negro clerical employment in New York and a few other states, the racial composition of the industry's aggregate employment changed slowly prior to 1960.

TABLE 9. *Insurance Industry*
Male Insurance Agents and Brokers by Race
Selected Standard Metropolitan Statistical Areas
1950-1960

Standard Metropolitan Statistical Area	1950			1960*		
	Total	Negro	Percent Negro	Total	Negro	Percent Negro
Boston	5,671	7	0.1	5,684	13	0.2
Hartford	2,153	1	**	2,301	8	0.3
New York	21,305	199	0.9	20,907	291	1.4
Chicago	13,581	517	3.8	13,059	403	3.1
Detroit	5,278	207	3.9	6,445	253	3.9
Los Angeles—Long Beach	10,948	160	1.5	13,436	164	1.2
San Francisco—Oakland	6,571	131	2.0	6,790	155	2.3
Atlanta	2,235	86	3.8	3,306	93	2.8
Dallas	2,360	86	3.6	3,472	75	2.2
Houston	2,180	86	3.9	2,834	74	2.6

Source: *U.S. Census of Population*

> 1950:   Vol. II, *Characteristics of the Population*, State volumes, Table 77.
>
> 1960:   Vol. I, *Characteristics of the Population*, State volumes, Table 122.

* 1960 includes underwriters.

** Less than 0.05 percent.

---

[26] William H. Wesson, Jr., *Negro Employment Practices in the Chattanooga Area*, NPA Committee of the South, Report No. 6:4 (Washington: National Planning Association, 1954), p. 403.

NEGRO EMPLOYMENT IN 1964

Table 10 is an analysis of 1964 employment data of ninety companies, covering 485 establishments throughout the country. The insurers in the sample are both large and small corporations. In addition, a number of the companies are members of Plans for Progress and therefore pledged to act affirmatively to increase Negro employment. These statistics cannot be strictly compared with the census data presented in the preceding section but are sufficiently representative to indicate the general employment situation for Negroes in the insurance industry in 1964—the year in which Title VII of the Civil Rights Act was enacted, and one year before it became effective.

Table 10 shows a continued paucity of Negroes in the insurers' work force. The total percent Negro employment, however, is somewhat higher in comparison to 1950 and 1960 data (2.8 percent versus 2.1 percent in 1950 and 1960). Table 10 also reveals that female Negro employees were much more prevalent than males and that the majority of all Negro employees were in the blue collar job categories. The number of male Negro employees exceeded the number of female Negroes in the blue collar jobs but were almost nonexistent in the white collar classifications.

Table 11 presents a summary of the 1964 sample by region.[27] These data show that the most favorable employment situation for Negroes in the insurance industry in 1964 was in the Northeast and West Coast areas; the least favorable in the Midwest and South, excepting, of course, the Rocky Mountain area which has a small Negro population.

Within the four regions, the Delaware-District of Columbia-Maryland and New York-New Jersey and California areas had a very high percentage of Negro employment. Delaware-District of Columbia-Maryland had a total 6.4 percent and a 4.1 percent white collar Negro representation. The sample for these three areas is small, however, and undoubtedly heavily weighted by the fact that the District of Columbia is the metropolitan area with the highest Negro population concentration in the country.

New York-New Jersey and California had, respectively, 3.3 and 4.1 percent total Negro employment and 3.3 and 3.4 percent Negro white collar employment. Within the white collar occupations, the ratio of managerial, professional, and technical Negro employees

---

[27] The detailed regional statistics are in Tables B-1 through B-12 of Appendix B.

TABLE 10. Insurance Industry
Employment by Race, Sex, and Occupational Group
90 Companies, 485 Establishments
Total United States
1964

Occupational Group	All Employees			Male			Female		
	Total	Negro	Percent Negro	Total	Negro	Percent Negro	Total	Negro	Percent Negro
Officials and managers	14,882	125	0.8	12,465	9	0.1	2,417	116	4.8
Professionals	14,485	52	0.4	12,970	30	0.2	1,515	22	1.5
Technicians	6,059	94	1.6	4,157	36	0.9	1,902	58	3.0
Sales workers	30,412	122	0.4	30,187	120	0.4	225	2	0.9
Office and clerical	92,160	3,681	4.0	13,694	353	2.6	78,466	3,328	4.2
Total white collar	157,998	4,074	2.6	73,473	548	0.7	84,525	3,526	4.2
Craftsmen	809	14	1.7	730	14	1.9	79	—	—
Operatives	477	20	4.2	446	15	3.4	31	5	16.1
Laborers	218	71	32.6	115	66	57.4	103	5	4.9
Service workers	3,881	443	11.4	1,875	233	12.4	2,006	210	10.5
Total blue collar	5,385	548	10.2	3,166	328	10.4	2,219	220	9.9
Total	163,383	4,622	2.8	76,639	876	1.1	86,744	3,746	4.3

Source: Data in author's possession.

in New Jersey-New York, although still low, was higher than that in most other areas.

New England, with a relatively sparse Negro population, had 1.9 percent Negro employment in white collar occupations and 2.2 percent Negro employment for all categories. In contrast, the more heavily Negro populated area of the Southeast had 0.4 percent Negro white collar employment and 1.1 percent Negro total employment.

The Negro sales representation in the Southeast (1.3 percent) possibly is attributable to the small sample for the area since there were only ten Negroes in this category. Whatever the cause, Negro sales employment in the Southeast exceeded that in New York and New Jersey, but in absolute terms was less than one-tenth of that in these two states. On the other hand, in Texas and Oklahoma, Negro representation was minute despite the concentration of insurers in Dallas and Houston where a substantial proportion of Negroes in the Southwest dwell.

In Pennsylvania, the ratio of Negro employment for both the white collar job categories and total employment was 1.5 percent. As the detailed analysis of the Pennsylvania experience in a later portion of this chapter indicates, however, a substantially higher percentage of Negro employment existed in Philadelphia than in the rest of the state.

The Midwest region includes many states that have a small total population but heavy Negro concentrations in several cities. Separate data for Illinois and Michigan reveal a higher Negro complement than the Midwest as a whole. For example, as is presented in Table 12, there was a 4.6 Negro employment ratio in Detroit insurance establishments in 1966. Nevertheless, the Negro employment for Illinois and Michigan was not as high as in comparable Northeastern or West Coast areas.

Overall, then, the regional data in Table 11 reveal that in 1964 the insurance industry was not a substantial employer of Negroes. Few Negroes held jobs as managers, professionals, technical employees, or salesworkers and consequently most Negro employment was in the clerical group. There were few blue collar employees but of these few, a sizeable percentage were Negroes.

TABLE 11. *Insurance Industry*
Percent Negro Employment
by Occupational Group and Region
1964

Region*	All Employees	Occupational Group							
		White collar						Office & clerical	Total blue collar
		Total	Officials & managers	Profes- sionals	Techni- cians	Sales workers			
Total United States	2.8	2.6	0.8	0.4	1.6	0.4	4.0	10.2
Northeast	3.1	2.9	1.2	0.5	1.4	0.4	4.8	6.1
New England	2.2	1.9	0.1	0.3	0.4	0.1	3.1	13.4
N.J.-N.Y.	3.3	3.3	1.7	0.7	2.7	0.4	5.4	5.0
Pennsylvania	1.5	1.5	0.3	—	0.3	0.8	2.4	14.3
Midwest	1.8	1.6	0.3	0.1	0.7	—	2.3	11.9
Ill. and Mich.	2.5	2.4	0.4	0.1	0.7	—	3.8	3.5
West Coast	3.7	3.1	0.4	0.1	1.1	—	4.2	28.3
California	4.1	3.4	0.5	0.1	1.4	—	4.7	29.1
South	2.1	1.1	0.1	0.3	3.8	1.1	1.3	46.1
Del.-D.C.-Md.	6.4	4.1	0.3	1.1	10.9	—	4.6	65.4

Southeast	1.1	0.4	—	—	1.3	0.4	53.4
Okla. & Texas	0.4	0.3	0.2	—	—	0.3	4.9

Source: Tables in Statistical Appendix B.

* No Negroes found in sample of 1,172 employees for Rocky Mountain states of Arizona, Colorado, Montana, New Mexico, Utah, and Wyoming (the states are included in United States total).

Regional definitions:

Northeast New England (Connecticut, Maine, Massachusetts, New Hampshire, Rhode Island, and Vermont), New Jersey, New York, and Pennsylvania.

Midwest Illinois, Indiana, Iowa, Kansas, Michigan, Minnesota, Missouri, Nebraska, North Dakota, Ohio, South Dakota, and Wisconsin.

West Coast California, Idaho, Nevada, Oregon, and Washington.

South Alabama, Arkansas, Delaware, District of Columbia, Florida, Georgia, Kentucky, Louisiana, Maryland, Mississippi, North Carolina, Oklahoma, South Carolina, Tennessee, Texas, Virginia, and West Virginia.

Southeast South except for Delaware, District of Columbia, Maryland, Oklahoma, and Texas.

NEGRO EMPLOYMENT IN 1966

Data are available on Negro employment in the insurance industry in 1966 on a national basis as a result of studies conducted by the Equal Employment Opportunity Commission (EEOC). The statistical information was obtained from a total sample of 8,247 establishments.

Before proceeding to an analysis of the 1966 EEOC report, it is important to note that although the study, in itself, is exhaustive and statistically reliable, comparisons cannot be made between the 1966 study and the 1964 data discussed in the first part of this chapter nor between the 1966 statistics and the 1967 figures included in the following chapter. The lack of comparability is caused by changes made by the EEOC in the technique insurers were to use in reporting their employment statistics. In 1966, the insurance companies were instructed to include all agents in the report under the occupational category of sales workers. As was explained in Chapter II, most of the salesmen in the industry are independent contractors rather than employees and are not subject to administrative control by their principals in such areas as field employment policies. Consequently, the total employment figures for 1966 are substantially inflated by the inclusion of these independent contractors and the overstatement generally is not offset by a corresponding increment in total Negro employment because the insurers have been unable to effect affirmative hiring practices in their field operations. In 1967 the reporting policy of the EEOC was reversed and the industry was instructed to exclude all independent contractors from the employment data reported in 1967. This modification results in a smaller total employment base to which the number of Negro workers is compared. Hence, an insurer that experienced no change in its total employment nor in its absolute number of Negro employees between 1966 and 1967 would have a higher (and somewhat more realistic) percentage of Negro representation in 1967 as compared to 1966 because of the reduction in the base employment figure reported in 1967. For the same reasons, the 1966 data are not commensurable with those for 1964. The 1964 employment figures, too, exclude all agents that are independent contractors.

Table 13 shows 1966 employment data by occupation for the entire industry. In general, the percent Negro employment in the white collar job classifications reveals little change in the industry's current employment status when compared to that existing

TABLE 12. *Insurance Industry*
Employment by Race and Type of Employment
Selected Standard Metropolitan Statistical Areas
1966

SMSA	All Employees			White Collar			Craftsmen			Blue Collar except Craftsmen		
	Total	Negro	Percent Negro	Total	Negro	Percent Negro	Total	Negro	Percent Negro	Total	Negro	Percent Negro
Boston	24,733	577	2.3	23,868	565	2.4	233	—	—	632	12	1.9
Detroit	10,207	473	4.6	10,023	447	4.5	17	—	—	167	26	15.6
Indianapolis	8,347	197	2.4	8,122	97	1.2	24	2	8.3	201	98	48.8
Pennsylvania: Sum of 6* SMSA's	4,369	26	0.6	4,321	25	0.6	2	—	—	46	1	2.2
Philadelphia	19,394	720	3.7	18,634	473	2.5	78	11	14.1	682	236	34.6
Pittsburgh	4,656	143	3.1	4,324	57	1.3	3	—	—	329	86	26.1
St. Louis	6,042	212	3.5	5,944	177	3.0	16	3	18.8	82	32	39.0

Source: Press releases of, and data compiled by, Equal Employment Opportunity Commission.

* Erie, Harrisburg, Lancaster, Reading, Scranton, and Wilkes-Barre.

TABLE 13. *Insurance Industry*
Employment by Race, Sex, and Occupational Group
United States,[a] *1966*

Occupational Group	All Employees			Male			Female		
	Total	Negro	Percent Negro	Total	Negro	Percent Negro	Total	Negro	Percent Negro
Officials and managers	91,044	1,346	1.5	84,324	1,130	1.3	6,720	216	3.2
Professionals	82,995	401	0.5	77,076	327	0.4	5,919	74	1.3
Technicians	34,430	344	1.0	26,182	208	0.8	8,248	136	1.6
Sales workers	178,621	5,420	3.0	172,904	3,924	2.3	5,717	1,496	26.2
Office and clerical	379,679	13,730	3.6	48,686	2,053	4.2	330,993	11,677	3.5
Total white collar	766,769	21,241	2.8	409,172	7,642	1.9	357,597	13,599	3.8
Craftsmen	3,017	129	4.3	2,678	126	4.7	339	3	0.9
Operatives, laborers, and service workers	17,471	4,415	25.3	10,450	2,954	28.3	7,021	1,461	20.8
Total blue collar	20,488	4,544	22.2	13,128	3,080	23.5	7,360	1,464	19.9
Total	787,257	25,785	3.3	422,300	10,722	2.5	364,957	15,063	4.1

Source: U. S. Equal Employment Opportunity Commission, *Job Patterns for Minorities and Women in Private Industry, 1966.* Report No. 1 (Washington: The Commission, 1968), Part II.

[a] Includes Alaska and Hawaii.

in earlier years. Within the total white collar grouping for 1966 the highest overall Negro employment ratio is in the office and clerical category. In addition, there is a greater percentage of female than male Negro employees in all white collar positions, except office and clerical. Both male and female Negro blue collar employment is substantially higher than that in the white collar categories. In contrast, however, to the white collar situation, the male Negro ratio is higher than the female employee percentage in all blue collar jobs.

Table 14 presents a summary of the 1966 data on a regional basis.[28] According to this tabulation, the most favorable total Negro employment ratios in 1966 were in the Southern and Middle Atlantic states. The ascendency of the South region over the other districts appears to be attributable to the former area's substantial number of blue collar workers. Hence, although total Negro representation is 4.5 percent in the South and 3.8 percent in the Middle Atlantic region, the rankings are reversed when total white collar employment only is analyzed (3.5 percent in the Middle Atlantic region and 3.2 percent in the South). The differential is even more apparent when only the office and clerical job category within the white collar classification is considered. In the clerical category, the Middle Atlantic region leads in Negro employment (5.2 percent), followed by the Far West (4.1 percent), New England (3.1 percent), the South (2.9 percent) and, finally, the Midwest (2.5 percent).

Negro employment in 1966 in the remaining white collar occupations that require higher skill levels still was minimal. And, as is to be expected, the largest concentration of Negro employees in each of the five regions was in the blue collar grouping.

Although, as previously stated, the 1964 and 1966 data are not strictly comparable, certain limited contrasts and similarities in the statistics for the two time periods may be noted. The broad conclusion drawn from such a comparison is that total Negro employment in the insurance industry has risen slightly between 1964 (2.8 percent) and 1966 (3.3 percent). Part of this increment may be due, however, to the increase in total blue collar employment recorded in 1966. Total white collar Negro employment rose by only 0.2 percentage points.

---

[28] The detailed regional statistics are in Tables B-13 through B-17 in Appendix B.

TABLE 14. *Insurance Industry*

Percent Negro Employment by Occupational Group and Region
1966

| | | Occupational Group | | | | | | |
| | | White collar | | | | | | |
Region[a]	All Employees	Total	Officials and managers	Professionals	Technicians	Sales workers	Office and clerical	Total blue collar
Total United States	3.3	2.8	1.5	0.5	1.0	3.0	3.6	22.2
South	4.5	3.2	2.5	0.4	1.2	4.7	2.9	53.5
Middle Atlantic	3.8	3.5	1.1	0.7	1.6	1.8	5.2	10.4
Midwest	2.4	2.1	1.3	0.4	0.6	2.6	2.5	17.4
Far West	2.8	2.6	1.1	0.5	0.8	1.8	4.1	14.3
New England	2.1	1.9	0.2	0.4	0.7	0.2	3.1	7.2

Source: U. S. Equal Employment Opportunity Commission, *Job Patterns for Minorities and Women in Private Industry, 1966.* Report No. 1 (Washington: The Commission, 1968), Part II.

[a] Geographic definitions are as follows:

South: Alabama, Arkansas, Delaware, District of Columbia, Florida, Georgia, Kentucky, Louisiana, Maryland, Mississippi, North Carolina, Oklahoma, South Carolina, Tennessee, Texas, Virginia, and West Virginia.

Middle Atlantic: New Jersey, New York, and Pennsylvania.

Midwest: Indiana, Illinois, Iowa, Kansas, Michigan, Minnesota, Missouri, Nebraska, North Dakota, Ohio, South Dakota, and Wisconsin.

Far West: Alaska, California, Colorado, Hawaii, Idaho, Montana, Nevada, New Mexico, Oregon, Utah, Washington, and Wyoming.

New England: Connecticut, Maine, Massachusetts, New Hampshire, Rhode Island, and Vermont.

Additional statistically valid comparisons between the data cannot be made. The sample for the 1966 analysis is much broader than the base for the 1964 study (respectively, 8,247 versus 485 establishments). Further distortion occurs because, as explained above, the employment figures for the two periods were not reported on a parallel base. Consequently the only conclusions that may be drawn are the very limited ones stated above and these do not vary significantly from the industry's employment pattern as observed from data of previous years.

CHAPTER IV

Negro Employment in the Insurance Industry in 1967

It is the purpose of this chapter to analyze the current Negro employment situation within the insurance industry on three broad bases: regionally, by Standard Metropolitan Statistical Areas (SMSA's),[29] and by individual companies. Each of these three bases is further refined to reveal, if possible, employment (1) in consolidated (i.e., all) locations, (2) in home offices, (3) in field offices, and (4) by occupational groups.

Insofar as possible, two statistical measures are applied to each of the three bases: (1) percent Negro to total employees and (2) percent changes in Negro employment.

One measure emphasized in the vast majority of tables in this chapter and in Appendix C [30] is the percentage of Negro employees in a given company's work force. It is immediately clear, of course, that there are significant defects in the accuracy of this measure. For example, if there are only ten employable Negroes in the geographic radius of a firm with 10,000 workers, and all ten are hired by the company, Negroes represent only 0.1 percent of the company's work force. If, however, these same conditions prevailed, with the exception of a geographic concentration of 5,000 employable Negroes, the ten Negro employees still would represent 0.1 percent of the insurer's work force. The fallacy, of course, is that in the first situation 100.0 percent of the area Negroes are employed, while in the second set of circumstances only 0.2 percent of the black community has been hired.

As is true of the percent Negro workers to total employees, percent changes in Negro employment from one time interval to another within a company or an entire industry has limitations.

---

[29] A Standard Metropolitan Statistical Area is defined as a city of at least 50,000 population and its contiguous metropolitan area.

[30] Each summary table in this chapter is based on a corresponding detailed tabulation which is included in Appendix C.

An insurer that hires one Negro employee in 1966 and a second in 1967 records a 100 percent increase in Negro employment between the two years. On the other hand, a company with the same number of employees as the first firm, and in the same geographic location, and which hires fifty Negro workers in 1966 and an additional five in 1967 experiences only a 10.0 percent increase in Negro employees. Yet, the second firm is accomplishing much more in the way of Negro employment in absolute terms than the first company.

Despite the inherent limitation, and because it is desirable to include in this analysis all feasible breakdowns of the data gathered on Negro employment in the insurance industry, a discussion of percent changes is included in the final portion of this chapter.

TOTAL NEGRO EMPLOYMENT

Tables 15 and 16 show the 1967 aggregate percent Negro employment among all insurers interviewed on the basis of three areas of operation: consolidated, home office, and field.

Aggregate Employment

According to Table 15, total Negro employment was 3.5 percent on a consolidated basis, 6.6 percent in the aggregate home offices, and 2.8 percent in the combined field offices. The 1967 consolidated figure, it should be noted, is very close to the corresponding 1966 figure: 3.3 percent.

Home office Negro employment for all insurers in 1967 was higher than in the other two areas of operation. Consolidated locations held the second highest position (3.5 percent) and field offices were last (2.8 percent).

In terms of categorizations by sex, there were more Negro female employees in all areas of operation than Negro male workers. Home office percentages for both males and females (4.9 and 7.7 percent, respectively) were higher than the percentages for the remaining two locales. Although the second highest female Negro employment percentage was in the consolidated category (4.8 percent) and was followed by the field classification (3.2 percent), male Negro employment in the combined field offices and in the consolidated grouping was 2.5 percent.

Finally, it is of interest to note that the percentages of Negro female workers exceeded all corresponding figures in the aggregate

TABLE 15. *Insurance Industry*
Employment by Race, Sex, and Area of Operation
United States, 1967

Area of Operation	Number of Companies	All Employees			Male			Female		
		Total	Negro	Percent Negro	Total	Negro	Percent Negro	Total	Negro	Percent Negro
Consolidated[a]	36	220,832	7,825	3.5	120,921	3,033	2.5	99,911	4,792	4.8
Home Office	26	48,927	3,215	6.6	19,107	927	4.9	29,820	2,288	7.7
Field	20	65,603	1,859	2.8	36,011	914	2.5	29,592	945	3.2

Source: Tables in Statistical Appendix C.

[a] Includes all geographic locations in which a company operates.

TABLE 15a. *Insurance Industry*
Employment by Race, Sex, and Area of Operation
17 Companies,[a] *United States, 1967*

Area of Operation	All Employees			Male			Female		
	Total	Negro	Percent Negro	Total	Negro	Percent Negro	Total	Negro	Percent Negro
Consolidated[b]	93,602	4,080	4.4	46,449	1,590	3.4	47,153	2,490	5.3
Home Office	32,248	2,291	7.1	12,759	701	5.5	19,489	1,590	8.2
Field	61,354	1,789	2.9	33,690	889	2.6	27,664	900	3.3

Source: Tables in Statistical Appendix C.

[a] Companies with data for all *three* areas of operation.

[b] Includes all geographic locations in which a company operates

employment classification and ranged from a high of 7.7 percent to a low of 3.2.

Table 15a presents a smaller group of seventeen companies. These companies reported data for each area of operation. The percent Negro employment follows the same pattern as the larger group: home office having the highest percent, 7.1, followed by consolidated with 4.4 percent, and field area the smallest, 2.9 percent. All percentages shown in Table 15a are higher than those in the larger group in Table 15.

Aggregate Employment by Occupational Groups

A more detailed analysis of some of the data in Table 15 appears in Table 16. The latter tabulation is a breakdown of the data by area of operation and sex in each of seven occupational groupings, where available.

In broad terms, total blue collar Negro employment within the industry in 1967 was much higher in all classifications than total white collar Negro employment. This situation is a reflection of the still-prevalent tendency of insurers of viewing Negroes primarily as potential maintenance type workers.

The white collar occupation with the highest percent Negro employment for all three areas of operation is the office and clerical category. This also is true when the male-female classifications are analyzed. In terms of a specific locale, the highest figures are in the home office classification of office and clerical workers.

Using the smaller sample shown in Table 16a, the same pattern prevails.

NEGRO EMPLOYMENT BY REGIONS

Negro employment in the insurance industry varies not only by area of operation but also by geographic location. For the purpose of determining these differences, data were obtained from insurers domiciled in five regions: East, Midwest, Mountain states, Pacific Coast, and South. Table 17 includes the results of this analysis for all areas except the Mountain states.[31] Each regional

---

[31] The Mountain states are excluded because of insufficient information. The inadequacy of data for this region is not due, however, to lack of industry cooperation. Rather, the necessity of acquiring statistical information applicable to comparable time periods forced a curtailment of the number of interviews with corporations in this area. The data actually obtained, therefore, are not representative of the companies domiciled in the mountain states region.

TABLE 16. *Insurance Industry*
Percent Negro Employment by Sex,
Occupational Group, and Area of Operation
United States, 1967

Occupational Group	Area of Operation	All Employees	Male	Female
Officials and managers	Consolidated	0.4	0.3	0.8
	Home Office	0.4	0.3	1.4
	Field	0.2	0.2	0.3
Professionals	Consolidated	0.5	0.5	0.4
	Home Office	0.7	0.7	0.8
	Field	0.5	0.5	0.4
Technicians	Consolidated	1.2	1.3	1.2
	Home Office	2.7	2.6	2.8
	Field	1.5	1.5	1.5
Sales workers	Consolidated	1.8	1.8	1.1
	Home Office	0.8	1.4	—
	Field	2.3	2.4	0.6
Office and clerical	Consolidated	5.1	6.8	4.9
	Home Office	8.1	8.8	7.9
	Field	3.3	4.7	3.2
Total white collar	Consolidated	3.0	1.7	4.6
	Home Office	5.8	3.3	7.3
	Field	2.2	1.5	2.9
Craftsmen	Consolidated	6.3	7.1	—
	Home Office	3.1	4.1	—
	Field	41.0	41.0	—
Operatives, laborers, and service workers	Consolidated	22.1	27.5	14.0
	Home Office	25.5	24.4	27.6
	Field	39.0	43.4	28.9
Total blue collar	Consolidated	20.0	23.7	13.4
	Home Office	22.3	21.1	24.6
	Field	39.1	43.2	28.9
Total*	Consolidated	3.5	2.5	4.8
	Home Office	6.7	4.9	7.8
	Field	2.9	2.6	3.3

Source: Tables in Statistical Appendix C.

* Consolidated, 29 companies; Home office, 23; Field, 17.

TABLE 16a. *Insurance Industry*
Percent Negro Employment by Sex,
Occupational Group, and Area of Operation
United States, 1967

Occupational Group	Area of Operation	All Employees	Male	Female
Officials and managers	Consolidated	0.3	0.3	0.7
	Home Office	0.6	0.4	1.7
	Field	0.2	0.2	0.3
Professionals	Consolidated	0.6	0.6	0.5
	Home Office	0.8	0.9	0.5
	Field	0.5	0.5	0.4
Technicians	Consolidated	1.7	2.0	1.1
	Home Office	1.7	2.2	0.9
	Field	1.5	1.5	1.5
Sales workers	Consolidated	2.2	2.3	0.5
	Home Office	0.7	1.3	—
	Field	2.3	2.4	0.6
Office and clerical	Consolidated	5.6	7.4	5.4
	Home Office	8.5	8.8	8.5
	Field	3.3	4.7	3.2
Total white collar	Consolidated	3.5	2.1	4.9
	Home Office	6.3	3.9	7.8
	Field	2.2	1.5	2.9
Craftsmen	Consolidated	12.2	16.5	—
	Home Office	2.8	4.2	—
	Field	41.0	41.0	—
Operatives, laborers, and service workers	Consolidated	28.5	30.9	23.6
	Home Office	21.6	22.1	20.6
	Field	39.0	43.4	28.9
Total blue collar	Consolidated	26.8	29.3	21.7
	Home Office	19.2	19.9	18.0
	Field	39.1	43.2	28.9
Total*	Consolidated	4.4	3.4	5.3
	Home Office	7.1	5.5	8.2
	Field	2.9	2.6	3.3

Source: Tables in Statistical Appendix C.

* 17 Companies with data for each area of operation.

tabulation contains three categories of percent Negro employment: consolidated, home office, and field.

Aggregate Regional Employment

The first step in determining the percentage of Negro employment for the three classifications within each area in Table 17 is the regional categorization of all insurers interviewed on the basis of the location of their corporate headquarters.

Consolidated Analysis. Table 17 reveals some employment patterns that generally are known to exist and others that perhaps are not anticipated. Total percent Negro employment is highest in the South (4.4 percent). The southern region is followed by the East (3.9 percent), then the Pacific Coast states (2.4 percent), and finally the Midwest, which has the lowest percentage of Negro employees (1.9 percent). The same pattern prevails when consolidated employment is analyzed by sex.

The percentages shown on Table 17a for companies reporting data for all three areas of operation follow the same pattern: total percent Negro employment is highest in the South (4.9 percent), slightly less in the East (4.7 percent), and lowest in the Midwest (2.8 percent). Again—as in Tables 15 and 15a—these percentages are slightly higher than those shown on Table 17 for the larger samples.

In addition to showing that the South has the highest Negro employment rate, Table 17 also reveals that the consolidated percent total Negro employment rate in the South is over twice that in the Midwest. A similar trend generally is observed in the male-female breakdown.

The pattern shown by the smaller group (Table 17a) follows the larger sample; but the gap between the percentages in the South and Midwest is smaller for total and male employees.

Several factors might possibly explain the ascendency of the South and why there is a large gap between the statistics in the latter area and in the Midwest.

One conceivable reason is based on the employment figures reported by each company. The data encompass all employees in all types of jobs—from executive to service positions. This system of reporting consolidated employment figures has a two-fold impact. First, most southern insurers employ their own building maintenance workers (along with cafeteria or janitorial personnel), especially in the home office areas. These workers usually are Negroes. In the East and Midwest, on the other hand, the

TABLE 17. Insurance Industry

Percent Negro Employment by Sex, Area of Operation, and Region
1967

Region[b]	Number of Companies	Area of Operation								
		Consolidated[a]			Home Office			Field		
		Total	Male	Female	Total	Male	Female	Total	Male	Female
East	14	3.9	2.4	5.7	7.7	5.1	9.5	3.1	2.6	3.5
Midwest	9	1.9	1.9	1.9	4.5	3.1	5.3	1.8	1.4	2.2
Pacific Coast	4	2.4	c	c	3.1	c	c	2.3	c	c
South	6	4.4	3.8	6.0	8.9	8.9	8.9	3.5	3.3	4.8
Total All Regions	33	3.4	c	c	6.5	c	c	2.8	c	c
Total All Regions less Pacific Coast	29	3.5	2.5	4.8	6.7	4.9	7.8	2.9	2.6	3.3

Source: Computed from tables in Statistical Appendix C.

[a] Includes all geographic locations in which a company operates.

[b] Geographic definitions are as follows:

East: Connecticut, Maine, Massachusetts, New Hampshire, New Jersey, New York, Pennsylvania, Rhode Island, and Vermont.

Midwest: Illinois, Indiana, Iowa, Kansas, Michigan, Minnesota, Missouri, Nebraska, North Dakota, Ohio, South Dakota, and Wisconsin.

Pacific Coast: California, Oregon, and Washington.

South: Alabama, Arkansas, Delaware, District of Columbia, Florida, Georgia, Kentucky, Louisiana, Maryland, Mississippi, North Carolina, Oklahoma, South Carolina, Tennessee, Texas, Virginia, and West Virginia.

c No data available.

TABLE 17a. *Insurance Industry*

Percent Negro Employment by Sex, Area of Operation, and Region
17 Companies, 1967

	Consolidated[a]			Home Office			Field		
Region[b]	All Employees	Male	Female	All Employees	Male	Female	All Employees	Male	Female
East	4.7	3.4	5.8	8.0	5.0	10.1	3.1	2.6	3.5
Midwest	2.8	2.4	3.1	4.3	4.4	4.2	1.8	1.4	2.2
South	4.9	4.2	6.8	8.1	8.9	7.7	3.5	3.3	4.8
Total	4.4	3.4	5.3	7.1	5.5	8.2	2.9	2.6	3.3

Area of Operation

Source: Computed from tables in Statistical Appendix C.

Note: 17 Companies, each reporting data in all areas of operation.

[a] Includes all geographic locations in which a company operates.

[b] For geographic definitions see Table 17.

majority of the insurers let contracts for this type work to building maintenance firms whose employees, of course, are not employees of insurers. Hence, these traditional Negro work areas
boost the number of Negro employees on the payroll of many
southern insurers but do not affect the proportion of Negroes
hired by midwestern corporations. This situation is emphasized
in greater detail in later sections which analyze Negro employment by job categories.

A second aspect pertinent to the total employment figures reported by insurance companies concerns each life company's
agency system. In delineating among the categories of life insurance, it was noted in Chapter II that one subdivision is industrial
(or debit) life insurance. The industrial insurance salesmen
(who frequently are referred to as "debit men") are considered
to be employees rather than agents. As employees, therefore,
these salesmen are included in the total employment figures of
the insurers whom they represent. The importance of this fact
becomes obvious once it is realized that the product of many of
the life insurers domiciled in the South is either predominantly
or exclusively industrial insurance. Since Negroes represent one
of the largest consumer groups that purchase industrial insurance,
many industrial-oriented insurers engage Negroes as salesmen.
Although there are midwestern companies that also market the
industrial product to some degree, the total number of potential
consumers (i.e., low income, usually Negroes) is not as great in
the East and Midwest as in the South. Insurers domiciled in the
East and Midwest thus find their need is not as great as that of
the southern companies for Negro salesmen *that are charged primarily with soliciting in Negro markets*. This factor alone would
cause insurers in the eastern and midwestern states to have a
lower percentage of Negro employees than southern insurance
companies.

A third, and intangible, factor that may explain the different
employment situation between insurers domiciled in the Midwest
and South is the recognition by the larger southern insurers of
the public (as well as governmental) scrutiny they are increasingly receiving. Most of the corporate executives interviewed
expressed great concern about their individual company's public
image and the extent to which it is adversely affected by being
categorized as a "southern company." This sensitivity especially
is evident among those insurers that wish to expand their operations to additional, nonsouthern, states. On the other hand, and

with significant exceptions, insurance companies headquartered in the Midwest seem to be less concerned about their public image with respect to Negro employment. Perhaps, as one executive noted, the insurers in this region have been "under fire" so much longer than their southern counterparts, and have tried to satisfy critics for as equally a long time, that the "revolutionary fires" of many midwestern insurers have been extinguished. This is not meant to imply, however, that insurance companies domiciled in the Midwest do not follow nondiscriminatory hiring practices or do not engage in extensive Negro recruiting and training programs; rather, they generally have not increased the existing number of such practices or been impelled to launch a "crash program" in hiring Negroes.

Whether one agrees or disagrees with the midwestern attitude is irrelevant. Further, it is impossible to assess how effective, in the long run, the southern insurers' approach will be as compared to that adopted by corporations in the Midwest. Still, intangible as it is, the attitude of insurers in a given locale toward public criticism of the companies' employment practices will influence Negro employment in that area.

Finally, the proximity of the eastern (3.9) and southern (4.4) percent Negro employment rates should be noted. (These percentages are even closer when the smaller sample is used, 4.7 and 4.9.) The general ascendency of insurers in the eastern region is not unexpected. The oldest, and largest, insurance companies are concentrated along the eastern seaboard. These insurers long ago captured a substantial part of the entire market for all types of insurance and their financial conditions generally are exceptional. In most cases, this established status has permitted the companies to develop a "social conscience." That is, the insurers have both the resources and desire (i.e., sense of obligation) not only to advocate Negro employment actively but also to hire so-called "unemployable" Negroes and provide the training necessary to improve their skills and abilities. This employment philosophy is especially (but not solely) applicable to life insurers whose operations, at this point, are substantially more profitably than those of property-liability insurers. Eastern life insurance companies are further aided in their relatively expensive Negro employment and training programs if they are mutual corporations. A stock insurer, which is the legal form of the vast majority of these corporations, cannot divert profits to somewhat intangible minority group employment programs as easily as can mutual companies. The owners of stock corporations (stockholders) tend to be more vocal in their insistence on minimizing operating expenses than are the owners of mutual insurers (policyholders).

The above analysis completely omits, however, the positive employment effects brought about by the very strong commitment of the executives of some eastern insurers to making equal employment opportunity a reality as well as a slogan [32] and the effects of the various states' nondiscriminatory employment laws. The presence of an attitude such as this former type and the influence of these state laws further enhance the extent of Negro employment in the East.

Home Office and Field Analysis. The percent total Negro employment for the corporate headquarters of insurers located in the South is 8.9 percent and is somewhat higher than the corresponding figure (7.7 percent) for home offices on the eastern seaboard. Both percentages are substantially higher than those in the Midwest (4.5 percent) or on the Pacific Coast (3.1 percent). The aggregate home office figures for all four regions, however, are significantly larger than their consolidated counterparts. (The smaller sample maintains the same relationship.) To some extent, and as was explained earlier, this is due to the southern corporations' traditional hiring practices and the eastern establishments' social philosophy, market strength, and legal form of organization. The relatively high eastern home office total Negro employment also is due to another, perhaps equally important, influence: the racial mixture of the available work force from which employees are drawn. Most of the insurers whose headquarters are in the East are located in center city, as opposed to suburban, areas. A sizable proportion of the populace in all but a few of these urban areas is Negro. The universe from which the insurers attract their home office employees, therefore, is so structured that a somewhat high percent of Negro employees is a natural development.

In general, the total home office Negro employment pattern is repeated in the corresponding male-female categories. The greatest concentration of Negro male employees is in the South and is attributable primarily to the number of Negroes in maintenance and service type positions. The largest percentage of Negro female employees, however, occurs in the East. (Again, the smaller

[32] Such sentiments are not confined to the eastern part of the United States. Nondiscriminatory employment policies were emphatically endorsed by at least some of the insurers interviewed in all the regions.

sample follows the same pattern.) Again, this is the result of the eastern insurers' social philosophy and the racial mixture of the companies' available work force.

Negro representation in the insurers' field locations is not as favorable as that in their corporate headquarters. This is true not only for the total Negro employment figures but also for Negro male-female employment. It is also of interest to note that the southern companies claim the highest percentage of total Negroes, although the percentages for two of the four regions fall within the same broad range.

The wide gap between the eastern insurers' total and female Negro home office and field employment primarily is attributable, as has been explained in Chapter II, to the formidable difficulties associated with long range enforcement of nondiscriminatory hiring practices. A disparity similar to that characterizing the eastern companies occurs in the South and Midwest. As already emphasized, such home office-field differences are due both to the maintenance type jobs that are more common to home than field offices and the supervision of the hiring practices in field locations.

The insurers headquartered in the Pacific Coast states deviate somewhat from the patterns established by inspection of total Negro employment figures for the other three regions. That is, although the percent total Negro employment figure is larger in the home office than the field category, the difference is not as great as between the other regions. There is no readily acceptable explanation for this variation. It cannot be rationalized in terms of corporate social philosophy or type of product marketed or type of agency system adopted. The only interpretations of the data that appear to be credible are as follows. First, the Negro market on the West Coast may be more attractive than that in the other regions because of generally higher Negro income levels in the Pacific Coast area. In 1964, for example, the median Negro (nonwhite) family income was $5,774 in the Pacific Coast area, $4,943 in the Northeast, $5,063 in the Midwest, and $2,898 in the South. According to various studies released by the Bureau of the Census, this pattern has occurred consistently in the past.[33] As a result, more Negroes may be hired in nonsales positions in an attempt to develop an awareness of the insurance product within the potential Negro market. A second reason for the unusual pattern is that the information obtained may be based on a

---

[33] U. S. Bureau of Labor Statistics, *The Negroes in the United States: Their Economic and Social Situation*, Bulletin No. 1511 (June 1966), 35, 139.

sample response that is not representative of actual home office and/or field employment.

Regional Employment by Job Categories

Negro employment by job categories (occupational group) for insurers domiciled in the various geographic regions generally follows the pattern that has been suggested in the preceding discussion. This section contains an analysis of the eastern, midwestern, and southern employment patterns in seven occupational groups. Statistics for total and male-female employment on a consolidated, home office, and field basis are included. Data were obtained from insurers located in the Mountain and Pacific Coast states but are not included in the regional analyses because the figures are insufficient for analytical purposes.

Consolidated Analysis. Table 18 shows that in each of the three regions the total and male-female percent Negro employment measures are generally the highest in the two blue collar categories (operatives, laborers, and service workers, and craftsmen).[34] The third position most heavily populated with Negro employees is office and clerical. Using the smaller sample, companies with data in all three areas of operation, the operatives, etc. are the highest in all three areas but the craftsmen only in the East.

Eastern corporations generally lead in the percent total Negro employee classifications of professional, office and clerical, and craftsmen. Data for the remaining four job categories reveal a more heterogeneous pattern. For example, the highest Negro total employment percentage in the technicians class, in the officials and managers, and in the sales workers is in the Midwest. The operatives, laborers, and service workers group is dominated by the South.

If the smaller sample had been used, the East would still dominate in the professional, office and clerical, craftsmen; and the technicians in the Midwest. The officials and managers and sales workers would shift to the South where the operatives, laborers, and service workers remained dominant.

Insurers domiciled in the South and in the East have the lowest percent Negro employment in the three regions—the South in of-

---

[34] The operatives, laborers, and service workers classification is a combination of three of the categories in the EEO-1 form referred to as operatives (semiskilled), laborers (unskilled), and service workers. The aggregation was made as a simplifying measure because of the relatively small number of employees in the insurance industry engaged in these capacities.

ficials and managers, professionals, and craftsmen, in the East, technicians, sales workers, and operatives, laborers, and service workers. Office and clerical workers were lowest in the Midwest.

Using the smaller group, the only changes would be two shifts to the Midwest: the officials and managers group from the South, and sales workers from the East.

The consolidated percent male-female Negro employment groupings follow no specific pattern. Each region has the largest figure in both the male and female classification in three job categories. With respect to consolidated Negro male employment, the Midwest region prevails in three job categories, the East and South in two. The highest percentages for consolidated Negro female employment, however, are divided among the three geographic areas: three in the East, two in the South, and one in the Midwest. There were no Negro female craftsmen.

The consolidated total Negro employment data for all three regions, it should be noted, fall within the same general range in the white collar categories except in the office and clerical classification. Negro clerical personnel in the eastern region are approximately three times more prevalent than in the Midwest and nearly one-third greater than in the South.

Home Office Analysis. As has been observed in preceding discussions, the total and male-female percent Negro employment in home offices frequently exceed the same measures in the consolidated and field categories. Table 18 demonstrates this pattern for total and male-female Negro employment in white collar jobs in the three regions with three major exceptions: (1) the percent Negro employment in the technician category in the East is lower for male employment and in the Midwest for female employment in the home office than in the field classification; (2) the ratios for sales workers in the South and Midwest are higher in the consolidated and in the field area for total and for male employment, and in the East for female employment than in the home office; (3) officials and managers in the Midwest consolidated total and male employment are higher than in the home office but in the field area only the males are higher.

It also is of interest to note that the eastern region's home office percent total Negro employment exceeds that of the other regions in two job categories—professionals and office and clerical.

Field Analysis. Finally, Table 18 shows the field percent Negro employment by job categories in the East, Midwest, and South.

TABLE 18. *Insurance Industry*
Percent Negro Employment by Sex, Occupational Group,
Area of Operation, and Region
1967

Occupational Group	Area of Operation	Total United States[a]			EAST[a]		
		Total	Male	Female	Total	Male	Female
Officials and managers	Consolidated	0.4	0.3	0.8	0.3	0.3	0.7
	Home Office	0.4	0.3	1.4	0.4	0.4	1.0
	Field	0.2	0.2	0.3	0.3	0.3	0.4
Professionals	Consolidated	0.5	0.5	0.4	0.6	0.6	0.4
	Home Office	0.7	0.7	0.8	0.8	0.8	0.8
	Field	0.5	0.5	0.4	0.6	0.6	0.4
Technicians	Consolidated	1.2	1.3	1.2	1.2	1.1	1.2
	Home Office	2.7	2.6	2.8	1.9	1.6	3.0
	Field	1.5	1.5	1.5	1.5	3.4	0.9
Sales workers	Consolidated	1.8	1.8	1.1	1.6	1.7	1.3
	Home Office	0.8	1.4	—	2.4	3.9	—
	Field	2.3	2.4	0.6	2.0	2.2	0.6
Office and clerical	Consolidated	5.1	6.8	4.9	6.3	6.8	6.2
	Home Office	8.1	8.8	7.9	9.7	8.2	10.1
	Field	3.3	4.7	3.2	3.7	4.3	3.7
Total white collar	Consolidated	3.0	1.7	4.6	3.6	1.8	5.7
	Home Office	5.8	3.3	7.3	7.2	3.9	9.3
	Field	2.2	1.5	2.9	2.4	1.4	3.3
Craftsmen	Consolidated	6.3	7.1	—	6.9	8.0	—
	Home Office	3.1	4.1	—	2.8	4.1	—
	Field	41.0	41.0	—	45.3	45.3	—
Operatives, laborers, and service workers	Consolidated	22.1	27.5	14.0	13.7	19.0	6.7
	Home Office	25.5	24.4	27.6	14.9	14.3	16.1
	Field	39.0	43.4	28.9	28.6	35.2	15.4
Total blue collar	Consolidated	20.0	23.7	13.4	12.7	12.7	6.4
	Home Office	22.3	21.1	24.6	13.0	12.6	13.7
	Field	39.1	43.2	28.9	30.1	36.5	15.4
Total[b]	Consolidated	3.5	2.5	4.8	3.9	2.4	5.7
	Home Office	6.7	4.9	7.8	7.7	5.1	9.5
	Field	2.9	2.6	3.3	3.1	2.6	3.5

TABLE 18. *Insurance Industry*
Percent Negro Employment by Sex, Occupational Group,
Area of Operation, and Region
1967
(Continued)

Occupational Group	Area of Operation	MIDWEST[a]			SOUTH[a]		
		Total	Male	Female	Total	Male	Female
Officials and managers	Consolidated	0.5	0.4	1.1	0.3	0.3	—
	Home Office	0.3	—	2.7	0.8	0.9	—
	Field	0.1	0.2	—	0.2	0.2	—
Professionals	Consolidated	0.4	0.4	0.2	0.2	0.2	—
	Home Office	0.7	0.7	0.9	0.2	0.2	—
	Field	0.4	0.4	—	—	—	—
Technicians	Consolidated	1.6	2.0	0.5	1.4	1.1	1.6
	Home Office	3.1	3.1	3.1	1.4	1.2	1.6
	Field	1.6	1.0	4.3	—	—	—
Sales workers	Consolidated	2.7	2.7	—	1.9	2.0	—
	Home Office	2.3	2.3	—	—	—	—
	Field	—	—	—	2.5	2.5	—
Office and clerical	Consolidated	2.1	5.3	1.9	4.4	8.7	3.7
	Home Office	6.0	10.8	5.6	7.7	9.6	7.2
	Field	2.5	8.9	2.3	1.1	—	1.2
Total white collar	Consolidated	1.6	1.4	1.9	2.4	2.0	3.4
	Home Office	4.1	2.1	5.3	5.8	4.1	6.6
	Field	1.5	0.8	2.1	2.0	2.1	1.2
Craftsmen	Consolidated	4.4	4.5	—	4.2	4.2	—
	Home Office	2.3	2.3	—	6.5	6.7	—
	Field	—	—	—	—	—	—
Operatives, laborers, and service workers	Consolidated	23.2	29.9	9.3	68.2	62.5	82.8
	Home Office	29.1	39.1	5.5	69.6	59.2	87.4
	Field	55.7	61.8	33.3	61.5	57.6	73.1
Total blue collar	Consolidated	19.8	23.7	9.2	66.2	60.0	82.8
	Home Office	25.2	31.8	5.5	64.4	52.8	86.7
	Field	50.0	54.0	33.3	61.5	57.6	73.1
Total[b]	Consolidated	1.9	1.9	1.9	4.4	3.8	6.0
	Home Office	4.5	3.1	5.3	8.9	8.9	8.9
	Field	1.8	1.4	2.2	3.5	3.3	4.8

Source: Table 16 and Tables in Statistical Appendix C.

[a] For geographic definitions see Table 17.

[b] Consolidated, 29 companies; Home Office, 23; and Field, 17.

TABLE 18a. *Insurance Industry*
Percent Negro Employment by Sex, Occupational Group,
Area of Operation, and Region
1967

Occupational Group	Area of Operation	Total United States[a]			EAST[a]		
		Total	Male	Female	Total	Male	Female
Officials and managers	Consolidated	0.3	0.3	0.7	0.3	0.3	0.6
	Home Office	0.6	0.4	1.7	0.5	0.4	1.1
	Field	0.2	0.2	0.3	0.3	0.3	0.4
Professionals	Consolidated	0.6	0.6	0.5	0.7	0.7	0.5
	Home Office	0.8	0.9	0.5	0.8	0.9	0.5
	Field	0.5	0.5	0.4	0.6	0.6	0.4
Technicians	Consolidated	1.7	2.0	1.1	1.2	1.3	1.0
	Home Office	1.7	2.2	0.9	1.1	1.1	1.2
	Field	1.5	1.5	1.5	1.5	3.4	0.9
Sales workers	Consolidated	2.2	2.3	0.5	2.0	2.2	0.6
	Home Office	0.7	1.3	—	2.4	3.9	—
	Field	2.3	2.4	0.6	2.0	2.2	0.6
Office and clerical	Consolidated	5.6	7.4	5.4	6.4	6.9	6.4
	Home Office	8.5	8.8	8.5	10.5	8.4	11.2
	Field	3.3	4.7	3.2	3.7	4.3	3.7
Total white collar	Consolidated	3.5	2.1	4.9	4.2	2.2	5.7
	Home Office	6.3	3.9	7.8	7.8	4.2	10.3
	Field	2.2	1.5	2.9	2.4	1.4	3.3
Craftsmen	Consolidated	12.2	16.5	—	14.4	20.9	—
	Home Office	2.8	4.2	—	3.0	5.2	—
	Field	41.0	41.0	—	45.3	45.3	—
Operatives, laborers, and service workers	Consolidated	28.5	30.9	23.6	17.5	20.9	11.3
	Home Office	21.6	22.1	20.6	10.8	11.8	9.0
	Field	39.0	43.4	28.9	28.6	35.2	15.4
Total blue collar	Consolidated	26.8	29.3	21.7	17.1	20.9	10.1
	Home Office	19.2	19.9	18.0	9.7	11.0	7.6
	Field	39.1	43.2	28.9	30.1	36.5	15.4
Total[b]	Consolidated	4.4	3.4	5.3	4.7	3.4	5.8
	Home Office	7.1	5.5	8.2	8.0	5.0	10.1
	Field	2.9	2.6	3.3	3.1	2.6	3.5

TABLE 18a. *Insurance Industry*
Percent Negro Employment by Sex, Occupational Group,
Area of Operation, and Region
1967
(Continued)

Occupational Group	Area of Operation	MIDWEST[a]			SOUTH[a]		
		Total	Male	Female	Total	Male	Female
Officials	Consolidated	0.3	0.1	1.3	0.4	0.4	—
and	Home Office	0.5	—	3.4	1.1	1.2	—
managers	Field	0.1	0.2	—	0.2	0.2	—
	Consolidated	0.6	0.6	0.4	0.2	0.2	—
Professionals	Home Office	1.1	1.2	0.7	0.2	0.2	—
	Field	0.4	0.4	—	—	—	—
	Consolidated	2.1	2.8	0.7	1.7	2.0	1.6
Technicians	Home Office	2.3	3.6	—	1.7	2.0	1.6
	Field	1.6	1.0	4.3	—	—	—
	Consolidated	—	—	—	2.4	2.5	—
Sales workers	Home Office	—	—	—	—	—	—
	Field	—	—	—	2.5	2.5	—
Office	Consolidated	3.5	9.4	3.2	5.2	9.0	4.5
and	Home Office	4.8	9.8	4.4	6.8	9.7	6.0
clerical	Field	2.5	8.9	2.3	1.1	—	1.2
Total	Consolidated	2.3	1.2	3.0	3.0	2.5	4.2
white	Home Office	3.5	2.2	4.2	5.2	4.7	5.5
collar	Field	1.5	0.8	2.1	2.0	2.1	1.2
	Consolidated	2.4	2.4	—	—	—	—
Craftsmen	Home Office	2.9	2.9	—	—	—	—
	Field	—	—	—	—	—	—
Operatives,	Consolidated	37.8	46.3	12.9	63.9	56.9	80.2
laborers, and	Home Office	31.7	40.7	7.3	66.7	55.9	86.2
service workers	Field	55.7	61.8	33.3	61.5	57.6	73.1
Total	Consolidated	33.1	38.9	12.9	62.2	54.8	80.2
blue	Home Office	27.6	33.7	7.3	63.1	51.4	86.2
collar	Field	50.0	54.0	33.3	61.5	57.6	73.1
	Consolidated	2.8	2.4	3.1	4.9	4.2	6.8
Total[b]	Home Office	4.3	4.4	4.2	8.1	8.9	7.7
	Field	1.8	1.4	2.2	3.5	3.3	4.8

Source: Table 16a and Tables in Statistical Appendix C.

[a] For geographic definitions see Table 17.

[b] 17 companies, each reporting data in all areas of operation.

The most favorable overall employment situation is in the East. There is substantial variance among the three region's job classifications, with the largest concentration of white collar type Negro field employees occurring in the office and clerical classification.

With the exception of the technicians category in general and the South's sales workers classification, the percentage of total and male-female Negroes in each region primarily is lower in all white collar job categories in the field as compared to home offices. The latter exception is not surprising, however, because of the amount of industrial life insurance marketed in the South and the corresponding number of Negro sales personnel employed and the general lack of need of sales personnel in home offices.

HOME OFFICE NEGRO EMPLOYMENT BY SELECTED STANDARD METROPOLITAN STATISTICAL AREAS

Table 19 presents home office Negro employment statistics for nine grouped Standard Metropolitan Statistical Areas (SMSA). All of the SMSA's included in a given category are closely related in terms of percentage of Negro population.

The grouping of the SMSA's was necessary to achieve statistically valid (and comparable) data which could not be accomplished by analyzing each city separately since in some (smaller) SMSA's only one insurer was interviewed while in other (substantially larger) SMSA's, information was obtained from several companies. In addition, in some cities only life insurers participated in this study; in other areas, property-liability companies were the sole participants. A comparison of life insurers in one SMSA to property-liability companies in a second SMSA prohibits the drawing of any type of meaningful conclusions about Negro employment by the insurance industry as an entity in the various SMSA's. Hence, the grouping of individual SMSA's was necessary to obtain a mixture of life and property-liability insurers.

SMSA Home Office Employment

The insurers participating in the study were separated according to the SMSA in which their home offices are domiciled and then the SMSA's were grouped according to the criteria set forth in the preceding paragraph.

TABLE 19. *Insurance Industry*
Home Office Percent Negro Employment by Sex
Grouped SMSA's
1967

SMSA[a]	Total	Male	Female
Los Angeles, Calif./San Francisco, Calif.	3.1	b	b
Atlanta, Ga./Birmingham, Ala./New Orleans, La.	6.8	5.7	7.4
Chicago, Ill./Bloomington, Ill./Evanston, Ill.	3.9	1.6	5.5
Baltimore, Md./District of Columbia/ Richmond, Va.	11.0	9.9	11.7
Kansas City, Mo./St. Louis, Mo./Nashville, Tenn./Chattanooga, Tenn.	7.2	9.2	6.3
Cincinnati, Ohio/Columbus, Ohio/Ft. Wayne, Ind./Indianapolis, Ind.	4.9	5.8	4.4
Philadelphia, Pa.	8.7	9.3	8.2
Newark, N. J./New York, N. Y.	9.9	5.4	13.6
Boston, Mass./Hartford, Conn./Springfield, Mass.	4.5	4.0	4.8
Total all SMSA's	6.6	4.9	7.7

Source: Tables in Statistical Appendix.

[a] SMSA (Standard Metropolitan Statistical Area) is defined as a city of at least 50,000 population and its contiguous metropolitan area.

[b] No data.

The data in Table 19 seem to reinforce the traditional Negro employment format: higher rates of Negro employment in the southern SMSA's than in their eastern counterparts. Although the percent total and male-female Negro employment in the South and the East are relatively close, in reality, the southern SMSA's employment record cannot be considered as favorable as that in the East because of the vast concentration of Negroes in the South and in eastern cities.

For example, the Boston/Hartford/Springfield percent Negro employment figure is one of the smallest (due to the minimum number of black individuals in the area) although the proportion of employed Negroes in the entire population is high (12.0

percent). The latter figure is a strong indication of the degree of Negro employment the insurance industry is able to achieve, at least in home office locations. The insurers in this SMSA have two characteristics in common: market and financial maturity and an absolute determination to eliminate job discrimination against Negroes. The latter characteristic is essential in executing nondiscriminatory hiring practices. Although market and financial maturity also would seem to be a necessary element, such a conclusion cannot be drawn unreservedly. Some insurers that were interviewed in other areas, and can be classified as neither financial giants nor as being in command of a substantial portion of the insurance market, were able to achieve substantial Negro employment.

SMSA Home Office Employment by Occupational Groups

Following the rationale behind the formulation of Table 19, the SMSA's presented in Table 20 and analyzed in this section are grouped into one of seven classifications. Each SMSA category included contains only data applicable to home office Negro employment in various job categories.

Table 20 displays the Negro employment pattern observed in other analyses: in general, a lower percent of total Negro employment is found among eastern SMSA's as compared to SMSA's in the South but higher than in the Midwest. The majority of both male and female Negro workers are concentrated in the service type, technical, and clerical occupations. The insurance industry's greatest deficiencies in Negro home office employment, therefore, are in the managerial and professional job categories.

NEGRO EMPLOYMENT BY INDIVIDUAL INSURERS

Although more than eighty insurers participating in this study freely disclosed their employment data, various internal administrative factors made it impossible to acquire from each corporation total employment figures in all its geographic areas of operation. Tables 21 through 25 present this information in summary form for those insurers from which it was obtainable. The insurers represent both life and property-liability, large and small, and geographically dispersed insurers.

TABLE 20. *Insurance Industry*

Home Office Percent Negro Employment by Sex and Occupational Group Grouped SMSA's,[a] 1967

Occupational Group	Atlanta/Birmingham/New Orleans			Baltimore/District of Columbia/Richmond			Chicago/Bloomington/Evanston		
	Total	Male	Female	Total	Male	Female	Total	Male	Female
Officials and managers	0.3	0.4	—	1.6	1.8	—	—	—	—
Professionals	—	—	—	0.2	0.2	—	0.2	0.2	0.7
Technicians	4.4	—	33.3	0.7	2.9	—	3.4	2.9	5.2
Sales workers	—	—	—	—	—	—	—	—	—
Office and clerical	4.8	4.5	4.8	12.3	14.5	11.8	5.9	8.6	5.7
Total white collar	3.4	1.1	4.7	8.6	6.0	10.1	3.8	1.6	5.5
Craftsmen	6.2	6.2	—	6.7	7.1	—	—	—	—
Operatives, laborers, and service workers	88.9	87.1	90.6	60.1	52.4	77.2	9.1	16.7	—
Total blue collar	72.2	59.6	90.6	56.1	47.9	75.9	9.1	16.7	—
Total	6.8	5.7	7.4	11.0	9.9	11.7	3.9	1.6	5.5

TABLE 20. Insurance Industry

Home Office Percent Negro Employment by Sex and Occupational Group
Grouped SMSA's,[a] 1967
(Continued)

Occupational Group	Cincinnati/Columbus Ft. Wayne/Indianapolis			Boston/Hartford/ Springfield			Kansas City/St. Louis/ Nashville		
	Total	Male	Female	Total	Male	Female	Total	Male	Female
Officials and managers	0.7	—	7.8	1.1	0.9	2.0	—	—	—
Professionals	1.7	1.8	1.2	1.1	1.2	0.8	2.2	2.4	—
Technicians	2.0	3.1	—	2.1	1.8	3.1	2.8	5.6	1.4
Sales workers	—	—	—	2.4	3.9	—	4.0	4.0	—
Office and clerical	5.0	12.6	4.5	5.0	5.2	5.0	4.6	5.6	4.5
Total white collar	3.9	2.7	4.4	3.7	2.0	4.5	4.1	3.6	4.3
Craftsmen	2.9	2.9	—	2.4	4.0	—	—	—	—
Operatives, laborers, and service workers	33.0	41.7	8.0	12.3	12.6	11.8	57.4	50.6	67.9
Total blue collar	28.5	34.3	8.0	10.3	11.0	8.9	54.0	45.7	67.9
Total	4.9	5.8	4.4	4.5	4.0	4.8	7.2	9.2	6.3

TABLE 20. *Insurance Industry*

Home Office Percent Negro Employment by Sex and Occupational Group Grouped SMSA's,[a] 1967

(Continued)

Occupational Group	Newark/New York City			Philadelphia		
	Total	Male	Female	Total	Male	Female
Officials and managers	—	—	—	—	—	—
Professionals	0.7	0.6	0.8	—	—	—
Technicians	0.8	1.1	—	16.7	—	20.0
Sales workers	—	—	—	—	—	—
Office and clerical	13.1	9.2	14.8	4.2	3.5	4.4
Total white collar	10.0	5.1	13.7	3.2	1.5	4.2
Craftsmen	—	—	—	17.6	17.6	—
Operatives, laborers, and service workers	10.0	9.6	10.6	57.8	48.1	78.4
Total blue collar	9.1	8.4	10.6	52.6	42.7	78.4
Total	9.9	5.4	13.6	8.7	9.3	8.2

Source: Tables in Statistical Appendix C.

[a] SMSA (Standard Metropolitan Statistical Area) is defined as a city of at least 50,000 population and its contiguous metropolitan area.

Consolidated Analysis

Table 21 reveals that the percentage of Negroes employed by the 36 consolidated insurers for whom data were available are clustered in the lower ranges. The largest concentration of total employment is in the interval of 3.0-3.9 percent (twelve insurers). None of these 36 corporations has a work force in which more than 10.9 percent of its total employees are Negroes. The typical company, therefore, has percent Negro employment of about 3 percent.

TABLE 21. *Insurance Industry*
Percent Negro Employment by Sex and Area of Operation
Individual Insurers, 1967

Percent Negro Employment	Number of Companies								
	Consolidated[a]			Home Office			Field		
	Total	Male	Female	Total	Male	Female	Total	Male	Female
0.0	—	—	—	—	—	—	4	4	4
0.1- 0.9	2	5	4	—	—	1	2	3	2
1.1- 1.9	7	11	4	2	5	—	3	4	2
2.0- 2.9	5	7	4	3	4	3	4	3	3
3.0- 3.9	12	7	8	3	2	4	2	1	3
4.0- 4.9	5	3	6	4	2	4	2	2	2
5.0- 5.9	1	1	3	4	4	1	—	—	—
6.0- 6.9	1	1	1	1	1	2	—	—	—
7.0- 7.9	1	—	—	2	3	3	—	—	—
8.0- 8.9	—	—	3	2	1	1	—	—	—
9.0- 9.9	1	—	1	1	2	2	—	—	1
10.0-10.9	1	1	1	3	2	2	—	—	—
11.0-11.9	—	—	1	—	—	1	—	—	—
12.0 & over	—	—	—	1	—	2	—	—	—
Total	36[b]	36[b]	36[b]	26[c]	26[c]	26[c]	17[d]	17[d]	17[d]

Source: Tables in Statistical Appendix C.

[a] Includes all geographic locations in which a company operates.

[b] 32 companies reported no breakdown by sex.

[c] 31 companies reported no breakdown by sex.

[d] 27 companies reported no breakdown by sex.

From the aspect of male-female Negro employment, the data are somewhat more evenly arrayed with the majority of male workers in the 1.0-1.9 range and the largest percent of female employees in the 3.0-3.9 and 4.0-4.9 categories. The heavier weighting in favor of Negro female workers is due, as indicated earlier, to the vast number of clerical jobs common to the insurance industry and which traditionally offer more employment opportunities for female as compared to male workers.

Home Office and Field Analysis

A summarized breakdown of each insurer's Negro employment on the basis of home office and field employees is included in Table 21. There are fewer insurers included in this tabulation than appear in the consolidated data because some of the companies were able to supply employment figures only on a consolidated basis and not by individual locations. It also should be noted that not all the organizations listed under home office and field are incorporated in the consolidated data—those insurers that were able to provide employment figures for only their home office or for only their field establishments necessarily were excluded from this section of the table.

The consolidated data exposes several significant employment factors that are not evident from examining the figures in the two other areas.[35] The percent Negro employment figures in the consolidated data obscure, and those in home office and field reveal, as emphasized earlier, that there are important differences in the extent of Negro employment in the insurance industry's home offices as compared to its field locations.

The total consolidated employment figures do not include a percent Negro employment interval above 10.0-10.9. This indicates that these consolidated maximums *understate* Negro employment in the home office and somewhat *overstate* the highest percentages in the field category. The greatest home office percentage is 12.0 and over for total Negro employment. This range is considerably higher than the maximum of 10.0-10.9 (total Negro employment) for the consolidated data.

Conversely, the aggregate tabulation obscures the very low Negro employment in the field. Slightly over one-third of the field offices (six out of seventeen) have a percentage of total Negro employment in the two lowest intervals. The maximum range of

---

[35] This is due to the inherent weaknesses in the averaging concept.

the male-female field employment coincides more closely, however, with the consolidated data.

Another important characteristic obscured by the consolidated data is the distribution of Negro employment ranges in home office establishments. The consolidated data show a clustering in the 0.1-0.9, 1.0-1.9, 2.0-2.9, 3.0-3.9, and 4.0-4.9 ranges. These five intervals contain 86 percent (total employment), 92 percent (male employment), and 72 percent (female employment) of the companies. There is no single outstanding percent interval applicable to the home office classification but rather the number of insurers are rather evenly distributed among most of ranges listed in the table. On the other hand, the percent Negro employment in the field is polarized in a manner similar to that characterizing the consolidated data.

The marked home office/field differences in Negro employment are largely due to the extreme difficulty that even the most progressive insurance companies experience in trying to enforce a nondiscriminatory hiring policy in their field offices. As indicated in Chapter II, an insurer's ability to assure that equal employment opportunities exist in all its locations is directly related to the distance between a given field office and corporate headquarters. The effects of this difficulty are emphasized by observing that none of the twenty-six home office establishments has a zero percent total Negro employment while four of the field locations (24 percent) have zero percent total Negro employment.

Consolidated Analysis by Job Categories

The total number of Negro employees in all locations of twenty-nine insurers in seven job categories is summarized in Table 22. This table reveals that the range of percent Negro total employment intervals among the insurers is the smallest in the officials and managers and professionals groups (0.0 to 2.9 percent). The second smallest range is that the sales workers category (0.0 to 4.9 percent). The range improves as the skills demanded by the remaining job categories decrease. For example, the craftsmen total employment class shows the widest range (0.0 percent to 100.0 percent).

When viewed in terms of a male-female employment breakdown, the above conclusions concerning the consolidated data must be slightly modified. For example, the smallest male employment range is in the officials and managers group and the largest is in the blue collar category. Female employment data reveal that the smallest grouping is professionals and the largest is in the blue collar class.

The white collar job category with the greatest number of insurers in intervals above 0.9 percent is the office and clerical classification. In the insurance industry's broad employment picture, therefore, the greatest white collar job opportunity for Negro applicants seems to be in the office and clerical area.

Home Office Analysis by Job Categories

Table 23 isolates the percent Negro employment within the home offices of individual insurers. There are fewer corporations included in Table 23 than in Table 22 because some insurers were able to provide only consolidated employment figures for all locations rather than separate data for home and field offices. Similarly, not all the companies listed in Table 23 appear in Table 22 —those insurers that could supply data for only their home office employees.

The summarized information included in Table 23 follows the same general pattern applicable to Table 22. That is, the range of the percent Negro employment intervals is quite narrow in the officials and managers, professionals, and sales categories and widens as positions that require less education, training, and experience are encountered. In addition, the job categories with the widest percent Negro employment range are the two blue collar groups.

Table 23 serves to reinforce the previous conclusion that the ripest area of employment opportunity for Negro men and women in the insurance industry is in clerical work. Moreover, by implication, the job categories in which there seems to be the greatest need for improvement are the managerial, professional, technical, and sales levels.

Field Analysis by Job Categories

The presentation of Negro employment in the insurance industry's field offices by job categories as delineated in Table 24 further emphasizes the disparity between Negro employment in home as compared to field offices.

This table contains an even smaller number of insurers than Tables 22 and 23 due to the difficulty of acquiring reliable field

TABLE 22. Insurance Industry

Consolidated ª Percent Negro Employment by Sex and Occupational Group
Individual Insurers, 1967

Number of Companies

Percent Negro Employment	Officials and managers			Professionals			Technicians			Sales workers		
	Total	Male	Female	Total	Male	Female	Total	Male	Female	Total	Male	Female
0.0	15	16	22	13	13	21	12	10	19	10	10	11
0.1-0.9	10	10	1	12	11	3	3	1	—	5	5	1
1.0-1.9	3	2	1	2	3	1	3	4	1	1	1	1
2.0-2.9	1	1	1	1	—	—	1	1	2	1	1	—
3.0-4.9	—	—	—	—	1	—	4	4	—	4	4	1
5.0-6.9	—	—	—	—	—	—	—	1	—	—	—	1
7.0-8.9	—	—	—	—	—	—	—	—	—			
9.0-10.9	—	—	—	—	—	—	—	—	—			
11.0-29.9	—	—	1	—	—	—	—	—	—			
30.0-49.9	—						1	—	—			
50.0-69.9	—						—	—	1			
70.0-99.9												
100.0												
No employees in occupation	—	—	3	1	1	4	5	8	6	8	8	14
Total	29	29	29	29	29	29	29	29	29	29	29	29

TABLE 22. *Insurance Industry*
Consolidated ᵃ *Percent Negro Employment by Sex and Occupational Group*
Individual Insurers, 1967
(Continued)

	Number of Companies								
Percent Negro Employment	Office and clerical			Craftsmen			Operatives, laborers, and service workers		
	Total	Male	Female	Total	Male	Female	Total	Male	Female
0.0	—	5	—	11	11	3	—	1	5
0.1-0.9	3	—	4	1	1	—	—	—	1
1.0-1.9	4	2	4	1	1	—	—	—	2
2.0-2.9	6	5	5	1	—	—	—	—	2
3.0-4.9	8	4	9	1	1	—	3	2	2
5.0-6.9	3	5	2	—	—	—	1	—	—
7.0-8.9	3	1	3	—	—	—	3	1	—
9.0-10.9	1	1	2	—	—	—	—	1	—
11.0-29.9	1	6	—	3	4	—	8	9	4
30.0-49.9				—	—	—	1	3	1
50.0-69.9				—	—	—	4	1	—
70.0-99.9				—	—	—	3	5	4
100.0				1	1	—	1	1	1
No employees in occupation	—	—	—	10	10	26	5	5	7
Total	29	29	29	29	29	29	29	29	29

Source: Tables in Statistical Appendix.

ᵃ Includes all geographic locations in which a company operates.

TABLE 23. *Insurance Industry*
Home Office Percent Negro Employment by Sex and Occupational Group
Individual Insurers, 1967

Percent Negro Employment	Number of Companies											
	Officials and managers			Professionals			Technicians			Sales workers		
	Total	Male	Female	Total	Male	Female	Total	Male	Female	Total	Male	Female
0.0	17	18	20	11	11	16	9	9	12	9	9	2
0.1-0.9	2	2	—	8	6	1	2	—	1	—	—	—
1.0-1.9	2	1	—	—	2	3	1	2	1	1	—	—
2.0-2.9	1	1	—	2	2	—	—	1	—	—	—	—
3.0-3.9	—	—	—	1	1	—	4	2	—	1	—	—
4.0-4.9	—	—	—	—	—	—	—	1	1	—	—	—
5.0-5.9	1	1	—	—	—	—	—	—	—	—	1	—
6.0-6.9	—	—	—	—	—	—	1	2	1	—	1	—
7.0-9.9	—	—	1	—	—	—	1	1	—	—	—	—
10.0-12.9	—	—	—	—	—	—	—	—	—	—	—	—
13.0-15.9	—	—	—	—	—	—	—	—	—	—	—	—
16.0-19.9	—	—	1	—	—	—	—	—	—	—	—	—
20.0-29.9	—	—	—	—	—	—	1	—	1	—	—	—
30.0-39.9	—	—	—	—	—	—	—	—	—	—	—	—
40.0-49.9	—	—	—	—	—	—	1	—	1	—	—	—
50.0-69.9	—	—	—	—	—	—	—	—	—	—	—	—
70.0-99.9	—	—	—	—	—	—	—	—	—	—	—	—
100.0	—	—	—	—	—	—	—	—	—	—	—	—
No employees in occupation	—	—	1	1	1	3	3	5	5	12	12	21
Total	23	23	23	23	23	23	23	23	23	23	23	23

TABLE 23. Insurance Industry

Home Office Percent Negro Employment by Sex and Occupational Group, Individual Insurers, 1967 (Continued)

Percent Negro Employment	Office and clerical			Craftsmen			Operatives, laborers, and service workers		
	Total	Male	Female	Total	Male	Female	Total	Male	Female
0.0	—	—	4	8	8	3	—	—	6
0.1-0.9	2	1	2	—	—	—	—	—	—
1.0-1.9	3	1	1	—	—	—	—	—	—
2.0-2.9	3	2	2	1	1	—	—	1	—
3.0-3.9	4	2	3	1	—	—	—	—	—
4.0-4.9	2	2	4	—	—	—	—	—	—
5.0-5.9	1	2	1	—	—	—	—	—	—
6.0-6.9	3	2	3	—	—	—	—	—	—
7.0-9.9	3	3	2	3	2	—	1	1	1
10.0-12.9	2	3	1	—	1	—	2	4	1
13.0-15.9	—	3	—	—	—	—	1	—	1
16.0-19.9	—	2	—	—	—	—	2	1	—
20.0-29.9	—	—	—	—	1	—	2	3	—
30.0-39.9	—	—	—	—	—	—	—	—	—
40.0-49.9	—	—	—	—	—	—	3	3	—
50.0-69.9	—	—	—	—	—	—	3	3	2
70.0-99.9	—	—	—	—	—	—	1	2	3
100.0	—	—	—	1	1	—	4	1	4
No employees in occupation	—	—	—	9	9	20	4	4	5
Total	23	23	23	23	23	23	23	23	23

Source: Tables in Statistical Appendix C.

TABLE 24. *Insurance Industry*

Field Office Percent Negro Employment by Sex and Occupational Group
Individual Insurers, 1967

Percent Negro Employment	Number of Companies											
	Officials and managers			Professionals			Technicians			Sales workers		
	Total	Male	Female	Total	Male	Female	Total	Male	Female	Total	Male	Female
0.0	8	8	6	3	3	5	2	2	2	6	7	5
0.1-0.9	6	6	1	4	4	1	—	—	—	3	2	1
1.0-1.9	—	—	1				—	1	—	—	—	1
2.0-2.9							2	1	1	1	1	—
3.0-3.9							—	—	—	2	2	—
4.0-4.9												
5.0-5.9							—	—	—			
6.0-6.9							—	—	—			
7.0-9.9							—	—	1			
10.0-12.9												
13.0-15.9												
16.0-19.9												
20.0-29.9												
30.0-39.9												
40.0-49.9												
50.0-69.9												
70.0-99.9												
100.0												
No employees in occupation	—	—	6	7	7	8	10	10	10	2	2	7
Total	14	14	14	14	14	14	14	14	14	14	14	14

TABLE 24. *Insurance Industry*
Field Office Percent Negro Employment by Sex and Occupational Group
Individual Insurers, 1967
(Continued)

Percent Negro Employment	Number of Companies								
	Office and clerical			Craftsmen			Operatives, laborers, and service wrokers		
	Total	Male	Female	Total	Male	Female	Total	Male	Female
0.0	5	5	5	2	2	—	1	1	2
0.1-0.9	1	1	1	—	—		—	—	—
1.0-1.9	3	—	3						
2.0-2.9	—	—	—						
3.0-3.9	4	1	3						
4.0-4.9	1	1	2						
5.0-5.9	—	—	—						
6.0-6.9	—	1	—						
7.0-9.9	—	3	—						
10.0-12.9	—	—	—						
13.0-15.9									
16.0-19.9							—	1	1
20.0-29.9							2	—	1
30.0-39.9							1	1	2
40.0-49.9				1	1	—	1	2	—
50.0-69.9							2	2	—
70.0-99.9							1	1	1
100.0							2	2	—
No employees in occupation	—	2	—	11	11	14	4	4	7
Total	14	14	14	14	14	14	14	14	14

Source: Tables in Statistical Appendix C.

employment figures from all the insurers interviewed. Neverthe-less, the fourteen companies that comprise the body of Table 24 are representative of the insurance industry in terms of geo-graphic location, market share control, and product mix (i.e., both life and property-liability insurers are included). The size of the sample, therefore, should not be interpreted as indicating poten-tial bias attributable to a small aggregation; rather, the tabula-tion should be viewed as simply a relatively small, but representa-tive, sample.

Table 24 emphasizes a conclusion drawn in earlier portions of this study: Negro employment in the industry's field locations generally is far inferior not only to that in the insurers' home offices, but to the level that could be achieved in the field.

There are, to reiterate previous statements, great difficulties in enforcing nondiscriminatory field hiring practices. It also should be noted, as a positive element, that the vast majority of all insur-ers interviewed realized the status of the industry's inadequate Negro employment in the field. Moreover, the executives state—without exception—that this employment area (and its shortcom-ings) is to be the next unfavorable employment condition within their companies to be remedied.

Ignoring the "traditional" service-type positions in which, in any case, there are very few Negro field employees, the percent Negro employment measure reveals a very limited amount of Negro employment in field locations. Employment opportunities —as well as currently held positions—as managers, professionals, and technicians are almost nonexistent for Negroes. Even the percent Negro employment in the office and clerical category is low in comparison to that in the home office. Moreover, one of the more favorable of all the classifications, sales workers must be discounted for the possible influence of the marketing of industrial life insurance that does not necessarily reflect *current* employment improvements since industrial companies have long utilized Negro sales representatives to solicit among potential Negro insureds.

PERCENT CHANGES IN NEGRO EMPLOYMENT

Table 25 details percentage changes in total employment and the corresponding changes in total Negro employment between 1966 and 1967 for twenty-seven individual insurers on a consoli-dated basis and the same data for twenty home office locations in Table 26. While no conclusions can be drawn regarding previous

TABLE 25.   *Insurance Industry*
Percent Change in Consolidated and Home Office Total and
Negro Employment
Individual Insurers, 1966-1967

Company Number	Consolidated		Home Office	
	Total	Negro	Total	Negro
3	—	—	— 3.4	+133.3
5	+ 1.5	+55.6	+ 1.2	+ 57.0
6	—	—	— 0.3	— 16.0
8	— 0.2	0.0	— 1.1	— 2.6
9	— 0.7	+17.0	+ 4.1	+ 15.8
10	—35.0	+27.5	— 0.2	+ 17.8
11	+ 6.7	—25.0	+ 0.9	— 25.0
13	—28.5	+20.5	+ 2.4	+ 36.0
14	—35.7	—26.5	—	—
15	+ 0.4	+25.0	—	—
17	+ 3.5	+75.3	—	—
18	—12.5	+29.9	—	—
19	+ 1.1	+80.0	—	—
20	+27.9	+ 9.1	—	—
21	— 1.3	+13.3	—	—
22	— 2.6	— 0.8	—	—
27	+ 4.3	+48.0	— 3.1	+100.0
28	+13.0	+25.0	+ 4.2	+ 53.6
29	+ 6.7	+23.7	+ 3.9	— 14.3
33	—70.4	*	—	—
35	+ 6.0	+25.0	— 0.2	+ 70.8
36	—50.2	+ 8.5	—	—
37	+ 1.6	+56.8	+ 0.2	+ 40.6
39	— 4.1	0.0	— 6.4	— 4.6
41	+ 9.4	+26.7	—	—
68	+ 1.6	+24.5	—	—
69	+16.5	+51.2	+16.5	+ 51.2
70	—43.1	+77.8	—43.1	+ 77.8
71	—	—	— 2.2	+125.3
72	—	—	+14.0	+ 44.1
75	—	—	+ 8.5	+ 38.1
76	—	—	+ 2.9	+ 27.1

Source: Tables in Appendix C.

* Cannot compute.

TABLE 26. *Insurance Industry*
Consolidated and Home Office Percent Negro Employment
Individual Insurers, 1966-1967

Company Number	Consolidated[a]		Home Office	
	Percent		Percent	
	1966	1967	1966	1967
3	—	—	1.1	2.8
5	4.8	7.3	7.0	10.8
6	—	—	6.6	5.6
8	1.7	1.7	1.9	1.9
9	3.7	4.3	5.8	6.5
10	0.8	1.6	2.1	2.4
11	1.5	1.1	1.9	1.4
13	3.7	6.3	6.4	8.5
14	1.7	1.9	—	—
15	2.6	3.2	—	—
17	2.0	3.5	—	—
18	2.4	3.5	—	—
19	1.8	3.2	—	—
20	3.5	3.0	—	—
21	1.1	1.3	—	—
22	3.2	3.2	—	—
27	2.2	3.2	3.5	7.2
28	1.3	1.4	1.7	2.6
29	2.4	2.8	5.7	4.7
33	0.6	—	—	—
35	2.2	2.7	2.1	3.6
36	2.5	5.4	—	—
37	2.4	3.7	3.9	5.5
39	4.2	4.3	9.8	10.0
41	2.7	3.1	—	—
68	7.6	9.3	—	—
69	7.8	10.2	7.8	10.2
70	1.4	4.5	1.4	4.5
71	—	—	1.8	4.2
72	—	—	7.6	9.6
75	—	—	6.8	8.6
76	—	—	4.2	5.1

Source: Tables in Appendix C.

a Includes all geographic locations in which a company operates.

practices or the number of employees involved, it is significant that Negro employment improved considerably over the one year period. The consolidated figures show that Negroes fared better in twenty-one of the twenty-seven companies and in the vast majority of cases the relative improvement was more than 20 percent. Only in three companies did the Negro position deteriorate. Particularly noteworthy are the seven companies which had total employment declines accompanied by substantial increases in Negro employment.

The home office figures in Table 25 exhibit a similar pattern. In fifteen of the twenty companies listed, the relative Negro position improved. Again, several insurers with total employment decreases experienced sharp percent increases in Negro employment.

Viewing the companies as a group, Table 26 indicates that the Negro portion of the consolidated employment in 1966 did not exceed 7.8 percent for any insurer and that the lowest percent was 0.6. In 1967, the highest Negro employment advanced to 10.2 percent—the individual company lower limit, however, decreased to 0.0 percent. On balance, the results were very favorable to percent Negro employment, with twenty-two companies registering an increase, two remaining the same, and three declining.

Most of the improvement revealed was attributable to home office increases. Consolidated Negro employment increased much less than that in home offices, which indicates that field employment is still lagging. Percent Negro employment declined in only three of the twenty home offices while one remained constant and the other sixteen showed increases. Also, several of the home offices with less than 3.0 percent Negro employment in 1966 added one percentage point or more by 1967.

NEGRO EMPLOYMENT IN 1967, FINAL COMMENTS

The Negro employment situation within the insurance industry, as described above, is placed in clearer perspective when viewed in combination with the elements that will advance and/or retard Negro employment in the future. These factors, which are discussed in detail in the following chapter, include the impact of such events as changes in operational procedures, product demand, and market development. It primarily will be the influence of these elements that alters the currently defined status of Negro employment within the insurance industry.

CHAPTER V

Factors Influencing Negro Employment in the Insurance Industry

The objective of this chapter is to isolate those factors in the insurance operation that favor the growth of Negro employment and those that deter its expansion within the business. To this end, therefore, the industry is analyzed according to primary occupational opportunities: sales, clerical, and managerial.

In assessing both the positive and negative factors, it must be noted that some of the positive influences identified are much less prevalent than certain of the negative ones. That is, while the elements retarding Negro employment seem to be common, with some exceptions, to the entire industry, the positive factors generally exist only in theory. The negative influences thus exist in most cases until and unless positive, or affirmative, employment action is taken. Hence, the current situation suggests that it will be individual (and perhaps isolated) action that will induce implementation of the positive factors by the industry as an aggregate.

NEGRO SALES EMPLOYMENT, NEGATIVE INFLUENCES

The extensive and severe factors that inhibit an increase in the number of Negroes in the industry's sales force are unlikely to be easily overcome. Among these restrictive influences are decentralization of recruitment, limitations on the Negro salesman's market potential, and failure of the industry to develop the Negro market.

Recruitment Decentralization

Except in the geographic area in which an insurer's home office is located, most of the recruiting of salesmen is decentralized. That is, hiring efforts are performed locally in a given region for an insurer by its salesmen or sales manager in that area.

Even though it is decentralized, the recruiting procedure supposedly is conducted according to the guidelines established by the home office. In addition, except for the "pure" general agency system (see Chapter II), each salesman recruited in the field must be approved by the home office. This approval is expressed when the insurer enters into a contractual arrangement with the new agent.

Despite the rather specific recruitment guidelines outlined by insurers, the control they exercise over the process is negative rather than positive. For example, although companies can efficiently screen and reject an unqualified sales applicant, they have not developed equally effective techniques for enforcing a philosophy of recruitment among all ethnic and racial groups. As a result, no matter how frequently an insurer's field representatives are urged to seek new agents actively from all ethnic, racial, and religious groups, these instructions can be ignored or circumvented by the simple statement that no Negro applicants can be located. A recruiter is able to exploit this degree of freedom because of the prohibitive expenses of enforcement attributable to the decentralized nature of the recruiter's duties and the substantial distance that usually exists between the locale of his realm of operations and that of the home office. The end result has been that the insurance industry *as a whole* has been unable to eliminate discriminatory hiring practices in its field operations.

Limitations on Negro Salesmen's Market

When asked whether they thought a Negro agent could develop a successful business composed of predominantly white clients, nearly all insurers interviewed responded emphatically with a negative answer. The only type of Negro agent that might be able to solicit primarily white prospects, in the opinion of these companies, is a celebrity, such as a well-known professional football player.

There are several known exceptions to this generalization. For example, the March 13, 1967 edition of *The Wall Street Journal* contains the profile of a Chicago based Negro agent who represents the New York Life Insurance Company. The article indicates that the agent works "in an integrated society." No mention is made, however, of the proportion of his sales activities that is directed toward white insurance prospects.

The reported exception, combined with an objective attempt to discover the reasons why a Negro salesman cannot develop an integrated clientele, causes doubt to be cast on the supposition that Negro agents would find it virtually impossible to build a market composed primarily of white insureds. The only basis for this hypothesis seemingly is the possibly questionable opinion of home office executives. A similar theory, for example, was held by drug manufacturers until they began to hire Negro salesmen and found that no market penetration difficulties actually did exist.[36] If it is true that resistance would be encountered, a Negro agent's market thus is restricted to Negro prospects.

Moreover, as long as "white" companies continue to deemphasize the insuring of Negro applicants—a factor discussed in the following section—the market of a Negro salesman who represents a "white" company necessarily is highly limited. As a result, the employment opportunities available to Negro agents are severely restricted by the narrow consumer market in which they usually are forced to operate.

Undeveloped Negro Market

A third major element retarding employment of Negro salesmen in the insurance industry is its failure to tap the Negro market for life insurance. According to Lloyd M. Levin, executive vice-president of Bennington Corporation, a St. Louis management consultant firm, the Negro market has a potential $30 billion to spend annually and is more heavily insurance oriented than any other segment of the population. In addition, it is asserted that it is a mark of social prestige for a Negro to buy life insurance from a "white" company.[37]

Despite these favorable factors very few life insurers are willing to incur the expenses necessary to recruit and to train nonwhite agents. This reluctance is the result of several factors: the higher mortality rate among Negro insureds, the monopoly of the Negro nonindustrial market by Negro owned insurers, and the comparatively low average annual income of Negroes. Moreover, the same life companies that are cognizant of these negative elements fail to see the factors favoring development of the Negro market: the presold nature of the market, the rising educational level and resulting higher income of Negroes, and the geographi-

---

[36] See the forthcoming study in this series dealing with the drug manufacturing industry.

[37] "Urges Small Stock Insurers to Take Plunge into Negro Market," *The National Underwriter*, December 9, 1967, pp. 1 and 6.

cally concentrated nature of the market, which increases the efficiency and production of agents.

As long as life insurers hesitate to cultivate the Negro market actively, the current aversion to the recruitment of Negro salesmen will persist and severely limit their employment opportunities.

A similar conclusion can be made about the employment opportunities for Negro salesmen in property-liability companies. A correspondingly favorable picture cannot be drawn, however, of the Negro market for property-liability as compared to that for life insurance. The property-liability Negro market is undeveloped not because of insurer inertia but because it is "undesirable."

Insurers must obtain what they conceive to be a proper aggregation or "book" of risks, the acquisition of which is based on two elements. First, the larger the number of risks insured, the more reliable will be the calculation of anticipated losses and the rate-making procedures. Second, the better the geographic dispersement or spread of the risks, the smaller the chance that a company will experience an excessive or catastrophic loss in a particular area. Ultimately, the success or failure of a company depends on the character of the business produced by its marketing system. An insurer, therefore, prefers to create a sales force that will seek a large number of widely dispersed insureds for whom, as an aggregate, there is little chance of a catastrophic loss. A company thus will not even attempt to develop a marketing system that is likely to gravitate toward a clientele that is unprofitable.

As far as the Negro market is concerned, the property-liability business produced must be considered, in terms of property concentrations in the northern and southern sections of the United States. Numerically, of course, there are more Negroes in the South than in the North. On the other hand, Negro owned property probably is of total greater value and is more geographically concentrated in the North than in the South.

Two types of Negro demand for property-liability insurance thus appear. In the South, smaller property values and lower incomes present neither an extensive demand nor a substantial insurance market; in the North—specifically in urban cores—both demand and need for property-liability insurance are strong. But insurers and their agents generally consider applications for coverage in urban core areas to be undesirable business because it is susceptible to losses that are in excess of the statutorily approved rate structure that the insurance companies must use.[38]

Just as two types of demand exist in the Negro property-liability market, two types of employment opportunities for Negro salesmen also are present. In the South, the relatively small amount of insurance demanded by the Negro consumers means that "white" companies need not undertake the expenses involved in recruiting and training Negro agents to capture an almost nonexistent market. Weak consumer demand, therefore, results in very limited employment opportunities in the South for Negro agents.

In the North, available evidence indicates that the number of Negro agents in urban core areas is very small. A survey of 108 property-liability companies revealed that the number of Negro agents is "practically nil."[39] This is not an unexpected situation, however, since insurers restrict the amount of protection they will provide in predominantly Negro areas in the North. No matter how great the demand, if there is no supply, there is no need for a facility to bring the forces of demand and supply together. Hence, the employment opportunities for Negro property-liability agents in the North are not promising.

NEGRO SALES EMPLOYMENT, POSITIVE INFLUENCES

The negative factors discussed above that inhibit the growth of Negro salesmen in the insurance industry are formidable. There are, however, some positive aspects to the attempts to increase Negro employment in the sales area. Some of these influences are general in nature, such as those relating to company employment policies and the activities of government agencies, both of which will be discussed in a later section of this chapter. Of major significance in the category of more specific affirmative factors by insurers is their recognition of the potential to capitalize on the vast untapped Negro market for life insurance. Through this recognition and the resulting sequential market development activities, the insurance industry will be able to provide substantial new employment opportunities for Negroes as salesmen.

---

[38] *Meeting the Insurance Crisis of Our Cities*, Report by the President's National Advisory Panel on Insurance in Riot-Affected Areas (Washington: Government Printing Office, 1968), p. 29.

[39] *Ibid.*, p. 25.

As also was indicated above, the Negro population represents a market that "understands" insurance and is one composed of a group of presold individuals. Hence, contrary to the attitude of other groups of life insurance purchasers, it will not be necessary to convince Negro consumers of their need for the product. The major responsibility of an insurer entering this market, therefore, will be to upgrade or increase the coverage of people who have what they consider to be adequate insurance.

The increasing quantity of the Negro market is emphasized by the report of the National Advisory Commission on Civil Disorders. The Commission predicts that by 1970, fourteen of the country's major cities will have a Negro population that comprises more than 50 percent of the cities' total. This means that insurers that decide to underwrite Negro applicants will be presented with a concentrated market: an agent will not have to extend his sales efforts to a large geographic area of several hundred miles, but will be able to solicit among a nucleus of prospects that have similar occupations, income, and insurance desires.

The quality, or profitability and premium paying ability, of the Negro market also is improving. There is a steadily increasing percentage of Negroes attending college. As this market becomes more educated, it should achieve a higher level of income which in turn will enable larger amounts of insurance to be purchased. Moreover, the average age of the Negro male is relatively low so that "brand loyalties" probably do not exist and can easily be cultivated by any aggressive insurer that decides to develop the Negro market.

The increasing quantity and quality of the Negro market thus create a favorable atmosphere for additional employment of Negro salesmen to solicit customers within this market. Whether this opportunity is developed will depend, of course, on the Negro market expansion actions of individual insurers. Nevertheless, the potential for growth of Negro employment does exist.[40]

---

[40] It is of interest to note that some of the "white" companies that already have entered the Negro market have proselyted agents (as well as other employees) from Negro-owned insurers. This action relieves the "white" corporations of training salesmen but it also is having an extremely detrimental effect on Negro-owned insurers.

NEGRO CLERICAL EMPLOYMENT,
NEGATIVE INFLUENCES

Several factors exist that may act as depressive forces on the insurance industry's attempts to increase its total number of Negro clerical employees. These deterring influences appear to be effective despite the tight clerical labor market presently encountered by most insurers and various positive elements that also are discussed in this section.

Declining Clerical Work Forces

Many insurers are initiating wide-range programs designed to improve methods and efficiency in clerical operations. The objective, of course, is to reduce total clerical employment or at least to contain its expansion. Such efforts, if successful, eventually could result in a net decrease in total clerical employment and, subsequently, a decline in employment opportunities for potential employees of all races.

The obvious solution to these particular causes of a declining Negro employment situation is an increase in the percentage of Negroes employed. Even if, however, there is a strong desire on the part of an insurer to raise the percentage of Negroes hired in a declining clerical work force, that company probably would hesitate to reject a qualified white applicant—especially in a tight labor market—in order to wait for a qualified Negro applicant to appear. This conflict between profit maximization and adoption of a corporate social philosophy gives additional credence to the conclusion that clerical employment opportunities of Negroes are affected adversely by the declining clerical work force in the insurance industry.

Low Clerical Salaries

As was briefly noted in Chapter II, the insurance industry has long been known for its low clerical salary scales. Various factors cause this situation, including the nonunion status of clerical employees, the low skill level necessary to perform the industry's clerical tasks, the willingness of employers to accept high turnover rates in the face of a (previously) seemingly unlimited supply of clerical employees.

Whatever the cause or causes, some portions of the insurance industry seem to be slowly moving away from the category of employers that offer only minimal, and sometimes the lowest, clerical salaries quoted in the labor market. According to the survey conducted by the Bureau of Labor Statistics (BLS), to which reference was made in Chapter II, average salaries for a large majority of clerical occupations in the industry were 15 to 25 percent higher in October-November 1966 than in May-July 1961.[41] Even when the 25 percent increment is considered, the average annual increase (about 4 percent) cannot be viewed as outstanding, but at least it is a move in the right direction. The study of the October-November 1966 period revealed that nationwide average weekly salaries for four numerically important clerical jobs in the insurance industry [42] were: class C file clerks—$63; class B [43] typists—$66.50; class B [44] keypunch operators—$70.50; and general stenographers [45]—$74.50.

These wage rates show the industry in an unfavorable position when compared to the wage rates for similar work in many other industries. Table 27 illustrates this situation by a comparison of

---

[41] U. S. Bureau of Labor Statistics, *Industry Wage Survey: Life Insurance-October-November 1966*, Bulletin 1569 (October 1967), p. 6.

[42] A class C file clerk is defined by BLS as one who "performs routine filing of material that has already been classified or which is easily classified in a simple serial classification system (e.g., alphabetical, chonological, or numerical). As requested, locates readily available material in files and forwards material; and may fill out withdrawal charge. Performs simple clerical and manual tasks required to maintain and service files."

[43] A class B typist is one that "performs *one or more of* the following: Types copy from rough or clear drafts; routine typing of forms, insurance policies, etc., and setting up simple standard tabulations, or copying more complex tables already set up and spaced properly."

[44] A class B keypunch operator is defined as an employee who, "under close supervision or following specific instructions, transcribes data from source documents to punched cards. Operates a numerical and/or alphabetical or combination keypunch machine to keypunch tabulating cards. May verify cards. Working from various standardized source documents, follow specified sequences which have been coded or prescribed in detail and require little or no selecting, coding or interpreting of data to be punched. Problems arising from erroneous items or codes, missing information, etc., are referred to supervisor."

[45] A general stenographer is designated as an employee whose "primary duty is to take and transcribe dictation from one person or more, either in shorthand or by Stenotype or similar machine, involving a normal routine vocabulary. May also type from written copy. May maintain files, keep simple records or perform other relatively routine clerical tasks. May operate from a stenographic pool. Does not include *transcribing-machine work*."

TABLE 27.   *Average Straight Time Weekly Earnings, Selected Occupations in Metropolitan Areas by Industry Division, United States, February 1967, and Life Insurance Industry, United States and Middle Atlantic Region October-December 1966*

Office Clerical Occupations (Female)	Total United States-Industry Division								Life Insurance	
	All Industries	All Manufacturing	All Nonmanufacturing	Public Utilities a	Wholesale Trade	Retail Trade	Finance b	Service	Total United States	Middle Atlantic Region
File Clerk C	$64.50	70.00	63.50	74.00	65.50	61.50	62.50	64.00	63.00	$66.50
Typist B	74.00	79.00	72.00	81.00	74.50	71.50	69.00	75.50	66.50	71.00
Keypunch Operator B	81.50	86.00	78.50	86.00	81.50	76.00	74.00	80.00	70.50	72.50
Stenographer-General	87.50	90.50	85.00	94.50	85.50	77.50	78.50	88.00	74.50	79.50

Source: *Monthly Labor Review*, Vol. XC (September 1967), p. 60; and Vol. XCI (April 1968), p. 45.

a Transportation, communication, and other public utilities.

b Finance, insurance, and real estate.

insurance industry salaries in four occupational categories with those of other industrial groups in metropolitan areas. As Table 27 demonstrates, when the average wages paid by life insurers in the Middle Atlantic region (which, according to the 1966 BLS survey, are the highest in the industry) are contrasted to average salaries in other industries, it is found that in three of the four occupational categories the earnings in the *highest paying region* in the life insurance industry (i.e., the Middle Atlantic) are below the *national average* for industry in general.

The insurance industry—a significant, if not the largest, employer among financial institutions—thus seems to follow a policy of paying minimal clerical salaries. Whether this is justified as the proper employment approach is irrelevant. What is of significance to this study is the end result of this practice, which is a general dampening of the clerical employment outlook for Negroes in the insurance industry. Most of the insurers interviewed indicated that the tight clerical labor market, combined with the salary competition presented by other industries, made attracting Negro clerical employees very difficult. One example cited by numerous insurers was their inability to compete in the clerical labor market against the federal government since the latter pays higher wages and demands a lower-skill level for certain clerical tasks identical to those in the insurance industry.

This general dampening effect on employment caused by low salary scales obviously applies to the hiring of all clerical employees and not just to Negroes. The effect is more severe in the case of Negro applicants, however, because of the increased efforts of some employers in other industries specifically to seek out and hire Negro clerical employees—even if higher than normal wages must be paid to do so.

A fairly apparent solution to the insurance industry's dilemma is simply to increase its clerical salary scale in total and lower its employment requirements. Many companies have eased their hiring standards, but raising their clerical salary scale is not so easily accomplished. The clerical staff utilized by the industry is enormous and a general increase in clerical wage levels would cause the cost of the insurance product to rise. This is an untenable prospect for most insurers in the property-liability lines who already are under heavy criticism because of continually rising rates for such coverages as automobile insurance, riot insurance (where it exists), fire insurance (especially in urban areas), and so on. Life insurers possibly could increase their levels of clerical pay but this suggestion runs contrary to the life industry's highly conservative business practices and lack of desire to disturb the status quo. Not all insurers, however, are reluctant to meet competitive pressures by altering their clerical salary scales. Of the companies interviewed, some cases were found—among both life and property-liability, small and large, and northern and southern based insurers—of deliberate realignment of salary scales to attract not only clerical employees in general but Negro clerical employees in particular. Unfortunately, the companies in this category, both in number and in the total amount of the market which they affect, do not outweigh the organizations that cling to the low clerical salary scales. The overall net effect of low salary scales, therefore, must be a negative one and will continue to retard a meaningful increase in total Negro clerical employment within the insurance industry.

NEGRO CLERICAL EMPLOYMENT, POSITIVE INFLUENCES

The outlook for Negro clerical employment within the insurance industry is affected by favorable as well as unfavorable factors. Among these positive stimuli are the educational requirements for most clerical jobs, the hiring standards of insurers, the turnover within the clerical work force, and the centralized location of most companies' corporate headquarters.

Educational Requirements

Most clerical occupations common to the insurance industry call for only a minimal level of education. In fact, much of the skill necessary to perform these tasks is acquired via informal on-the-job training and supervision. Some clerical jobs, of course, require the previous attainment of skills, such as typing. In the majority of the cases, however, a high school education is not necessary for the *performance* of clerical tasks. Some insurers require that an employee have a high school diploma but this does not mean that twelve years of formal education are necessary for the execution of all clerical jobs. The high school diploma requirement often is used merely as a method of selecting potentially better employees.

Most companies interviewed indicated that the following operations entail on-the-job training and do not necessitate previous experience: filing; transcribing from a dictaphone; operating a keypunch (knowledge of a keyboard generally is required) ; and performing simple clerical tasks such as typing form letters, calculating premiums from premium rate books, and assembling policy forms. The last example includes a substantial portion of all clerical tasks involved in the insurance industry.

Since the level of education of Negroes is on average lower than that of whites, the relatively less demanding educational requirements actually needed by clerical employees in the insurance industry is one inherent factor favoring Negro employment growth. Insurers thus are in the position of being able to offer job opportunities to the black community that industries which require highly-skilled employees cannot provide. The potential exists; it is now up to the insurance industry to make certain that this potential is fully realized.

The Selection Process

Changes in the selection criteria have also been beneficial in terms of increasing Negro employment within the industry. Most executives interviewed in connection with this study stated that the present quality of the clerical employee market has forced a downward revision of hiring standards. Some companies indicate that their employment prerequisites have been softened to the point where there are practically no criteria; others state that their hiring standards have been lowered only slightly. Hence, the degree of easing varies not only by region and by demand for clerical employees, but by insurers within a given location. The criteria also are influenced by a company's philosophy concerning the hiring of minority group employees.

It is in the selection process, of course, that the industry's overall lowering of hiring standards is most evident. The two steps in which the most significant change in the selection criteria has occurred are (1) testing of an applicant's skill and/or general intelligence and (2) evaluating the test scores and results of the initial interview.

Nearly all of the insurance companies participating in this study indicated that they have made some changes in their clerical testing procedures. Some insurers no longer administer a general intelligence test and instead test only for skills (such as typing speed) relevant to a given job. A few companies do not test experienced applicants in any manner. The vast majority of the insurers interviewed stated that the clerical tests in use were being, or had been, re-evaluated to determine their effectiveness in view of the aptitudes of current applicants. At least a half of the companies revealed that they had discarded the tests that were being used prior to the current employment situation in favor of allegedly easier tests. In addition, nearly all the life insurers that have moved to the use of less difficult tests indicated that they had adopted or were in the process of adopting the new Life Office Management Association (LOMA) test that supposedly is validated for cultural, that is, racial, differences. The expressed objective of utilizing the test is to increase the number of Negroes and other minority group members employed by the industry.

In evaluating test results, all the insurers interviewed stated that they had lowered the minimum test scores required of new clerical hirees. Moreover, this leniency has been extended both to general intelligence and to skill tests. Two sources of pressure seem to be responsible for the lowering of minimum score requirements. First, the continuously decreasing quality of applicants—attributable by most insurers to inadequate instrucion in secondary schools—made such an adjustment necessary if insurance companies were to hire clerical employees in the quantity needed. Second, employers in other industries, and especially the federal government, are willing to pay a higher salary to those applicants that were being rejected by insurers on the basis of their previous test score minimums. It was partially in self-defense, then, that acceptable test scores were lowered in the evaluation process.

In addition to establishing lower test standards, nearly all insurers have eased evaluation standards applied in analyzing the results of the initial interview with an applicant. For example, many of the few companies that previously had a retail credit check conducted on all applicants have deleted this evaluation requirement.[46] Further, *all* of the insurers queried will employ an individual who has a "minor" criminal record—if it is revealed during the interviewing process and not indirectly learned by the company while checking the applicant's references. The revelation usually must be voluntary since very few insurers include questions in their application forms designed to obtain informa-

---

[46] Retail credit checks provide information about a person's background, credit rating, possible infractions of the law and so on. These tests have been curtailed largely because of rising administrative costs.

tion about criminal convictions. The criminal record factor, however, will influence the position for which an applicant is eligible. Bonding requirements may eliminate some employment areas, such as in the cashier's department, for an applicant with a criminal record. In this case, another type job that does not require bonding generally is offered the individual. The willingness of some companies to hire individuals with a minor criminal record is of special significance to Negroes in large urban areas. This new attitude has made possible the employment of many responsible Negroes who, generally in their youth and because of a variety of circumstances, had acquired a criminal record.

These two examples of liberalized interview evaluations (eliminating retail credit investigations and ignoring minor criminal records) are by no means the only areas in which such appraisals have been eased. The illustrations merely are indicative of the measures that the vast majority of all insurers have adopted in an attempt to capture a larger portion of the supply of available clerical employees, whether black or white. Certainly, however, these moves are favorable to increased Negro employment.

High Turnover of Clerical Employees

The high rate of turnover among clerical employees, which is an inherent characteristic of the insurance industry, creates continual job openings and an almost perpetual demand for clerical workers. The industry, therefore, can be characterized as an employer that has almost endless work opportunities for Negroes. To the extent that insurers actively seek Negro applicants and present them with competitive employment offers, the high turnover rates in the industry could react favorably upon Negro employment.

Accessible Home Offices

As previously indicated in Chapter II, approximately two-thirds of those individuals whose employment is connected with the insurance industry are engaged in nonsales activities. Of this percentage, slightly over half are employed in a home office. The location of the home offices of the insurance industry within given geographic locales thus is relevant since most employees will be drawn from immediately surrounding areas.

The headquarters of nearly all insurers are in centrally located, urban areas. These offices, moreover, generally are accessible by the use of public transportation. It is these location and accessibility factors that create a very favorable outlook for increased Negro employment, and especially for greater Negro clerical employment, within the insurance industry.

For example, most of the insurance corporations domiciled in Washington, D. C. are in the downtown area, which is both adequately serviced by public transportation and heavily populated by Negroes. (Approximately 50 percent of the population is black.) It thus follows that Negroes should be in an advantageous employment situation; and, as the number of Negroes in Washington continues to increase, the total Negro employment in that area correspondingly should rise.

NEGRO MANAGERIAL EMPLOYMENT

In assessing the status of Negro employment within the industry's management hierarchy, and the elements favoring and retarding future growth, it first should be noted that the classification of employees as executives and managers includes many persons who actually have professional or technical skills. Such individuals are sometimes categorized by insurance companies as "managerial" rather than "professional and technical" employees. In addition, it also is important to recognize that all employees from the level of building maintenance supervisor to chairman of the board (in most insurance organizations the latter is a full-time employee) are included in the managerial classification. Finally, it is essential that any analysis of current Negro managerial employment data be tempered by the fact that the majority of all managerial employees within the industry are in the lower management echelon and primarily are supervisors, department managers, and so on. Hence, the number of individuals in the industry in the higher management groups is not in reality very large.

Recruitment and Promotion

A significant detriment to enlarging the number of insurers' Negro managerial employees is the industry's very limited *external* management recruitment activities. The prevailing and very firm philosophy among more than 90 percent of all insurers is that **every** vacant managerial position should be filled by promoting lower-management employees. Recruitment and promotion of managerial talent, therefore, are intimately connected. The only time that management openings are not filled by drawing on existing intracompany talent is when a vacancy occurs in an area where professional or technical skill is needed and cannot be supplied from a company's then-present staff.

Two conclusions emerge as a result of this recruitment/advancement philosophy. First, there is almost a complete absence of recruitment activities directed toward experienced executive-level personnel or management trainees. Second, the internal pool from which executives and managers are drawn, especially in the case of higher, more responsible positions, obviously is quite small and is defined in terms of, and limited by, an insurer's existing organizational structure. Hence, the managerial recruitment and promotion policies of the insurance industry as a whole are such that the opportunity to achieve executive status is, in effect, almost nonexistent except for a small number of individuals.

Changes in the Number of Executives and Managers

It is unlikely that the number of existing executives and managers employed by insurance companies will decrease. When viewed as a whole, the organizational structure of the insurance industry is clearly "top heavy," a condition that has existed since the early 1900's and which gives all indication of being permanent.

Opinion appears to be divided, however, on whether the managerial and executive staff of insurers will increase proportionately. There is a consensus that the ranks of the higher executive hierarchy will not expand substantially and that most growth, if any, will be in the area of new departments created because of product expansion, marketing changes, and other new developments.

On the other hand, the total number of lower-level managers and supervisors probably will fluctuate. Any changes in clerical operations and procedures will affect the number of managers needed to direct these functions. If the adjustment in clerical activities results in an employment decline, the change will have a depressing effect on the number of low-level managers in the industry. A positive influence, however, will be exerted if insurers increase the employment of management trainees. It is questionable, of course, whether they should be considered as part of the industry's managerial staff. They are so classified in this portion of the study because the majority of the insurers questioned categorize their management trainees as a part of the corporations' managerial force.

It seems, then, that the number of executives and managers with the rank of second vice-president or higher will remain fairly stable. The lower and middle management portion of the insurance industry will fluctuate and possibly may increase if the functions and products of insurers expand to a degree sufficient to offset the decline in supervisory personnel attributable to a decreasing clerical staff.

Effect on Negro Employment

The implication of the managerial recruitment and promotion policies of insurers, along with the hypothesized changes concerning the number of executives needed in the future, is not promising from the viewpoint of Negro employment.

The fact that there are few higher-level managerial positions in the industry, combined with the promotion-from-within philosphy, results in a virtual exclusion of Negroes from the insurers' executive echelon. Negroes have not been white collar workers in insurance corporations for a long enough period of time to meet the industry's unwritten—but generally widespread—tenure requirements that precede promotion into the higher managerial ranks. A growth in the number of Negro managers and executives, therefore, should not be expected so long as insurers perpetuate their current promotion practices.

THE IMPACT OF GOVERNMENT

As was observed in Chapter III, the insurance industry did not begin to employ Negroes in any number until the labor shortage of World War II compelled it to reassess its labor source and supply. Following World War II, the forceful policies of the New York State Commission Against Discrimination gave the impetus to further minority employment among domestic companies that are based in New York City. Investigations, however, by other state or local bodies—for example, by the Philadelphia Human Relations Commission—in the post-World War II period do not appear to have had widespread effect on the employment practices of insurers. It was not until the civil right's activities of the early 1960's, combined with the shortage of labor, that a significant impact was made on the industry as a whole.

In terms of future influences, perhaps one of the more important factors that will increase Negro employment in the insurance industry is the influence on hiring practices that can be exercised by the federal government. This impact probably will be felt more in the future by smaller insurers, however, since most of the giants in the industry have been striving for some time to achieve Negro employment goals even higher than those sought by the federal government.

Insurers become federal contractors and so are subject to control by the Office of Federal Contract Compliance (OFCC)—which polices nondiscriminatory employment practices of federal contractors—by participating in any number of government-connected services and programs. Examples of such activities include the following: (1) reinsuring health benefits available to federal civil service employees, (2) acting as administrators of the Medicare program, and (3) providing group life insurance (through a pool of insurers) to members of the armed forces.

Participation in these programs, of course, is voluntary on the part of an insurer. Hence, it would seem that an insurer that does not wish to become a federal contractor—and subject to any corresponding employment requirements—could decline to participate in the programs. It might also be noted at this point that of the insurers interviewed in connection with this study, the vast majority are *not* government contractors.

To the pressures that may be exerted by the OFCC, however, must be added the potential influence of the Equal Employment Opportunity Commission (EEOC) established by Title VII of the Civil Rights Act of 1964 to assure nondiscrimination in employment generally. The activities of the EEOC should result in increased Negro employment in the insurance industry since all insurers, and not just those designated as federal contractors, are subject to it. Interestingly, the insurers interviewed in connection with this study revealed that they have experienced very little governmental pressure other than that exerted by the OFCC. It also appears that the OFCC has restricted its investigative activities to the largest companies. The conclusion drawn among those interviewed seems to be that it will be simply a matter of time before the OFCC extends its efforts to smaller companies that fall within its jurisdiction and before the EEOC becomes active in relation to the insurance industry as a whole.

AFFIRMATIVE ACTION IN PRACTICE, SOME EXAMPLES

One of the most encouraging factors favoring Negro employment growth in the insurance industry is the progressive attitude
of many of the insurers interviewed toward increasing the number
of Negro employees in the industry and generally assisting the
Negro population as a whole. This attitude does not prevail, of
course, among all insurers: some are too small to engage in such
activities; a few admit to having been (intentionally) a "totally
white" company prior to enactment of the Civil Rights Act of
1964. On the other hand, it must be stated that of the companies
interviewed, no more than 5 percent created the *impression* in the
ensuing discussions of only giving superficial adherence to the
concept of equal employment opportunity.

The data that follow detail some of the more progressive hiring
practices encountered in four companies, each in a different geographical location, while this study was being conducted. Although these insurers are emphasized in particular, it should be
noted that these are not the only companies with exceptional Negro
employment records. There are other, equally aggressive, insurers with comparable records that simply were not selected for
inclusion as examples or were not asked to participate in the
overall study. Their exclusion, therefore, should not be con-
strued as an indication of categorization in an unjustifiably unfavorable Negro employment classification.

Aetna Life and Casualty Insurance Company

The first Negro hired by the Aetna (in other than a service
capacity) was employed about 1946. The insurer, confronted by
the current tight labor market, found it necessary to lower its
hiring standards about three years ago. As a result, the organization's overall home office hiring ratio (number hired to number
of applicants) has increased from 18 percent to 40 percent. During the time the 18 percent ratio prevailed, 8 to 10 percent of all
Negro applicants were hired by the company. Currently, of the
existing 40 percent hiring ratio, about 40 percent of the applicants
hired are Negroes.

The Aetna recruits in local high schools and specifically seeks
out those institutions whose students are predominantly Negro
and Puerto Rican. In addition to this direct recruiting, the insurer conducts a student part-time work program that has been
in effect approximately fifteen years. There were about 130 stu-

dent participants employed at the time this information was obtained and 50 percent of those students were Negroes.

Three years ago the company instituted an eight week clerical training program in its home office for "young women from disadvantaged backgrounds" [47] to qualify them for jobs with the company and other local firms. The plan was the first of its kind in the country and one class has been conducted each year since the program's initiation. Recruiting of all participants for the training school is conducted through the local Urban League. On the average, sixteen students have participated in the eight-week all day long sessions and almost 100 percent of the trainees have been hired by the company upon completion of the course.

The students are given instruction in such areas as spelling, grammar, arithmetic, and telephone techniques. The cost to the insurer of conducting one of the annual programs averages around $7,000, which includes a weekly allowance for each student (initially $15 and now $35) to cover transportation and incidental costs. The company justifiably considers the project to be an outstanding success.

Nationwide Insurance Companies

In 1954 the Board of Directors of Nationwide adopted a nondiscriminatory personnel policy that was developed as a result of the culmination of the work of the insurer's officers that began in 1952. Between 1954 and the addition of Title XVIII (Medicare) to the Social Security Act of 1935, the company candidly admits that although it did not discriminate in its hiring practices, it did not actively seek out Negro applicants. Since 1965, the company has adopted and executed exceptionally aggressive programs designed to increase the number of its white collar Negro employees. At the time the Medicare amendment was enacted, the percentage of minority group employees in Nationwide's home office (other than in the service area) was about 0.5 percent. The current proportion now is in excess of 9.5 percent. It might also be noted at this point that Nationwide is one insurer that has been able to implement its nondiscriminatory hiring policies in its regional offices.

The home office recruiting activities of the company purposely are directed toward the inclusion of as many predominantly Negro high schools as possible. Attempts also have been made to obtain

---

[47] From the files of the author.

Negro nonservice employees by sending interviewers into Negro neighborhoods for the purpose, in effect, of taking the labor market employment demand to the supply. Moreover, these efforts extend not only to increasing its clerical employees but also to attracting Negro management personnel and agents.

It is of special note that the recruiting efforts of Nationwide are directed not necessarily toward qualified but *qualifiable* applicants. The insurer will hire so-called unqualified minority employees for on-the-job training and attempt, within three or four months, to bring the trainee's skills up to the necessary level of performance.

Nationwide's activities have not been restricted to aggressive recruiting methods. The organization is, for example, a member of Plans for Progress and was a "Pace Setter" in its contribution to the United Negro College Fund. As indicated, efforts also have been, and are being, made to provide on-the-job training for Negroes. The first venture into this program brought in twelve employees (referred by the local Urban League), nine of whom completed the program. Of these nine, about five elected to remain as employees of the insurer. The company accepted twenty-five additional on-the-job trainees during 1968, and plans to hire twenty-four more of these type workers during 1969-1970.

Although Nationwide has never hired summer employees, as such, about four weeks prior to the beginning of the 1967-1968 school year, the insurer was requested to participate in a city-sponsored program to employ Negro youths that had not completed their secondary education. About twenty firms (including, of course, Nationwide) were asked to participate in the goal of providing employment for a total of 300 male minority group youths for a three-week period prior to the beginning of school. Although the city asked for immediate commitments, the desired responses were not very vocal. Nationwide was one of the few corporations that immediately agreed to take part in the project. The insurer offered to hire fifty of the 300 quota for the three-week period and to place them in other than service-type positions. Of the 300 youths whom the city wished to have employed, only 189 were placed in positions offered by the twenty companies originally approached. Of these 189, fifty-nine (rather than the fifty initially accepted) were employed on meaningful jobs. (Five of these youths were still employed a year later on a part-time, after-school-hours basis because of a temporary need and the demonstrated performance of the youths.) To obtain employment for the approximate 100 of the unfilled quota, a company officer spearheaded a movement to raise the funds (about $9,000) from other local employers necessary for the city to hire those 100 youths not already employed.

Nationwide Insurance is engaged continuously in other minority group recruiting and community actions too numerous to detail. What gives the insurer's efforts and results such dramatic impact, and demonstrates what can be achieved by the industry, is the fact that the company is not the largest of its type in the industry and is heavily engaged in the property-liability in addition to the more profitable life area.

New York Life Insurance Company

This corporation was the first insurance company to join the federal Plans for Progress program and the first "white" company to hire a Negro agent. It is obvious from both their actions and their reputation that the president and the chairman of the board of New York Life strongly endorse a policy of nondiscriminatory hiring practices, in both the insurer's home and field locations.

The company exercises extensive recruiting efforts in local, and predominantly Negro high schools as well as in a number of colleges. The results of these efforts are noteworthy: at the time the study of New York Life was being conducted, 30 percent of the new employees being hired in its home office were nonwhite and the insurer had approximately 100 Negro agents, many of whom successfully solicit business from markets that are integrated to some degree. At present, 50 percent of the new employees hired in its home office are nonwhite and the number of Negro agents is over 250. In addition, not all of the company's Negro employees are in clerical positions: at the time of the interviewing process, the insurer had already advanced a number of Negro employees to higher-level technical and supervisory positions, including an assistant field manager, a general manager, an investment assistant vice-president, an actuarial student, and several electronic technicians.

The Negro recruiting/hiring and promotion policies of New York Life are among the most progressive and the earliest in the industry and its other activities involving the Negro population emphasize its basic nondiscriminatory employment practices. For example, the insurer participates in the National Urban League's program that enlists companies to host a professor or placement officer from a Negro college. The objective is to expose the visitor to the actual employment conditions and opportunities in the participating company for transmission to the college's students. Then, during the summer of 1968, the company fulfilled the first of two pledges to the National Alliance of Businessmen (NAB) by hiring 113 minority youths in summer jobs. The second NAB commitment was to hire and train ninety hard-core unemployed before July 1969. By mid-September 1969, that commitment had been fulfilled and the insurer is about to undertake an additional commitment to NAB to hire ninety more employees.

To prepare employees for promotion, the insurer encourages all employees who wish to prepare for higher-level jobs to continue their education at night. In addition to reimbursing tuition costs, the insurer places its most promising night school students in a "cadet" program of on-the-job training. The benefits of this program include the previously mentioned tuition refund and other advantages, such as premium wages and an intensive program of extra training designed to further promotion. Special efforts are made to recruit Negroes who can take advantage of this program.

To combat the problem of an insufficient supply of qualified Negro applicants for stenographic jobs, New York Life—again in cooperation with the National Urban League—initiated a special "Stenographic Development Program" in July 1964. The insurer absorbs all costs of the program, which is conducted over a fifteen-hour week, six-week period. Since 1964, over 100 women have completed the course, about half have been hired by the company. Most of the other participants have obtained jobs with other employers.

In addition to the insurer's many so-called minor projects—such as its keypunch operators' program—one final project should be mentioned. New York Life is contemplating establishing a special training program for high school graduates to instruct them in the very basic fundamentals of reading, writing, and other elementary skills. As New York Life and other local insurers explained, this type training is essential since the actual level of education obtained in the public school system is far below what is necessary to perform clerical tasks that require even the most minimal level of education.

Pan-American Life Insurance Company

In comparison to the three insurers discussed above, Pan-American is both small and new to the ranks of progressive insurers that follow nondiscriminatory hiring practices. It is included here not only because it is one of the leading insurers in the deep South in terms of its Negro employment policies but also because of the rapid advances it is making in this area. The latter situation almost seems inevitable, for, after talking with the officers of this company, it was clear that the insurer is exceptionally sincere and determined in its efforts to integrate its home office work force (its agency system almost precludes enforcement of a nondiscriminatory field hiring policy).

Pan-American voluntarily became an Equal Opportunity Employer early in 1965. This fact was communicated at that time to every home office employee through a letter bearing the signature of the insurer's president; the new status was inserted in the company's personnel advertisements and revealed to all local employment agencies; and, an Equal Opportunity Policy statement was inserted in the insurer's supervisory administrative manuals.

These measures were followed by actions designed to implement the corporation's nondiscriminatory hiring policy. Meetings were held with company supervisors to orient them with the company's newly stated employment philosophy and, literally, to explain how to interview Negroes. Moreover, at these meetings, and through other devices, the personnel department's strong supervision over *all* home office hiring, promotions, and terminations was underscored. *Absolute* authority over employment is vested in the insurer's department heads. The personnel department's employment and promotion recommendations, however, are weighed very heavily by the supervisors. If it is felt that a department head rejects Negro applicants on a basis other than merit, the manager is told quite directly that if his action results in a charge of discrimination against the company, he will have to attend any hearings that are conducted. This usually encourages a supervisor to reverse any discriminatory decisions he has made.

An elaborate—and effective—feedback system was developed concerning all employment, promotions, and terminations to enforce the insurer's nondiscriminatory stand. The details of the system are much too numerous for explanation here; nevertheless, its effectiveness was demonstrated quite sufficiently during the process of interviewing the company.

Pan-American has not experienced a tight labor market except in some of the clerical areas that require higher-skill levels, such as secretarial positions. Many of the applicants (and resulting employees) are "walk-ins"; hence, the insurer does little recruiting, as such. It does recruit, however, at predominantly Negro high schools and has conducted on-campus recruitment at several Negro colleges to secure applicants from college graduates for entry-level jobs. The insurer also has been in continuous contact with the local Urban League for personnel development purposes, but has not participated in any of the Urban League's specific programs. As a result of the recruiting activities in which it has engaged, Pan-American had been able to employ at least one Negro in all but two or three small departments in the home office by mid-1967, even though the insurer's first nonmaintenance Negro employee was not hired until March 1966.

Despite the absence of a tight labor market environment, the company has adopted a more flexible policy in its minimum entry test scores for Negro clerical applicants. Also, entry tests that have been validated for cultural differences are currently being used.

Of all the organization's recruiting and hiring activities, one of the most noteworthy is the New Orleans' "cooperative education program" in which it participates with several area high schools. The company agrees to employ during an academic year approximately a dozen seniors who work and attend school on a half-time basis. At the end of the year, the students are offered permanent white collar jobs with the insurer, on the condition that they are able to meet the testing requirements of the personnel department. Pan-American has such an arrangement with four predominantly white and two predominantly Negro high schools. At the time the interview with the company was conducted, it had employed thirteen students under the program, four of whom were Negroes.

Further, Pan-American has taken part in the National Alliance of Businessmen Program and, as a result, has hired eight hardcore unemployables. The insurer also actively participated in several programs for Negroes supported by the Manpower Training and Development Act. Under these programs, approximately sixty Negroes were trained in basic educational areas and, in addition, were counseled in such concepts as conduct during an employment interview. Of those engaged in the programs, ten were hired by the company to fill white collar positions.

THE PRO AND CON FACTORS, FINAL COMMENTS

There are many factors which weigh heavily against increased Negro employment in the insurance industry. If, however, there is a change in certain negative attitudes, such as those regarding the capability of Negroes to produce sales in an integrated society; if the federal government continues its nondiscriminatory hiring pressures; and, above all, if cases such as those just described become more common, these negative factors may be overcome.

CHAPTER VI.

Concluding Observations

EMPLOYMENT STATUS OF NEGROES

It would seem essential that this study be concluded with an assessment of the overall effectiveness of the insurance industry in its role as an employer that does not practice discrimination in the hiring and promotion of Negro employees. Any evaluation of this type should include not only an analysis of the equal employment progress of insurance companies as a group, but also their accomplishments in relation to those of other industries.

Unfortunately, even if these two bases of comparison were made, the results would be inconclusive. If, for example, other industries are found to have an unusually low percent Negro employment, the insurance industry, with perhaps only a slightly higher Negro employment ratio, would appear in an unjustifiably favorable light. Similarly, an attempt to categorize the entire insurance enterprise as discriminatory or nondiscriminatory really only produces an "average" employment view of the industry. And, like all averages, it will be influenced by extremes at both ends of the scale. The effect of these analytical difficulties is obvious: inaccurate inferences very likely would arise from any attempts to generalize about Negro employment in the insurance industry as a whole or in comparison with other industries. Any appraisal of the industry's effectiveness, therefore, must be made on a regional and individual insurer basis.

Regional Status

The insurance companies domiciled in the eastern region are by far the most progressive as compared to the insurers headquartered in other locales. This is objectively evident from the statistics presented in Chapters III and IV. Perhaps equally as important, the subjective impression gained while interviewing the eastern companies participating in this study was even more favorable. The majority of the insurers genuinely appear to want to eliminate discriminatory employment and promotion practices.

This attitude is not present to the same degree, of course, in all companies located in the East. Nevertheless, the outstanding measurable accomplishments of some of the eastern establishments compensate for the less favorable efforts of other insurers in that area and thus elevate the aggregate results above those of insurers in other regions.

It is much more difficult to determine on the basis of statistical evidence whether the insurers in the Pacific Coast area, the South, or the Midwest should be assigned to the position following the East. Too many variables, such as the following, are present for an objective judgment to be made: the number of Negroes in blue collar positions, the statistical anomaly caused by the Negro salesmen usually employed in the marketing of industrial life insurance; and the size of some of the corporations, as well as the portion of the total insurance market they command.

Subjectively, however, a surprising and unexpected Negro employment pattern was observed. Some Midwest and Pacific Coast insurers of a given size demonstrated much less willingness than southern companies of a comparable size to actively pursue non-discriminatory employment practices. It must be stressed, however, that information concerning the Pacific Coast is limited. Moreover, the author's pre-interview employment expectations for the Midwest and Pacific Coast were higher than for the South and this undoubtedly affected the judgment.

Changes in Negro Employment

Whether or not the growth in Negro employment in the insurance industry as described in Chapter IV may be termed sufficient or inadequate, the fact remains that an overall increase did occur. It is the impression of the writer that the increment was at least adequate.

Somewhat more definite conclusions may be drawn concerning the effectiveness of the industry in improving Negro employment in the higher-level white collar positions. In this area, the insurers' record is not at all favorable and there is much room for improvement. Any advances by the industry as a whole, however, probably will not occur for some time. The restraining factor is the companies' policy of promoting from within their own ranks and largely on the basis of seniority. Advancement from a clerical to even a lower managerial position usually requires long years of service by employees. Hence, since Negroes are a relatively new (although hopefully permanent) factor in the industry's white collar work force, they (as a group) may expect to remain in the lower-level clerical and supervisory jobs for a substantial period of time before promotions into executive positions occur.

There are, and will be, of course, exceptions to this generalization. Nevertheless, the industry seems to be trapped by its own advancement customs. The insurers appear to fear, in all earnestness, that if the promotion system is changed to accelerate the upgrading of only Negro employees, accusations of reverse discrimination will be made, employee morale in general will suffer and productivity will be adversely affected. The validity of these arguments might well be questioned, but such a challenge probably would be to no avail. The insurance industry, with the exception of a very few companies, apparently is determined not to change its promotion procedures. As long as the present advancement system is maintained, therefore, Negro employees in insurance companies will be concentrated in clerical jobs and their promotion into managerial positions will proceed at a rate far below that which might occur in other industries.

Impact of Unions

Beginning in approximately 1895, numerous and persistent attempts have been made to unionize the clerical and sales staff of various insurers.[48] With only rare exceptions, however, the organizing efforts have not met with substantial success. Clerical personnel—for all intents and purposes—are entirely nonunion employees. Of the several types of sales representatives common to the insurance industry, it is primarily the industrial agent that has been successfully organized to some extent. The numerical inroads made by unions among these sales personnel, however, are very limited and seem to be confined primarily to the industrial sales force of the giant insurance corporations, such as the Metropolitan Life Insurance Company.[49]

The general absence of unionism in the insurance industry has been attributed to many elements. Most of the hypotheses concerning the various contributing causes are based on a good deal of subjective analysis. Several widely accepted reasons for the unorganized status of insurance workers include (1) the negative

---

[48] Harvey J. Clermont, *Organizing the Insurance Worker: A History of Labor Unions of Insurance Employees* (Washington, D. C.: The Catholic University of America Press, 1966), pp. 219-222.

[49] *Ibid.*, pp. 223-224.

attitude of insurers toward unionization—as expressed in passive terms as compared to active opposition; (2) the apparent indifference of the vast majority of insurance personnel toward the entire concept of the collective bargaining process; (3) the high turnover of clerical staff which hampers organizing drives; and (4) the strong emphasis given by most companies to the policy of stressing the professional status, independence, and importance of their salesmen.

There is no indication that the factors hindering the organization of insurance workers will be eliminated in the near future. Hence, because of their absence, unions are not expected to be an important factor in altering Negro employment patterns within the insurance industry—whether for better or worse.

SUGGESTIONS FOR
IMPROVING THE EMPLOYMENT STATUS OF NEGROES

It is not difficult to offer proposals for increasing the number of Negroes hired by the insurance industry and accelerating promotions once they are employed. Effecting the changes is a much more complicated process.

For example, it is simple to suggest that tradition, company policy, and effect on employee morale be ignored and that Negroes be promoted in a different, more advantageous manner than that applicable to other employees. To endorse this suggestion— regardless of its moral correctness or incorrectness—requires an executive staff both courageous and perhaps endowed with a strong social philosophy. (Such executives, it might be noted, do exist—if as a minority—in the insurance industry.) The following suggestions are proposed, therefore, with full cognizance of the obstacles blocking their acceptance.

One approach for increasing Negro employment within the insurance industry is the specific lowering of hiring standards applicable to Negroes. A few insurers tacitly do this; most, however, expect all new hires in a given category to possess the same skills and abilities. The adoption of this suggestion for varying employment criteria clearly would require an insurer to decide whether it has the right to expect its owners to subsidize (via reduced profits) the hiring of less efficient personnel in lieu of individuals with greater ability.

A second possibility is the introduction of training programs especially designed to upgrade the skills of Negro employees so that they may be promoted to higher-level jobs. Again, the very basic question that must be answered before such a plan can be inaugurated is whether society is justified in expecting a business firm to divert part of its income to philanthropically oriented projects, especially when such projects are designed to benefit only one group.

A third technique is for other companies to adopt the internal practices of those insurers that have made significant progress in hiring and promoting Negroes. The greatest difficulty in utilizing this method is the vast differences in size between the pace-setting insurers and those that might hope to adopt the formers' procedures. That is, the more progressive companies are giants in the industry whose financial condition is, to say the least, very sound. It is much easier for this type insurer to engage in socially oriented advancement activities for the benefit of the black community than it is for a corporation that is still struggling to achieve and/or maintain its market and financial strength. The larger companies, for example, can absorb the expenses of extensive, country-wide recruiting activities at Negro colleges which would be prohibitively expensive for smaller insurers. Despite the validity of this generalization, however, it should be noted that one so-called "small" property-liability stock insurer that participated in this study is as insistent on the use of the recruiting example cited as the largest of the mutual life companies.

A fourth, and perhaps the most practical and feasible suggestion, is a change in the monitoring activities of the Office of Federal Contract Compliance (OFCC).[50] Three modifications would seem to be in order. First, the compliance reviews conducted by OFCC should not be directed primarily toward the larger insurers but should encompass those smaller insurance companies that are federal contractors. It became apparent very early during the interviewing process that the Negro employment practices of only the very largest insurers were being investigated. Ironically, those organizations were the industry leaders in providing equal employment opportunities for Negroes well before the initiation of OFCC's compliance reviews.

Perhaps the theory of OFCC is that maximum results from a given amount of effort can be obtained by examining those corporations with the greatest number of employees. The results of this study indicate, however, that it is actually the smaller federal

---

[50] The same line of reasoning can be applied to the Equal Employment Opportunity Commission.

contractors that need policing. It can only be assumed that the OFCC is conducting its investigations of insurers in descending order of magnitude and market control and that smaller insurers eventually will be examined.

The second proposal for modification of OFCC's procedures of inquiry involves a shift in its objectives. Rather than merely acting as auditors (as all insurers indicated is the case), the agency should facilitate the circulation of ideas and positive approaches that eliminate economic discrimination against Negroes. Most corporations interviewed did not express displeasure with the concept of a compliance review per se, but rather with its almost exclusively negative aspects. As several executives noted, they are willing to be told the incorrect hiring, promotion, and administrative procedures they are following, but they also would be receptive to positive suggestions for alleviating undesirable employment practices and/or conditions. These companies believe that the OFCC can perform a very valuable service by acting as both a monitor and disseminator of ideas in order to further non-discriminatory employment procedures.

The third proposal applicable to the OFCC's functions is better coordination by EEOC and OFCC so that the situation is eliminated where two visits are made to some insurers and none to other companies.

Despite the negative aspects so clearly evident in the insurance industry, it would be a mistake to lose sight of the recent improvements that have been made by insurers as a whole in the employment of Negroes. The continuation of the leadership demonstrated by the more prominent insurers, combined with the increasing influence and pressure exerted by the federal government, should result in additional advances in the elimination of discrimination against Negro employees. No matter how slowly these advances seem to be taking place, they should be viewed at the very least as a positive step forward in the quest of Negroes for equal employment opportunities.

Appendix A

HISTORY OF NEGRO LIFE INSURANCE COMPANIES

Negro life insurance companies have existed in the United States since 1787 [1] in the form of "church relief societies, crude but effective units" that were first organized by free Negroes in the North. These societies were established, initially in the North and later in the South, because of the precarious economic condition of the free Negroes. The societies also served as centers of social activities and religious worship and were important factors in the social and economic life of the free Negroes and to some extent of the slaves.[2] In New York City, for example, prior to 1914

> Negroes, foreign-born and native, established benevolent, fraternal and protective societies to keep up old friendships and provide insurance for themselves and families in sickness and death. The vast majority of New York's Negro population belonged to insurance and fraternal societies. The largest Negro insurance company of Virginia, the True Reformers [organized in 1881], has a branch office in the city.[3]

The leaders of these organizations had neither insurance knowledge nor training. They operated the societies on the basis of a small initiation fee and small periodic payments, both of which were arbitrarily determined. These rather uncomplicated efforts, however, laid the foundation for the structure of what is now the largest, most successful, and longest sustained business conducted by Negroes—life insurance.[4]

Although some insurance enterprises were organized as cooperative ventures by Negroes for self-protection or grew out of church

---

[1] W. J. Trent, Jr., "Development of Negro Life Insurance Enterprises" (unpublished Master's dissertation, Graduate School of Business Administration, University of Pennsylvania, 1932), p. 2.

[2] Joseph A. Pierce, *Negro Business and Business Education* (New York: Harper and Brothers, 1947), p. 8.

[3] Gilbert Osofsky, *Harlem: The Making of a Ghetto* (New York: Harper and Row, Torchbook edition, 1968), p. 31.

[4] Pierce, *op. cit.*, p. 8.

relief, mutual benefit societies, fraternal orders, or undertaking businesses, others were started by enterprising Negro entrepreneurs who took an "economic detour" to use their talents and to serve their clients.[5] The Negro life industry's growth was slow, however, because of the difficulty in obtaining capital. This was due, in part, to numerous publications that emphasized the hazardous financial consequences caused by unfavorable Negro mortality rates. The best known of these publications was Frederick L. Hoffman's *Race Traits and Tendencies of the American Negro,* which appeared in 1896. The author endeavored to show that, because of social diseases, living conditions and other undesirable circumstances, Negroes were undesirable insurance risks.[6]

Despite these difficulties, Negro owned life insurers continued to appear and generally were established in those cities that had a sizeable Negro population. The latter tendency still prevails since Negro business is, for the most part, solely dependent upon Negroes for its patronage and therefore must be located in sections of the country where large Negro populations are found, such as in urban areas in the South and a few cities in the East and Middle West where large groups of Negroes have settled.[7]

By 1930 there were fifty life insurance companies owned and operated by Negroes, thirteen of which were legal reserve corporations, with the remainder being assessment associations.[8] By 1937, these Negro owned life companies employed more than 9,000 persons.[9] In 1947, according to one study, the number of Negro insurers of all types had increased to 211, the vast majority of which were some type of life company.[10] The same study

---

[5] M. S. Stuart, *An Economic Detour: A History of Insurance in the Lives of the American Negroes* (New York: Wendell Mallet and Company, 1940), Chapter I-III.

[6] Pierce, *op. cit.,* p. 12.

[7] Durham, North Carolina was described by the late E. Franklin Frazier as the capital of the black bourgeois because of the location there of several very successful Negro owned enterprises, including the largest Negro life insurance company, North Carolina Mutual Life Insurance Company. Later Chicago and Detroit claimed this titular honor. See E. Franklin Frazier, *The Black Bourgeouise: The Rise of a New Middle Class* (New York: The Free Press, 1957), pp. 124-25.

[8] Trent, *op. cit.,* p. 91.

[9] Stuart, *op. cit.,* p. 49.

[10] Robert H. Kinzer & Edward Sagarin, *The Negro in American Business* (New York: Greenberg, 1950), pp. 93-96.

contends that employment among these 211 insurance organizations included "literally thousands of home office executives and minor officials, and about 10,000 agents." [11] The employment total appears somewhat exaggerated, however, since data from the 1950 Census of Population, as noted earlier, indicate that total Negro employment in the *entire industry* was 15,600. Even after allowing for the possible distortion in the employment figures included in the 1947 study, those data indicate that the number of Negroes employed by white companies in the 1945-1950 period was very small.

Perhaps the most detailed profile of Negro owned life insurers during the 1945-1950 period is found in a 1945 study of the forty-four member companies of the National Negro Insurance Association.[12]

Geographically, in 1945 the member firms of the National Negro Insurance Association operated most frequently in the South. In addition, in terms of their assets, the insurance capital concentration of Negro insurers also was located in the South. The companies as an aggregate had been doing business on an average for 23.7 years. Six insurers had been operating, as they were then organized, for less than ten years; nine had been established for forty or more years and two companies had been in existence for more than fifty years. The insurers were classified as follows: thirty legal reserve companies, eight assessment and mutual aid companies, five burial insurance companies, and one fraternal society. Twenty-seven of the forty-four firms were organized as stock insurers.

In terms of types of policies issued, ordinary life insurance and endowment insurance were written by 20 companies, industrial life insurance by 38 companies, industrial health and accident by 29 companies, other industrial insurance by 5 companies, group life insurance by 3 companies, ordinary annuities by 2 companies, and ordinary health and accident insurance by 1 company. The median number of policies in force per company was 59,999.5. The total number of policies in force for the insurers as an aggregate was 3,940,704, of which 232,441 were ordinary policies, 3,860,890 were industrial or health and accident policies and 79,-814 were not specified as to type. The average size of ordinary policies was $690 and the median size of all industrial contracts

---

[11] *Ibid.*, p .98.

[12] Pierce, *op. cit.*, Chapter 4.

was $140.28. As an aggregate, the insurers issued in 1945 a total of 1,314,583 policies, which amounted to $267,496,314 of insurance in force.[13]

The total income, during 1945, of the forty-four member companies of the National Negro Insurance Association was $42,253,-526.29. This income was dispersed primarily in the form of compensation to employees and in payments to policyholders, and the data on these two items indicate the importance of life insurance at that time as a business in the economy of the Negro. In 1945, for example, the forty-four companies paid to policyholders approximately $8.8 million. The compensations of workers in forty of the forty-four insurers amounted to about $14.5 million, an indication of the part which life insurance played as a source for the employment of Negroes. The payments were divided as follows: field forces, $12.2 million; home office employees, $2.3 million.

In addition to the data on salaries, twenty-seven insurers were sampled in order to determine the characteristics of the Negro insurers' management and other personnel. It was found that, among the twenty-seven companies included in the survey, 232 persons were employed at the executive level in the companies' home offices. Of these executives, 204, or 87.9 percent, were men and 28, or 12.1 percent, were women. Men predominated in the top executive positions of Negro owned life insurance companies, but women also were found in some of the highest positions. For example, there was one woman president, one secretary, and one treasurer. In the highly specialized positions, however, except that of medical director, women were well represented. For example, of 16 auditors, 3 were women; of 19 cashiers, 14 were women; and of 13 actuaries, 3 were women. The ages of the executive personnel ranged from 35 years to over 65 years. Presidents and treasurers, who on the average were about 60 years old, were generally older than any other executives. In general, the younger executives were found as cashiers, actuaries, superintendents of underwriting, and superintendents of ordinary departments. The latter individuals were usually in their early 40's.

Other than at the management level, Negro owned life insurers offered substantial employment opportunities for persons to perform general or routine tasks. The twenty-seven companies were found to employ 884 persons in their home offices and 5,667

---

[13] *Ibid.*

individuals in their branch offices, or a total of 6,551 persons. The employees in the home offices were about one-third male, whereas the branch office workers were about one-third female. These employees had, on the average, 8.2 years of business experience. Their experience had been gained in a wide variety of lines of business, although the insurers themselves provided the training for the largest percentage of their employees. In terms of occupations, clerks, salesmen, and office secretaries constituted, as an aggregate, about two-thirds of all the employees of the twenty-seven insurers sampled. The usual employee, however, had a wide variety of duties to perform, some of which were not consistent with the title of the individual's position. Similarly, the wages of employees in a single occupation covered an unusually wide range. For example, the monthly salaries of accountants ranged from $140 to $265 and for clerks average from $60 to $182.[14]

In contrast to the characteristics of the forty-four companies discussed above are the traits of the forty-six companies that, at present, are members of the National Insurance Association (formerly known as the National Negro Insurance Association).[15] In 1968, the forty-six companies that belong to the Association employed 12,000 persons, including 8,000 agents.[16] As of December 31, 1967, these insurers had assets of $418 million, insurance in force of $2,330 billion, and a premium income in excess of $115 million.[17]

These Negro life insurance companies range in size from the numerous organizations that market industrial insurance to several major concerns that are outstanding entrepreneurial successes. Foremost among the latter group of corporations is the North Carolina Mutual Life Insurance Company, Durham, North Carolina. It not only is the largest Negro life insurer but also ranks among the 150 largest life insurance companies in existence in the United States. Other major Negro life insurance firms in-

---

[14] *Ibid.*

[15] In addition to the National Insurance Association member companies, there are at least seven other fairly well-known Negro life companies and a number of fraternal benefit associations that provide life insurance for their members. Letter from Chester A. Davis, Executive Secretary, National Insurance Association, January 24, 1969.

[16] *Ibid.*

[17] National Insurance Association, *Report of the Actuary for Year Ending December 31, 1967.*

clude Golden State Mutual Life Insurance Company, Los Angeles; Supreme Life Insurance Company of America, Chicago; Atlanta Life Insurance Company, Atlanta, Georgia; and Universal Life Insurance Company, Memphis, Tennessee.

Negro entrepreneurship in the property-liability field is not nearly so prevalent as in the life area. There apparently is only one Negro owned multiple line company currently in existence and it is domiciled in Atlanta, Georgia.[18] The general absence of Negro entrepreneurs in all types of business activities and the problems of underwriting coverages such as automobile and fire insuarnce for black consumers appear to be basic factors limiting the organization of Negro owned property-liability firms.

Negro owned life insurance companies historically have been significant in providing protection for a market generally neglected by the main stream of the industry. At the same time the Negro insurers were a source of employment and training for people who otherwise would have been denied work opportunities. It is this very prominence in furthering employment of the black community that currently is affecting the Negro companies in an adverse manner. White insurers anxious to increase their ratio of Negro employees have found in the Negro companies' personnel a prime source of proficient and experienced black workers. The Negro firms thus are major targets for a vast number of recruiters. Concurrent with the Negro concerns' difficulties in preventing a crippling drain on their work force are the increasing efforts by white firms to capture the Negro market. The combined effect of these two events will ultimately have an impact—and probably detrimental—on those Negro firms that have pioneered in developing both the Negro life insurance market and employment skills and opportunities among black employees.

---

[18] Harding B. Young and James M. Hund, "Negro Entrepreneurship in Southern Economic Development," in Melvin L. Greenhut and W. Tate Whitman, *Essays in Southern Economic Development* (Chapel Hill: University of North Carolina Press, 1964), pp. 132-133.

Appendix B

Basic Statistical Tables, 1964, 1966

TABLE B-1. Insurance Industry

Employment by Race, Sex, and Occupational Group Northeast Region 1964

Occupational Group	All Employees			Male			Female		
	Total	Negro	Percent Negro	Total	Negro	Percent Negro	Total	Negro	Percent Negro
Officials and managers	9,010	112	1.2	7,643	3	*	1,367	109	8.0
Professionals	7,880	42	0.5	6,989	22	0.3	891	20	2.2
Technicians	4,049	56	1.4	2,719	26	1.0	1,330	30	2.3
Sales workers	28,278	112	0.4	28,189	112	0.4	89	—	—
Office and clerical	61,397	2,935	4.8	9,870	286	2.9	51,527	2,649	5.1
Total white collar	110,614	3,257	2.9	55,410	449	0.8	55,204	2,808	5.1
Craftsmen	655	9	1.4	592	9	1.5	63	—	—
Operatives	404	10	2.5	379	7	1.8	25	3	12.0
Laborers	201	59	29.4	101	55	54.5	100	4	4.0
Service workers	3,063	185	6.0	1,414	89	6.3	1,649	96	5.8
Total blue collar	4,323	263	6.1	2,486	160	6.4	1,837	103	5.6
Total	114,937	3,520	3.1	57,896	609	1.1	57,041	2,911	5.1

Source: Data in author's possession.

* Less than 0.05 percent.

Note: For regional definitions, see Table 11.

TABLE B-2. *Insurance Industry*
Employment by Race, Sex, and Occupational Group
New England Region
1964

Occupational Group	All Employees			Male			Female		
	Total	Negro	Percent Negro	Total	Negro	Percent Negro	Total	Negro	Percent Negro
Officials and managers	1,705	1	0.1	1,504	1	0.1	201	—	—
Professionals	2,901	9	0.3	2,629	9	0.3	272	—	—
Technicians	2,053	9	0.4	1,459	3	0.2	594	6	1.0
Sales workers	2,056	3	0.1	2,054	3	0.1	2	—	—
Office and clerical	12,885	399	3.1	1,457	56	3.8	11,428	343	3.0
Total white collar	21,600	421	1.9	9,103	72	0.8	12,497	349	2.8
Craftsmen	56	—	—	56	—	—	—	—	—
Operatives	53	—	—	41	—	—	12	—	—
Laborers	199	57	28.6	100	54	54.0	99	3	3.0
Service workers	213	13	6.1	87	6	6.9	126	7	5.6
Total blue collar	521	70	13.4	284	60	21.1	237	10	4.2
Total	22,121	491	2.2	9,387	132	1.4	12,734	359	2.8

Source: Data in author's possession.

Note: For regional definitions, see Table 11.

TABLE B-3. Insurance Industry
Employment by Race, Sex, and Occupational Group
New Jersey and New York
1964

Occupational Group	All Employees			Male			Female		
	Total	Negro	Percent Negro	Total	Negro	Percent Negro	Total	Negro	Percent Negro
Officials and managers	6,576	109	1.7	5,571	2	*	1,005	107	10.6
Professionals	4,428	33	0.7	3,861	13	0.3	567	20	3.5
Technicians	1,691	46	2.7	1,030	22	2.1	661	24	3.6
Sales workers	26,100	108	0.4	26,021	108	0.4	79	—	—
Office and clerical	46,162	2,479	5.4	8,320	225	2.7	37,842	2,254	6.0
Total white collar	84,957	2,775	3.3	44,803	370	0.8	40,154	2,405	6.0
Craftsmen	598	9	1.5	535	9	1.7	63	—	—
Operatives	351	10	2.8	338	7	2.1	13	3	23.1
Laborers	2	2	100.0	1	1	100.0	1	1	100.0
Service workers	2,837	170	6.0	1,317	82	6.2	1,520	88	5.8
Total blue collar	3,788	191	5.0	2,191	99	4.5	1,597	92	5.8
Total	88,745	2,966	3.3	46,994	469	1.0	41,751	2,497	6.0

Source: Data in author's possession.

*Less than 0.05 percent.

TABLE B-4. *Insurance Industry*
Employment by Race, Sex, and Occupational Group
Pennsylvania
1964

Occupational Group	All Employees			Male			Female		
	Total	Negro	Percent Negro	Total	Negro	Percent Negro	Total	Negro	Percent Negro
Officials and managers	729	2	0.3	568	—	—	161	2	1.2
Professionals	551	—	—	499	—	—	52	—	—
Technicians	305	1	0.3	230	1	0.4	75	—	—
Sales workers	122	1	0.8	114	1	0.9	8	—	—
Office and clerical	2,350	57	2.4	93	5	5.4	2,257	52	2.3
Total white collar	4,057	61	1.5	1,504	7	0.5	2,553	54	2.1
Craftsmen	1	—	—	1	—	—	—	—	—
Operatives	—	—	—	—	—	—	—	—	—
Laborers	—	—	—	—	—	—	—	—	—
Service workers	13	2	15.4	10	1	10.0	3	1	33.3
Total blue collar	14	2	14.3	11	1	9.1	3	1	33.3
Total	4,071	63	1.5	1,515	8	0.5	2,556	55	2.2

Source: Data in author's possession.

TABLE B-5. Insurance Industry
Employment by Race, Sex, and Occupational Group
Midwest Region
1964

Occupational Group	All Employees			Male			Female		
	Total	Negro	Percent Negro	Total	Negro	Percent Negro	Total	Negro	Percent Negro
Officials and managers	2,765	7	0.3	2,283	3	0.1	482	4	0.8
Professionals	2,868	2	0.1	2,615	2	0.1	253	—	—
Technicians	880	6	0.7	636	2	0.3	244	4	1.6
Sales workers	766	—	—	748	—	—	18	—	—
Office and clerical	12,737	297	2.3	1,380	24	1.7	11,357	273	2.4
Total white collar	20,016	312	1.6	7,662	31	0.4	12,354	281	2.3
Craftsmen	55	2	3.6	43	2	4.7	12	—	—
Operatives	22	—	—	22	—	—	—	—	—
Laborers	2	—	—	2	—	—	—	—	—
Service workers	392	54	13.8	222	36	16.2	170	18	10.6
Total blue collar	471	56	11.9	289	38	13.1	182	18	9.9
Total	20,487	368	1.8	7,951	69	0.9	12,536	299	2.4

Source: Data in author's possession.

Note: For regional definitions, see Table 11.

TABLE B-6. *Insurance Industry*
Employment by Race, Sex, and Occupational Group
Illinois and Michigan
1964

Occupational Group	All Employees			Male			Female		
	Total	Negro	Percent Negro	Total	Negro	Percent Negro	Total	Negro	Percent Negro
Officials and managers	1,237	5	0.4	1,037	3	0.3	200	2	1.0
Professionals	1,182	1	0.1	1,069	1	0.1	113	—	—
Technicians	444	3	0.7	306	—	—	138	3	2.2
Sales workers	275	—	—	272	—	—	3	—	—
Office and clerical	5,030	189	3.8	440	18	4.1	4,590	171	3.7
Total white collar	8,168	198	2.4	3,124	22	0.7	5,044	176	3.5
Craftsmen	48	—	—	36	—	—	12	—	—
Operatives	16	—	—	16	—	—	—	—	—
Laborers	—	—	—	—	—	—	—	—	—
Service workers	252	11	4.4	140	6	4.3	112	5	4.5
Total blue collar	316	11	3.5	192	6	3.1	124	5	4.0
Total	8,484	209	2.5	3,316	28	0.8	5,168	181	3.5

Source: Data in author's possession.

TABLE B-7. Insurance Industry
Employment by Race, Sex, and Occupational Group
West Coast Region
1964

Occupational Group	All Employees			Male			Female		
	Total	Negro	Percent Negro	Total	Negro	Percent Negro	Total	Negro	Percent Negro
Officials and managers	1,223	5	0.4	937	2	0.2	286	3	1.0
Professionals	1,265	1	0.1	1,069	—	—	196	1	0.5
Technicians	280	3	1.1	208	3	1.4	72	—	—
Sales workers	361	—	—	355	—	—	6	—	—
Office and clerical	7,459	316	4.2	1,145	19	1.7	6,314	297	4.7
Total white collar	10,588	325	3.1	3,714	24	0.6	6,874	301	4.4
Craftsmen	40	2	5.0	36	2	5.6	4	—	—
Operatives	18	2	11.1	14	2	14.3	4	—	—
Laborers	1	—	—	—	—	—	1	—	—
Service workers	195	68	34.9	110	31	28.2	85	37	43.5
Total blue collar	254	72	28.3	160	35	21.9	94	37	39.4
Total	10,842	397	3.7	3,874	59	1.5	6,968	338	4.9

Source: Data in author's possession.

Note: For regional definitions, see Table 11.

TABLE B-8. *Insurance Industry*
Employment by Race, Sex, and Occupational Group
California
1964

Occupational Group	All Employees			Male			Female		
	Total	Negro	Percent Negro	Total	Negro	Percent Negro	Total	Negro	Percent Negro
Officials and managers	1,084	5	0.5	817	2	0.2	267	3	1.1
Professionals	1,094	1	0.1	919	—	—	175	1	0.6
Technicians	211	3	1.4	167	3	1.8	44	—	—
Sales workers	255	—	—	251	—	—	4	—	—
Office and clerical	6,685	312	4.7	1,116	19	1.7	5,569	293	5.3
Total white collar	9,329	321	3.4	3,270	24	0.7	6,059	297	4.9
Craftsmen	34	2	5.9	34	2	5.9	—	—	—
Operatives	13	2	15.4	13	2	15.4	—	—	—
Laborers	—	—	—	—	—	—	—	—	—
Service workers	187	64	34.2	105	29	27.6	82	35	42.7
Total blue collar	234	68	29.1	152	33	21.7	82	35	42.7
Total	9,563	389	4.1	3,422	57	1.7	6,141	332	5.4

Source: Data in author's possession.

TABLE B-9. Insurance Industry
Employment by Race, Sex, and Occupational Group
South Region
1964

Occupational Group	All Employees			Male			Female		
	Total	Negro	Percent Negro	Total	Negro	Percent Negro	Total	Negro	Percent Negro
Officials and managers	1,659	1	0.1	1,425	1	0.1	234	—	—
Professionals	2,330	7	0.3	2,168	6	0.3	162	1	0.6
Technicians	770	29	3.8	541	5	0.9	229	24	10.5
Sales workers	934	10	1.1	826	8	1.0	108	2	1.9
Office and clerical	9,922	129	1.3	1,260	24	1.9	8,662	105	1.2
Total white collar	15,615	176	1.1	6,220	44	0.7	9,395	132	1.4
Craftsmen	59	1	1.7	59	1	1.7	—	—	—
Operatives	33	8	24.2	31	6	19.4	2	2	100.0
Laborers	14	12	85.7	12	11	91.7	2	1	50.0
Service workers	224	131	58.5	124	73	58.9	100	58	58.0
Total blue collar	330	152	46.1	226	91	40.3	104	61	58.7
Total	15,945	328	2.1	6,446	135	2.1	9,499	193	2.0

Source: Data in author's possession.

Note: For regional definitions, see Table 11.

TABLE B-10. *Insurance Industry*
Employment by Race, Sex, and Occupational Group
Delaware, District of Columbia, and Maryland
1964

Occupational Group	All Employees			Male			Female		
	Total	Negro	Percent Negro	Total	Negro	Percent Negro	Total	Negro	Percent Negro
Officials and managers	340	1	0.3	287	1	0.3	53	—	—
Professionals	523	6	1.1	488	5	1.0	35	1	2.9
Technicians	267	29	10.9	149	5	3.4	118	24	20.3
Sales workers	34	—	—	34	—	—	—	—	—
Office and clerical	2,077	96	4.6	266	15	5.6	1,811	81	4.5
Total white collar	3,241	132	4.1	1,224	26	2.1	2,017	106	5.3
Craftsmen	8	1	12.5	8	1	12.5	—	—	—
Operatives	16	6	37.5	14	4	28.6	2	2	100.0
Laborers	—	—	—	—	—	—	—	—	—
Service workers	106	78	73.6	61	37	60.7	45	41	91.1
Total blue collar	130	85	65.4	83	42	50.6	47	43	91.5
Total	3,371	217	6.4	1,307	68	5.2	2,064	149	7.2

Source: Data in author's possession.

TABLE B-11. Insurance Industry
Employment by Race, Sex, and Occupational Group
Southeast Region
1964

Occupational Group	All Employees			Male			Female		
	Total	Negro	Percent Negro	Total	Negro	Percent Negro	Total	Negro	Percent Negro
Officials and managers	997	—	—	857	—	—	140	—	—
Professionals	1,270	—	—	1,185	—	—	85	—	—
Technicians	346	—	—	274	—	—	72	—	—
Sales workers	758	10	1.3	650	8	1.2	108	2	1.9
Office and clerical	5,839	26	0.4	686	8	1.2	5,153	18	0.3
Total white collar	9,210	36	0.4	3,652	16	0.4	5,558	20	0.4
Craftsmen	30	—	—	30	—	—	—	—	—
Operatives	10	1	10.0	10	1	10.0	—	—	—
Laborers	14	12	85.7	12	11	91.7	2	1	50.0
Service workers	64	50	78.1	48	34	70.8	16	16	100.0
Total blue collar	118	63	53.4	100	46	46.0	18	17	94.4
Total	9,328	99	1.1	3,752	62	1.7	5,576	37	0.7

Source: Data in author's possession.

Note: For regional definitions, see Table 11.

TABLE B-12. *Insurance Industry*
Employment by Race, Sex, and Occupational Group
Texas and Oklahoma
1964

Occupational Group	All Employees			Male			Female		
	Total	Negro	Percent Negro	Total	Negro	Percent Negro	Total	Negro	Percent Negro
Officials and managers	322	—	—	281	—	—	41	—	—
Professionals	537	1	0.2	495	1	0.2	42	—	—
Technicians	157	—	—	118	—	—	39	—	—
Sales workers	142	—	—	142	—	—	—	—	—
Office and clerical	2,006	7	0.3	308	1	0.3	1,698	6	0.4
Total white collar	3,164	8	0.3	1,344	2	0.1	1,820	6	0.3
Craftsmen	21	—	—	21	—	—	—	—	—
Operatives	7	1	14.3	7	1	14.3	—	—	—
Laborers	—	—	—	—	—	—	—	—	—
Service workers	54	3	5.6	15	2	13.3	39	1	2.6
Total blue collar	82	4	4.9	43	3	7.0	39	1	2.6
Total	3,246	12	0.4	1,387	5	0.4	1,859	7	0.4

Source: Data in author's possession.

TABLE B-13. *Insurance Industry*
Employment by Race, Sex, and Occupational Group
South Region
1966

Occupational Group	All Employees			Male			Female		
	Total	Negro	Percent Negro	Total	Negro	Percent Negro	Total	Negro	Percent Negro
Officials and managers	25,823	649	2.5	24,330	599	2.5	1,493	50	3.3
Professionals	18,143	73	0.4	17,203	55	0.3	940	18	1.9
Technicians	5,482	65	1.2	4,333	27	0.6	1,149	38	3.3
Sales workers	67,411	3,198	4.7	64,591	1,957	3.0	2,820	1,241	44.0
Office and clerical	80,143	2,359	2.9	8,724	461	5.3	71,419	1,898	2.7
Total white collar	197,002	6,344	3.2	119,181	3,099	2.6	77,821	3,245	4.2
Craftsmen	617	36	5.8	539	35	6.5	78	1	1.3
Operatives, laborers, and service workers	4,336	2,616	60.3	2,563	1,674	65.3	1,773	942	53.1
Total blue collar	4,953	2,652	53.5	3,102	1,709	55.1	1,851	943	50.9
Total	201,955	8,996	4.5	122,283	4,808	3.9	79,672	4,188	5.3

Source: U. S. Equal Employment Opportunity Commission, *Job Patterns for Minorities and Women in Private Industry, 1966.* Report No. 1 (Washington: The Commission, 1968), Part II.

Note: For regional definitions, see Table 14.

TABLE B-14. *Insurance Industry*
Employment by Race, Sex, and Occupational Group
Middle Atlantic Region
1966

Occupational Group	All Employees			Male			Female		
	Total	Negro	Percent Negro	Total	Negro	Percent Negro	Total	Negro	Percent Negro
Officials and managers	20,903	232	1.1	18,859	109	0.6	2,044	123	6.0
Professionals	20,120	135	0.7	18,575	111	0.6	1,545	24	1.6
Technicians	9,432	149	1.6	7,312	107	1.5	2,120	42	2.0
Sales workers	26,557	487	1.8	25,981	462	1.8	576	25	4.3
Office and clerical	100,866	5,264	5.2	17,179	832	4.8	83,687	4,432	5.3
Total white collar	177,878	6,267	3.5	87,906	1,621	1.8	89,972	4,646	5.2
Craftsmen	885	26	2.9	850	26	3.1	35	—	—
Operatives, laborers, and service workers	5,629	651	11.6	3,157	442	14.0	2,472	209	8.5
Total blue collar	6,514	677	10.4	4,007	468	11.7	2,507	209	8.3
Total	184,392	6,944	3.8	91,913	2,089	2.3	92,479	4,855	5.2

Source: See Table B-13.

Note: For regional definitions, see Table 14.

TABLE B-15. Insurance Industry
Employment by Race, Sex, and Occupational Group
Midwest Region
1966

Occupational Group	All Employees			Male			Female		
	Total	Negro	Percent Negro	Total	Negro	Percent Negro	Total	Negro	Percent Negro
Officials and managers	23,847	315	1.3	22,270	298	1.3	1,577	17	1.1
Professionals	22,585	85	0.4	21,303	73	0.3	1,282	12	0.9
Technicians	9,175	53	0.6	7,121	35	0.5	2,054	18	0.9
Sales workers	48,539	1,242	2.6	47,313	1,061	2.2	1,226	181	14.8
Office and clerical	102,671	2,608	2.5	11,465	371	3.2	91,206	2,237	2.5
Total white collar	206,817	4,303	2.1	109,472	1,838	1.7	97,345	2,465	2.5
Craftsmen	689	50	7.3	612	49	8.0	77	1	1.3
Operatives, laborers, and service workers	3,759	723	19.2	2,362	542	22.9	1,397	181	13.0
Total blue collar	4,448	773	17.4	2,974	591	19.9	1,474	182	12.3
Total	211,265	5,076	2.4	112,446	2,429	2.2	98,819	2,647	2.7

Source: See Table B-13.

Note: For regional definitions, see Table 14.

TABLE B-16. *Insurance Industry*
Employment by Race, Sex, and Occupational Group
Far West Region
1966

Occupational Group	All Employees			Male			Female		
	Total	Negro	Percent Negro	Total	Negro	Percent Negro	Total	Negro	Percent Negro
Officials and managers	12,408	135	1.1	11,445	114	1.0	963	21	2.2
Professionals	12,962	70	0.5	11,968	54	0.5	994	16	1.6
Technicians	5,555	45	0.8	3,984	20	0.5	1,571	25	1.6
Sales workers	26,989	475	1.8	26,073	426	1.6	916	49	5.3
Office and clerical	54,014	2,216	4.1	7,007	265	3.8	47,007	1,951	4.2
Total white collar	111,928	2,941	2.6	60,477	879	1.5	51,451	2,062	4.0
Craftsmen	239	8	3.3	196	7	3.6	43	1	2.3
Operatives, laborers, and service workers	1,360	221	16.2	898	134	14.9	462	87	18.8
Total blue collar	1,599	229	14.3	1,094	141	12.9	505	88	17.4
Total	113,527	3,170	2.8	61,571	1,020	1.7	51,956	2,150	4.1

Source: See Table B-13.

Note: For regional definitions, see Table 14.

TABLE B-17. *Insurance Industry*
Employment by Race, Sex, and Occupational Group
New England Region
1966

Occupational Group	All Employees			Male			Female		
	Total	Negro	Percent Negro	Total	Negro	Percent Negro	Total	Negro	Percent Negro
Officials and managers	8,063	15	0.2	7,420	10	0.1	643	5	0.8
Professionals	9,185	38	0.4	8,027	34	0.4	1,158	4	0.3
Technicians	4,786	32	0.7	3,432	19	0.6	1,354	13	1.0
Sales workers	9,125	18	0.2	8,946	18	0.2	179	—	—
Office and clerical	41,985	1,283	3.1	4,311	124	2.9	37,674	1,159	3.1
Total white collar	73,144	1,386	1.9	32,136	205	0.6	41,008	1,181	2.9
Craftsmen	587	9	1.5	481	9	1.9	106	—	—
Operatives, laborers, and service workers	2,387	204	8.5	1,470	162	11.0	917	42	4.6
Total blue collar	2,974	213	7.2	1,951	171	8.8	1,023	42	4.1
Total	76,118	1,599	2.1	34,087	376	1.1	42,031	1,223	2.9

Source: See Table B-13.

Note: For regional definitions, see Table 14.

Appendix C

Basic Statistical Tables, 1966, 1967

TABLE C-1. *Insurance Industry*
Consolidated [a] *Employment by Race and Company*
1967

Company	All Employees	Negro	Percent Negro
1	1,406	28	2.0
2	1,418	118	8.3
3	988	7	0.7
4	4,973	124	2.5
5	15,198	1,117	7.3
6	620	21	3.4
7	9,796	393	4.0
8	2,695	46	1.7
9	3,989	172	4.3
10	4,013	65	1.6
11	285	3	1.1
12	8,484	361	4.3
13	10,768	676	6.3
14	1,293	25	1.9
15	9,040	290	3.2
16	3,300	15	0.5
17	55,382	1,916	3.5
18	6,369	226	3.5
19	1,686	54	3.2
20	806	24	3.0
21	1,359	17	1.3
22	3,957	128	3.2
23	1,000 [b]	17 [b]	1.7
24	1,128	27	2.4
25	818	19	2.3
26	18,504	772	4.2
27	12,495	398	3.2
28	6,075	85	1.4
29	12,742	360	2.8
30	3,600 [b]	85 [b]	2.4
31	3,211	120	3.7
32	19,313	90	0.5
33	96	—	—
34	3,351	33	1.0
35	3,456	93	2.7

TABLE C-1. *Insurance Industry*
Consolidated [a] *Employment by Race and Company*
1967
(Continued)

Company	All Employees	Negro	Percent Negro
36	1,187	64	5.4
37	1,559	58	3.7
38	669	25	3.7
39	2,027	88	4.3
40	1,250	17	1.4
41	9,274	285	3.1
42	1,280	34	2.7
43	324	9	2.8
44	10,300	265	2.6
45	2,400 [b]	135 [b]	5.6
46	4,825	53	1.1
47	861	32	3.7
48	842	9	1.1
49	1,600 [b]	35 [b]	2.2
50	1,477	23	1.6
51	1,150	24	2.1
52	475	6	1.3
53	1,500	5	0.3
54	5,043	60 [b]	1.2
55	1,524	24	1.6
56	627	6	1.0
57	2,500	35	1.4
58	2,823	5	0.2
59	2,856	195	6.8
60	440	5	1.1
61	4,400 [b]	25 [b]	0.6
62	1,100	14	1.3
63	25,000 [b]	900	3.6
64	231	2	0.9
67	1,400	35	2.5
68	2,014	188	9.3
69	3,022	307	10.2
70	357	16	4.5
Total (68 Companies)	329,951	10,909	3.3

Source: Data in the author's possession.

[a] Includes all geographic locations in which a company operates.

[b] Estimated.

TABLE C-1a. *Insurance Industry*
Consolidated [a] *Employment by Race and Company*
1966

Company [b]	All Employees	Negro	Percent Negro
5	14,971	718	4.8
8	2,701	46	1.7
9	4,016	147	3.7
10	6,172	51	0.8
11	267	4	1.5
13	15,053	561	3.7
14	2,011	34	1.7
15	9,004	232	2.6
17	53,507	1,093	2.0
18	7,283	174	2.4
19	1,668	30	1.8
20	630	22	3.5
21	1,377	15	1.1
22	4,061	129	3.2
27	11,977	269	2.2
28	5,374	68	1.3
29	11,938	291	2.4
33	324	2	0.6
35	3,259	71	2.2
36	2,383	59	2.5
37	1,534	37	2.4
39	2,113	88	4.2
41	8,479	225	2.7
68	1,982	151	7.6
69	2,595	203	7.8
70	627	9	1.4
Total (27 companies)	175,306	4,729	2.7

Source: Data in the author's possession.

[a] Includes all geographic locations in which a company operates.

[b] Company numbers correspond to those enumerated in Table C-1.

TABLE C-2. *Insurance Industry*
Consolidated [a] *Employment by Race, Sex, and Company*
1967

Company [b]	Male Employees			Female Employees		
	Total	Negro	Percent Negro	Total	Negro	Percent Negro
1	505	14	2.8	901	14	1.6
3	729	1	0.1	259	6	2.3
5	7,462	361	4.8	7,736	756	9.8
6	212	6	2.8	408	15	3.7
7	7,699	318	4.1	2,097	75	3.6
8	641	8	1.2	2,054	38	1.9
9	3,100	96	3.1	889	76	8.5
10	916	27	2.9	3,097	38	1.2
11	132	2	1.5	153	1	0.7
12	3,793	137	3.6	4,691	224	4.8
13	5,950	284	4.8	4,818	392	8.1
14	517	8	1.5	776	17	2.2
15	6,785	249	3.7	2,255	41	1.8
17	35,617	566	1.6	19,765	1,350	6.8
18	3,604	134	3.7	2,765	92	3.3
19	1,232	16	1.3	454	38	8.4
20	402	1	0.2	404	23	5.7
21	1,079	16	1.5	280	1	0.4
22	3,006	95	3.2	951	33	3.5
24	384	1	0.3	744	26	3.5
25	213	4	1.9	605	15	2.5
27	5,742	131	2.3	6,753	267	4.0
28	2,804	20	0.7	3,271	65	2.0
29	5,218	51	1.0	7,524	309	4.1
31	1,248	24	1.9	1,963	96	4.9
32	10,333	46	0.4	8,980	44	0.5
34	1,109	19	1.7	2,242	14	0.6
35	1,606	38	2.4	1,850	55	3.0
36	470	31	6.6	717	33	4.6
37	778	13	1.7	781	45	5.8
38	184	4	2.2	485	21	4.3
39	1,241	43	3.5	786	45	5.7
41	4,269	119	2.8	5,005	166	3.3
68	579	20	3.5	1,435	168	11.7
69	1,226	122	10.0	1,796	185	10.3
70	136	8	5.9	221	8	3.6
Total (36 Companies)	120,921	3,033	2.5	99,911	4,792	4.8

Source: Data in the author's possession.

[a] Includes all geographic locations in which a company operates.

[b] Company numbers correspond to those enumerated in Table C-1.

TABLE C-3   *Insurance Industry*
Home Office and Field Employment by Race and Company
1967

Company*	Home Office Employees			Field Employees		
	Total	Negro	Percent Negro	Total	Negro	Percent Negro
1	790	28	3.5	616	—	—
2	827	118	14.3	591	—	—
3	252	7	2.8	736	—	—
4	2,224	95	4.3	2,749	29	1.1
5	7,279	788	10.8	7,919	329	4.2
6	375	21	5.6	245	—	—
7	1,571	91	5.8	8,225	302	3.7
8	1,950	37	1.9	745	9	1.2
9	679	44	6.5	3,310	128	3.9
10	2,169	53	2.4	1,844	12	0.7
11	214	3	1.4	71	—	—
12	2,687	200	7.4	5,797	161	2.8
13	4,752	404	8.5	6,016	272	4.5
23	500[a]	15[a]	3.0	500[a]	2[a]	0.4
26	6,300	327	5.2	12,204	445	3.6
27	1,778	128	7.2	10,717	270	2.5
28	1,673	43	2.6	4,402	42	1.0
29	2,031	96	4.7	10,711	264	2.5
30	950[a]	45[a]	4.7	2,650[a]	40[a]	1.5
31	1,200	84	7.0	2,011	36	1.8
35	1,152	41	3.6	2,304	52	2.3
37	814	45	5.5	745	13	1.7
38	669	25	3.7	[b]	[b]	—
39	827	83	10.0	1,200	5	0.4
42	657	30	4.6	623	4	0.6
43	253	9	3.6	71	0	0.0
44	1,300	49	3.8	9,000	216	2.4
45	1,000[a]	65[a]	6.5	1,400[a]	70[a]	5.0
46	1,000	13	1.3	3,825	40	1.0
47	230	32	13.9	631[a]	—	—
48	194	8	4.1	648	1	0.2
49	1,150	35[a]	3.0	450[a]	[c]	—
50	442	23	5.2	1,035	—	—

TABLE C-3. *Insurance Industry*
Home Office and Field Employment by Race and Company
1967
(Continued)

Company*	Home Office Employees			Field Employees		
	Total	Negro	Percent Negro	Total	Negro	Percent Negro
51	350	—	—	800	24	3.0
52	315	6	1.9	160	—	—
53	500	5	1.0	1,000	—	—
54	1,600	50	3.1	3,443	10 a	0.3
55	200	4	2.0	1,324	20 a	1.5
56	494	6	1.2	133	—	—
57	550	1	0.2	1,950	34	1.7
58	957	5	0.5	1,866	—	—
59	1,206	137	11.4	1,650	58	3.5
60	240	5	2.1	200	—	—
61	1,800	25 a	1.4	2,600	c	—
62	1,100	14	1.3	b	b	—
63	6,000 a	400 a	6.7	19,000 a	500 a	2.6
64	204	2	1.0	27	—	—
67	700	25	3.6	700	10	1.4
69	3,022	307	10.2	b	b	—
70	357	16	4.5	b	b	—
71	8,085	338	4.2	c	c	—
72	886	85	9.6	c	c	—
73	292	2	0.7	c	c	—
74	210	20	9.5	c	c	—
75	675	58	8.6	c	c	—
76	1,189	61	5.1	c	c	—
77	565	4	0.7	c	c	—
Total	81,386 (57 Companies)	4,661	5.7	135,794 (44 Companies)	3,398	2.5

Source: Data in the author's possession.

a Estimated.

b No field offices.

c No data.

* Company numbers correspond to those enumerated in Table C-1 (through company No. 70).

TABLE C-3a. *Insurance Industry*
Home Office and Field Employment by Race and Company
1966

Company[a]	Total Employees	Negro Employment	Percent Negro
3	261	3	1.1
5	7,191	502	7.0
6	376	25	6.6
8	1,971	38	1.9
9	652	38	5.8
10	2,174	45	2.1
11	212	4	1.9
13	4,642	297	6.4
27	1,835	64	3.5
28	1,605	28	1.7
29	1,955	112	5.7
35	1,154	24	2.1
37	812	32	3.9
39	884	87	9.8
69	2,595	203	7.8
70	627	9	1.4
71	8,269	150	1.8
72	777	59	7.6
75	622	42	6.8
76	1,156	48	4.2
Total (20 Companies)	39,770	1,810	4.6

Source: Data in the author's possession.

[a] Company numbers correspond to those enumerated in Table C-3.

TABLE C-4. *Insurance Industry*
Home Office Employment by Race, Sex, and Company
1967

Company[a]	Male Employees			Female Employees		
	Total	Negro	Percent Negro	Total	Negro	Percent Negro
1	207	14	6.8	583	14	2.4
2	253	25	9.9	574	93	16.2
3	86	1	1.2	166	6	3.6
4	657	18	2.7	1,567	77	4.9
5	3,236	190	5.9	4,043	598	14.8
6	127	6	4.7	248	15	6.0
7	438	43	9.8	1,133	48	4.2
8	500	6	1.2	1,450	31	2.1
9	278	15	5.4	401	29	7.2
10	727	23	3.2	1,442	30	2.1
11	74	2	2.7	140	1	0.7
12	976	77	7.9	1,711	123	7.2
13	2,179	101	4.6	2,573	303	11.8
27	865	64	7.4	913	64	7.0
28	743	8	1.1	930	35	3.8
29	777	17	2.2	1,254	79	6.3
35	593	22	3.7	559	19	3.4
37	334	6	1.8	480	39	8.1
38	184	4	2.2	485	21	4.3
39	377	41	10.9	450	42	9.3
69	1,226	122	10.0	1,796	185	10.3
70	136	8	5.9	221	8	3.6
71	3,324	56	1.7	4,761	282	5.9
72	266	22	8.3	620	63	10.2
75	231	18	7.8	444	40	9.0
76	313	18	5.8	876	43	4.9
Total	19,107 (26 Companies)	927	4.9	29,820	2,288	7.7

Source: Data in the author's possession.

[a] Company numbers correspond to those enumerated in Table C-3.

TABLE C-5. *Insurance Industry*
Field Employment by Race, Sex, and Company
1967

Company[a]	Male Employees			Female Employees		
	Total	Negro	Percent Negro	Total	Negro	Percent Negro
1	298	—	—	318	—	—
3	643	—	—	93	—	—
5	4,226	171	4.0	3,693	158	4.3
6	85	—	—	160	—	—
7	7,261	275	3.8	964	27	2.8
8	141	2	1.4	604	7	1.2
9	2,822	81	2.9	488	47	9.6
10	189	4	2.1	1,655	8	0.5
11	58	—	—	13	—	—
12	2,817	60	2.1	2,980	101	3.4
13	3,771	183	4.9	2,245	89	4.0
27	4,877	67	1.4	5,840	203	3.5
28	2,061	12	0.6	2,341	30	1.3
29	4,441	34	0.8	6,270	230	3.7
35	1,013	16	1.6	1,291	36	2.8
37	444	7	1.6	301	6	2.0
39	864	2	0.2	336	3	0.9
Total	36,011 (17 Companies)	914	2.5	29,592	945	3.2

Source: Data in the author's possession.

[a] Company numbers correspond to those enumerated in Table C-3.

TABLE C-6. *Insurance Industry*
Consolidated Employment by Race, Sex, and Occupational Group
United States, 1967

Occupational Group	All Employees			Male			Female		
	Total	Negro	Percent Negro	Total	Negro	Percent Negro	Total	Negro	Percent Negro
Officials and managers	23,400	85	0.4	21,463	70	0.3	1,937	15	0.8
Professionals	22,622	116	0.5	20,366	108	0.5	2,256	8	0.4
Technicians	6,174	76	1.2	4,005	51	1.3	2,169	25	1.2
Sales workers	56,503	1,036	1.8	55,389	1,024	1.8	1,114	12	1.1
Office and clerical	91,131	4,666	5.1	9,694	661	6.8	81,437	4,005	4.9
Total white collar	199,830	5,979	3.0	110,917	1,914	1.7	88,913	4,065	4.6
Craftsmen	853	54	6.3	759	54	7.1	94	—	—
Operatives, laborers, and service workers	5,507	1,216	22.1	3,303	907	27.5	2,204	309	14.0
Total blue collar	6,360	1,270	20.0	4,062	961	23.7	2,298	309	13.4
Total	206,190	7,249	3.5	114,979	2,875	2.5	91,211	4,374	4.8

Source: Data in the author's possession.

TABLE C-7. *Insurance Industry*
Home Office Employment by Race, Sex, and Occupational Group
United States, 1967

Occupational Group	All Employees			Male			Female		
	Total	Negro	Percent Negro	Total	Negro	Percent Negro	Total	Negro	Percent Negro
Officials and managers	5,208	22	0.4	4,641	14	0.3	567	8	1.4
Professionals	6,015	42	0.7	4,995	34	0.7	1,020	8	0.8
Technicians	1,922	51	2.7	1,308	34	2.6	614	17	2.8
Sales workers	368	3	0.8	219	3	1.4	149	—	—
Office and clerical	29,792	2,401	8.1	5,043	445	8.8	24,749	1,956	7.9
Total white collar	43,305	2,519	5.8	16,206	530	3.3	27,099	1,989	7.3
Craftsmen	359	11	3.1	270	11	4.1	89	—	—
Operatives, laborers, and service workers	2,108	538	25.5	1,391	340	24.4	717	198	27.6
Total blue collar	2,467	549	22.3	1,661	351	21.1	806	198	24.6
Total	45,772	3,068	6.7	17,867	881	4.9	27,905	2,187	7.8

Source: Data in author's possession.

TABLE C-8. *Insurance Industry*
Field Employment by Race, Sex, and Occupational Group
United States, 1967

Occupational Group	All Employees			Male			Female		
	Total	Negro	Percent Negro	Total	Negro	Percent Negro	Total	Negro	Percent Negro
Officials and managers	8,928	22	0.2	7,760	18	0.2	1,168	4	0.3
Professionals	9,240	48	0.5	8,444	45	0.5	796	3	0.4
Technicians	261	4	1.5	131	2	1.5	130	2	1.5
Sales workers	15,002	341	2.3	14,276	337	2.4	726	4	0.6
Office and clerical	26,678	887	3.3	2,187	102	4.7	24,491	785	3.2
Total white collar	60,109	1,302	2.2	32,798	504	1.5	27,311	798	2.9
Craftsmen	83	34	41.0	83	34	41.0	—	—	—
Operatives, laborers, and service workers	1,162	453	39.0	809	351	43.4	353	102	28.9
Total blue collar	1,245	487	39.1	892	385	43.2	353	102	28.9
Total	61,354	1,789	2.9	33,690	889	2.6	27,664	900	3.3

Source: Data in author's possession.

TABLE C-9. *Insurance Industry*
Consolidated [a] Employment by Race, Sex, and Occupational Group
East Region,[b] 1967

Occupational Group	All Employees			Male			Female		
	Total	Negro	Percent Negro	Total	Negro	Percent Negro	Total	Negro	Percent Negro
Officials and managers	13,270	44	0.3	11,840	34	0.3	1,430	10	0.7
Professionals	12,387	73	0.6	10,650	66	0.6	1,737	7	0.4
Technicians	5,043	58	1.2	3,205	36	1.1	1,838	22	1.2
Sales workers	37,619	619	1.6	36,729	607	1.7	890	12	1.3
Office and clerical	61,552	3,890	6.3	7,496	512	6.8	54,056	3,378	6.2
Total white collar	129,871	4,684	3.6	69,920	1,255	1.8	59,951	3,429	5.7
Craftsmen	670	46	6.9	578	46	8.0	92	—	—
Operatives, laborers, and service workers	4065	557	13.7	2,300	438	19.0	1,765	119	6.7
Total blue collar	4,735	603	12.7	2,878	484	16.8	1,857	119	6.4
Total	134,606	5,287	3.9	72,798	1,739	2.4	61,808	3,548	5.7

Source: Data in the author's possession.

[a] Includes all geographic locations in which a company operates.

[b] For regional definitions, see Table 17.

TABLE C-10. *Insurance Industry*

Consolidated ª Employment by Race, Sex, and Occupational Group
Midwest Region,ᵇ 1967

Occupational Group	All Employees			Male			Female		
	Total	Negro	Percent Negro	Total	Negro	Percent Negro	Total	Negro	Percent Negro
Officials and managers	7,175	33	0.5	6,707	28	0.4	468	5	1.1
Professionals	9,631	42	0.4	9,174	41	0.4	457	1	0.2
Technicians	910	15	1.6	708	14	2.0	202	1	0.5
Sales workers	6,860	186	2.7	6,853	186	2.7	7	—	—
Office and clerical	23,017	488	2.1	1,258	67	5.3	21,759	421	1.9
Total white collar	47,593	764	1.6	24,700	336	1.4	22,893	428	1.9
Craftsmen	159	7	4.4	157	7	4.5	2	—	—
Operatives, laborers, and service workers	721	167	23.2	485	145	29.9	236	22	9.3
Total blue collar	880	174	19.8	642	152	23.7	238	22	9.2
Total	48,473	938	1.9	25,342	488	1.9	23,131	450	1.9

Source: Data in the author's possession.

ª Includes all geographic locations in which a company operates.

ᵇ For regional definitions, see Table 17.

TABLE C-11. *Insurance Industry*
*Consolidated [a] Employment by Race, Sex, and Occupational Group
South Region,[b] 1967*

Occupational Group	All Employees			Male			Female		
	Total	Negro	Percent Negro	Total	Negro	Percent Negro	Total	Negro	Percent Negro
Officials and managers	2,955	8	0.3	2,916	8	0.3	39	—	—
Professionals	604	1	0.2	542	1	0.2	62	—	—
Technicians	221	3	1.4	92	1	1.1	129	2	1.6
Sales workers	12,024	231	1.9	11,807	231	2.0	217	—	—
Office and clerical	6,562	288	4.4	940	82	8.7	5,622	206	3.7
Total white collar	22,366	531	2.4	16,297	323	2.0	6,069	208	3.4
Craftsmen	24	1	4.2	24	1	4.2	—	—	—
Operatives, laborers, and service workers	721	492	68.2	518	324	62.5	203	168	82.8
Total blue collar	745	493	66.2	542	325	60.0	203	168	82.8
Total	23,111	1,024	4.4	16,839	648	3.8	6,272	376	6.0

Source: Data in the author's possession.

[a] Includes all geographic locations in which a company operates.

[b] For regional definitions, see Table 17.

TABLE C-12. Insurance Industry
Home Office Employment by Race, Sex, and Occupational Group
East Region,ᵃ 1967

Occupational Group	All Employees			Male			Female		
	Total	Negro	Percent Negro	Total	Negro	Percent Negro	Total	Negro	Percent Negro
Officials and managers	2,535	11	0.4	2,235	8	0.4	300	3	1.0
Professionals	2,629	22	0.8	1,899	16	0.8	730	6	0.8
Technicians	411	8	1.9	312	5	1.6	99	3	3.0
Sales workers	84	2	2.4	51	2	3.9	33	—	—
Office and clerical	14,644	1,416	9.7	3,436	282	8.2	11,208	1,134	10.1
Total white collar	20,303	1,459	7.2	7,933	313	3.9	12,370	1,146	9.3
Craftsmen	285	8	2.8	197	8	4.1	88	—	—
Operatives, laborers, and service workers	1,516	226	14.9	999	143	14.3	517	83	16.1
Total blue collar	1,801	234	13.0	1,196	151	12.6	605	83	13.7
Total	22,104	1,693	7.7	9,129	464	5.1	12,975	1,229	9.5

Source: Data in the author's possession.

ᵃ For regional definitions, see Table 17.

TABLE C-13. *Insurance Industry*
Home Office Employment by Race, Sex, and Occupational Group
Midwest Region,[a] *1967*

Occupational Group	All Employees			Male			Female		
	Total	Negro	Percent Negro	Total	Negro	Percent Negro	Total	Negro	Percent Negro
Officials and managers	1,946	5	0.3	1,762	—	—	184	5	2.7
Professionals	2,786	19	0.7	2,563	17	0.7	223	2	0.9
Technicians	1,304	40	3.1	916	28	3.1	388	12	3.1
Sales workers	43	1	2.3	43	1	2.3	—	—	—
Office and clerical	10,273	612	6.0	725	78	10.8	9,548	534	5.6
Total white collar	16,352	677	4.1	6,009	124	2.1	10,343	553	5.3
Craftsmen	43	1	2.3	43	1	2.3	—	—	—
Operatives, laborers, and service workers	247	72	29.1	174	68	39.1	73	4	5.5
Total blue collar	290	73	25.2	217	69	31.8	73	4	5.5
Total	16,642	750	4.5	6,226	193	3.1	10,416	557	5.3

Source: Data in the author's possession.

[a] For regional definitions, see Table 17.

TABLE C-14.　Insurance Industry
Home Office Employment by Race, Sex, and Occupational Group
South Region,[a] 1967

Occupational Group	All Employees			Male			Female		
	Total	Negro	Percent Negro	Total	Negro	Percent Negro	Total	Negro	Percent Negro
Officials and managers	727	6	0.8	644	6	0.9	83	—	—
Professionals	600	1	0.2	533	1	0.2	67	—	—
Technicians	207	3	1.4	80	1	1.2	127	2	1.6
Sales workers	241	—	—	125	—	—	116	—	—
Office and clerical	4,875	373	7.7	882	85	9.6	3,993	288	7.2
Total white collar	6,650	383	5.8	2,264	93	4.1	4,386	290	6.6
Craftsmen	31	2	6.5	30	2	6.7	1	—	—
Operatives, laborers, and service workers	345	240	69.6	218	129	59.2	127	111	87.4
Total blue collar	376	242	64.4	248	131	52.8	128	111	86.7
Total	7,026	625	8.9	2,512	224	8.9	4,514	401	8.9

Source:　Data in the author's possession.

[a] For regional definitions, see Table 17.

TABLE C-15. *Insurance Industry*
Field Employment by Race, Sex, and Occupational Group
East Region,[a] *1967*

Occupational Group	All Employees			Male			Female		
	Total	Negro	Percent Negro	Total	Negro	Percent Negro	Total	Negro	Percent Negro
Officials and managers	5,905	17	0.3	4,976	13	0.3	929	4	0.4
Professionals	5,404	33	0.6	4,737	30	0.6	667	3	0.4
Technicians	136	2	1.5	29	1	3.4	107	1	0.9
Sales workers	6,047	121	2.0	5,371	117	2.2	676	4	0.6
Office and clerical	19,102	716	3.7	1,878	80	4.3	17,224	636	3.7
Total white collar	36,594	889	2.4	16,991	241	1.4	19,603	648	3.3
Craftsmen	75	34	45.3	75	34	45.3	—	—	—
Operatives, laborers, and service workers	783	224	28.6	523	184	35.2	260	40	15.4
Total blue collar	858	258	30.1	598	218	36.5	260	40	15.4
Total	37,452	1,147	3.1	17,589	459	2.6	19,863	688	3.5

Source: Data in the author's possession.

[a] For regional definitions, see Table 17.

TABLE C-16. *Insurance Industry*
Field Employment by Race, Sex, and Occupational Group
*Midwest Region,*ᵃ *1967*

Occupational Group	All Employees			Male			Female		
	Total	Negro	Percent Negro	Total	Negro	Percent Negro	Total	Negro	Percent Negro
Officials and managers	1,380	2	0.1	1,141	2	0.2	239	—	—
Professionals	3,836	15	0.4	3,707	15	0.4	129	—	—
Technicians	125	2	1.6	102	1	1.0	23	1	4.3
Sales workers	115	—	—	114	—	—	1	—	—
Office and clerical	6,097	154	2.5	248	22	8.9	5,849	132	2.3
Total white collar	11,553	173	1.5	5,312	40	0.8	6,241	133	2.1
Craftsmen	8	—	—	8	—	—	—	—	—
Operatives, laborers, and service workers	70	39	55.7	55	34	61.8	15	5	33.3
Total blue collar	78	39	50.0	63	34	54.0	15	5	33.3
Total	11,631	212	1.8	5,375	74	1.4	6,256	138	2.2

Source: Data in the author's possession.

ᵃ For regional definitions, see Table 17.

TABLE C-17. *Insurance Industry*
Field Employment by Race, Sex, and Occupational Group
South Region,[a] *1967*

Occupational Group	All Employees			Male			Female		
	Total	Negro	Percent Negro	Total	Negro	Percent Negro	Total	Negro	Percent Negro
Officials and managers	1,643	3	0.2	1,643	3	0.2	—	—	—
Professionals	—	—	—	—	—	—	—	—	—
Technicians	—	—	—	—	—	—	—	—	—
Sales workers	8,840	220	2.5	8,791	220	2.5	49	—	—
Office and clerical	1,479	17	1.1	61	—	—	1,418	17	1.2
Total white collar	11,962	240	2.0	10,495	223	2.1	1,467	17	1.2
Craftsmen	—	—	—	—	—	—	—	—	—
Operatives, laborers, and service workers	309	190	61.5	231	133	57.6	78	57	73.1
Total blue collar	309	190	61.5	231	133	57.6	78	57	73.1
Total	12,271	430	3.5	10,726	356	3.3	1,545	74	4.8

Source: Data in the author's possession.

[a] For regional definitions, see Table 17.

TABLE C-18. *Insurance Industry*
Home Office Employment by Race, Sex, and Occupational Group
Atlanta/Birmingham/New Orleans (Grouped) SMSA's
1967

Occupational Group	All Employees			Male			Female		
	Total	Negro	Percent Negro	Total	Negro	Percent Negro	Total	Negro	Percent Negro
Officials and managers	321	1	0.3	281	1	0.4	40	—	—
Professionals	90	—	—	72	—	—	18	—	—
Technicians	45	2	4.4	39	—	—	6	2	33.3
Sales workers	44	—	—	44	—	—	—	—	—
Office and clerical	1,027	49	4.8	112	5	4.5	915	44	4.8
Total white collar	1,527	52	3.4	548	6	1.1	979	46	4.7
Craftsmen	16	1	6.2	16	1	6.2	—	—	—
Operatives, laborers, and service workers	63	56	88.9	31	27	87.1	32	29	90.6
Total blue collar	79	57	72.2	47	28	59.6	32	29	90.6
Total	1,606	109	6.8	595	34	5.7	1,011	75	7.4

Source: Data in the author's possession.

TABLE C-19. *Insurance Industry*
Home Office Employment by Race, Sex, and Occupational Group
Baltimore/District of Columbia/Richmond (Grouped) SMSA's
1967

Occupational Group	All Employees			Male			Female		
	Total	Negro	Percent Negro	Total	Negro	Percent Negro	Total	Negro	Percent Negro
Officials and managers	313	5	1.6	273	5	1.8	40	—	—
Professionals	497	1	0.2	448	1	0.2	49	—	—
Technicians	153	1	0.7	35	1	2.9	118	—	—
Sales workers	197	—	—	81	—	—	116	—	—
Office and clerical	2,491	307	12.3	502	73	14.5	1,989	234	11.8
Total white collar	3,651	314	8.6	1,339	80	6.0	2,312	234	10.1
Craftsmen	15	1	6.7	14	1	7.1	1	—	—
Operatives, laborers, and service workers	183	110	60.1	126	66	52.4	57	44	77.2
Total blue collar	198	111	56.1	140	67	47.9	58	44	75.9
Total	3,849	425	11.0	1,479	147	9.9	2,370	278	11.7

Source: Data in the author's possession.

TABLE C-20. Insurance Industry
Home Office Employment by Race, Sex, and Occupational Group
Chicago/Bloomington/Evanston (Grouped) SMSA's
1967

Occupational Group	All Employees			Male			Female		
	Total	Negro	Percent Negro	Total	Negro	Percent Negro	Total	Negro	Percent Negro
Officials and managers	1,201	—	—	1,085	—	—	116	—	—
Professionals	2,016	5	0.2	1,880	4	0.2	136	1	0.7
Technicians	907	31	3.4	695	20	2.9	212	11	5.2
Sales workers	—	—	—	—	—	—	—	—	—
Office and clerical	5,837	347	5.9	475	41	8.6	5,362	306	5.7
Total white collar	9,961	383	3.8	4,135	65	1.6	5,826	318	5.5
Craftsmen	—	—	—	—	—	—	—	—	—
Operatives, laborers, and service workers	11	1	9.1	6	1	16.7	5	—	—
Total blue collar	11	1	9.1	6	1	16.7	5	—	—
Total	9,972	384	3.9	4,141	66	1.6	5,831	318	5.5

Source: Data in the author's possession.

TABLE C-21. *Insurance Industry*
Home Office Employment by Race, Sex, and Occupational Group
Cincinnati/ Columbus/Ft. Wayne/Indianapolis (Grouped) SMSA's
1967

Occupational Group	All Employees			Male			Female		
	Total	Negro	Percent Negro	Total	Negro	Percent Negro	Total	Negro	Percent Negro
Officials and managers	670	5	0.7	606	—	—	64	5	7.8
Professionals	694	12	1.7	611	11	1.8	83	1	1.2
Technicians	299	6	2.0	191	6	3.1	108	—	—
Sales workers	18	—	—	18	—	—	—	—	—
Office and clerical	3,875	193	5.0	215	27	12.6	3,660	166	4.5
Total white collar	5,556	216	3.9	1,641	44	2.7	3,915	172	4.4
Craftsmen	34	1	2.9	34	1	2.9	—	—	—
Operatives, laborerrs, and service workers	194	64	33.0	144	60	41.7	50	4	8.0
Total blue collar	228	65	28.5	178	61	34.3	50	4	8.0
Total	5,784	281	4.9	1,819	105	5.8	3,965	176	4.4

Source: Data in the author's possession.

TABLE C-22. Insurance Industry
Home Office Employment by Race, Sex, and Occupational Group
Boston/Hartford/Springfield (Grouped) SMSA's
1967

Occupational Group	All Employees			Male			Female		
	Total	Negro	Percent Negro	Total	Negro	Percent Negro	Total	Negro	Percent Negro
Officials and managers	1,030	11	1.1	878	8	0.9	152	3	2.0
Professionals	1,090	12	1.1	736	9	1.2	354	3	0.8
Technicians	283	6	2.1	218	4	1.8	65	2	3.1
Sales workers	84	2	2.4	51	2	3.9	33	—	—
Office and clerical	4,684	235	5.0	462	24	5.2	4,222	211	5.0
Total white collar	7,171	266	3.7	2,345	47	2.0	4,826	219	4.5
Craftsmen	212	5	2.4	124	5	4.0	88	—	—
Operatives, laborers, and service workers	819	101	12.3	557	70	12.6	262	31	11.8
Total blue collar	1,031	106	10.3	681	75	11.0	350	31	8.9
Total	8,202	372	4.5	3,026	122	4.0	5,176	250	4.8

Source: Data in the author's possession.

TABLE C-23. *Insurance Industry*
Home Office Employment by Race, Sex, and Occupational Group
Kansas City/St. Louis/Nashville (Grouped) SMSA's
1967

Occupational Group	All Employees			Male			Female		
	Total	Negro	Percent Negro	Total	Negro	Percent Negro	Total	Negro	Percent Negro
Officials and managers	168	—	—	161	—	—	7	—	—
Professionals	89	2	2.2	85	2	2.4	4	—	—
Technicians	107	3	2.8	36	2	5.6	71	1	1.4
Sales workers	25	1	4.0	25	1	4.0	—	—	—
Office and clerical	1,918	89	4.6	303	17	5.6	1,615	72	4.5
Total white collar	2,307	95	4.1	610	22	3.6	1,697	73	4.3
Craftsmen	9	—	—	9	—	—	—	—	—
Operatives, laborers, and service workers	141	81	57.4	85	43	50.6	56	38	67.9
Total blue collar	150	81	54.0	94	43	45.7	56	38	67.9
Total	2,457	176	7.2	704	65	9.2	1,753	111	6.3

Source: Data in the author's possession.

TABLE C-24. Insurance Industry

Home Office Employment by Race, Sex, and Occupational Group
Newark/New York (Grouped) SMSA's
1967

Occupational Group	All Employees			Male			Female		
	Total	Negro	Percent Negro	Total	Negro	Percent Negro	Total	Negro	Percent Negro
Officials and managers	1,239	—	—	1,120	—	—	119	—	—
Professionals	1,454	10	0.7	1,101	7	0.6	353	3	0.8
Technicians	122	1	0.8	93	1	1.1	29	—	—
Sales workers	—	—	—	—	—	—	—	—	—
Office and clerical	8,579	1,123	13.1	2,682	248	9.2	5,897	875	14.8
Total white collar	11,394	1,134	10.0	4,996	256	5.1	6,398	878	13.7
Craftsmen	56	—	—	56	—	—	—	—	—
Operatives, laborers, and service workers	581	58	10.0	363	35	9.6	218	23	10.6
Total blue collar	637	58	9.1	419	35	8.4	218	23	10.6
Total	12,031	1,192	9.9	5,415	291	5.4	6,616	901	13.6

Source: Data in the author's possession.

TABLE C-25. *Insurance Industry*
Home Office Employment by Race, Sex, and Occupational Group
Philadelphia SMSA
1967

Occupational Group	All Employees			Male			Female		
	Total	Negro	Percent Negro	Total	Negro	Percent Negro	Total	Negro	Percent Negro
Officials and managers	199	—	—	173	—	—	26	—	—
Professionals	85	—	—	62	—	—	23	—	—
Technicians	6	1	16.7	1	—	—	5	1	20.0
Sales workers	—	—	—	—	—	—	—	—	—
Office and clerical	779	33	4.2	172	6	3.5	607	27	4.4
Total white collar	1,069	34	3.2	408	6	1.5	661	28	4.2
Craftsmen	17	3	17.6	17	3	17.6	—	—	—
Operatives, laborers, and service workers	116	67	57.8	79	38	48.1	37	29	78.4
Total blue collar	133	70	52.6	96	41	42.7	37	29	78.4
Total	1,202	104	8.7	504	47	9.3	698	57	8.2

Source: Data in the author's possession.

Index

Part Three

CONCLUDING ANALYSIS

by

Armand J. Thieblot, Jr.

TABLE OF CONTENTS

LIST OF TABLES

Concluding Analysis

Banking and insurance are the two major components of the vast financial structure of the country. Together they controlled over $600 billion of assets in 1967. Their 18,000 firms employed more than two million persons. In many respects the industries are similar. In not only structure and activities, but also in personnel requirements and in their history concerning hiring and using Negroes as work force participants, their experiences reflect similar philosophies and policies.

The two independent studies which comprise this volume have demonstrated the enormous complexity attendant to these industries. Although low levels of Negro representation were found in both as compared with other types of firms, the studies demonstrated by their analyses that simple pronouncements purporting to have discovered the reason for this relative lack of participation—whether in managerial discrimination or bigotry, in Negro lack of preparedness, or in some other specific cause—are almost invariably oversimplifications.

It has been the goal not only of this volume but also of other studies in this series to go beyond simply demonstrating the evolving level of Negro employment and to include analyses of the factors which have caused that level to be at its indicated position. There is much to be learned from the individual industry studies. This final chapter seeks to gain additional insight by comparing and contrasting the joint experiences of banking with insurance, and the common experiences of both with other industries. It should be no secret at this time in history, for example, that firms employing large numbers of blue collar unskilled persons will tend, other things being equal, to show larger proportions of Negroes in their work forces. Blue collar requirements, therefore, would be one such factor which might help explain differences in Negro employment levels. We shall try to examine all such differences which are critical to the employment requirements and patterns in banking and insurance.

The earlier compendium study in this series covering six manufacturing industries directed specific attention to hypotheses seeking to explain the varying racial employment patterns found among different American industries. Although those hypotheses will be outlined briefly here along with the presentation of evi-

1

dence responsive to them from the financial industries, the reader who desires more complete explanations is referred to Part One, "Introduction and Overview," in Volume I of this series.[1]

NATURE OF THE INDUSTRY

There can be no question but that the nature of any industry—the time and place of its growth, its structure, and its market orientation—has considerable impact on the acceptance of Negro work force participants by the industry. Perhaps the most significant variable concerning the nature of the industry is its demand for labor.

Demand for Labor

One of the most consistently supported hypotheses concerning Negro employment growth has been that such growth is disproportionately affected by swings in the business cycle and employment conditions. During periods of only moderate general unemployment, minority group persons, and particularly Negroes, have tended to be unemployed in disproportionate numbers. Although Negro unemployment tends to remain higher than the national average even in prosperous times, it is only during periods of labor shortage or significant economic expansion that Negroes have been able to make inroads to new types of jobs. This has been amply supported in manufacturing industries, many of which first employed Negroes during the periods of war-related labor shortages.

Negro employment patterns in banking and insurance did not change until even later—until the 1960's. Both industries have had steady and considerable employment growth throughout their histories, and both are participating in the burgeoning service industries boom which began in the early 1950's. The nature of their work is such that most of their jobs can be held equally well either by males or females, and it was very largely for this reason that neither industry had gained previous experience with Negro employees prior to the 1960's. Before then, in periods of tight labor markets, they replaced departing males with female employees.

---

[1] Herbert R. Northrup, et al., *Negro Employment in Basic Industry*, Studies of Negro Employment, Vol. I (Philadelphia: Industrial Research Unit, Wharton School of Finance and Commerce. University of Pennsylvania, 1970).

During the racially quiet years from 1940 through the late 1950's, the overall Negro employment patterns in banking and insurance were almost identical. The work forces of each hovered at around 2 percent Negro during this entire time. Manpower shortages brought about by World War II began to be felt early in the 1940's, and as a result a few Negroes were brought in—generally into blue collar jobs. But from after the War until 1960, there was practically no change in Negro employment proportions in either industry, despite the rapidly changing sociology of the country and the increasing skill levels and aspirations of many Negro citizens. Banking employment rose from a low 1950 Negro proportion of 1.8 percent to a 1960 level of only 1.9 percent. Insurance remained at 2.1 percent during the same period.

The civil rights activities and the beginnings of government pressures during the early 1960's, as well as other social and economic changes, brought about a sharp rise in Negro employment in both industries after 1960. High turnover rates, partially attributable to the heavily female employment structures, and the general service industry boom have sustained the rise. Table 1 illustrates the evolving pattern.

There has been no significant economic downturn nor any lessening in the tightness of the labor supply since the financial industries began making expanded job opportunities available to

TABLE 1. *Banking and Insurance Industries*
Percent Negro Employment
United States, 1940-1968

Year	Banking	Insurance
1940	1.5	1.9
1950	1.8	2.1
1960	1.9	2.1
1964	2.9	2.8
1966	4.4	3.3
1967	4.9	3.5
1968	5.6	4.0[a]

Source: Data in author's possession.

[a] Estimated.

Negroes. Nevertheless, in a few specific instances where individual firms have suffered retractions, there is scant evidence either from banking or insurance to support the contention that Negroes, although the last hired, are necessarily the first fired. Nevertheless, without an expanding demand for labor and a generally tight labor market, it is obvious that changes in employment patterns would have been modestly positive at best.

Personnel Expansion and Community Mores

The time period during which an industry underwent its major expansionary personnel changes has been found again and again to have been significant in forming current personnel patterns. The most obvious examples of this are perhaps to be found in the racial patterns of the various construction trades. In the carpentry and the trowel trades—bricklaying, plastering, cement finishing—which developed in the South before the Civil War, Negroes were a key labor source. In other construction trades which developed with the new technologies of the late nineteenth century—electrical installing, pipefitting, heating, etc. —Negroes were excluded from competition with the poor whites. In the North, the mores of the community were such that European immigrants were the preferred labor source at all times. The initial patterns, once established in each set of trades have been perpetuated to this day.

The finance industries have not been subject to massive growth inspired by particular events or technologies. Rather than springing forth fully formed as was seemingly the case with, for example, the electrical machinery or aircraft industries, financial firms grew to what they are today through evolution. If any period over the past two hundred years can be said to be one of rapid expansion in personnel demands for the finance industries, it is the 1960's; and during that time, both industries studied showed their clear intentions to follow the community mores.

It is no secret that the North and South do not share unanimity concerning racial questions. Industries which developed outside the South often show less severe racial barriers. Yet in both the banking and the insurance studies, it is usually in the South that greater proportions of Negroes are found in financial work forces. One factor helping to explain this anomoly is the adherence of both banking and insurance to aspects of community mores which are not directly race related. Most of the employment differences can be explained by noting that banks and insurance companies in the South continue to perform their own maintenance, cleaning, and guarding operations whereas their counterparts in other areas of the country have turned these functions over to independent contractors for servicing.

Market Orientation

It has generally been supported by earlier studies in this series that firms having close association with the final product of their industry tend to be more responsive to sociological values than intermediaries selling to other producers. More specifically, we would expect that firms dealing extensively with Negro customers would tend to have more Negro employees.

The experience of the financial industries tends to be contradictory on this point, and there are certain complexities concerning the nature of the financial industries' product which prohibit perfect resolution. Between the two industries, it would have to be said that insurance is more oriented to the potentials of a Negro market and to marketing as a function. On the other hand, the "product" of banking is such that the market is more oriented to the industry. Customer contact with employees is probably more widespread in banking but more intensive in insurance. Thus comparisons between the two industries on the basis of market orientation are probably not worthwhile. Therefore, let us look at differences within each industry.

Within the banking industry, comparisons can be made between the federal reserve banks—which have very little customer contact—and the commercial banks—where such contact is often the basis for business. In this example, the hypothesis is not supported, as the federal reserve banks show much higher Negro employment ratios.

There are several arguments concerning the structure and operations of federal reserve banks which might explain at least some of the divergence noted here, but it is also quite possible that the analysis underlying the hypothesis does not apply to the banking industry. Short of organized disruptions or publicized boycotts, Negroes in general can bring little economic pressure to bear on banks, and even now have but modest potentials as either depositors or borrowers. Until quite recently, most banks held that the loss of one or two important white customers would greatly outweigh the gains from many Negro customers who only possibly might be attracted by a personnel philosophy allowing Negroes greater job opportunities. Thus it appears that because of the special economic conditions of the industry, the reverse of the hypothesis actually held true until the mid-1960's: the closer the relationship between the firm and its customers, the smaller were the chances for increased Negro employment. (During the later 1960's this was no longer the case as, increasingly, white customers took up the cause of augmenting Negro employment opportunities.)

In the insurance industry, the case is much more straightforward and reflects the findings of other industries in supporting the hypothesis. In the first place, the product of the insurance industry must be actively rather than passively sold. For reasons which find their origins in the earliest mutual burial associations, Negroes have always been predisposed in favor of collective action for mutual protection and are therefore a prime market group, especially for industrial (or debit) life insurance which is paid for on small weekly installments. The firms, most of them in the South, which specialize or deal heavily in this type of insurance employ many more Negro salesmen than do other firms.

The analysis is also supported within the life insurance group, where it has found that mutual corporations, owned by the insured, tended to employ greater proportions of minority group members than did stock corporations which perhaps have to be more concerned with the expense of sociological experimentation with minority group employment programs.

Size of Firm

The size of firm or economic unit within an industry has not been a significant factor in differentiating Negro employment proportions in many of the industries we have reviewed in other volumes in this series. One reason for this is that the technological structure of many of the industries studied required firms of a specific size—usually large—to take advantage of inherent economies of scale. Additionally, we have concentrated on studying those employers within each industry whose policies have the greatest impact of their communities or on general employment trends. Therefore, we have generally examined only the larger firms.

Nevertheless, it seems reasonable to hypothesize that within a fairly broad range of sizes,[2] the larger a firm (or employment

---

[2] Below a certain size the presence of a single minority group person in perhaps a janitorial or custodial position can have an overwhelming effect on the statistics.

center within a firm), the greater the economic horizons and job opportunities within that firm. Larger firms tend to be more impersonal, have greater facility for horizontal shifts (lateral transfers) to relieve specific interpersonnal clashes which might develop, have more training abilities, have fewer requirements for immediate productivity from new employees, and have broader promotional opportunities. In short, they are better able to absorb and utilize marginal employees.

The banking industry provides an excellent vehicle for testing this hypothesis. A tremendous number of autonomous units exist in the industry, and they are of all sizes. The structure of the industry is such that even in those states where extensive branch structures are allowed, hiring is typically done at the home office for the entire firm. In this industry, the evidence is very strong that a direct correlation does exist between size of firm and Negro proportion of total employment.

The insurance industry also supports the hypothesis but the evidence is somewhat less clear because of the more complex structure of the industry. The seventy firms interviewed as part of the insurance industry study ranged in size from 96 to 55,382 employees, but the differing sales and organizational structures necessary to appeal to different markets with different products prohibit any direct correlation between size and Negro employment. Decentralization of personnel control is a significant differentiating factor in the industry, however. Nonsales personnel are about equally divided between home office and agency (field, brokerage, or other) offices, and the findings of the study were definitely that the independently managed decentralized field, agency, or brokerage offices afforded less Negro employment potential. If we consider each of these independently managed units as a separate "firm" for the purpose of testing this hypothesis, then the supporting evidence is quite clear: the larger the firm, the greater the proportion of Negro employment.

Industrial Location

The financial industries are with few exceptions national in scope even if individual firms within them are not. In both industries, we found that similar regional employment patterns existed. The high proportion of entry-level clerical jobs in both industries which can generally be handled by high school graduates directly out of school has meant that both industries have tended to reflect population patterns in their home office areas.

In the East, both industries are city oriented, and the increased cencentration of Negroes in the center city areas, combined with growing geographical decentralization of many manufacturing industries, have tended to increase the numbers of Negroes seeking jobs in finance. On the other hand, the flight of whites to suburbia and the difficulties usually experienced with urban transit have tended to decrease the number of whites seeking jobs in finance. The result has been increased possibilities for Negroes to find work in the industry.

In the West, except in California, Negroes are not significant population concentrations in most cities and are often outnumbered by Orientals, Spanish-speaking Americans, and occasionally, by Indians. Additionally, the insurance industry is more often located in suburban areas in the West. These factors would lead us to expect fewer Negro employees in the West—and this in fact was found to be the case.

In the South, cities where insurance companies and banks of any size are located have about the same Negro population concentrations as cities in the Northeast, but show surprisingly large proportions of Negroes in their work forces. Negroes employed there, however, tend to be lower in the organizational structure and, as mentioned, the finance industries in this area have more blue collar jobs available than they do elsewhere.

NATURE OF THE WORK

The nature of the work in both of the industries studied has been extremely significant in determining the degree of Negro employment. The occupational mix, the demands of the job—its character or relative unpleasantness—the pattern of occupational progression, and the significance and impact of technological change are all meaningful in this regard.

The Occupational Mix and Patterns of Employment Progression

Table 2 shows that the banking and insurance industries have extremely high proportions of salaried and white collar personnel. Whereas white collar employment at all industries reporting to EEOC in 1966 averaged less than half of total employment, almost all of the work forces of banking and insurance were in this category. The table also shows that Negroes have made considerable inroads into nontraditional jobs. More than six out of ten Negroes employed by banks are in white collar jobs, and

TABLE 2. *Banking and Insurance Industries Compared with All Industries
Percentage Distribution of Employees by Race and Occupational Group
United States, 1966*

Occupational Group	All Industries		Banking		Insurance	
	Total	Negro	Total	Negro	Total	Negro
Officials and managers	8.2	0.9	17.3	1.5	11.6	5.2
Professionals	6.6	1.1	2.1	0.4	10.5	1.6
Technicians	4.5	2.2	0.7	1.1	4.4	1.3
Sales workers	7.0	2.0	0.5	0.1	22.7	21.0
Office and clerical	16.7	7.2	73.1	62.3	48.2	53.2
Total white collar	43.0	13.4	93.7	65.4	97.4	82.4
Total blue collar	57.0	86.6	6.3	34.6	2.6	17.6
Total	100.0	100.0	100.0	100.0	100.0	100.0

Source: U.S. Equal Employment Opportunity Commission, *Job Patterns for Minorities and Women in Private Industry, 1966.* Report No. 1 (Washington: The Commission, 1968), Part II.

TABLE 3. *Banking and Insurance Industries*
Compared with All Industries and with Manufacturing Industries
Employment by Race and Occupational Group
United States,[a] *1966*

Occupational Group	All Industries			Manufacturing Industries			Banking and Insurance		
	Total	Negro	Percent Negro	Total	Negro	Percent Negro	Total	Negro	Percent Negro
Officials and managers	2,077,663	18,106	0.9	878,497	4,991	0.6	179,151	1,689	0.9
Professionals	1,689,886	22,333	1.3	670,818	3,732	0.6	93,782	484	0.5
Technicians	1,137,952	46,503	4.1	448,217	6,563	1.5	38,241	587	1.5
Sales workers	1,796,574	42,417	2.4	346,136	4,160	1.2	181,269	5,433	3.0
Office and clerical	4,264,770	151,105	3.5	1,307,982	26,193	2.0	752,930	27,810	3.7
Total white collar	10,966,845	280,464	2.6	3,651,650	45,639	1.2	1,245,373	36,003	2.9
Total blue collar	14,543,857	1,808,783	12.4	9,090,218	964,959	10.6	52,759	12,363	23.4
Total	25,510,702	2,089,247	8.2	12,741,868	1,010,598	7.9	1,298,132	48,366	3.7

Source: U.S. Equal Employment Opportunity Commission, *Job Patterns for Minorities and Women in Private Industry, 1966.* Report No. 1 (Washington: The Commission, 1968), Part II.

[a] Excludes Alaska and Hawaii.

insurance companies have an even more impressive record, with eight of every ten Negroes employed holding these higher positions.

Generally speaking, however, given the occupational mix and the disadvantaged status of Negroes in educational attainment, training, and industrial experience, we would expect the proportion of Negroes would be higher in those industries having greater demand for unskilled labor—that is, those having higher blue collar employment requirements. Table 3 shows this to be the case. The financial industries, represented by banking and insurance, have a far smaller Negro employment proportion than either manufacturing industries or than the average of all industries.

Incidently, there is an interesting statistical situation evident here which illustrates the need for continual care in interpreting numerical results. In every occupational category noted (with the unimportant exception of professional workers) the financial industries employ higher proportions of Negro workers than do manufacturing industries, and in the case of blue collar workers, quite substantially higher. And yet, when all employment is taken together, the finance industries' total Negro employment proportion is less than half that of manufacturing firms. Obviously, this comes about because of the few blue collar jobs in finance and their consequently small statistical weight. Nevertheless, it could be said that it is only the technology of the financial industries and their resultant high-level employment structures which have condemned these industries to compare unfavorably with others in racial employment patterns.

Let us return to the basic argument and note that although banking and insurance both have high-level job requirements, banking does have more of what could be considered entry-level positions in the office and clerical category. (Table 2.) Under the hypotheses being investigated, we should expect relatively higher Negro employment proportions. Table 4 shows this to be the case.

Job Demands

Table 2 points up the fact that banking and insurance are both very definitely industries requiring high levels of skill development at the point of entrance into the industries. As we have already pointed out, neither industry has much of a demand for unskilled, muscle-type labor, and the typical entry point is into a

TABLE 4. *Banking and Insurance Industries*
Employment by Race and Occupational Group
United States, 1966

Occupational Group	Banking and Insurance			Banking			Insurance		
	Total	Negro	Percent Negro	Total	Negro	Percent Negro	Total	Negro	Percent Negro
Officials and managers	179,151	1,689	0.9	88,107	343	0.4	91,044	1,346	1.5
Professionals	93,782	484	0.5	10,787	83	0.8	82,995	401	0.5
Technicians	38,241	587	1.5	3,811	243	6.4	34,430	344	1.0
Sales workers	181,269	5,433	3.0	2,648	13	0.5	178,621	5,420	3.0
Office and clerical	752,930	27,810	3.7	373,251	14,080	3.8	379,679	13,730	3.6
Total white collar	1,245,373	36,003	2.9	478,604	14,762	3.1	766,729	21,241	2.8
Total blue collar	52,759	12,363	23.4	32,271	7,819	24.2	20,488	4,544	22.2
Total	1,298,132	48,366	3.7	510,875	22,581	4.4	787,257	25,785	3.3

Source: U.S. Equal Employment Opportunity Commission, *Job Patterns for Minorities and Women in Private Industry,*
1966. Report No. 1 (Washington: The Commission, 1968), Part II.

white collar job. The skills required in these clerical jobs in the beginning are not excessive. Nevertheless, they were not skills for which the Negro, especially the Negro male, had typically prepared himself. Although both banking and insurance have shown willingness during the later part of the 1960's partially to atone for past exclusionary practices by providing specialized industrial training and by lowering induction standards, the fact remains that such positions will continue to show an underrepresentation of Negro employees until such time as education levels improve and the industries succeed in convincing the Negro community that lines of progression and job opportunities have been opened in earnest.

Sales positions have typically been among the most difficult for Negroes to break into, largely because of the demands of the job and fears that the company will be hurt by racist customer reaction to Negro salesmen. In the insurance industry, however, the proportion of salesmen who are Negro is considerably higher than that of all industries reporting to EEOC. The reasons for this are detailed in the insurance study, and are basically the result of the existence of a Negro market for insurance and the fact that salesmen catering to this market have traditionally been employees of the companies rather than independent agents. But even under these conditions, the proportion of salesmen in the industry who are Negro is only 3 percent and there are few indications that all of the barriers are down in this area.

Overall, the financial industries support the national pattern of inverted Negro representation. The more demanding the job the less Negro representation in it.

Impact of Technology

Technological change usually has the greatest impact on those who are lowest in the organization. In the financial industries, the group most sensitive to technological change would presumably be the clerical-level employees whose jobs might be threatened by the rapidly spreading use of computers. The statistics show, however, that there has been no apparent diminution in the requirements for clerical workers in these industries. Our study of the insurance industry found some fears that nonsales employment would decrease as a result of automation and adversely affect Negro employment. We doubt that this argument can be sustained, however, in light of the tremendous augmentation in demand for keypunch operators and computer-related personnel which now exists in the finance industry. Large numbers of Negroes have been going into this line of work during the past few years, and we feel the potentials for Negro employment have been and will continue to be improved by the introduction of computers.

Late in 1969, pressures began to be raised to force firms in the banking industry to abandon the concept of the one-bank holding company and restrict themselves to the deposit and lending business which had been their original stock in trade. At the time of this writing, it is still too early to tell what effect these pressures will eventually have on banking credit card operations and certain other services which banks originated to make better use of their excess computer capacity. But it seems clear that if banks are forced to divest themselves of these computer based services, the adverse effect on Negro employment in that industry will be severe.

NATURE OF MANAGEMENT

Every organization reflects to at least some degree the philosophical bent of its policy-making executives. It is therefore safe to assume that the personal, sociological, and organizational views of top managerial personnel will result in a climate less or more amenable to Negro employment advancement in different firms.

Management Ethnic Orientation

It is often assumed that companies headed by individuals of minority ethnic stock will be more sympathetic to programs designed to expand minority group employment. In the banking and insurance industries, we have virtually no evidence one way or the other on the impact of management ethnic origin on racial policies. There are a few ethnically-oriented banks and some moderately-sized branches of foreign banks—mostly in New York City. Although these organizations do give positive preference to persons of their same ethnic origins seeking employment, there is little to show that they are in general either more or less receptive to the special employment needs of Negroes.

Image Concern

Managements in both banking and insurance have always felt it part of their duty to preserve and protect the high image of their industry. This is economically understandable for both of them, in that a bond of trust must exist between the institutions and their customers which is based partially on the image which the industries manage to convey. Protection of this image was one of the most serious obstacles to increasing Negro employment in both industries until quite recently. During the 1960's, sociological and workplace advancement of Negroes began to be a concern of a great many white persons who had previously been disinterested at best. As this group began to make its views felt, both banking and insurance found that their overall images would be enhanced by a posture of sociological concern. In many cases that posture has been translated into improved opportunity for black persons.

Organizational Philosophies

Although changes in organizations are seldom undertaken from racial motives, they can often have considerable effect on the racial employment levels in a firm. One example of this we have already noted in the discussion of decentralization. Fewer Negroes are usually employed in those firms which have a dispursed hiring function. Even in firms where the hiring function is centralized, Negro employment potentials are affected by the hiring methodology used. In those firms, for example, where the final decision to hire a particular candidate is made by the supervisor or department head, fewer Negroes are typically employed than in those firms in which the final hiring decision is made by the personnel department.

Overall, our findings in both banking and insurance have indicated that unless the chief executive officer and top policy-making personnel are committed to the idea of expanding Negro employment potentials, traditional racial employment patterns continue to exist. Government agencies have acted wisely when they have sought to secure commitments from chief executive officers.

NATURE OF INDUSTRIAL ENVIRONMENT

The final factors which we shall consider are those which arise outside the financial industries themselves. What have been the effects of unions, racial disturbances, and government activities on the level of Negro employment found in the financial community?

Union Organization

Because of the overwhelmingly nonunion traditions in both insurance and banking, there is very little evidence to bear one way or the other on the impact of unions. Only one nationally affiliated union exists in the insurance industry, and that is made up almost entirely from the diminishing group of industrial life agents. In the banking industry there are only two or three local unions. In neither industry do the unions have an important effect on racially-related policy making.

Community Crises

In recent years, community crises such as those arising from the southern school closings or from the racial riots in the cities have had considerable effect on production, location, and other corporate policy decisions. Also, there were often secondary effects related to employment policies; in areas where racial unrest threatened firms' capacity to produce, many firms found it impossible to remain neutral and moved towards instituting more liberal employment policies in efforts to restore tranquility.

Community crises probably had a greater primary effect on the financial industries than a secondary one. This is particularly true for the property and liability insurance firms with respect to the highly destructive city riots. A secondary effect in the insurance industry was the famous "billion dollar pledge" to support Negro programs, but there is little evidence to show that hiring patterns of the companies themselves were much changed by the riots.

In the banking industry, urban unrest seems to have greatest effect on branch offices in the slum neighborhoods. Partially for public relations purposes, and partially because of the difficulties involved with convincing white employees to work in heavily Negro neighborhoods during periods of racial turmoil, the riots did have the effect of accelerating the promotion to branch management or assistant branch management of a number of Negroes to work in these locations. The banking industry, too, has made substantial contributions to urban redevelopment programs, special job training centers, and other programs for the benefit of Negro city dwellers. Although in some senses this seems to reward antisocial behavior, it must be acknowledged that community crises have had beneficial effects in augmenting and upgrading Negro employment.

Role of Government

The effect of government pressures on Negro employment have been greater in the banking industry than insurance primarily because almost all of the firms in the banking industry are considered to be contractors to the federal government, and therefore subject to the Office of Federal Contract Compliance as well as to the Equal Employment Opportunity Commission. In addition to being more active, the OFCC has more stringent regulations and greater enforcement power than does EEOC. Nevertheless, there are no substantive differences in employment patterns between the two industries that can be attributed directly to differences in government pressures. At this time it is still too early to tell what effect the recent requirements for employment test validification—required of banking but not of insurance —will have.

In both industries, however, the evidence is quite strong that had it not been for pressures from agencies of local, state, and federal governments to make increased opportunities available to Negroes, progress would have been considerably slower in the 1960's. Perhaps the most important aspect of governmental pressures was that rules and regulations promulgated provided those managements which supported the principals of equal opportunity but were afraid to practice them for fear of employee or customer reaction the wherewithall to put their ideas into practice. On the other hand, the continuance of the profusion of programs developed by agencies on all levels of government has lessened the salutary effect of those regulations. Proliferating reporting requirements are adding to the administrative burden of many firms. Some employers have been harassed by repeated compliance reviews, and many have been antagonized by duplication and interagency rivalries. Firms in both banking and insurance often reported a lack of constructive suggestions from the governmental agencies and a basic lack of familiarity with, or sympathy for, the special problems arising from the structure and nature of their industries.

Progress in the future towards equal opportunity in practice will depend in part on government and industry working together towards a common goal. The future of harmonious racial relations will depend on our ability to eliminate the special racially-oriented programs which have mushroomed during the 1960's by eliminating the need for them. This cannot be accomplished if antagonisms are allowed to grow and barriers solidify between government and industry.

Additionally the need for innovative management continues to exist in this area as it has in all other aspects of development of the American industrial system. In the past, American managements have shown themselves remarkably able to overcome difficulties of a technological, organizational, or economic nature. The great problem which continues to remain before managements now is a sociological one. We hope that in these studies and others in this series we have detected the beginnings of the solution to that problem.

FINAL COMMENT

The finance industries offer great hope for the employment of Negroes in large part by virtue of their center city location, and the increasing urban concentration of blacks, North and South. The increasing utilization of Negroes by these relatively cyclical free industries is both promising and by all indications will tend to continue.

The big task ahead is greater emphasis on black male employment in the managerial, professional, and sales functions. As manufacturing industry has dispersed to suburb and even farther from the urban centers, the jobs left in the cities have more and more been office, clerical, and service occupations for which females are generally preferred. Much of the improved employment of Negroes by financial institutions has been in these occupations. This adds to family income and reduces discrimination and unemployment. But it leaves unsolved the key problem of black male employment and exacerbates the difficult Negro family problem. The greatest contribution to improved Negro employment and to resolution of our urban problems must involve improved employment of male Negroes and their greater participation in the mainstream of American industry. The two great finance industries are ideally located and structured to contribute substantially to such improvement.

Research Reports
Racial Policies of American Industry Series

Ten more Industry Report studies are scheduled in late 1970 and 1971.
Order from University of Pennsylvania Press or the
Industrial Research Unit, Philadelphia, Pennsylvania 19104

Research Reports
Labor Relations and Public Policy Series

1. *Compulsory Arbitration and the NLRB*, by Paul A. Abodeely. 1968. $2.50

2. *Union Authorization Cards and the NLRB*,
   by Alan R. McFarland and Wayne S. Bishop.   1969. $2.50

Forthcoming studies will deal with various aspects of government labor policy including bargaining unit determination, picketing and boycott regulation, and government intervention in labor disputes.

Miscellaneous Series

14. *Economics of Carpeting and Resilient Flooring: A Survey of Published Material and a Questionnaire Summary*, by David C. Stewart. 1966. $1.00

15. *Job Mobility and Occupational Change: Philadelphia Male Workers, 1940-1960*, by Carol P. Brainerd.   1966. $2.00

16. *Improving the Potential for Negro Employment and Skill Development in the Delaware Valley Fabricated Metals Industry*, by Armand J. Thieblot, Jr., and William N. Chernish.   1967. $2.00

Order from University of Pennsylvania Press or the
Industrial Research Unit, Philadelphia, Pennsylvania 19104